UNIVERSITY OF GLAMORGAN
LEARNING RESOURCES CENTRE

Pontypridd, Mid Glamorgan, CF37 1DL
Telephone: Pontypridd (01443) 482626

Books are to be returned on or before the last date below

18 MAR 1998

2 5 SEP 1998   1 5 DEC 2000   1 1 FEB 2006

2 4 MAR 1999   2 6 FEB 2001   8 JUN 2007

- 5 MAY 2000   0 5 MAR 2001

2 5 MAY 2000   2 7 MAR 2001

                - 4 MAY 2001
                2 7 FEB 2002

1 6 JUN 2000   1 9 APR 2002
                2 0 APR

D1345971

332·1532
PAY

The World Bank

The World Bank

A Critical Analysis

Cheryl Payer

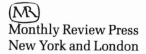
Monthly Review Press
New York and London

This book is also listed in the PRIO Monograph Series of the International Peace Research Institute, Oslo

Library of Congress Cataloging in Publication Data

Payer, Cheryl, 1940–
   The World Bank.
   Includes bibliographical references.
   1. World Bank. I. Title
HG3881.P37   332.1'532   81–84738
ISBN 0-85345-601-1
ISBN 0-85345-602-X (pbk.)

Monthly Review Press
62 West 14th Street, New York, N.Y. 10011
47 The Cut, London SE1 8LL

Manufactured in the United States of America
10 9 8 7 6 5 4 3 2 1

2 X 4308

Contents

Preface and Acknowledgments

Most people who write about "development" and "development lending" have very little acquaintance with the concrete realities of development projects. This, at least, has been my observation as I compiled the material for this book. Nor do development lending institutions such as the World Bank make it easy for the curious researcher to find out what is going on. It is not that the Bank does not publish information about itself; it does, in such copious volume that one is reminded of J. S. Furnivall's epigram about the British Colonial Office, that it "concealed itself, like a cuttlefish, in a cloud of ink."[1] A great deal of what the Bank publishes is self-serving propaganda; much of the rest is research that has little or nothing to do with the actual projects that absorb several billion dollars yearly. As Aart van de Laar observed, "Some staff members may be prolific writers, but it does not follow that they have much impact on Bank policy. The contrary conclusion could also be drawn: they have time to write so much because they have so few other responsibilities within the Bank!"[2]

Nevertheless it is fair to surmise that in so much public relations fodder, some indication of what the Bank is really doing must be available; the problem is finding the Ariadne's thread which will lead one to the relevant documents with some efficiency. For me, the first step in this quest was the discovery that all International Bank for Reconstruction and Development (IBRD) loans and International Development Association (IDA) credits are formalized in "loan agreements" or "credit agreements" which are published as UN treaties and thus available in all libraries that are UN depositories. As these documents number over 3,000 at present and are issued chronologically, they are of little use without some sort of index; happily one is also available, free, from the Bank's publications office in its Washington headquarters, in the form of the "Statement of Loans" (IBRD) and "Statement of Development Credits" (IDA): regularly updated computer print-outs giving cumulative lists of loans, arranged by borrowing countries and identified by brief project titles. With these indices one can find the identifying numbers of particular loans and so find the pertinent loan or credit agreement for the project one wishes to study.

As the formal agreements reveal very little about the operation of the project, the search has only begun; with the identification of projects, one must then set out to discover from other sources enough about the operation of that project to allow some kind of evaluation. In writing this book, I have utilized the following procedure. The chapters are organized by "sectors" which correspond, roughly, to the Bank's own sector categories.[3] In each chapter I have used the Bank's own publications to build a sort of "ideal type" (or types) of Bank project for that sector. The Bank publications which have proved most useful as guides to loan operations are the following:

Sector policy papers, produced at intervals during Robert McNamara's presidency, are summaries of Bank thinking and of lending guidelines for a particular sector or subsector, approved by the executive directors. The papers are periodically bound together and published in book form by the Bank: examples include *World Bank Operations* (1972) and *The Assault on World Poverty* (1975). Information on specific projects has been compiled from a number of sources; in addition to the official loan and credit agreements already mentioned, one can be informed of current lending by getting on the Bank's mailing list for press releases announcing new loans as they are approved. Each press release contains one or two pages of information about the project. In addition, each *Annual Report* contains a paragraph summary of all IBRD loans and IDA credits approved during the year.

Two publications aimed at a popular audience contain articles which summarize sector activity and policy and also occasional descriptions of specific projects: one is a slick color magazine, *Finance and Development*, jointly published with the International Monetary Fund (IMF), which appears four times a year; the other is a black and white tabloid, *Report: News and Views of the World Bank Group*, which is published six times a year.

Much more important than any of these, but more difficult to obtain because they are not published, are the project appraisals which the Bank produces for each project. Each of these documents contains dozens of pages of detailed information on the physical, technical, economic, and financial aspects of the project; and although even these internal documents are heavily edited to suppress embarrassing revelations, they provide far more information than is available from all other Bank sources together for particular projects. Although officially restricted in circulation, they are not terribly secret and there are quite a few floating around in UN libraries and in private hands. Although I was not always able to find the project appraisal for a specific project, I had little trouble obtaining a fair sampling for each sector which I examined, and the Bank itself even supplied a few of these at my request. I have also been informed that the U.S. Department of Commerce has a collection of these, compiled for the convenience of businesses interested in supplying materials or services for projects, which can be requested by the public at the Commerce Department building in Washington.

For this work, information in the Bank publications was supplemented by a large number of analyses by independent observers in published or unpublished form. In collecting these, the indices of Bank loans and credits were very important, for once one knew that the Bank had aided a particular project, e.g., the Selebe-Pikwe copper-nickel mining project in Botswana, then all information about that particular project could be utilized as evidence, whether or not the Bank was mentioned in the article or report.

With all these various leads to follow, it became necessary to narrow the field of investigation somewhat. Clearly, one researcher could not investigate all 3,000 loans and credits even in a library-based investigation. A scientific sampling of projects would also have been unfeasible with the resources at my disposal. It was therefore necessary to impose some criteria of

selection for projects which would be scrutinized more intensively. This book is primarily an overview of available information, and for the most part I was limited to investigations which
had already been performed and reported by others. It would
have been quixotic to ignore such information and I have not
done so; however, a passive reliance on preexisting studies does
pose a real danger of distorted vision, since it is likely to be
the spectacularly unsuccessful projects which attract the most
critical attention.

It was not my intention to criticize the Bank for making mistakes; any individual or institution which is achieving anything
is bound to make some mistakes. Therefore I tried to counteract
such bias by concentrating my own investigations on successful, typical, or important (judging by sheer size of the funds
committed by the Bank) projects. "Successful" or "typical" projects were selected according to two criteria: first, those which
are cited as successful in the Bank's own promotional literature,
and second, loans which were part of a long series to a particular
borrower in a particular sector in one country. Whereas one
isolated loan for a particular project may not be typical of Bank
operations or may not work out as it was planned, the presump-
tion must be that when the Bank makes eight or twelve or fifteen
loans to one sector in a particular country (as for example,
irrigation in Indonesia or palm oil production in the Ivory Coast),
it is in general well pleased with the progress in that sector and
with the local institution which administers those loans. By
using these criteria of selection I have tried to obtain a fair
picture of the Bank's "ideal" type project; in fact if I have seriously erred in my evaluation, I think it is not in choosing the odd
failure or mistake and generalizing from those, but in assuming
too easily that projects actually work the way that the Bank
wants them to work. There is a fairly large body of evidence of
errors and miscalculations in Bank projects, but I have not based
my critique on these.

Although this work is based primarily on published and unpublished written sources, I conducted interviews at the World
Bank headquarters in Washington on two occasions: in May
1979, when I focused exclusively on agriculture and rural de-

velopment, and in April 1981, when most of my written research had been concluded. On both occasions I utilized the interviews to clarify specific questions raised by my previous research. On both occasions I was received with courtesy by the public relations office and the Bank officials with whom they arranged interviews. Although a number of my questions and requests for documents remained unanswered, I wish to thank all those Bank employees who tried to help me within the limits of their official responsibilities. Those interviews, though they do not merit specific attention in the text, did save me from some errors of fact and interpretation.

I did not conduct any field research of World Bank projects for this book, not because I do not believe in the value of such research, but because with limited time and money I could have visited at best a few projects in one or a few countries, which could have distorted the findings of what is intended as an overview of all projects in all countries. Needless to say, these findings and hypotheses remain tentative and will need to be confirmed, challenged, and revised by other research. I hope that this book will stimulate a debate on the meaning and value of what we call economic development, in the hope of finding new and different directions which will mean genuine progress for poor people./Capitalist economic "development" makes people poor by depriving them of their share of the world's natural resources and of access to political power. It is to these people, the victims of development, that this book is dedicated.

The preface and acknowledgments contained in my first book (*The Debt Trap*) have gained a certain notoriety apart from that of the contents of the book itself. The key paragraph, which seems to have touched exposed nerves in many places, read:

> I have rejected the invidious division of labor, typical of the academic and publishing world, which assigns the more tedious tasks to persons who never enjoy the rewards of authorship. Both from necessity . . . and from conviction, I have no research assistants, secretaries, or typists to thank in this space; I did the work myself. Nor did I have a spouse who would take charge of the time-consuming mechanics of living while I carried on the higher intellectual labor.

The wide response to this paragraph is proof that it needed to be said. For the most part, that paragraph also holds true for the writing of this volume.

Nevertheless, on rereading these lines I now find them disturbingly arrogant and individualistic. For one thing, in them I ignored the unacknowledged workers in the publishing houses which issued the book, many of whom I never met and could not know by name; we are none of us truly independent in the division of labor.

More important, this work has been a truly collective effort. On this occasion I have many more people to thank, and it is no mere graceful flourish to state that without their help this book could not have been written. This is a work of synthesis, and as the perpetrator of it I am standing on the shoulders of a small army of colleagues whose collective professional experience (including fieldwork in many of the Bank's borrower countries) is truly impressive. Many of them have aided me, not merely by reading and correcting drafts which I have submitted, but in shaping some of the hypotheses which guided my investigations and the very form of the chapters. If the book nevertheless bears my name alone, it is because I alone have decided which of my colleagues' insights to utilize and which to ignore or criticize. In other words, this work is more of a personal viewpoint than an individual achievement.

It would be impossible to thank by name everyone who has aided me in the course of five years' study of the World Bank by supplying documents, names, references, and other types of moral and practical support. I hope that those whom I have not been able to name will nevertheless accept these thanks for their contribution.

There are many, nevertheless, whose contribution is so great that they must be named. These include Roger Burbach and Patricia Flynn, who gave me the first push into World Bank research; Elias Davidson, who first informed me of the existence of the published loan agreements and the index to them; old friends such as Moss and Florence Roberts, Dorothy Friesen, Lynn Payer, and Chen-Ie Lie who supported me in a variety of ways; Jim Boyce and Betsy Hartmann who have become good friends as we worked on related critiques of the Bank (and who also gave me Sandino, my literary kitten); all of my colleagues in the Rome Declaration Group, but particularly Anne-Marie Holenstein, Jacques Berthelot, and Hannes Lorenzen; new friends first met as I pursued the research on this book, including Doug Smith, Peter Hayes, Carol LeGrasse, Jack Westoby, and Erna Bennett; and veteran critics of the World Bank who have been generous in their comradeship: Teresa Hayter, Gavin Williams, and Ernest Feder. A (nonexhaustive) list of those who have helped would also have to include Jane Fearer Safer of Survival International U.S.A., Lars Søftestad, Timothy Weiskel, Peter Odell, Richard Stren, William Goldsmith, Walden Bello and the Congressional Task Force, David Kinley of the Institute for Food and Development Policy, Joel Rocamora and Martha Winnaker of the Southeast Asia Resource Center, Fred Goff of the Data Center; Robin Broad, Arthur Domike, Ellen Seidensticker, Richard Curtain, Ben Crow, Helen Hill, Meredith Turshen, Steve Zorn, Ben Kerkvliet, Lindy Washburn, Robert Williams, Fereidun Fesharaki, Robert Stauffer, Marc Herold, Hank Frundt, Harris Gleckman, the Middle East Research and Information Center, the Center for International Policy, the Center for Development Research, North American Congress on Latin America, and the Corporate Data Exchange.

There are also some individuals who wish to remain nameless. In a few cases this is because they live under repressive governments and acknowledgment could endanger their work or their lives; in the other cases the individuals involved have previously been employed by or closely associated with the World Bank. Most of the latter group, although willing to help my project, asked that their names not be used because "my friends in the Bank wouldn't understand." Perhaps, if those friends ponder the message of this book, they may begin to understand; I hope so.

Major financial support for this book came from unemployment payments; I also wish to acknowledge grants from the Rome Declaration Group and from the Rabinowitz Foundation, and two summers spent at the Peace Research Institute of Oslo as a visiting researcher.

1

The Institution and Its Power

The World Bank is the foremost international development agency. Some call it the best, some call it the worst; but no one escapes its influence. It was the first bank of its type, founded in 1945, and is still the largest, with an administrative budget of $410 million in fiscal year 1981. It also moves more money, by far, than any other development agency: in fiscal year 1981 its three components—the International Bank for Reconstruction and Development (IBRD), the International Development Association (IDA), and the International Finance Corporation (IFC)— made lending and investment commitments of more than $13 billion dollars in seventy-six countries.

The Bank has in addition magnified its power of financial leverage by coordinating and subordinating a number of other international financial and technical organizations, bilateral aid agencies, and export credit institutions. This "coordination" of aid efforts has both financial and intellectual aspects. Financially, the World Bank puts great emphasis on "cofinancing." It persuades other (and potentially rival) funding agencies to contribute their capital to projects that have been prepared and appraised by the Bank for its own funding. Regional development banks and funds such as the Inter-American Development Bank (IDB), the Asian Development Bank, and the African Development Bank (all of which are modeled on the general pattern of the World Bank), a number of new funds based in the Middle East and formed for the purpose of dispensing excess oil revenues, bilateral aid programs—especially those of Scandinavia, the Netherlands, Great Britain, and Canada—frequently invest or contribute money to projects selected, defined, appraised, and supervised by the World Bank. Even the International Fund for Agricultural Development, which began operations in 1978 and was intended specifically as a rival lending institution controlled by developing country members, has signed a cooperation agreement with the Bank and has contributed its funds to several Bank projects.

Another important source of cofinancing for World Bank projects is commercial banking and finance institutions. In fiscal year 1980, private sources provided $1.8 billion cofinancing for twenty-one Bank projects. The total amount of cofinancing from all lenders in fiscal year 1980 was $6.5 billion, or more than 50 percent of the total extended by the World Bank group.[1]

This financial hegemony is combined with an attempt at intellectual hegemony, the co-optation of technical expertise from a number of specialized agencies of the United Nations. The World Bank and its sister agency, the International Monetary Fund (IMF), are themselves nominally specialized organs of the UN, but their structure of control (weighted voting which ensures the predominance of the capital-exporting nations) is very different from that of the United Nations. In fact, the agreement of liaison which the Bank signed with the UN in 1947 has been described as "more a declaration of independence from than cooperation with the United Nations." The Bank was fearful that association with the UN would subject it to political control or influence and hurt its credit rating on Wall Street, and insisted on a number of special privileges which had the effect of keeping the central UN bodies at arm's length.[2]

In recent years the Bank has had close and continuing relationships with a number of the UN's specialized technical organizations, mostly involving the use of experts from these agencies to prepare projects for Bank funding. Formal agreements for this purpose have been concluded with the Food and Agriculture Organization (FAO), whose cooperative program with the World Bank fielded 178 agricultural and rural development missions in forty countries, which assisted in preparing about one-third of the agriculture and rural development programs approved for Bank financing in fiscal 1980. In the same period the Bank's cooperative program with the United Nations

Educational, Scientific and Cultural Organization (UNESCO) carried out sixty-three missions in twenty-seven countries for the identification and preparation of education sector projects. A cooperative program with the World Health Organization (WHO) concentrated on water supply and sanitation facilities, and a cooperative program with the United Nations Industrial Development Organization (UNIDO) prepared projects in industrial development.[3] For a number of years the Bank has utilized the United Nations Development Program (UNDP) to prepare projects for Bank financing.[4] These agencies supply expertise to the Bank but have no policy input into the lending process. On the contrary, the Bank formulates its own in-house policy statements on agriculture, education, health, and industry, and these, rather than the ideas of the specialized agencies, dominate the cooperative work, because it is the Bank that has large sums of money to lend. The intellectual hegemony of the Bank complements, and is dependent upon, its financial hegemony.

In addition to these networks of cooperation for the preparation and appraisal of project lending, the Bank plays a critical role in the coordination of the overall aid programs of bilateral and IMF lending to individual countries through its position as convener of almost all the existing consortia or consultative groups. Such groups, or "donors' clubs," are formed for a select group of countries that receive aid from a number of different developed countries. The impetus for their organization may be an imminent debt crisis, when a rescheduling of the debt is seen as necessary, and the various donors wish to coordinate their debt relief efforts. Or, in exceptional cases, they may be formed at the request of a borrower country that hopes to qualify for higher amounts of aid. As Aart van de Laar points out, however, these groups act in practice as a creditors' cartel, whereas a country might well receive better terms if it tried to negotiate with creditors separately for maximum counterleverage. Just Faalands' important case study of the Bangladesh aid group led him to conclude that "the role of the World Bank as a determined organiser of creditors, not primarily an international instrument of mediation, was seen as being exposed beyond doubt."[5]

Finally, it must not be forgotten that the borrowing governments are also expected to contribute funds to Bank projects, usually in the form of infrastructure or operating expenses necessary for the success of the project. For example, in eight loans to Algeria approved between April 1978 and July 1980, the World Bank provided a total of $528 million in financing, while the Algerian government eventually will contribute $443.56 million.[6] This is the "matching funds" technique, which, wherever it is used, is a powerful way to induce governments to spend their own money for purposes determined by the funding agency. This circumstance would not attract notice if in every case the government eagerly desires the project and agrees with all expenditures required. In many cases, however, it is probable that the government has committed itself to expending money that might have found a better, or at least a different, use if the Bank had not insisted on such contributions. Of course, as Bank loans have to be repaid, it could be said that even the Bank's portion of the investment is the government's own money.

The effect of this network of cooperative and cofinancing agreements is to give the Bank an influence over development lending which extends far beyond its own, already large, monetary contribution. The World Bank is admired by some as "more productive, less bureaucratic, certainly less corrupt . . . and more ready to take a stand on principle, than is the case with most development agencies."[7] But its power is frequently resented even by those in the cooperating agencies ("arrogant" and "sanctimonious" were two words I heard frequently in interviews). The World Bank is also the agency that has done the most to formulate a self-conscious philosophy of development and development lending, as expressed in a series of "sector policy papers," "issues papers," "working papers," and simply "papers," which despite their disparate titles are published in uniform editions that express their status as official statements. The World Bank is thus not only the biggest and richest development finance institution in the Western capitalist world; it is generally considered the "best" as well, and it provides the dominant model that other aid and finance institutions imitate, cooperate with, and react against. It is not my purpose in this book to compare and contrast the World Bank with any of these other competing and cooperating agencies, but rather to take it at its own evaluation as the ultimate development finance agency. And, although my findings are very critical, these criticisms apply not only to the Bank as an institution, but to the whole of Western efforts to promote "development" in the Third World, with the Bank taken as the leading exemplar rather than as an individual offender.

How has the enormous financial power of the World Bank been used in practice? To what purpose does it exert the leverage of several billions of dollars that it dispenses yearly?

As the following chapters will demonstrate, the World Bank has deliberately and consciously used its financial power to promote the interests of private, international capital in its expansion to every corner of the "underdeveloped" world. It has worked toward this end in many different ways:

—By acting as intermediary for the flow of funds abroad, with taxpayers' money from its developed member countries serving to guarantee the safety of the bonds it sells;
—By opening up previously remote regions through transportation and telecommunications' investments, thus destroying the natural protection such regions had previously enjoyed;
—By directly aiding certain multinational corporations, notably, but not exclusively, in the mining sector;
—By pressuring the borrowing governments to improve the legal privileges for the tax liabilities of foreign investment;
—By insisting on production for export, which chiefly benefits the corporations that control international trade;
—By selectively refusing to loan to governments that repudiate international debts or nationalize foreign property;
—By opposing minimum wage laws, trade union activity, and all kinds of measures that would improve the share of labor in the national income;
—By insisting on procurement through international competitive bidding, which favors the largest multinationals;
—By opposing all kinds of protection for locally owned business and industry; and
—By financing projects and promoting national policies that deny control of basic resources—land, water, forests—to poor people

and appropriate them for the benefit of multinationals and their collaborative local elites.

In summary, the World Bank is perhaps the most important instrument of the developed capitalist countries for prying state control of its Third World member countries out of the hands of nationalists and socialists who would regulate international capital's inroads, and turning that power to the service of international capital.

There are at least four levels at which the influence of the World Bank will touch, for better or worse, the lives of the poor people in the countries to which it lends.

The first level is that of the individual projects financed by its loans. Although the evidence in the following chapters may suggest otherwise, I by no means insist that poor people *never* gain any benefit from these projects. It is clear that the figures put out for public relations purposes about the number of poor people helped are fantastic calculations that bear little relationship to reality, but it would be equally foolish to maintain that all the projects supposedly designed to help poor people are actually malicious tricks to deceive them. Some poor people do benefit from some projects. But poverty is not abolished, and is not even alleviated, if only a few people step up a notch or two in the hierarchy of wealth. By the Bank's own admission the type of projects it has designed so far cannot reach the very poorest people.

The second level of influence is at the "sector" level. When, for example, the Bank lends for a mining project, it demands changes in the legal and taxation code concerning mining investment. Similar procedures occur in the case of every loan and every sector. If no major changes are demanded, it is because the Bank finds the situation in that sector to be basically satisfactory. To the extent that greater advantage for foreign investment is incompatible with the alleviation of poverty and the satisfaction of human needs (a possibility that is never entertained in the Bank's ideology), poverty in the sector, and society, is likely to *increase* as a result of the Bank's intervention.

The following chapters explore these first two levels of influence in detail. However, two other levels should be borne in mind throughout.

The third level is the overall thrust and direction of national policies. The Bank's influence on policy at this level is called "leverage" and has already been explored in previous works.[8] Usually working in cooperation with the IMF and with the governments that control both these institutions, the Bank is able to force borrowing governments to abandon progressive policies in favor of harsh austerity programs. They are without exception disastrous for the poor people of the country which the Bank claims to be trying to help.

The fourth level is the most fundamental of all. It will be noted in the following chapters that many projects have proved to be detrimental to the interests of the poor for reasons which do not seem to be directly the fault of the World Bank, but are an inevitable consequence of the type of society in which the project is situated. A very high proportion of these societies are inegalitarian, corrupt, and unjust, and it is almost impossible to run a progressive, beneficial, and at the same time successful project within such a society, however well-designed and well-intended it may be. Is this the responsibility of the Bank? Absolutely. If the Bank chooses to lend its support to the government of such a society by making loans to it—and a very high proportion of the Bank's largest borrowers are notorious for extremely inequitable income distribution and/or violations of human rights—*this is not an accident*. It is a natural consequence of the Bank's preference for lending to governments that offer favorable conditions for foreign investment, and of its unwillingness to jeopardize the power of such governments by exerting pressure on behalf of the underprivileged it champions in its rhetoric.

A Brief History of the World Bank

The International Bank for Reconstruction and Development (IBRD), the original institution of what is now the World Bank Group, was founded at the Bretton Woods conference in 1944. It was something of a neglected sibling of the IMF, the designs for which generated the most attention and controversy at Bretton Woods and the subsequent Savannah conference. Whereas the IMF was designed to provide short-term balance of payments relief, the IBRD's function was to be to provide longer-term funds for investment in productive endeavors. Membership in the IBRD (and access to its funds) was made conditional on membership in the IMF. As one of the drafters later remarked, "Basically we wanted to force countries to agree to standards in the monetary field as a condition to get the benefits of the Bank."[9]

The planners who designed both institutions were haunted by the depression of the 1930s and the breakdown of international trade and investment which was its consequence, or—as they believed—its cause. In Robert W. Oliver's words,

> Their major objective was to provide a world within which competitive market forces would operate freely, unhampered by government interference, for they supposed that market forces would produce optimum results for the entire world. . . . As Jacob Viner put it, they were "trying to reverse the whole trend of policy and practice of the world at large in the field of international economic relations since 1914 and especially in the ill-fated years since 1929."[10]

It was the expectation of the founders that the Bank's primary function would be to guarantee private investments. It was conceived as a "safe bridge" across which private investment could move again into distant and politically volatile territories that had appeared much too risky since the debacle of the 1930s.

The IBRD, like the IMF, was designed primarily by officials of the U.S. government, notably Harry Dexter White, working under Secretary of the Treasury Henry Morgenthau, with a minor input from Lord Keynes of Great Britain. U.S. predominance was absolute at the time of the founding of the IMF and IBRD; as the only major power which had escaped devastation in World War II it was at first the only feasible source of loanable funds. At the time of its founding the United States held over 37 percent of its voting power. Its headquarters were located in Washington, its charter providing that the "principle office of the Bank shall be located in the territory of the member holding the greatest number of shares."[11] The choice of Washington over New York reflected the victory of the U.S. view that the World Bank and the IMF should be subject to rather close control by national governments over Keynes's hope that they could be operated as autonomous, technocratic institutions divorced from the vicissitudes of national politics.[12]

The first year of the Bank was inauspicious. The first president, Eugene Meyers, found himself preoccupied with recruiting staff and trying to raise money for the Bank from an initially suspicious financial community. It was also marked by conflict between a brash United States executive director and the president, which ended in the president's resignation only six months after assuming office.

John J. McCloy, when asked to become the next president, made the ascendancy of the president over the executive board a condition of his acceptance, a pattern which has prevailed ever since. Under McCloy's presidency the Bank made its first four loans. These were all program loans, which are disbursed to governments and function as virtually untied balance of payments support, and were designed for the reconstruction of four European countries: France, Netherlands, Denmark, and Luxembourg. The first loan for a specific project (which became the preferred form of Bank lending) was made to Chile in 1948, with loans to Brazil and Mexico made in the following year.

When the Bank first opened for business Poland and Czechoslovakia joined as members, and soon both submitted requests for reconstruction loans. Their ties with the Soviet Union, which had been present at Bretton Woods but had not subsequently joined the IMF or the Bank, prevented them, however, from participating in the Marshall Plan, the program of governmental aid which played the major role in financing European reconstruction. The IBRD, responding to U.S. pressure, subsequently decided that it could not grant any loans to "member countries in Europe which are not participants in [the Marshall Plan.]"[13]

As McCloy resigned the presidency in 1949, he could say with accuracy that "the reconstruction phase of the Bank's activity is largely over," and "the development phase is underway."[14] Although the Bank did make loans subsequently to a number of developed countries in Europe, to Japan, Israel, and South Africa, its orientation toward Latin America and toward the areas of Asia and Africa in process of formal decolonization was set, and its membership rose from the original 45 to 139 in mid-1981. It has suffered a few withdrawals: Poland withdrew from membership in 1950, Czechoslovakia in 1955, and Cuba in 1960. Indonesia withdrew in 1965 under Sukarno's presidency and rejoined in 1967 after Sukarno was deposed.

The Bank was connected with the decolonization process in other ways as well. Employment with the Bank provided a haven for a number of ex-colonial officers no longer able or willing to continue in their previous posts.[15] The Bank has also made loans to colonial powers for use in their territories, including to Australia for Papua New Guinea, to the United Kingdom for Kenya and a number of other colonies, and to Belgium for development of the Belgian Congo. This last loan is notable as one of the closest approaches to "what one director declared the Bank would never do, that is 'grant a loan to any country for general purposes to be determined by the country itself.' "[16] And not only the critics of the Bank, but one of its presidents, have remarked that a great deal of the work of the Bank involves carrying on the work of empire, such as irrigation works, ports and railways, dams, roads, mines—and even projects for "small farmers."[17]

Eugene Black's presidency of the Bank (1949–1963) saw lending expand as the institution found its niche. Black is usually credited, or blamed, for the conservative orientation of the bank in his years there; it was during the 1950s that infrastructure lending—roads, railroads, electric power, ports, and so on—became the characteristic project type, and an emphasis on GNP growth was the primary, if not the only, definition of development. This conservatism is somewhat belied by the fact that it was during Black's presidency that the IBRD was joined by two new institutions to become the "World Bank Group." These institutions were both created as a response to perceived inadequacies of the Bank's own operations. The International Finance Corporation (IFC) was created in 1956 after it was recognized that private corporations were in general unwilling to borrow directly from the World Bank because the government guarantee required by the IBRD usually brought with it more government scrutiny of the corporation's books than they found desirable. The International Development Association (IDA), on the other hand, was created as the answer to two kinds of challenge. For one, the growing group of Third World countries was lobbying so intensely for a more liberal type of development fund that (after first opposing the creation of such a fund) the World Bank decided it would be wiser to co-opt the demand by incorporating the new institution into its own structure than to oppose it. For another, the Bank perceived that it could enhance its own powers of leverage if it controlled the disbursal of concessionary aid funds.

George Woods, the next president (1963–1968), was determined to make the Bank a more innovative organization. "I never saw a more rigid institution—it is an institution, not a bank, why they call it a bank I don't know," he told David Lilienthal as he sat in what Lilienthal termed "the huge Mussolini-sized President's room."[18] Woods's years at the Bank were transitional; many of the trends that came to fruition under McNamara were initiated during the Woods years. Among other changes, the Bank started financing local currency expenses of projects, it started to make loans for education, and it began to modify its rigid opposition to state-owned industry and development finance companies.[19] This was also the period in which the Bank began to expand its agricultural lending by making loans to individual farmers (fairly wealthy ones) for on-farm investments rather than, as previously, loans for infrastructure only.

It was President Robert McNamara, however, who received the most publicity for his innovations at the Bank. Extremely astute at public relations, he is best known to the public for his eloquent speeches on the degrading effects of absolute poverty and his radical expansion both of the amounts of money moved by the Bank and of the types of projects which it was permissible for the Bank to finance (two categories that are without a doubt very closely related). It should be emphasized that the Bank, and McNamara, in no way repudiated the conservative old-style projects; lending for these continued and even increased under McNamara, but with the radical expansion of lending it was possible to reduce the relative predominance of such projects by expanding the new types even more rapidly. Under McNamara's leadership the Bank began to make loans which purport to benefit "small farmers," and for the poor in the cities the Bank began to lend for urban upgrading and "sites and services" projects. It was also during the McNamara years that the Bank decided to expand lending for natural resource extraction by expanding its modest program of mineral development financing and breaking its traditional taboo against lending for oil and gas production and, later, exploration.

Within the Bank, McNamara is at least as famous for his organizational reforms as for his advocacy of poverty-oriented lending. Coming to the World Bank directly from the U.S. Department of Defense, where he had managed the prosecution of the Vietnam war, McNamara brought his "whiz-kid" business school management techniques into the world's biggest development lending institution and made it even bigger.[20] Two of his characteristic innovations were forward planning and personnel budgeting. The process of forward planning is an attempt to assess resource needs and match them with aid availabilities for a five-year period for the Bank's major borrowers (the key documents, the Country Program Papers, are supposed to be prepared for each of the 100-odd active borrowers, but this requirement has never been met).[21] McNamara's introduction of personnel budgeting (cost effectiveness or "Taylorism" in development lending) is analogous to his reorganization of the Pentagon in 1961. In fact, according to van de Laar, "several Pentagon hands came to the Bank with McNamara and introduced their techniques, as though the output of the organizations was comparable and amenable to standardization to a similar extent."[22] Van de Laar also points out that this "efficiency expert" approach directly subverted McNamara's professed aim of experimenting with innovative approaches to development projects:

> If . . . staff output is measured by the speed with which a "product" is delivered, staff are strongly tempted to avoid anything that detracts from welltrodden paths; any deviant or more ambitious course of action introduces additional uncertainty and possible delays in completion dates, which look bad on staff records. . . .

The prevailing work-environment entails that any novel approaches come about not *because* of the organizational style adopted but *in spite of it*.[23]

In the view of some observers, however, the most important and damaging aspect of McNamara's presidency was the rapid expansion of annual lending. This has led to charges that the Bank is "pushing money" by rushing through unsound projects, and by overfunding projects.[24] "McNamara started by borrowing much more than his predecessor and afterwards instructed his staff to find ways to spend the money. The increased availability of loanable funds has thus generated demand for more projects."[25]

But perhaps this is not merely McNamara's personality quirk, but a structural demand of the system. As McNamara steps down from the presidency to make way for A. W. Clausen (who, like every previous president except McNamara, comes from the commercial banking community), it is interesting to note that the incoming president has stressed the imperative need to continue to expand lending.

In my opinion, the changes in the World Bank's lending style under presidents Woods and McNamara do not represent fundamental changes, but merely incremental adaptation to a rapidly changing environment, combined with the systemic imperative to expand loans in order to keep net capital transfers to borrowers positive. Both old-style and new-style projects are examined in the following chapters, with relevant differences noted, but the fundamental similarity in intent cannot be overly stressed.

The International Bank for Reconstruction and Development

The World Bank Group includes the International Bank for Reconstruction and Development (IBRD), established in 1946, the International Development Association (IDA), founded in 1960, and the International Finance Corporation (IFC), which dates from 1956. This work will follow Bank usage: references to the World Bank will refer to the activity of the IBRD and IDA, as

Table 1.1

Major shareholders of IBRD, percent of voting power
(June 30, 1981)

United States	20.84	China	3.47
United Kingdom	7.44	India	3.28
Germany, Fed. Republic	5.06	Canada	3.22
France	5.05	Italy	2.94
Japan	5.04	Netherlands	2.25
percent held by top five	43.43	Belgium	2.13
percent held by top twelve	62.62	Australia	1.90

Major borrowers from IBRD with percent of loans outstanding
(June 30, 1981)

Brazil	9.73	Thailand	3.60
Mexico	7.92	Rumania	3.24
Indonesia	6.59	India	3.15
Korea	5.63	Nigeria	2.84
Turkey	5.11	Morocco	2.64
Colombia	5.02	Argentina	2.10
Philippines	4.90	Malaysia	2.10
Yugoslavia	4.65	Egypt	2.01
percent held by top eight	49.55	Algeria	1.91
percent held by top seventeen	73.14		

both institutions have the same staff and follow the same policy guidelines and similar, if not identical, procedures in appraising and supervising project work. While the IDA has a different source of funds and country eligibility for its loans is not the same, it is essentially a "legal fiction," a separate account in the same organization and not a different institution.[26]

The original entity, the IBRD, makes loans on relatively conventional terms. It is "owned" by its shareholders, the 139 member countries, who hold voting rights proportional to their shareholdings. The subscribed capital of the IBRD totaled roughly $37 billion in 1981. One-tenth of this share capital is paid-in and is used in the Bank's operations; the rest is callable capital and can be used only as a guarantee to the Bank's

Major contributors to IDA (June 30, 1981)

	percent of contributions	percent of voting power
United States	30.56	21.35
United Kingdom	12.20	7.32
Japan	12.03	5.59
Germany	11.78	6.57
Canada	5.52	3.80
France	5.40	3.85
Sweden	3.64	2.59
Netherlands	2.95	1.95
Part I members:	95.86	63.53

Major recipients of IDA credits, percentages (June 30, 1981)

India	40.33	Indonesia	3.94
Bangladesh	7.41	Tanzania	2.63
Pakistan	5.93	Sudan	2.42
Egypt	4.01	Kenya	1.90
Total of top four	57.68	Total of top eight	68.57

Source: World Bank, *Annual Report 1981.*

creditors.[27] In January 1980 the Bank's Board of Governors authorized a doubling of the authorized capital stock of the Bank, effective in October 1981. Only 7.5 percent of the new stock subscription will be paid-in.

The bulk of the IBRD's loanable funds are borrowed on the capital markets and from governments and central banks. Thanks to the guarantee of the uncalled portion of the Bank's capital, it can borrow at very favorable rates, close to or identical with the rates obtained on the securities of governments of the countries in which it sells its bonds. The World Bank is a major factor in world capital markets and is the largest nonresident borrower in virtually all countries where its issues are held.[28]

The Bank borrows chiefly from countries that have surpluses in their balance of payments, because it is easier and less costly in nominal terms. During the first ten years of its existence, the Bank was chiefly a "dollar" bank, reflecting the international strength and dominance of the U.S. economy. With the growing strength of the European economies and the balance of payments problems of the U.S., the sources of borrowing became more diversified: "The Federal Republic of Germany was the principal source in the late 1960s, Japan in the early 1970s, certain members of the Organization of Petroleum Exporting Countries (OPEC) in 1974, and the United States in 1975. In fiscal years 1976 and 1977, the Bank raised the majority of its funds in the United States, Germany, and Switzerland."[29] Although by the end of June 1980 the Bank had borrowed in a total of eighteen currencies, 95 percent of outstanding borrowings were made in only four: U.S. dollars (33 percent), Deutschemarks (30 percent), Swiss francs (18 percent), and Japanese yen (14 percent).[30] The currency of borrowing does not necessarily coincide with the nationality of investors; according to the Bank's treasurer, OPEC members held approximately $3.6 billion of the securities at the end of 1977, or about 17 percent of total outstanding borrowings.[31]

This borrowing is divided between official placements (borrowing from governments and central banks), which accounts for about one-third of the total, and private capital markets. In 1977 over 80 percent of the government placements were held in eight countries: Abu Dhabi, Germany, Iran, Japan, Libya, Nigeria, Saudi Arabia, and Venezuela.[32] All but Germany and Japan are oil-exporting nations. Although the Bank has been accused of subservience to the Organization of Petroleum Exporting Countries (OPEC), the dispute in September 1980 over the seating of the Palestine Liberation Organization (PLO) as an "observer" at the annual World Bank-IMF meeting in which OPEC backed down seems to indicate that OPEC will not pull its funds out of the Bank on a matter of political principle (or that the PLO is not really important to OPEC, compared with a relatively safe channel for investing surplus funds).[33]

The IBRD lends money at rates that are significantly more favorable for most borrowers than those they could obtain on the market, despite the fact that the Bank itself raises most of its funds on the capital market. Several factors contribute to this apparently paradoxical situation.

First, the shareholders of the Bank (its member governments) receive no interest or dividends on their contributions. The Bank charges all its borrowers the same interest rate, which may however be adjusted at quarter-year intervals. This rate is determined by figuring the average cost of borrowing in a given period and adding a spread of .5 percent. In fiscal year 1981, the cost of total borrowings by the Bank averaged 9.1 percent. The average cost of all funds, including paid-in capital and accumulated earnings, was only 6.1 percent. Borrowers at the end of fiscal year 1981 were paying interest rates of 9.6 percent, only slightly more than the Bank's cost of borrowing. The paid-in capital contributed by the taxpayers of its member countries, which is available free of cost to the Bank, allows it nevertheless to enjoy a substantial spread of over 3.5 percent while still charging subsidized rates to its borrowers.

Second, the Bank can borrow at extremely favorable rates because creditors have the guarantee that, if ever needed, the Bank's callable capital is committed to meeting its obligations. That is, the taxpayers again would have to shoulder the burden of any catastrophic deterioration of the Bank's financial position and make good its debts to the financial markets.

Third, the Bank's interest rates are not as good as they look, at least if one is comparing them to comparable rates in the dollar market. Under the regime of floating exchange rates, currencies change value in respect to one another at frequent intervals. It is the Bank's policy never to bear this currency risk. But in order to obtain *nominally* low rates of interest, the Bank borrows chiefly the strongest currencies, as we have seen—the dollar, the Deutschemark, the Swiss franc, and the yen. Loans are disbursed in the currencies held by the Bank, which do not necessarily match the currency needed for the project being financed, and they must be paid back in the same currency which is disbursed (even though all loans are still officially denominated in dollars). The nominal interest rates on marks, Swiss francs, and yen are low because these currencies are expected to appreciate in value relative to dollars and pounds; when borrowers have to pay back loans in appreciated currencies they are actually paying a hidden interest charge which may be quite substantial.

Complaints from borrowers about the unfair incidence of this burden recently prompted the Bank to adopt a currency pooling system. Under this system the borrowers would still bear the exchange risk, but it would be evenly distributed among them, in contrast to the previous practice in which, for example, a borrower might have to assume the risk on sharply appreciating yen which was not even usable on the project in question. At least under the new system it should be easier to calculate the hidden interest charge which is inherent in the exchange risk system.[34]

Finally, World Bank loans are attractive to borrowers because they are made at fixed interest rates for relatively long periods. This is an anomaly in the current international market, in which commercial banks now insist on "floating" interest rates which vary during the life of the individual loans according to the cost of funds to the banks.

The International Development Association

When the IDA was founded in 1960, it saved the Bank from a threatening crisis of irrelevance, according to the Bank's semi-official history. In the words of historians Mason and Asher:

> The outlook in 1960 for an agency equipped only to make loans at close-to-commercial rates of interest to countries unable to borrow elsewhere would have been bleak indeed. The Western Europeans and the Australians were becoming too creditworthy to borrow from the Bank. The Japanese were still large borrowers but obviously not destined to remain so. Among the less developed countries, on the other hand, India, Pakistan, and some other major borrowers were piling up external debt so rapidly as to call into question their continued creditworthiness for loans on Bank terms. The creditworthiness of newly independent countries in Africa for interest-bearing loans was also questionable. *IDA, in short, had to be invented to keep the Bank preeminent, or at least eminent, in the growing complex of multilateral development agencies attempting to facilitate international development.*[35]

The creation of IDA was also a means of heading off the

demand of Third World countries for a more radical form of soft-loan or grant agency under the auspices of the United Nations, a demand largely prompted by dissatisfaction with the conservative lending policies of the IBRD. The best-known of these proposed soft-loan agencies was the Special United Nations Fund for Economic Development (SUNFED). The Bank management, initially hostile to the idea of a soft-loan agency, eventually made a 180-degree turn on the matter, pushed by U.S. government officials who adopted the idea and explored it with other potential donor governments, "stressing the growing need of the less developed countries for soft loans and the specter of SUNFED under UN auspices if IDA were not set up as an affiliate of the Bank."[36] Eugene Black, president of IBRD at the time, admitted in an interview that IDA "was really an idea to offset the urge for SUNFED."[37]

IDA has its own constitution that declares it to be "an entity separate and distinct from the Bank" (article 6, section 6 [a]), but it is simply a separate account managed by the Bank officers and staff, which finances the same type of projects as the Bank (in some cases the same projects), selected according to the same standards. Membership in the Bank is a condition of membership in IDA, although a few IBRD members have chosen not to join. The elaborate emphasis on the separate nature of the IDA was necessary to assure the capital markets from which the IBRD borrows that their funds would not be endangered by the soft-loan affiliate of the Bank.

IDA's funds come almost entirely from grants made by its Part I (capital-exporting) member governments, with a small proportion deriving from gifts made by the IBRD out of its retained profits, which are not distributed to IBRD shareholders. Thus all of its funds are derived directly or indirectly from the taxpayers of the member governments. The IDA "credits" are nominally loans which must be repaid, but no interest is charged (except an administrative charge of only .75 percent and a recently instituted fee of .5 percent on undisbursed credits) and the grace period and maturity of the credits are so long (ten and fifty years, respectively) that it is virtually grant aid.

Unlike the IBRD, which could in theory operate as a revolving fund requiring no additional financial support from member governments, the IDA requires frequent infusions of new appropriations and is extremely vulnerable to shifts in the political climate for aid. Budgets are made, and financial replenishments are required, at three-year intervals, which means that in practice the lobbying activity on behalf of IDA must be virtually constant. The United States is the key contributor, and replenishments cannot come into force without the U.S. contribution, but to date the United States has been late five out of five times with its share.[38] As amendments to the Bank's constitution, the Articles of Agreement, require three-fifths of the members holding four-fifths of the voting power, the United States with slightly more than one-fifth of the votes holds an effective veto power over amendments.[39]

As the soft IDA credits are more valuable to recipients than the "harder" IBRD loans, there is a great deal of competition and politicking centered around eligibility for these credits. As the criteria for project selection are supposed to be identical to that of the IBRD, eligibility is determined on a country basis. There are two basic criteria: per capita GNP is supposed to be below a given level (at present $730), and the country is not supposed to be creditworthy for loans on IBRD terms. The second condition has its paradoxical aspects, as van de Laar has pointed out. Good economic "performance" is supposed to be a condition for both IBRD loans and IDA credits, with the test being, if anything, more severe in the case of IDA. A country cannot qualify for IBRD loans if it is not deemed "creditworthy." But, as he goes on to note:

> On the one hand, a country that does well on the economic front rates high on the performance scale, to the point of being penalized by having to graduate to hard Bank loans. Good performance is frequently equated with "good" economic management and contributes to creditworthiness. On the other hand, a country that does poorly qualifies for IDA on lack of creditworthiness grounds, and is rewarded with soft IDA credits rather than hard Bank loans.[40]

The so-called Asian giants—India, Pakistan, Bangladesh (after 1971), and Indonesia—consume such a large proportion of IDA credits that it is sometimes nicknamed the "India Development

Association." A number of African countries also qualify for IDA, but it is insignificant in Latin America. Indonesia was taken off the eligibility list in 1974 because of its high oil revenues, but qualified again after 1978, as heavy and indiscriminate foreign borrowing damaged its credit standing—a perfect example of the paradox outlined by van de Laar. The promise of IDA credits is a particularly valuable bargaining tool with which to bribe a potential defaulter to resume payments on IBRD debt—which is probably what the Bank's treasurer implied when he reassured investors that "whatever financial questions might arise in connection with IDA, it is the Association's member governments that are at risk, not the World Bank or the investors in its securities. . . . IDA does cost something to taxpayers, but in no way does it add to their risk as World Bank bondholders. On the contrary, it reduces it."[41]

A Multibillion Dollar Market

Loans and credits disbursed by the World Bank are, for the most part, project-tied, which means the money is paid directly to the corporations that win contracts for constructing and/or supplying projects financed by the Bank. This is a multibillion dollar market, as total loans and credits amounted cumulatively to nearly $80 billion at the end of fiscal year 1980, of which about $48 billion had been disbursed at the end of January 1981. About 80 percent of these funds is allocated through international competitive bidding (ICB) supervised by the Bank, in which corporations based in Bank member countries—rich and poor—and in Switzerland, which is not a member but has opened its capital markets to the Bank, are eligible to compete.

This international "public spending" could be regarded as a sort of international Keynesianism which, taken together with expenditures financed through bilateral aid programs and other international institutions, plays an important role in maintaining the capitalist system by providing a taxpayer-financed market for goods produced in the creditor countries. It has been estimated that shipments to non-OPEC Third World nations comprised 26 percent of all U.S. exports in 1976, and that the United States ran a $16 billion trade surplus with those nations in that year.[42] The World Bank finances a substantial proportion of that market, and because of its key position in enforcing debt repayment through expansion of its own lending, its role is far more important than absolute shares indicate.

Because bidding on World Bank contracts is competitive among member countries, procurement does not correspond exactly to contributions for each member nation, and some are considered "winners" and "losers" in the competition for contracts. Japan is the big winner, with a surplus of procurements over contributions in the period to mid-1977 of $2 billion, while other winners include West Germany ($1.7 billion), Britain ($1 billion), Italy ($919 million), France ($666 million), and the United States ($422 million).[43]

Although international competitive bidding is supposed to eliminate the abuses, such as overpricing of aid-financed supplies, which are endemic to the system of tying aid donations to exports of a given country, some problems persist. For one thing, World Bank projects are often cofinanced with bilateral aid which is country-tied, thus diluting the presumed beneficial effect of the competitive bidding. Another is that ICB offers no defense against price-fixing cartels found, for example, in the electrical equipment supply industry. This becomes an important element in World Bank procurement given that large sums are disbursed every year for electric power loans.[44]

A more serious problem is the fact that ICB is designed to keep or pry open markets in the poorer countries that might otherwise be covered by local suppliers. This is relatively insignificant in the poorest countries that have no industry and are forced to import all modern equipment, but it is a serious concern in the more industrialized Bank clients such as Brazil, India, and Pakistan. The promise of bilateral or multilateral aid constitutes, in Richard Newfarmer's words, "a lucrative incentive for host governments to keep the door open to imports."[45] Brazil, for example, was nearing self-sufficiency in electrical equipment production in 1965. "If external financing were confined to equipment which had to be imported, the scope for foreign aid would be limited," according to a World Bank report at the time. But, as Newfarmer noted:

> Today in Brazil, international aid finances more than 80% of heavy electrical equipment purchases for hydroelectric projects (including generation, transmission, and distribution and equipment such as hydraulic generators, turbines, transformers, and cables). About three-quarters of the funding now comes from the Interamerican Bank and the World Bank.[46]

After many complaints from borrowing countries that their suppliers should be allowed a margin of preference in competitive bidding on Bank projects, a decision was made in 1962 to allow a preference of 15 percent or the existing tariff rate, whichever was lower, when local companies wished to bid on Bank projects. This concession was made in order to stave off demands for higher levels of protection, and is at such a modest level that it poses no serious threat to international suppliers. As a Bank attorney once admitted:

> At least in the experience of our Bank, there has been some feeling at times that by insisting on international competitive bidding we do a disservice to the borrower in special cases. On the other hand we have to take into account that the providers of our capital are very interested and we have to strike a balance between the interest of exporters of equipment and goods and recipients of loans.[47]

At least in the past, the Bank has been strict in insisting that the procurement "packages" offered for bidding should be big enough to attract the international firms.[48]

At least one analyst believes that ICB may be more ideally suited to the purposes of the largest multinational or transnational corporations (TNCs) than tied aid, which demands procurements within the nation supplying the aid: "By and large, aid programs allow transnational conglomerates to allocate their lowest bids to the highest profit point in the parent system while exposing the less-developed economy to international agreement between TNCs."[49]

Corporations that are potential bidders on Bank-financed projects have received, since 1978, a publication designed specifically to give them an early warning about projects coming up for bidding in the future. In June 1978 the Bank began quarterly publication of an "Operational Summary of Proposed Projects (IBRD/IDA)" which, for a subscription fee of $20 per year, gave information on (1) projects that the Bank and IDA are actively considering for financial assistance, with a brief description of each project; (2) the member country and the agency responsible for the project; (3) the amount of financing to be provided and colenders, if known; and (4) the stage to which a proposed project has progressed.[50] The following year the publication was made into a monthly and the price was raised to $60 per year. It is now available as an insert in the *Development Forum/Business Edition*, which is published by the United Nations' Division for Economic and Social Information in Geneva. Advertising itself to multinational executives as "the unique UN source of advance notices for more than $16,000,000,000 of world-wide projects," *Develoment Forum/Business Edition* sells for $250 per year or Swiss francs 420 in the wealthy countries and $170 or Swiss francs 370 in the underdeveloped ones. It is worthy of note that no such advance notice of projects that are under preparation is available to the people who will be affected by the projects, or to researchers who cannot afford the stiff subscription price.

It is also remarkable that an institution such as the World Bank, which indefatigably grinds out compilations of statistics on all conceivable matters relating to the social, economic, and financial affairs of its member countries, has kept no breakdown of procurement awards by corporations, except for the United States, where it is also broken down by state in order to facilitate lobbying of Congress by corporations winning Bank contracts. (This breakdown hinders perception of the sales of a large international corporation.) The Caterpillar Tractor Company of Peoria, Illinois is said to be the biggest contractor in the United States.[51] Under a new policy, contracts let under Bank loans approved after November 1980 will begin appearing in *Development Forum/Business Edition* when approved. In the future, researchers who can afford the subscription will be able to do more than speculate about who are the real beneficiaries of Bank finances.

U.S. Dominance in the Bank

The World Bank is formally ruled by its Board of Governors. Each member nation has a governor, who is usually that country's minister of finance or equivalent acting ex officio. Certain important decisions are reserved for the Board of Governors, but as that body comes together only once a year, at the annual meeting in the last week of September, and as a body of 100-plus is rather cumbersome, the day-to-day business of the Bank is conducted by the executive directors and the president.

There are twenty executive directors, of which five are appointed by the five members having the largest number of shares (currently the United States, United Kingdom, Germany, France, and Japan), and the remainder elected by the other, smaller members. The country groupings that elect directors are relatively stable, and Escott Reid has noted the existence of "virtually permanent non-permanent" directorships. Of the "virtually permanent" directorships he noted in 1973,[52] four were still held by the country in question in 1981 (Canada, India, Belgium, and Italy).

According to the Bank's Articles of Agreement, the president is appointed and fired by the executive directors. In practice, the president has always been a U.S. citizen, as this was deemed necessary for retaining the confidence of the capital markets and the U.S. government, and the executive directors have been confined to approving a candidate selected by the president of the United States. When nominating A. W. Clausen of the Bank of America to succeed Robert McNamara in the fall of 1980, President Carter found it prudent to clear the nomination with his eventually successful rival in the presidential campaign, Ronald Reagan. It was also reported that the selection was made hurriedly, in order to head off the growing drive among member countries to name someone from a country other than the United States to the post this time.[53]

The United States is still the largest shareholder in the World Bank, although its voting power has shrunk from the 35 percent plurality it held in 1947 to 21 percent in the IBRD and 31 percent in the IDA in fiscal year 1981. The plurality it now holds in the

IBRD is barely large enough to preserve a U.S. veto on certain important decisions, but the economic power of the United States is a more powerful constraint on the decisions of the World Bank than the percentage of voting power would indicate. If the U.S. executive were ever seriously displeased by a decision of the Bank, it could withdraw from the organization, or simply refuse to contribute to IDA, which would leave the Bank financially impotent.

The U.S. executive director is not free to vote according to whim in the Bank's board meetings. He is subordinate to the instructions of the secretary of the treasury, who is advised on policy matters relating to the IMF, World Bank, and the regional development banks of which the United States is a member by the National Advisory Council (NAC). This little-known body was created by the legislation that authorized U.S. participation in the Bretton Woods institutions when they were first established. Members of the NAC are the secretaries of treasury, state, and commerce; the Federal Reserve Board chairman, the president of the Export-Import Bank (Ex-Im Bank), and the administrator of the Agency for International Development.[54] Representatives of other nations are presumably also subordinate to the instructions of their nation's highest financial officer.

The U.S. secretary of the treasury is, of course, supposed to be responsible to the U.S. Congress, but in discussing U.S. dominance over the decision-making process it is important to distinguish between the interventions of the executive and those of the legislative branch of the U.S. government. Both branches have injected politics into the operations of the World Bank (and the IMF and regional development banks as well), but they have also been at loggerheads with each other over what type of prolitics to inject.

The process of government in the United States may be described in oversimplified but basically valid fashion as a constant struggle by the executive branch to maintain its autonomy and freedom of action from the Congress, which must appropriate all funds expended by the government. The executive branch is itself subject to constraints that, without detailing them here, can be inferred to be much more directly linked to the power of

U.S.-based multinational corporations and financial institutions as well as to the maintenance of U.S. power, influence, and credibility vis-à-vis the rest of the world.[55] The Congress, by contrast, is a confusing patchwork of conservative and liberal ideologies, but tends to be much more responsive to particularistic pressures in contrast to the executive's concept of elite management.

In order to avoid limitations and restrictions imposed by congressional scrutiny, there has been until recently a marked trend to channel less aid funds through bilateral channels and more through multilateral banks and institutions such as the Ex-Im Bank that are not answerable to Congress, except when they must request replenishment of capital.[56] Congress has responded to this challenge by directing much closer scrutiny to the multilateral institutions than they had previously, leading to such legislation as the Gonzalez Amendment, which limits the freedom of the U.S. executive directors in these institutions to vote as the NAC might advise them.

The Gonzalez Amendment of 1972 required U.S. executive directors to vote against loans to any country which has nationalized, expropriated, or otherwise restricted the use of property owned by U.S. citizens, thus paralleling the Hickenlooper Amendment that had done the same thing for bilateral aid.[57] Even though the executive branch by no means favors such expropriations, it has protested, resisted, and evaded these mandatory instructions in order to maintain its freedom of maneuver in politically sensitive situations.

During most of its history the Bank tried to operate by "consensus," avoiding formal voting by settling divisive issues before they came before the executive board. In 1972, however, in response to congressional direction the United States cast its first formal vote in opposition to a proposed loan, which was nevertheless approved by the other executive directors. Since that time the U.S. director has frequently cast a negative vote or abstained on particular loan decisions. These votes are reported in the *Annual Report* of the National Advisory Council on International Monetary and Financial Policies.

In the late 1970s, congressional critics of multilateral aid tried to direct the U.S. representatives to vote against loans to countries found to be violating human rights standards, loans for the production of sugar, palm oil, and citrus fruits for export, and loans to Vietnam, Laos, Cambodia, Cuba, Angola, Mozambique, and Uganda. In order to head off such legislation, President Carter promised to instruct U.S. directors to vote against such loans. This action dismayed the international institutions and their advocates, who argued that such pledges would politicize and undermine the institutions.[58] President McNamara said in 1977 that the Bank "could not accept funds so conditioned,"[59] but two years later he was himself promising the U.S. Congress that the Bank would make no loans to Vietnam in order to prevent the passage of a legislative amendment to that effect. By doing so he provoked a sharp rebuke from the executive directors, who accused him of exceeding his authority by communicating directly with members of Congress.[60]

That there should be an uproar about injecting "politics" into Bank operations is ironic, for in fact the Bank has been obedient to the wishes of the U.S. *executive branch* ever since it was founded. The only new element introduced in the 1970s was that the politics came this time from the elected representative body of the United States rather than the bipartisan foreign policy establishment sometimes called the "permanent government."[61]

It was also doubly ironic that loans to Vietnam figured so prominently in the most recent crisis. Not only was Robert McNamara the secretary of defense who had prosecuted the U.S. war against Vietnam during the phase of its most rapid escalation, but in 1974 the U.S. executive had attempted to strengthen the puppet government which they supported in South Vietnam by mustering multilateral support for a large loan to Saigon from the World Bank. This effort, which would have paralleled, if it had been successful, the programs of IMF support for Cambodia and Laos during the war years,[62] became moot when the United States was forced to withdraw from Saigon in April 1975.[63]

The United States government, as the largest shareholder in the Bank and contributor to IDA, has always been able to control the direction of its lending. During the formative years, when the Bank was considering loans to postwar Poland and Czechoslovakia, the United States made it clear to the management that it would vote against such loans if presented to the executive board. It was decided that the loans would not be presented, negotiations were suspended, and eventually both countries withdrew from membership.[64] Negotiations for a World Bank loan to build the Aswan Dam in Egypt were suspended when U.S. Secretary of State John Foster Dulles decided to refuse financing for the project.[65] On the other hand, when the World Bank wanted to discipline a country by suspending its lending program, but the United States continued to supply aid for military or other reasons, the World Bank found it had no leverage at all, as happened in Turkey in the mid-1950s.[66]

The United States got the World Bank to cease lending to Chile during the Allende years, although several of its European allies maintained cordial relations with the Allende government and continued to provide aid. Now the United States is trying to use the Bank as a channel for multilateral support for the ruthless regime in El Salvador, over European opposition. A Treasury Department report on multilateral development banks prepared for the Reagan administration boasts of several instances in which the United States was able to impose its wishes on the World Bank, including the cessation of lending to Chile, Vietnam, and Afghanistan in 1979.[67]

Major changes in the type of loans made by the Bank also seem to be made more in response to initiatives from its major shareholder than as a result of autonomous management and staff decisions. The decision to give high priority to agricultural projects in the 1960s followed a phone call made by a "very high official of the U.S. government" to President George Woods, or so Woods confided to David Lilienthal.[68] And while Robert McNamara has garnered much praise for his redirection of Bank focus toward poverty-oriented lending, van de Laar notes that this shift in World Bank policy followed closely on the changed focus of the 1973 U.S. Foreign Assistance Act.[69]

Quite apart from the more blatant attempts to use Bank lending for political purposes in volation of its own charter, the pattern of loans over the years shows an unsubtle preference for governments that put out the welcome mat for foreign investment. The Bank insists that its loan decisions are always based on economic criteria. It is easy enough to find fault with the economic management of Chile under Allende, Brazil from 1958 to the military coup of 1964, Indonesia under Sukarno, and other governments to which the Bank has refused to lend, whether one's critique comes from the Right or from the Left. It is less easy to accept the Bank's story that only economic criteria are decisive if one looks at the blatant economic mismanagement of many of the borrowers who remain in good standing, such as Mobutu's Zaire, Marcos' Philippines, and the current regimes of Chile, Turkey, and Indonesia. Clearly, the Bank equates good economic management with policies favorable to foreign investors and is quite willing to overlook the fact that such policies may be incompatible with a genuine commitment to abolish poverty.

The Crisis of the World Bank

The continued viability of the Bank depends on two factors: the confidence of the financial markets from which the IBRD does its borrowing, and the continued support of its developed member governments, of which the most important is the United States. There is reason to believe that the Bank is facing a crisis in its relations with both of these pillars of support.

The crisis of relations with the U.S. government is overt: the accession of Ronald Reagan to the presidency means that for the first time in its history, the support of the U.S. executive branch for continued expansion of the World Bank is in question. There is no open crisis on the financial markets yet, but the following analysis of the Bank's relationship with these markets suggests that a crisis may be just waiting in the wings.

The Bank's obligations are considered very high quality in the capital markets: they carry a Triple A rating from the three major U.S. bond rating services. This high rating is apparently based on two factors: the government guarantees that callable capital will be used to make good the Bank's obligations in case of any serious financial trouble (there has up to now been no necessity to call in any capital for this purpose), and the claim that there has never been a default on a Bank loan.

The treasurer of the Bank likes to emphasize in his communications to the financial community that under the Bank's charter, the Articles of Agreement, the total amount of outstanding loans held by the Bank may not exceed the total of its subscribed capital (paid-in and callable), surplus, and reserves.

> The point here is that unlike in the case of private commercial institutions, an express provision limits how much we can have outstanding in loans as compared with capital and reserves. That limitation is "one-to-one." I would suggest that is an extremely prudent proscription. How many commercial lending institutions limit their outstanding loans receivable to their capital and reserves?[70]

This statement is somewhat disingenuous, as it does not mention that while virtually all the Bank's obligations are in "strong" currencies, only a little over half of the Bank's callable share capital is in the form of currencies that would be acceptable as payment for these obligations. In its early days, when it was a "dollar" bank, the World Bank attempted to borrow only to the extent of the U.S. capital share. Although article 2, section 7 (ii) provides that in case of a call on capital the members must pay in gold, dollars, or the currency required to meet the obligation, there is considerable doubt that the weak-currency members would be able to pay up in such a case. Therefore, analysts sometimes only count the uncalled capital subscription of the Group of Ten (wealthy countries), which comprises about 56 percent of the total.[71]

If this practice is followed, the ratio of Bank lending to reserves is more on the order of 1.7:1 than 1:1. The massive expansion of Bank lending under the McNamara presidency (1968–1981) came up sharply against this constitutional limitation, and led to McNamara's insistence on the necessity for a doubling of the authorized capital, which was agreed in January 1980. Hardly was that matter settled than McNamara proposed, in his annual address to the Board of Governors on September 30, 1980, that the limiting clause in the Articles of Agreement be scrapped so that the purported one-to-one ratio be abandoned.

This ratio, he suggested, "contrasts with the standard practice of large commercial banks, whose capital to risk-asset ratios run to less than 6 percent. And yet none of these banks has the IBRD's repayment record; none of them relies on such long-term sources of funds; and none has such a strong liquidity position."[72] Asking rhetorically whether a thirty-five-year-old provision still makes financial sense in this modern, heavily leveraged world, McNamara's answer is no: "The tentative answer is that the 1 to 1 ratio, established at Bretton Woods in the closing months of World War II, is no longer really relevant to the Bank's financial condition or to the economic situation of its principal shareholders, and that the result now is an unnecessary underutilization of the Bank's capital base."[73] The effect of dropping this limitation and adopting a higher debt-equity ratio, van de Laar points out, would be to increase the importance of the criteria of international financial markets, at the governments' expense, in decisions about the Bank's scope for lending, and would most likely raise the interest rates it would have to pay.[74] McNamara's successor, A. W. Clausen, has, at least for the time being, rejected any tampering with this 1:1 ratio.

The Bank likes to boast that it has never suffered a default.

> We have not had any losses on loans. We have never had a write-off of a loan. We have never had a nonaccruing loan. We have a firm policy against debt rescheduling. We do not tolerate late payments.[75]
>
> There are substantial pragmatic reasons why borrowers do not default on World Bank loans. In the event of a default, no further disbursement would be made on that loan or any other loan we had outstanding in the country. And, no new loans would be committed until the default had been cured. Borrowers know our policies in this regard, and given the substantial amount of our undisbursed loans, I suggest they would be extremely reluctant to take steps to jeopardize the transfer of future resources.
>
> A default to the Bank also carries serious consequences that would affect the credit of the country involved, both with other countries and with commercial suppliers of resources.[76]

According to van de Laar, no provisions are made for bad debts as a matter of principle![77] The Bank's treasurer says, "While our financial statements include a 'general reserve' (previously called 'reserve against losses on loans') that item constitutes, in fact, our accumulated retained earnings. We have no actuarial basis for our 'reserves' simply because we have never had a 'bad loan.' "[78]

It is probably true that a government in financial trouble is less likely to default on a World Bank loan than on other types of international commitments; this was demonstrated when the government of Ghana selectively repudiated some of its debt in 1972 but agreed to honor its obligations to the World Bank.[79] Nevertheless, the Bank's claim that it has never had a bad debt has to be qualified somewhat in light of the facts, and though it may not "tolerate" late payments, they have occurred. A case in point is provided by the Bank's relationship with Allende's Chile.

The U.S. executive director of the Bank, responding to inquiries from the House Appropriations Subcommittee on Foreign Assistance, gave a detailed history of the Bank's relationship with Chile during the government of Popular Unity. In mid-October 1972 the World Bank suspended work on new loans for Chile, claiming that the government's economic policies would prevent the effective utilization of Bank lending. The nationalization of the large U.S.-owned copper companies without payment of what the companies considered "adequate" compensation also loomed large in the background, a moot point only because the Bank claimed to regard Chile as ineligible for credit in any case.

Chile suspended service on all payments of interest and principal to the Bank as of January 1, 1973, an action which the executive director's report to the subcommittee did not shrink from calling a default. The Bank's response was swift and conciliatory. Although the resumption of normal development lending was not deemed possible, the Bank promised to "give the highest priority to accelerating disbursements on existing loans to Chile," to amend two earlier loan agreements to ease the interest burden during construction, and to extend a small technical assistance loan "as evidence of the Bank's desire to assist Chile's future economic development when circumstances permitted." The Chileans then agreed to resume service on loans and credits from the Bank group from July 1, 1973, and to make good all debt in arrears by December 31, 1973. The Allende government was displaced by a right-wing military coup on September 11, 1973, and the Bank moved as quickly as its cumbersome procedures allowed to decide that normal lending should be resumed as "substantial progress is being made in overcoming the country's economic problems."[80]

The political significance of this pattern of suspension and resumption of lending is obvious, but the point I want to emphasize here is that Chile *did* default on its debt to the Bank, and the Bank administration, caught between the refusal of the United States to permit normal lending to Chile and the horror of an open default, did everything within its power to bribe the Chilean government to resume debt service. (Despite the promises, it was decided that the technical assistance loan and the interest refinancing proposal could not get a favorable vote in the executive board and they were not presented—until after the coup.)

It is very likely, though difficult to prove as clearly as in the Chilean case, that other defaults have occurred and have been covered up in similar fashion—by promising new loans if the payments are resumed. It is rumored that Burma was in default on payments to the Bank for years before resuming a loan relationship in 1973 (and then it received soft-term IDA credits). Although the Bank has a "firm policy" against rescheduling its own loans, it did reschedule in one case, that of India in 1968.[81]

Clearly, the Bank is convinced that any further participation in debt rescheduling would have a disastrous effect on the volume and cost of capital that it borrows.[82] A well-publicized default that could not be quickly papered over would be, if anything, even worse. To be sure, from a financial point of view the Bank could probably tolerate one or two defaults as isolated events. In 1976 the Bank's treasurer attempted to reassure lenders that the Bank could easily meet such a challenge:

> Nonetheless, I am asked what impact a default would have on the finances of the Bank and on its ability to meet service on its indebtedness. Let us take one exaggerated example. Assume that a sizable borrower repudiates all of its debt to the World Bank and stops payment of debt service immediately. The reasons may be

irrational, but let us assume it happens. The effect of this action might be that the Bank incurs a loss against its current income.

As far as the ability of the Bank to meet service on its debt is concerned, however, the default would have little, if any, impact. In the immediate period following the default, our cash flow very likely would increase, since we would stop all disbursements on loans to the defaulting country. Further, since our debt structure consists primarily of long-term and intermediate-term obligations, the effect on the market for our outstanding obligations would be minimal. It would be a nonevent, in terms of its effects on our bondholders. Our reserves are adequate. Our capital is huge. And, most important for the bondholder, the very real and substantial liquid position of the Bank of over $6 billion, as well as its access to worldwide markets, afford protection not available elsewhere. The uncalled capital is simply icing on the cake. All this is available, along with the cash flow from the repayments of the pool of disbursed loans, to support the credit of the Bank and the security of those who invest in its bonds and notes.[83]

International financial markets rely far more on government guarantees of the Bank's obligations than on its questionable claim that there has never been a default. Aside from the fact that the past is not always a reliable guide to the future, it is probable that the claim is true only in the sense that, technically speaking, a default is simply what the creditor decides to call a default. In the current atmosphere of heavy unease over unviable Third World debt structures, the Bank has apparently decided it would be better not even to the mention the possibility; the 1978 edition of Rotberg's pamphlet omits the paragraphs quoted above.

In the last analysis, the Bank's power to avoid defaults on its own loans, as well as its considerable powers of leverage on the politics of borrowing countries, depends on the prospect of continuing large flows of new loans from the Bank. And it is not only the Bank's own repayment prospects which are at stake, but those of the entire panoply of Western lending institutions, public and private, who have chosen to make the IMF and the World Bank the keystone of the debt enforcement system. Commercial bankers are quite openly calling upon the Fund and the Bank to salvage their dubious loans to debt-laden Third World borrowers, and one of their own, Bank of America president A. W. Clausen, has been appointed the successor to Robert McNamara as World Bank president.

The Bank's powers to enforce debt repayment depend on its power to extend new loans; but unless the gross total of Bank lending expands constantly, the burden of repaying old loans will eventually surpass the amount of new loans that can be expected. This would not be a problem for a country that was using the borrowings to develop successfully, and to begin earning balance of payments surpluses out of which the loans could be repaid, but this is manifestly not the case with most of the Bank's borrowers, particularly that large number who every year run deficits that must be financed by new borrowings and thus see their total debt burden pyramid.

Unless the lending of the Bank, and the financial system as a whole, expands constantly, a point will come when it will be clearly more advantageous for a given country to repudiate its debts than to continue to pay them. This means that, in order to protect its considerable powers of leverage and its own strong but vulnerable record of no (highly visible) defaults, the Bank must constantly expand its volume of new loans in order to maintain a positive net transfer of resources. In this light, the radical expansion of Bank lending under McNamara's presidency, often viewed as the product of an idiosyncratic and even megalomaniac personality, can be seen rather as a systemic imperative. Net transfers of funds from the Bank to all its members reached a very low level in 1969, the year after McNamara assumed the presidency, and was actually negative in 1970. The urgency of the problem has only increased in the decade of the 1970s, as the massive spate of commercial bank lending temporarily eased repayment problems in the short run but exacerbated them as soon as the newer loans began to fall due. Continued expansion is an institutional imperative for the World Bank. No one has stated this more bluntly than president-elect Clausen, in an interview shortly after his appointment was announced:

> I am a banker, and . . . in my professional judgment we have no choice but to support this approach. All the facts are there to prove that it is in America's self-interest to support the international

agencies. . . . And if we don't produce this expanded level of support—comes the revolution. It's as simple as that. We have to do it
or else we will destroy ourselves.[84]

As several analysts have pointed out,[85] there are only three
ways in which net transfers can be increased: first, by softening
the terms of lending; second, by accelerating the rate of gross
commitments; and third, by debt renegotiation. As we have
seen, the Bank abjures renegotiation for fear of its repercussions
on its terms of borrowing. Terms of IBRD borrowing have got-
ten harder rather than softer in recent years. In the present
atmosphere of inflation and escalating interest rates, the Bank
could find that fixed-rate loans are not financially viable. It has a
policy of matching maturities, which is supposed to minimize
this risk, but clearly it has to borrow on shorter terms than it
lends: in 1978, according to the treasurer, the average life of its
outstanding debt was 6.5 years while the average life of outstanding loans was 10.5.[86]

The Bank attempts to minimize this risk by keeping a large
liquidity position (roughly 40 percent of its portfolio), which
allows it to time its entry into financial markets so as to obtain
the most favorable terms and avoid the necessity of borrowing
when rates are high; it permits high earnings when short-term
rates are high, which may partially compensate for low rates on
long-term assets. But this may not be enough in the current
situation, when interest rates are very high and may not come
down at all. The Bank is now finding it more difficult and
expensive to raise funds in the international bond markets than
in past years,[87] and these costs are reflected in rates to borrowers.
In 1976 the Bank hardened its terms to borrowers by shortening
the average maturities and grace periods on its loans and by
changing the repayment formula. In early 1982 new "front-end
fees" on IBRD loans and commitment fees on IDA credits further
raised the costs to borrowers.[88]

Overall terms of lending could be softened by expanding the
proportion of IDA soft loans in the Bank's total portfolio, but in
order to do this the Bank must have the support of the United
States as well as other governments. It has been difficult enough
in the past to get funds for IDA through the U.S. Congress when

the executive branch was firmly in favor of the action; but now the Reagan administration has decided to reduce the U.S. commitment to IDA. This will only hasten the further hardening of Bank lending terms.

The third way—acceleration of the rate of commitments—cannot continue unless the Bank asks its member governments for increases in subscribed capital (as was successfully accomplished at the end of the 1970s) or by diluting the coverage of those guarantees by abandoning the one-to-one ratio, which might make its borrowings even more expensive. For individual countries in trouble, however, the use of program loans can temporarily plug the gap; they can be disbursed rapidly because there is no need to wait until a project is designed and executed, and they provide free foreign exchange, which can be used to pay back debts that have fallen due. Under the circumstances it is not surprising that the Bank has decided to extend new forms of program loans (see Chapter 5) that resemble those of the IMF; the wonder is that it has not expanded such lending even more rapidly, given the enormous temptations.

2

Malignant Growth: A Preliminary Explanation

> Labour is *not the source* of all wealth. Nature is
> just as much the source of use values. . . . The
> bourgeois have very good grounds for falsely
> ascribing *supernatural creative power* to labour;
> since precisely from the fact that labour depends
> on nature it follows that the man who possesses
> no other property than his labour power must,
> in all conditions of society and culture, be the
> slave of other men who have made themselves
> the owners of the material conditions of labour.
> He can then work only with their permission,
> hence live only with their permission.
> —Karl Marx, *Critique of the Gotha Programme*

Who are the poor, and how did they get that way? These questions are basic to poverty programs. The way in which they are posed, and answered, in large part determines the prescriptions for overcoming poverty.

One of the most famous solutions was provided by Thomas Malthus, who held that population growth must inevitably exceed the growth in production of the means of subsistence, since food production increases according to arithmetical progression, while population increases geometrically. Malthus' evidence for this proposition is extremely dubious, consisting of an assertion that the population in the United States "had been found to double itself in twenty-five years" on the one hand, and pure ungrounded supposition about food production on the other.[1] However dubious Malthus' reasoning, it had two merits that have ensured it a long life (or frequent resurrections). The first was that it was simple, and seemed to explain the observed facts: in early nineteenth-century England people were going hungry, and even starving. The second virtue was a political one: it was extremely convenient to the ruling class to have the evident scarcity explained in this way.

> Malthus proved to the satisfaction of the ruling classes that they had no responsibility for the existing state of affairs. They were not about to raise questions about subjects such as the effect of private property on the availability of resources . . . who among the ruling classes would question the doctrine that the road to salvation lay not in furthering the struggle between classes but in eliminating the lust between sexes?[2]

Through the years since it was first published, Malthus' doctrine (though clearly disproved by technological advances in the nearly two centuries since he wrote, as well as by demographic changes consequent upon urbanization and industrialization) still finds its followers, among which we can number the World Bank. Past president Robert McNamara made population control a high priority Bank policy at the same time he began to expand lending into other new fields purportedly designed to aid the poor. "The greatest single obstacle to the economic and social advancement of the majority of peoples in the underdeveloped world is rampant population growth," he asserted in his 1969 address to the Board of Governors.

In April 1977 he devoted a major address at the Massachusetts Institute of Technology to the population problem. And in 1979 he asserted, "To put it simply: excessive population growth is the greatest single obstacle to the economic and social advancement of most of the societies in the developing world. . . ."[3]

But a one-sided emphasis on population growth as an explanation for increasing immiseration in the current world could be counterproductive for McNamara's goal of attracting more governmental and public support for the Bank's lending program. Such figures may make the task seem so hopeless that there is no point in giving aid; "lifeboat" and "triage" theories are becoming increasingly popular as a result of such exercises of population extrapolation. So McNamara's ideology departed from

Malthus' by stressing *both* the terrors of population growth and the world's potential to increase productivity:

> The lifeboat isn't full. The world capacity is not being utilized. I don't care whether it's food, or what it is you're talking about. We have a capacity to expand production in the countries that need it, in the Indias, the Bangladeshes, and elsewhere, to expand production— to expand production to begin to deal with these problems.[4]

Malthusian disaster *without* the Bank, but a chance for salvation if the Bank is supported with adequate funds—this was the McNamara scenario.

McNamara has delivered some very moving speeches about the devastating effect of poverty in limiting the development of human potential. But if we examine more closely the Bank's efforts to define poverty and identify the poor that it intends to "aid," it becomes clear that its programs are not designed, and *cannot be designed under current Bank assumptions,* to reach the "poorest of the poor."

The Bank has suggested several definitions of poverty. There are the absolute poor, defined as those people with an average annual per capital income of less than $100—a monetary criterion that may be wholly inadequate for judging real levels of living standards, as I demonstrate later on in the discussion of the "small farmer" strategy. Then there is the concept of the "relative poor," whose average yearly income is less than one-third the national average in their own country.[5] This concept has the interesting corollary that a nation with a highly unequal distribution of income would contain more "relative poor," for whom Bank lending could be rationalized, than one with a commitment to social justice which had resulted in a more equitable income distribution.

Most of the Bank's rhetoric, however, speaks of the "bottom 40 percent" of the population of the Bank member countries. With such an array of definitions to draw upon, the Bank has a wide choice of potential poor "beneficiaries" to constitute "target populations."[6] (But then, by comparison with the extremely well-paid Bank officials and professionals, nearly everyone—and not only in the poor countries—would be relatively poor!) More than one commentator has noted the similarity of the Bank's counting of poor people with the Pentagon's Vietnam "body counts"—during Robert McNamara's tenure as U.S. secretary of defense.[7]

In its projects the Bank has found it easiest to assist the poor with "some tangible assets, however meager (a small farm, a cottage industry, or a small-scale commercial operation in the urban centers)."[8] But the people who own such tangible assets are not the poorest of the poor; they are more likely to hire labor themselves. The stress on tangible assets might even lead us to suspect that the Bank and its sponsors are more interested in the assets than in their owners—particularly when the assets include arable land.

Despite some efforts on the part of Bank intellectuals to devise ways of reaching the very poor—those with no tangible assets— they have found no satisfactory answers within their capitalist framework. Only regular, decently paid employment can be a solution to poverty. I will examine the Bank's suggested solution to the employment problem below; here it is sufficient to note that while the Bank has announced a few token projects for creating employment, it has more typically exerted its influence to keep wage levels low in order to encourage foreign investment and export enterprises. This passage from the Bank's country report on Papua New Guinea of July 14, 1976, provides a good example:

> continuously increasing wages without increased labor productivity may hamper Papua New Guinea's agricultural export growth by reducing its competitive strength vis-à-vis other exporters of traditional agricultural products. The Government is, however, becoming increasingly aware of this problem [and has] assured the mission that it will continue to advocate wage restraint in the interest of satisfactory growth of Papua New Guinea's agricultural exports.[9]

The landless of the rural areas are excluded by definition from the Bank's small farmer program, while in the urban areas the Bank's "shelter" (i.e., subhousing) projects cannot, by its own admission, be designed to reach the bottom 10 to 20 percent of the urban proletariat.[10] But if the Bank's definition of poverty allows it to count hundreds of thousands, and even millions, of poor that it has "aided" (although it does not touch the core of the poverty problem), its etiology of poverty is designed to obscure the real reasons for that heart-rending deprivation upon which it builds its humanitarian appeal. "Throughout the developing world, the rural poor have neither shared adequately in their country's progress, nor have themselves been able to contribute significantly to it. Their destitution has in effect ruled them out of the entire development process," McNamara was quoted as saying in a 1974 press release. This was a reformulation of a statement which first appeared in his address to the Board of Governors in 1972, when he first broached the Bank's new concern for the poor. After first mentioning countries that are poor in natural resources, and depressed areas in otherwise booming countries, he continued:

> But it is the third category that is the largest, the most pervasive, and the most persistent poverty of all. It is the poverty of the low-income strata—roughly the poorest 40 percent—of the total population in all developing countries. It is they who—despite their country's economic growth—remain entrapped in conditions of deprivation which fall below any rational definition of human decency.
>
> This is not simply the poverty of a highly disadvantaged country, nor of a particularly backward geographical region in an otherwise rapidly advancing country. Rather, it is the poverty of those people widely dispersed throughout every developing country who, for whatever reason, lie *beyond the reach of traditional market forces* and present public services. It is the poverty of those masses of the population which current government policies do not adequately encompass and which external assistance cannot directly reach. (Emphasis added)

In the same forum a year later, he reiterated this theme: "The basic problem of poverty and growth in the developing world can be stated very simply. The growth is not equitably reaching the poor. And the poor are not significantly contributing to growth."

In the Bank's paradigm, people are poor not because they have been crowded off the best lands in their country or deprived of land altogether by local elites and foreign agribusiness. Ignoring the historical, and in many cases quite recent, origins of inequality and poverty, McNamara's rhetoric assumes that the poor are poor because they have been "left behind" or "ignored" by their country's progress, when in fact most are poor because they are the *victims* of that so-called progress. Despite McNamara's words, the poor have contributed most to that progress: they have contributed, unwillingly, lands they used to cultivate, which have been taken over by large (sometimes foreign) commercial farmers; and they are thereby condemned to contribute their labor, insofar as it is still needed, to those large farms. Their destitution has not "ruled them out" of the development process: the development process is responsible for their destitution.

The relationship between the poor of the world and the resources that they need in order to lead a decent life is indeed central to the diagnosis and cure of poverty, but the Bank's neo-Malthusianism is not the correct explanation. Half a century after Malthus dveloped his grim algebra, Karl Marx and Friedrich Engels proposed a theory of population specific to the capitalist mode of production. According to this theory, which was at the same time an explanation of the existence of poverty, population growth pressed not against the means of subsistence, which had been removed from the control of the poor anyway, but upon the means of employment, which were firmly in the control of the classes that controlled the resources—the capitalists. In order to create a working class dependent upon the capitalist employer for its means of subsistence, it was necessary to first drive the producers off the land, to separate them forcibly from their means of subsistence.[11] To illustrate the importance of this expropriation (achieved by means of the English and Scottish enclosure movement, which reached a peak in the eighteenth century), Marx recounts the amusing story of Mr. Peel, who

> took with him from England to Swan River, West Australia, means of subsistence and of production to the amount of £50,000. Mr. Peel had the foresight to bring with him, besides, 3,000 persons of the working class, men, women, and children. Once arrived at his destination, "Mr. Peel was left without a servant to make his bed or fetch him water from the river." Unhappy Mr. Peel, who provided for everything except the export of English modes of production to Swan River![12]

Those who can find enough land on which to sustain themselves do not need or desire to sell their labor to capital.

The wages of labor (like other commodities) are determined

by supply and demand. But under capitalism wages cannot rise so high that they can wipe out the margin of profit, for investment ceases if they approach that limit. Worse, the rise in the price of labor becomes itself a stimulus to the entrepreneur to introduce technological change which increases the productivity of labor; in other words, to make the operation more capital-intensive and less labor-using. Such technological change enables the capitalist to employ fewer workers to produce the same amount of goods. This means also that the quantity of resources transformed by each worker will increase. Thus the demand for labor rises less rapidly than does the quantity of resources processed and of goods produced by the capitalist; and in most cases the demand for labor rises less rapidly than the absolute growth of population. This is the process of creation of what Marx termed the "relative surplus population." It may take the form of actual layoffs of employed workers (often blamed on "automation" in modern industrial societies) or the less evident, but no less real, form of the slower absorption of the additional laboring population through the usual channels. The relative surplus population itself suffers from lack of employment, but it also keeps the wages of the working population down, a process which Marx called "the condemnation of one part of the working class to enforced idleness by the over-work of the other part."[13]

The "overpopulation" that results is not a consequence of scarcity in any absolute sense, but simply an oversupply of labor relative to the immediate need of capital for employees. The scarcity that results is not a scarcity of food, but a scarcity of employment with which to buy the food that is produced and, repeatedly, overproduced. Engels wrote ironically in 1895:

> I do not understand how anyone can today speak of a completion of the Malthusian theory that *the population presses against the means of subsistence*, at a time when corn in London costs twenty shillings a quarter, or half the average price of 1848–70, and when it is generally recognized that *the means of subsistence are pressing against the population*, which is not large enough to consume them![14] (Emphasis in original)

It follows directly that if the increasing productivity of labor under capitalism means the transformation of a larger quantity of means of production, capitalism will be a more voracious consumer of the raw materials it needs than would be a small peasant or artisan producer. And it is clear that if the effect of capitalist production is to reduce the cost of production of goods by reducing the demand for labor, it is bound to undersell the precapitalist forms of production; indeed this is the meaning of the industrial revolution.[15]

Capitalist forms of agriculture and industry thus compete with simpler forms of production both for its raw materials and its markets. The competition is inevitably unequal. Despite Marx's nineteenth-century background, some of the consequences he describes have a very modern ring: the inability of capitalism to employ all the labor driven off the farms or thrown out of work by automation, for example. But while Marx saw this as an inevitable consequence of the spread of capitalism, the World Bank sees this as a problem to be solved within the parameters of capitalist production. Let us now take a closer look at the solutions proposed by the World Bank.

The Question of Productivity

Throughout its literature on poverty-oriented lending, the World Bank stresses that the poor can be helped only by aid which increases their productivity. For example, McNamara said in a 1978 interview:

> There is only one way by which poverty in the developing countries can be attacked successfully, and that is by producing more in those nations. In no one of those countries can human needs be satisfied by the simple redistribution of existing wealth and income. In these countries, small is not beautiful. National incomes must rise.[16]

McNamara asserts that the redistribution of existing wealth and income in poor countries cannot help because the existing wealth is too meager. This is nonsense. It may well be true that not *all* human needs could be satisfied this way, but it is also true that it is precisely the poorest societies that can least afford distributional inequalities, whereas even the richest have never satisfactorily solved the problem of poverty, though they can demonstrably afford to do so. Clearly the Bank is strongly opposed to redistribution policies, and presents the "productivity" argument as a counter to arguments for redistribution.[17]

Productivity is simply the amount of goods produced by each laborer within a given time period, and it can be increased in several ways: by more, and longer, working days or greater exertions by the laborer; by organizing the labor process more efficiently; by introducing machinery that multiplies the effects of labor; and, under conditions that will be discussed below, by making more raw materials available where their lack has been the limiting factor. The possibilities and the effect of productivity increases are somewhat different for industry, agriculture, and extractive enterprises, so we will examine each of these in turn.

Increasing the productivity of labor in a privately owned factory can be done through "speed-up," which demands more exertions from each laborer; or it can be done by the introduction of labor-saving machinery. In either case, it does not necessarily follow that entrepreneurs will reward their employees for increased productivity with higher wages. Both methods are, rather, typically used to reduce labor costs and thus improve profitability; and the introduction of machinery historically has enabled employers to substitute lower wage, unskilled labor for higher paid, skilled workers.[18] Payments to labor are determined primarily by the situation of supply and demand in the local labor market and in most underdeveloped countries the massive reserve army of unemployed and underemployed labor will keep the prevailing wage rate very low. Workers in the modern sector, however, may receive somewhat higher remuneration because, for the smooth operation of high-technology enterprises, they must be "well fed, healthy, punctual, and clothed," in the words of Frances Stewart.[19] Higher than average pay also helps to prevent even more costly labor disturbances and reduces labor turnover.

Even the so-called labor aristocracy suffers, however, for their increased productivity generates more unemployment for the society at large and thus helps to keep their own wage levels down. Increased productivity, then, is no solution for the employee in the modern capitalist sector. But what about agriculture?

Agriculture can be carried on either in small family units or in large organizations modeled on industrial units. Except in labor-scarce societies (which are found today only in limited areas of black Africa and Polynesia) the important measure of productivity is not that of individual members of units, but that of the land itself and the distribution of the produce to the whole society. The (labor) productivity of commercial agriculture is high because in most cases it employs fewer people per hectare than the overcrowded small farm sector. Despite this higher productivity, the hired labor on commercial farms does not benefit; their wages remain at an extremely low level, and are usually paid for only part of the year at that, while the farm owners enjoy the productivity gains in the form of profit. Thus, the expansion of this type of high-productivity farming cannot solve society-wide problems of poverty, which are in part *the result of the increased productivity of the larger units,* which control larger amounts of land per worker and often dominate markets as well. This is even more serious in the case of agriculture than in that of industry, because while more factories are constantly being built, the supply of farmland is relatively limited.

As for the small farm sector, now so heavily favored by the World Bank—in countries where the land resource itself is unequally distributed, the productivity of small farmers could be raised simply by a redistribution of land, without the addition of industrial inputs. In such a case the farm family (if unencumbered by debt) could immediately appropriate its own enhanced productivity by eating part of the harvest. But the World Bank almost never supports redistributive land reform (in part because its borrowing governments are mostly dominated by landed elites, in part because redistribution might threaten the interests of international as well as local capital) and the rural development strategy it favors, which is discussed in detail in Chapter 8, saddles the farmers with heavy repayments for inputs and services they have not chosen, ensuring that productivity improvements will be mostly siphoned off for the repayment to the project of debts incurred.

There is a third type of enterprise where productivity is of a somewhat different nature: such activities as forestry and fishing (not fish farming), which involve the harvesting of resources not cultivated on private land.

Forests and fish populations, if harvested at a judicious rate, can regenerate themselves without further human expense and interference, but in many parts of the world they are being exploited too rapidly to allow for natural regeneration, and the resource base is being rapidly depleted. In such a situation of resource scarcity, increasing the productivity of a few operators only heightens the difficulty of the rest in finding resources. This would be true even if the World Bank aided *individual* lumberers and fishers, which it does not.

The usual World Bank lending operation in forestry or fishing involves credit to fairly large, and usually privately owned, enterprises for capital equipment, which allows the entrepreneurs to increase the productivity of their employees by harvesting larger amounts of logs (or fish). Unless the area in question has unlimited resources, an unlikely case in today's world, the privileged entrepreneurs will thus increase their share of the harvest, depleting the local resources and virtually robbing those who have traditionally taken a smaller harvest for their own or local use. The employees' productivity will have increased, but for the profit of the capitalist, not necessarily the employees, and at the expense of the rest of society.[20]

The Tragedy of the Commons, Revisited

Such resources as forests, ocean and river fish, rangelands, fresh water, and, lately, minerals found on the ocean floor can be quite valuable and even essential to human life and industry. All of these resources pose certain problems for private and (in the case of oceans) even national appropriation; yet although they may be owned by no one they are still valuable and subject to private exploitation. These types of resources are all, to a varying extent, still in the realm of the "commons" even in the highly privatized developed capitalist economies, where they are, however, usually subject to some sort of national management or licensing.

About a dozen years ago, an influential article entitled "The Tragedy of the Commons" by Garrett Hardin appeared in *Science*. In it, Hardin argued:

> The tragedy of the commons develops in this way. Picture a pasture open to all. It is to be expected that each herdsman will try to keep as many cattle as possible on the commons. . . .
>
> As a rational being each herdsman seeks to maximize his gain. Explicitly or implicitly, more or less consciously, he asks, "What is the utility *to me* of adding one more animal to my herd?" This utility has one negative and one positive component.
>
> 1) The positive component is a function of the increment of one animal. Since the herdsman receives all the proceeds from the sale of the additional animal, the positive utility is nearly +1.
>
> 2) The negative component is a function of the additional overgrazing created by one more animal. Since, however, the effects of overgrazing are shared by all the herdsmen, the negative utility for any particular decision-making herdsman is only a fraction of −1.
>
> Adding together the component partial utilities, the rational herdsman concludes that the only sensible course for him to pursue is to add another animal to his herd. And another; and another. . . . But this is the conclusion reached by each and every rational herdsman sharing a commons. Therein is the tragedy. Each man is locked into a system that compels him to increase his herd without limit—in a world that is limited. Ruin is the destination toward which all men rush, each pursuing his own best interest in a society that believes in the freedom of the commons. Freedom in a commons brings ruin to all.[21]

Presented thus, as a formal, logical parable, Hardin's reasoning seems faultless. It is also representative of the predominant mode of thinking about the resources of the Third World among World Bank policymakers and in general among the establishment in the developed countries that control its policies.

The problems with Hardin's parable arise from the fact that he is, willfully or not, ignorant of the real history and sociology of the appropriation of the "commons." His first fallacy is the assumption that the solution to the "tragedy" (he also calls it the "horror of the commons") is "private property, or something formally like it." The second fallacy is that it is formally equal individuals—by implication, the little people—that are responsible for the problem. (The real purpose of the article is not to argue for private property, but for enforced population control, and Hardin reveals his mean-spiritedness by making it clear that he means for the poor people, not for those who own the resources to support their offspring.) The third fallacy (perhaps "half-truth" would be more accurate) is that national management of resources in the realm of the commons is the solution to the problem.

In building his theory Hardin ignores the fact that private appropriation has by no means solved the problem of ecological destruction, even for those forms of resources which are most easily appropriated. Privately owned mines are exploited for quick returns rather than sustained yields over longer time periods.[22] Privately owned agricultural land is similarly "mined" with devastating consequences for topsoil erosion; conservationist measures go contrary to the demands of the market and must be enforced or subsidized.[23] Even privately owned forests (despite much propaganda to the contrary) are stripped of standing timber and abandoned to devastation—not reforested—so long as unexploited stands are available elsewhere.[24]

Even if private appropriation were the answer to resource conservation, Hardin's analysis ignores another very important point: the conservation is purchased at the cost of the people who are fenced off the land, excluded from the produce which is then privately appropriated by the owners. For the appropriation rarely if ever happens in such a fashion that everyone who wishes can have his or her plot of land. And for those who are excluded by private property from the use of the land it is an immediate tragedy, equal to or greater than the "tragedy of the commons."

From the beginnings of private property in land it has been the wealthy and powerful who have excluded the poor and powerless from land they had previously farmed on a communal or nonexclusive basis. In recent years the locally based wealthy and powerful elites have been joined by foreign owners and multinational corporations as appropriators of the land. These private appropriators always take the best located and/or most fertile territory, leaving the powerless to areas that either have limited access to the national and world market and/or are marginal in terms of productive potential. In the first case, communities may live a content and healthy life as "subsistence" farmers until they are threatened by the building of a reservoir, or until new transportation projects destroy their isolation and open their lands up for exploitation by national or international elites. In the second case, the marginalized farmers destroy the poor land to which they have been driven because they have no choice; they must do so in order to live.

In *Losing Ground: Environmental Stress and World Food Prospects*, perhaps the most influential publication to issue from the U.S. ecology establishment, Erik Eckholm cites examples of such expropriation of the poor by the rich:

> [L]atifundia occupy El Salvador's most fertile and productive lands . . . a third of the cropland is annually planted to coffee, cotton and sugar cane. Meanwhile, hundreds of thousands of subsistence farmers, struggling to grow food for their families, are crowded onto the remaining land. (P. 168)
>
> [In Haiti] wealthy farmers and North American sugar corporations own the best valley lands, crowding peasants onto slopes where cultivation is a futile, temporary proposition. (P. 169)
>
> In Costa Rica, the spread of cattle ranching to supply the North American market is forcing smaller farmers onto poor-quality, easily eroded lands, even as per capita beef consumption within Costa Rica drops. (Pp. 170–71)

Further, it is the international corporations that are the most destructive "shifting cultivators" of our day, as they move their operations from one country to another in search of cheaper labor and/or uneroded soils. Pineapple corporations transplant their operations from Hawaii to the Philippines and Thailand, leaving stripped and devastated soils behind them. Timber companies denude the hills of the Philippines and then move on to Malaysia and Indonesia to repeat their good work. Some corporations do not even make a success of their operations (e.g., Bud Corporation in Senegal and the Iran-California Company in

Iran, see Chapter 9) and sell out or close down, in the meantime having destroyed local social relations and possibly discredited all ideas of progressive change. It is these entities, and not the poor marginalized farmers, herders, and fuel gatherers, who are the proper studies for a "tragedy of the commons," because under cover of the legal protection of private property they are appropriating the world commons for their own use, excluding all others from the resources needed to sustain life.

Hardin's parable further errs in assuming a Hobbesian competition of individual rational actors. Historically, or perhaps in this case one should say prehistorically, communal exploitation of resources has usually been carried out by closely organized communities which often had a good empirical idea of the carrying capacity of the land they used and overexploited it only unwillingly, as a necessity for survival. In any case, their modest levels of consumption ensured that they were a lighter burden on the available resources than the overconsuming wealthy societies serviced by the multinational corporations.

Finally, collective management of restricted access to the resources of the commons (Hardin's solution where private appropriation is not possible) can only be as effective and honest as the entity that issues the licenses to exploit those resources. When that entity is a government dominated by domestic elites and international corporations, it is unrealistic to expect that the common resources will be protected from the ravages of those corporations or that poor people will be allowed to have the right to utilize a fair share of those resources. The history of forest and rangeland management by federal agencies in the United States is instructive in this regard, where national management has not prevented overgrazing or destructive timber cutting, under pressure of the demands of the powerful ranchers and lumber companies for access to "national" resources. How effective, then, could we expect the weak comprador states of the Third World to be in this respect, especially when, as we shall see, the World Bank is steadily pressuring these governments to impove conditions for the international corporations? It is one of the most reprehensible of hypocrisies that while Hardin, Eckholm, and the World Bank deplore the ecological damage caused by the small, marginalized entrepreneurs of the Third World, they refuse to condemn the depradations of the large corporations, which are siphoning off Third World resources for their greater profits, from those who need them for simple survival. (See Chapter 10.)

The Problem of Employment

As we have seen, under capitalism the trend of increasing productivity of labor has been the problem, not the solution. The growth in labor productivity brought about by technological advances, which could lead to diminished labor and improved consumption for everyone, instead, under capitalism has meant increased drudgery and boredom for the ever-decreasing proportion of employed and marginalization of the rest of the working class.

As noted above, only regular, decently paid employment can provide a solution to the problem of poverty. Direct resource redistribution is not feasible for most branches of industry and even in agriculture, where it is still an aspiration of many to possess their own land (or more of it), there are severe limits to the security and independence of small farmers. The Bank is not unaware that employment is desperately needed by the poor of the Third World. The subject recurs frequently in Bank literature, most notably in McNamara's report to the Board of Governors in 1979 and in the literature on aid to "small enterprises." In McNamara's words,

> But whatever can be done to increase employment in the country-side both on and off the farm—and a great deal can be done—migration to the city is going to continue, and the massive under-employment problem there must be faced and dealt with directly.
> How?
> The honest answer is that no one really knows yet.[25]

The honest answer is that no one really knows how to do it *within a capitalist framework.* The best, and only, way to deal directly with the employment problem is to guarantee employment to everyone who is able and willing to work. It is likely that in a rationally planned society productive employment could be found for everyone. In those socialist societies that have not yet become enamored of capitalist definitions of labor productivity, there has long existed a chronic labor shortage. Even the wealthiest capitalist societies, on the other hand, cannot provide work for their entire labor force; when the point of full employment is approached, the capitalists import labor from less advantaged countries and/or depression ensues which reestablishes the scarcity of employment. How then could an institution controlled by these same wealthy countries and their capitalists be prepared to recognize the real solution to unemployment in the much more difficult situation of the Third World? As McNamara admitted, they cannot, but it is necessary nevertheless to make a show of activity around the problem. Having admitted that no one really knows how to deal with the employment problem directly, McNamara proceeded in the same speech to assert that "the emphasis on low capital investment per job . . . is the key to the solution."

Borrowing a page from E. F. Schumacher's book on alternative technology, *Small is Beautiful*, the Bank has embraced the idea of "low capital investment per job" and is now promoting the idea of loans to small enterprises. Although Marx's name is never invoked, the truth of his observations is confirmed by such statements as this one: "In Latin America, between 1960 and 1969, the rate of growth in manufacturing employment was only 40 percent that of output for the sector."[26] The Bank reasons, following Schumacher, that if large capital-intensive industrial enterprises are not creating enough employment to match the growth in the labor force, the answer is to spend less capital per job created, i.e., with $1 million to invest, only 10 jobs can be "created" at a capital intensity of $100,000 per work place, but 1,000 can be created at a capital intensity of $1,000 per work place.

Formally, the reasoning is faultless, but as a practical solution to the employment problem this is a nonstarter. In the first place, capitalist enterprises simply do not make decisions this way. They do not set about to allocate their capital expenditures in such a way as to create the maximum number of jobs; they decide what they want to produce, and the least cost technology for achieving that end, and then hire the labor they need for the task. Indeed, for a variety of reasons many entrepreneurs will choose the more capital-intensive technique even when it would seem to be more profitable to employ a labor-intensive technique, because they do not want to face the difficulties of managing a large labor force (with the potential for strikes, etc.).[27]

Second, even the Bank propaganda does not claim that labor-intensive technologies are viable except in a very few product lines—shoes, cotton cloth, cotton yarn, bricks, cornmeal, sugar, beer, leather, and fertilizer are the ones cited in one article—and it is not clear what kind of fertilizer is meant, as it is also admitted that large, capital-intensive units are mandatory for other lines of production including synthetic fertilizer and petrochemicals, basic steel, and heavy equipment.[28]

Third, it is clear that the ideology of small enterprises can be used by the Bank, when it so wishes, to discourage investment in the branches of industry which require large, capital-intensive development, in favor of "alternatives that are more in keeping with the country's human and natural resources and capital availability."[29] This can be particularly useful in blocking state investments that threaten to compete with the large, capital-intensive enterprises established by foreign private capital, and thus to perpetuate a very unfavorable international division of labor for the poorer countries.

The Bank does not have the power, even if it so wished, to prevent foreign private capital from employing capital-intensive technology in the factories it builds in developed and in under-developed countries. Further, the Bank does not even propose to devote the major part of its own industrial lending to so-called small enterprise, but proposes merely a "major increase in this share"—to about one-third of total industry lending by fiscal year 1981.[30] Far from intending to supplant capital-intensive technology, it is made clear that the Bank intends the labor-intensive enterprises to complement the technologically advanced sector through subcontracting and marketing links, described as "mutually advantageous cooperation between small and large firms" which will permit small businesses "to function alongside and reinforce big firms in doing the things that they, as small undertakings, do best."[31]

Further, if Bank loans to small enterprises have the effect of increasing their labor productivity (and it is hard to see that they could have any other effect), these "small" businesses could still outcompete yet smaller operations in handicraft production of shoes, cotton cloth, cotton yarn, bricks, cornmeal, sugar, beer, leather, etc.[32] for raw materials and/or markets. Labor demands would thus still decline in proportion to the total output, albeit at a slower pace than with very high technology enterprises. Small businesses are still capitalist enterprise, and limiting the extent of the technology they use does not suspend the law of creation of the relative surplus population. Thus, as David Dickson has remarked, "despite its many radical implications, we can see how all too easy intermediate technology becomes little more than a formula for small-scale capitalism, with all the inequality and uneven distribution of social rewards that this inevitably brings."[33] McNamara was right the first time; the Bank does not know how to solve the employment problem. Its proposed solution, lending to "small enterprises," must be seen as an attempt to do something, but in reality is no solution at all.

3

Project Lending: Some General Considerations

There are benefits, of course, which may be
    countable, but which
Have a tendency to fall into the pockets of the
    rich,
While the costs are apt to fall onto the shoulders
    of the poor.
So cost-benefit analysis is nearly always sure
To justify the building of a solid concrete fact
While the Ecologic Truth is left behind in the
    abstract.
—Kenneth E. Boulding,
    "A Ballad of Ecological Awareness"

Well over 90 percent of the loans and credits made by the Bank and IDA are made for specific projects. While the following chapters will discuss the various types of project by sectors, something should first be said about the features they all have in common. Each loan goes through a series of six stages, which the Bank calls the "project cycle."

    1. Identification: Selection by Bank and borrowers of suitable projects that support national and sectoral development strategies and are feasible according to Bank standards. The projects are then incorporated into the lending program of the Bank for a particular country.
    2. Preparation: Borrowing country or agency examines technical, institutional, economic and financial assistance available for preparation or helps borrower obtain assistance from other sources. This takes time, typically one to two years.[1]

When the Bank first opened for business in 1947, it considered its function to be that of saying yes or no to projects presented for loans by the borrowers. Its dissatisfaction with the quality of projects thus presented soon led it into the business of assisting the borrower to identify and prepare projects that the Bank would consider suitable for financing. Judith Tendler describes this as analogous to the "backward integration" of industrial firms: in order to ensure an adequate supply of projects to finance, the Bank had to start producing them itself.[2] Today project selection is made within the context of Country Economic Surveys prepared by the Bank for each borrowing country, which identify the priority sectors for investment. These surveys are widely regarded as the most comprehensive and sophisticated compilations of information available on any given nation's economy and are widely cited even by authors who may vehemently oppose the World Bank's operations and philosophy. Fawzi Mansour identifies the Bank's function as an "economic intelligence bank" as one of the sources of its hegemonic power in the development community. He makes two important criticisms of the way in which this power is exercised. First:

> The information the Bank gathers is in one way or the other, to this or that extent, usually available to all interested parties; the government of the country itself and other governments, other aid-givers, private lenders and investors—*all except the party most concerned*: the people of the country reported upon, where the Bank's unpublished documents, wherever they are made available to its government, are normally kept a top state secret, except for the odd or slanted leakage, mostly when it suits the government's purposes—or those of others—to provide the leakage.

And second, there is no way to ensure the "objectivity" of the information so provided, or to protect the country concerned from the slants it may contain.[3] One should add that it is necessary not to exaggerate the omniscience of the Bank; if its reports are the best, that is probably simply because no other organization has the resources or the motive to attempt such a massive gathering of data. Two examples given by van de Laar are useful in demystifying the competence of the data gatherers.

Firstly, the civil war between the Hutus and the Tutsis in Burundi in late 1972 reportedly cost the lives of perhaps three percent of the country's population in about two months. Only after this had been reported in the *New York Times* could the Bank's Area Department be persuaded that tribal antagonism went deeper than an occasional killing in a bar fight, as was maintained in the review cycle of Burundi which was in progress at that very time.

Secondly, in CPPs [Country Program Papers] for the early 1970s of several Sahel countries little could be deduced about the severity and consequences of the drought in the area which, as has become clear since, had lasted already for five years.

Government bureaucrats in the countries concerned rarely stray from their capital city, and are thus often uninformed of what is going on. Short-stay World Bank missions who, because of the pressure, have talks only with those capital-based officials, will invariably receive misinformation. Only after conditions in the countryside had become desperate—the nomads with the remnants of their herds came into the towns—could the seriousness of the situation no longer be denied by the national authorities, and only then did the Sahel tragedy break into the open.[4]

Even if we assume that the information contained in the Country Surveys is accurate, it is clear that the issuing of these surveys, and their use as guides to project identification, is a powerful means by which the Bank can impose the priorities desired by its capital-supplying members. Within this context, projects may be proposed by the borrowing government, by private sponsors (many of which are identified in subsequent chapters), or by the Bank itself. Proposed projects must meet the Bank's initial tests of feasibility before they are considered to be "identified."

Once identified, formal responsibility for preparation of the project rests with the borrower, but the Bank hovers close at hand during the process. "At one time the Bank was reluctant to assist in project preparation, on the banker's principle that such involvement might prejudice its objectivity at appraisal. But experience has demonstrated that the Bank must have an active role in ensuring a timely flow of well-prepared projects."[5] Consequently, "the IBRD found itself working both sides of the street. It would help a potential borrower locate a promising investment, help to prepare a feasible project, and then appraise the results of its own efforts.'"⁶ The Bank may itself make special technical assistance loans for the purpose of preparing projects that qualify for more loans, and project preparation is the chief function of the cooperative programs with the Food and Agriculture Organization (FAO), UN Educational, Scientific and Cultural Organization (UNESCO), World Health Organization (WHO), and UN Industrial Development Organization (UNIDO) discussed in the previous chapter. The UN Development Program (UNDP) is a particularly important source of aid in project preparation; while this is provided on a grant basis, the UNDP then hires the Bank as the executing agency for the study! As such, it "draws up the 'plan of operations' for the study in consultation with the host government, negotiates the terms of reference with the government, employs the consultants, supervises the field work, and reviews the consultants' report. It also submits to UNDP a confidential assessment of their work.'"⁷ The net effect is that the UNDP has been "relegated to picking up the preinvestment tab for the World Bank."⁸ However financed, the project preparation is inevitably a socialization process that instructs the borrowers in the requirements for qualifying for a Bank loan.

   3. Appraisal: Bank staff review comprehensively and systematically all aspects of the project. This may take three to five weeks in the field and covers four major aspects: technical, institutional, economic and financial. An appraisal report is prepared on the return of Bank staff to headquarters and is reviewed extensively. This report serves as the basis for negotiations with the borrower.

The staff appraisal report, a "restricted distribution" document bound in a yellow cover, is typically between 50 and 100 pages long. It contains chapters on sector background (which includes a general justification of the need for the project together with information on any previous Bank lending to that sector in the borrowing country); project components, costs and finance (including a detailed project description); borrowing and executing agencies, an analysis of the borrower's institutions that will be administering the project; design standards and project specifications; project implementation; financial analysis; economic analysis; and recommendations. Annexes and maps are included at the end of the report.

Almost all project appraisals include an economic cost-benefit analysis, sometimes broken down for individual components of a project, which yields a single-figure rate of return expressed in percentage. This procedure differs from the financial analysis of the project (which concerns the actual expenditures and receipts of the implementing organizations) by taking into account "externalities"—i.e., costs and benefits accruing to individuals and organizations other than the one directly implementing the project. The idea is that costs and benefits to the society as a whole should be taken into account and that the Bank should lend only if the consequent rate of return is greater than what the same amount of funds could earn elsewhere (its "opportunity cost").

The technique of social cost-benefit analysis deserves a chapter of its own, which happily does not need to be supplied here since Jacques Berthelot has produced a detailed critique.[9] It will suffice to mention some of the most important points mentioned by Berthelot and others.

Social cost-benefit (SCB) analysis is a sophisticated procedure with a large body of literature and a sort of priesthood of practitioners who have been initiated into the esoteric art.[10] But, as one proponent explained:

> The basic notion is very simple. If we have to decide whether to do A or not, the rule is: Do A if the benefits exceed those of the next best alternative course of action, and not otherwise. If we apply this rule to all possible choices we shall generate *the largest possible benefits*, given the constraints within which we live. *And no one could complain at that.*[11]

As Frances Stewart comments, it would seem logically perverse to object to the maximization of social welfare as the aim of social choice. SCB analysis is in theory simply the application on a large scale of the way most of us evaluate decisions, although few of these can be made in terms of simple numbers.

But many ideological problems become apparent when this concept is put into practice. In the first place, as Stewart points out, the very idea assumes that there is a high degree of unity and consensus in the society, and that costs and benefits can be fairly distributed among the components of that society. But this is clearly not the case.

> In any society there are individuals, groups and classes with different interests, and objectives. . . . [T]o select projects in such a way that net benefits are maximized is meaningless as a criterion of selection, until one has defined whose benefits one is talking about. . . . [A]dvocates of social welfare functions never clarified the key question with which we are concerned, namely, *who* should determine society's preferences. . . .[12]

The problem is solved in practice by looking to the government to establish the values. But to assume that governments represent a social consensus "depends on a theory of governments as being above the fray, impartial, if sometimes misguided, brokers between the different interests in society," an assumption which "is not so, because the government itself is part of the class and interest struggle."[13]

Stewart therefore concludes that

> SCB is thus used as an instrument, rather than other instruments, because governments do not represent the "social" interest, but their own class interests, and yet wish to appear to represent the "wider" social interests. . . . SCB does not show governments stepping outside their normal activities to represent the interests of all; rather it is another instrument in the class struggle.[14]

Stewart is quite correct in her analysis of the nature and intentions of government, but there is a serious omission in her argument. She assumes that it is the governments in whose territory the project will be built that are using SCB in this way, when in practice it is the aid institutions, primarily the World Bank, who insist on the use of SCB to evaluate every project.

At this point it is necessary to explain the way in which "economic" or "social" cost-benefit analysis differs from plain old financial analysis. The method starts from the financial analysis used by private business, but it is embellished and modified in a number of ways:

  —By the use of "shadow" prices, wages, and/or exchange rates that vary from market prices (sometimes they are called "accounting" or "reference" prices);
  —By the addition to the model of costs and benefits accruing to other actors in the society ("externalities"); and, more recently

—By the weighting of benefits accruing to certain social categories that the government (or aid agency) is supposed to favor.

The use of "shadow" pricing attempts to substitute world market for actual local prices in the analysis. This is an ideological ploy with which the aid agency criticizes protectionist measures in the borrowing country. By using world market prices as the standard, the agencies imply that they should be the "real" ones, and that any measures that the government may take to insulate its citizens from the effects of the world market are illegitimate.[15]

The use of shadow wage rates also has more ideological than practical significance. The assumption is that for unskilled labor, the opportunity cost is zero, or close to zero, because in most countries the agricultural sector cannot absorb any more labor. Giving unskilled labor a "shadow wage" of zero implies that the real cost to the economy of the labor employed is less than the wages that actually have to be paid. The idea is to slant the analysis somewhat in the direction of labor-intensive technologies, but the actual impact of this device on employment is dubious, as real wages still have to be paid. Another effect is to enhance the rate of return and thus help justify the project. More ominous, as Berthelot warns, are the psychological and political consequences of this practice: not only are wages of agricultural laborers already very low in these countries, but it is suggested that they are *not low enough* to justify the completion of projects.[16]

The weighting of distributional benefits to favor projects that provide income to poorer sectors of the population also has a progressive veneer which dissolves when the practice is examined closely. Stewart provides one critique:

> Income distribution is incorporated in general by weighting income receipts . . . and not by looking at income levels among consumers of the project. . . . Thus if a project to produce Rolls-Royce cars were to guarantee more incomes among the lowest 40 percent than a project to produce low-income housing, the Rolls-Royce project would be accepted on income distribution grounds, whereas on these criteria the low-cost housing project might not.[17]

Berthelot puts it more bluntly: "the fact of weighting revenues to certain beneficiaries does not mean that the project will benefit them."[18]

In fact, Berthelot charges, the specifics of the methods used are strongly class-biased. For example, the "opportunity cost" of capital—the rate of return that must be exceeded if projects are to be considered "economic"—is determined by reference to international interest rates; therefore if investors (or in this case, the government) can get a better rate of return by investing its resources in London or New York, the method implies that they should do so, regardless of the consequence to the country of this decapitalization. In practice, this figure, like most others used by project evaluators, varies according to what needs to be proved. If the calculated rate of return exceeds the international cost of capital, fine; if not, it can be judged satisfactory on less rigorous grounds.[19]

The use of the discount rate, which is copied directly from private capital's adoption of the discounted rate of return for its own investment calculation, also replicates private capital's excessive concern with short-term profitability by assigning higher values to present income than to future income. For example, projects with a long-term aim of improving the ecology of an area, but which involve present costs and will produce significant benefits only after fifteen or twenty years, would show up very badly in a discounted rate of return analysis in contrast to one which produced quick profits, but caused long-term damage to soil and forests (even assuming that the damage was factored into the analysis, which in practice is not likely to be the case).

In practice, however, social cost-benefit analysis looks quite different than it does in academic circles. It turns out that the sophisticated methodology is simply too complicated for use in the field, and "shortcuts all around" is the rule. The choice of shadow prices, wages, and interest rates, for example, is largely arbitrary; the role of "hunch, guesstimate, and judgment" is enormous.[20] What is the world market price, for example, of an agricultural commodity or raw material that has fluctuated widely in the last five years, but for which the evaluator must choose a value for the next twenty or thirty years? Is the "opportunity cost" of labor zero, or 50 percent of the real wage? (Berthelot observed two different IBRD-FAO teams using these different rates at the same time in the same country, for no apparent reason.)[21] The use of distributional weights is in practice extremely rare. And there is virtually no end to the calculation of externalities, and therefore an enormous range of choice of what to include in the calculations and what to ignore. With a system of shadow prices, anything can be justified. And is.

For the emperor has no clothes. Cost-benefit analysis is used (after two years of project preparation, remember) as an ex post* justification for decisions that have long since been made on political grounds, not as an objective means for selecting one project in preference to another. Both Berthelot and van de Laar, who have participated in such exercises for the World Bank, have expressed themselves in print to this effect.

> [C]ost-benefit analysis becomes "cosmetic analysis" as the projects are of course chosen *a priori* on purely political grounds. . . . (the complexity of methods offering sufficient freedom of interpretation to the experts so that they can produce the high rate of return which will give a good conscience to the decision-makers on both sides).[22]

And,

> Many Bank staff not surprisingly feel that the calculation of project rates of return is principally intended to put the "icing on the cake" after all interesting decisions have been made.[23]

My own interviews with economists working in or with the Bank, who did not want to be quoted by name, confirmed these statements. According to one, "It is a game we play. We ask what number they want, and we give it to them." And another said that the first time he worked on an evaluation for the Bank, "I couldn't understand why my figures didn't come out right. I did them over a number of times before I realized that it was not my calculations that were wrong, but the conclusions that I was supposed to reach."

For this purpose the subtleties of social cost-benefit analysis

---

Ex post and *ex ante* are the two terms commonly used in this context.

are ideally suited. Overoptimistic price projections and under-estimation of costs can make a dubious project look profitable. I am told that World Bank estimates of mineral prices, for example, are consistently much higher than the best industry forecasts, and have led to the financing of some unviable mines.[24] And, just as private companies can slough off to host governments the essential, but unprofitable, infrastructure elements of their in-vestments, so the World Bank itself has been said to indulge in the same practice:

> It has sometimes occurred that the Bank cut out vocational and training components of projects if the calculated internal rate of return tended to be reduced below levels acceptable to the Board by their inclusion in the project. Such components were then shifted to the government, or to some other agency for financing, or never materialized.[25]

It is probable that negative externalities would wipe out the viability of many Bank projects if they were, or could be, fully quantified. David Hart's study of the Volta River project is one attempt to take fuller account of the negative effects of a project in an ex post analysis;[26] one can only imagine what this, or any other dam project, might look like if the tens of thousands of people displaced by the reservoir were able to demand full monetary compensation for their permanent loss of home and livelihood, instead of a token payment for houses that the ad-ministrators (conveniently for them!) consider virtually worth-less in monetary terms.

Having examined the appraisal process, we can proceed to the fourth stage of the project cycle:

> 4. Negotiations: This stage involves discussions with the bor-rower on the measures needed to ensure success for the project. The agreements reached are embodied in loan documents. The project is then presented to the Executive Directors of the Bank for approval. After approval the loan agreement is signed. The project can now go into its implementation stage.

It is at this stage that the World Bank secures commitments from the borrowing government on such matters as the pricing of inputs for and outputs of the project (utility rate tariffs are a good example, see Chapter 4), government actions or guarantees that are considered necessary for the success of the project, the creation of special administrative units for the project, etc. Every loan or credit is formalized by a loan agreement, in the case of IBRD, or credit agreement, in the case of IDA, which is registered as an international treaty with the UN, published, and made available through UN depository libraries and through the Bank's own publication office. Sometimes other supplementary agreements are signed at the same time (guarantee agreements with the host government if the government is not itself the borrower; shareholders' agreements if private corporations are closely involved in the project, etc.), which are also published with the loan agreements. Although these legal documents set forth some of the conditions agreed upon during negotiations, additional information on commitments made by the borrower can be found near the end of the appraisal documents, which are not published.

Although my interest here is on the conditions imposed on borrowers by the Bank, it must be understood that each agreement is the product of negotiations between at least two parties, one of which is always the borrowing, or guaranteeing, government. It is therefore implicated in the decision to undertake the project, and in the conditions imposed as a condition for the loan.

"It is an *affaire* between two consenting adults," one Bank official told a journalist, adding:

> Governments call in the Bank either because they want the money or because somebody related to the government needs a road built in order to increase the value of his land-holdings. The young bureaucrats ... know that their job may be on the line if they appraise the Bank's proposals too critically. Furthermore, there is always the possibility of landing a plush job in Washington, D.C. in the future if the young official shows he has the "correct" mentality.[27]

The most sophisticated picture of the relationship between the Bank and the national elites with which it negotiates is given by A. A. Fatouros, who criticizes "the usual confrontation images, where an alien 'World Bank' meets a totally autonomous 'national government.' "

"From the very start," he notes, "the Bank has a special relationship with certain groups in the member countries, a relationship symbolized (and strengthened) by the constitutional requirement that the members' Treasury or Finance Departments be in charge of relations with the Bank." The Bank's views "are largely shared by officials of central banks and national financial agencies and by groups of influential private persons (e.g., private bankers) in the borrowing countries." He continues:

> The multinational character of its staff, moreover, makes possible considerable mobility between the Bank (and IMF) and the national economic bureaucracies. It would be slanderous and unfair to allege that the ex-Bank officials within a borrowing country's civil services are, so to speak, the Bank's fifth column. At the same time, they are often imbued with the approach and point of view of the Bank, they think in the same terms as Bank officials, they use the same economic and other techniques that the Bank uses and they are thus peculiarly receptive to the Bank's arguments and positions. . . . Their perception coincides with the Bank's because the outlook (and the interests) of such elites are closely tied to the Bank and to the forces and ideas the Bank represents.[28]

Negotiations are also carried on between the Bank staff and the executive directors, particularly those of the United States and other developed countries that have a particular interest in the project and/or in the borrowing country. These negotiations are informal and thus difficult to document, but they are extremely important. Continuing consultation between the Bank's "management" and the executive directors "ensures that by the time an issue is brought for formal action before the executive directors, rejection or even serious opposition is unlikely."[29] By the time of presentation, the "yellow cover" staff appraisal has metamorphosed into a "gray cover" project appraisal document which is approved by the Executive Board. The loan agreement is signed at a later date by a representative of the borrowing country and one from the Bank, usually the vice president for the geographical region in which the borrower is situated.

The loan agreements incorporate a number of standard provisions that are printed in the Bank's *General Conditions for Loans* and not repeated in the individual loan agreements. Fatouros, discussing the impact of World Bank lending on the borrower's legal system, mentions a few of these general conditions. One category of clauses consists of those which attribute to the Bank sole authority to decide (in the future) whether particular requirements or conditions have been met. In some cases, specific security is required for the repayment of a loan (e.g., a lien on revenues of the project or a guarantee from a private sponsor). In all other cases a "negative pledge" clause requires the state to undertake that no other external debt will take priority over the debt to the Bank. Other common clauses "limit considerably the state's freedom of action within its territory and drastically reduce the legal and policy options initially open to it concerning the manner in which the project itself will be realized and concerning state action affecting the national economy."[30]

> 5. Implementation and supervision: The borrower is responsible for implementation of the project that has been agreed with the Bank. The Bank is responsible for supervising that implementation, through progress reports from the borrower and periodic field visits. An annual review of Bank supervision experience on all projects underway serves to continually improve policies and procedures. Procurement of goods and works for the project must follow official Bank guidelines for efficiency and economy.

During this stage the Bank has the dual function of "watchdog" to ensure the proper use of the proceeds of the loan, including supervision of international competitive bidding or other procurement procedures, and "troubleshooter," working with the implementing agency to identify and solve problems that threaten the timely execution of the project. The Bank may at any time suspend disbursements if it feels that the project is not being satisfactorily implemented. The method of sending Washington-based staff out for short supervision missions may not be the most effective, however. In one case, nine successive missions failed to discover a basic technical problem involving water leakage from a reservoir; it seems that each successive mission noted that the reservoir was empty when it should not be, but then passed the buck on to the following mission, which like the others stayed too short a time to get to the bottom of the problem.[31] The evaluation remarks that "the Bank concentrated its supervision efforts almost entirely on enforcing the covenants on agricultural services and water charges, ignoring the main problem confronting the project."[32]

6. Evaluation: This is the last stage. It follows the final disbursement of Bank funds for the project. An independent department of the Bank, the Operations Evaluation Department, reviews the completion report of the Bank's projects staff, and prepares its own audit of the project, often by receiving materials at headquarters, though field trips are made where needed. This *ex post* evaluation provides lessons of experience which are built into subsequent identification, preparation or appraisal work.

The operations evaluation department is "independent" in the sense that it is separate from the operating staff of the Bank and reports directly to the executive directors and the president through its own director general. Their audits are concerned primarily with whether there were time and cost overruns on the project, whether the anticipated rate of return has been achieved, and so on, rather than on the broader social questions raised in this book. The audit is in most cases based on material submitted to the department by the operating staff—which does not prevent it from occasionally being sharply critical.

According to van de Laar, the Bank management resisted the introduction of independent evaluations and was forced to do so only by strong pressure from the U.S. Congress. The first chief of the evaluation activities, he claims, had to threaten to resign almost every week for a period of time to ward off pressure to undermine his autonomy in the evaluations.[33]

The operations evaluation department publishes an *Annual Review of Project Performance Audit Results* that summarizes the audits carried out in that year. These are presented in a rather homogenized form: no country names are used, for example, although a few cases (as "a bauxite mining project in a West African country") are easy to figure out. The publication stresses positive results; the 1976 audit of 70 projects found, in summary, that "90 percent of the Bank's investments had economic returns similar to, or substantially better than, estimates made at the time of their appraisal," while the one for the following year, studying 109 projects, found that "over 91 percent of the investments have been 'worthwhile' in the sense that the projects

materially achieved the objectives set for them.''[34] Both the
supervision and evaluation stages of the project cycle are concerned to see that Bank projects achieve the objectives they were
designed for. Neither addresses questions about the nature and
validity of those objectives.

4
Infrastructure: The Traditional Sectors

It is usually assumed that roads and railways
act as an instrument of civilization and promote
welfare by bringing people into contact with the
modern world, but negro slavery was formerly
defended on the same grounds. Whether closer
contact is beneficial depends upon its nature
and the results, and where as has happened
sometimes on railway construction large numbers die, or where as also has happened, a whole
people fades away, it can be regarded as beneficial to them only on the ground that they are
better dead.
—J. S. Furnivall, *Colonial Policy and Practice*

Infrastructure projects—transportation, communications, and
electric power—are the traditional areas of Bank lending. They
dominated the lending pattern in the 1950s, and even after the
expansion of lending for agriculture and so-called social infrastructure projects in the past two decades, they remain among
the largest sectors in volume of money lent. The rationale of this
emphasis has always been aid to private industry:

Costly equipment from abroad, it was clear, would be required for
electric power plants, transportation and communication systems,
and other basic facilities that were no longer attractive to private
capital, although they could be regarded as prerequisites for the
attraction of private capital to industry, agriculture, and the services. Public utilities had attracted private capital to less developed
countries in pre-World War II days, but it would have been un-

realistic to expect them to do so on any appreciable scale after the war. The investment was too large, the return to the investor too small, and the prospect of government intervention too great. Projects to develop electric power and transport facilities were accordingly considered especially appropriate for Bank financing.[1]

Almost from the beginning, this emphasis on infrastructure for industry was criticized for its failure to improve the lives of the poor. However, it might fairly be asked, does not every society that aspires to development, socialist as well as capitalist, need roads, railroads, and electric power? They do, of course, and infrastructure projects can be criticized only in the context of the specific changes they promote, and the industries they service. Personally, I find less to criticize here than in the social projects with which the Bank became so enamored under McNamara's presidency. That said, however, it is useful both to reiterate the old criticisms and to note some specific features of the way in which the Bank has carried out its lending for infrastructure projects.

Transportation

First, while every society uses some form of transportation, it is accorded a special importance in an internationally open economy where regional specialization and division of labor are paramount. Both require facilities for long hauls of massive quantities of goods and materials. A policy of self-sufficiency in basic goods, on the other hand, while still requiring and permitting the transport of goods and persons, does not demand the massive transport investment of a highly specialized international economy. This is clearly expressed in the introduction to the Bank's sector working paper on transportation:

> Transportation is a necessary concomitant of the *exchange economy* and is indispensable to *economic growth*. Where there is no transportation, economic activity is restricted to hand-to-mouth *subsistence levels. Specialization* and the generation of *surpluses for exchange* on the basis of *comparative advantage* are not possible

without the capability to move resources and goods from one place to another.[2]

But even within this framework, transportation has a unique place in colonial and neocolonial economies which supply raw materials to the overseas metropolis. The pattern of transportation development of colonial Africa, which has not been significantly altered in postcolonial times, is the clearest illustration of this: ports were built all around the continent's coastline, and railroads were built from mines to ports, or from agricultural developments to ports. All the productive areas of Africa were tied to the European and world economy through their ports, while remaining for the most part totally separate from each other.

The Bank's working paper also emphasizes the special nature of the transportation problem in raw materials exporting economies:

> Investigations in developed economies suggest that transportation costs are not a significant proportion of the final price of most manufactured and some mining products. . . . The situation is radically different in less developed economies where a larger proportion of the economically important movements are likely to be high-bulk, low-value agricultural and mineral products. The threshholds of viable production or export of these primary products are often determined by externally defined prices. Transport costs on the feeder roads, on the trunk road or railway to the coast, through the port, and on the ship to foreign markets often account for as much as 50% of the receipts from these commodities. Maize in Kenya and iron ore in Brazil are cases in point. Where transportation is particularly costly due to a lack of adequate facilities or inefficient operation, the impact on profitability and output can be decisive.[3]

Railroads, ports, and airports are types of Bank-financed transportation investments which clearly illustrate the neocolonial nature of the type of development promoted by the Bank and its sponsors. Whereas before the age of the automobile, railroads served a variety of customers and purposes, today new rail lines are constructed almost exclusively for a single purpose and a "captive" client. The railroads financed by the Bank in connection with mines in countries like Mauritania, Botswana, and Brazil are typical illustrations of this (see Chapter 6). (Rehabilitation of old railway lines and the puchase of new rolling stock and equipment, however, are frequently financed by the Bank.)

Ports are the key interface for the vast bulk of import-export trade and thus have always had a place in the Bank's designs. Fifteen percent of all transport sector funds have gone into port development. Most of these loans involve port "improvements" that will allow the Third World port to accommodate the largest supertankers in the multinational shipping fleets or to handle the labor-saving "container" shipping now favored by the wealthy countries, however inappropriate to labor-surplus economies.

Even the Bank admits that aviation projects "serve foreigners to a large extent."[4] Most of the Bank's aviation loans have financed the modernization of airports, the major purpose of which is to speed the transit of passengers through the airports. This may facilitate the introduction of large-scale tourism into the country, or it may merely provide greater convenience for business travelers, diplomats, and World Bank missions.

By far the largest category of transport investment financed by the Bank is highway construction, which requires closer investigation. It is not merely a large but also a complex topic, as the highways financed range in size and technical sophistication from multilane limited-access expressways, on which tolls are charged, to relatively simple "feeder" roads in rural areas. There has been a relative shift of emphasis to the latter, as the lending program overall has changed to favor agricultural lending and the propaganda has shifted to stress the benefits of loans to poor people and rural residents. Most rural development projects now contain a component for the improvement of roads, and several of the highway loans have been announced as concomitant with or preceding rural development projects.

Most residents of rural areas in the Third World desire and welcome the building or the improvement of roads connecting their area with market centers and the capital (in this differing from the sophisticated residents of Pacific Palisades and New York, who have discovered they don't always like what comes down the pike). The social change induced by the introduction of motor transport into an area is complex and by no means merely detrimental. But the important fact to remember is that these investments are planned and executed at the center, for the purposes of the administrative and commercial classes. As M. K. McCall asserts, in an important contribution on the impact of transport investment:

> As a general rule, the purposes of transport investment under colonialism and neocolonialism are to exploit, pacify and administer, and integrate rural areas into the economic and socio-political mainstream of national life; and integration into the national economy implies integration into the world-wide capitalist system.[5]

The building of a road or, more frequently, the upgrading of a track to accommodate motor traffic, is an essential precondition of both political and economic integration. According to McCall: "Historically, transport has been a keystone in the control of resources, the extraction of surplus and the formation of class."[6] Thirty years earlier, the great historian of colonialism, J. S. Furnivall, had reached a similar conclusion:

> Thus the general belief in the intrinsic value of roads, railways and other forms of public works as instruments of native welfare must be dismissed as an illusion; only too often they do more harm than good to those whom they are supposed to benefit. . . . Public works in general, whether roads, railways, airways, ports or irrigation, serve to expedite development, and thereby enhance the difficulty of protecting natives against its evil consequences.[7]

Paved roads serve motor vehicles, all of which are owned and most of which are used by the elites. Poor people, using animal carts or going on foot, are better served by dirt roads. Bullock carts with pneumatic wheels quickly shake to pieces on paved roads; horses can travel much farther on unpaved roads than on paved; and even with heavy shoes, feet blister on pavement over the same distance that walk on a dirt road comfortably.[8] And the use of high-speed motorized vehicles on the same road as slow-moving carts, rickshas, bicycles, tricycles, and pedestrians is dangerous to all, but particularly to the slow-moving forms of transport owned and used by poorer people.

In evaluating transport projects the World Bank first ascertains if there is a "need" for the project, then tries to quantify the benefits in order to achieve a figure for the rate of return. Traditionally, the bank has tried to quantify "user savings" on the benefit side of the account—that is, the savings accruing to vehicle operators from fewer repairs, accidents, and the reduction of time spent by vehicles, cargoes, and drivers on the road (an important component of turnover time). Recently, with the new popularity of feeder roads in rural areas, there has appeared a new conceptual benefit, that of new production induced by the enhanced possibility of transporting produce. In the words of the sector working paper, "reductions in transport costs are likely to have a larger impact in terms of bringing into production the marginal piece of land."[9] But McCall is skeptical:

> when impacts are restricted to simplistic and positivistic measures regarding agricultural change, it is not surprising that nearly all feeder roads turn out to be evaluated positively. If agricultural production is assumed to depend directly on the reduction in transportation costs, than any road improvement will lead to induced production.[10]

The reduction in transport cost brought about by investment in roads, according to McCall, in no way benefits the farmer: "The savings due to improved transport technologies rarely if ever accrue to the peasant, falling instead into the laps of the railway companies, private truckers, marketing boards, trading companies, and the metropolitan purchaser."[11] While this judgment is probably too sweeping, it is likely that the changes introduced by the commercialization of agriculture into the region opened by the road will further marginalize the poor and polarize rural society. For one thing, the value of lands near the road tend to rise in direct proportion to the fall in transport cost, and the increased value is then appropriated by those who own the land—or those who can obtain it by fair means or foul from its original occupants. McCall cites an example from northwestern Tanzania under German rule where the chiefs took advantage of the transport links constructed by the Germans to extend a quasi-feudal form of land tenure that expropriated the best coffee lands for the chiefs and reduced peasants to sharecropping. A more recent case from South Korea showed that an increase in land prices was the first impact of rural expressways, which "in turn led to the new social activity of land disputes, brought about by forging of land documents, illegal disposal of communal lands, double disposal of land and other such manifestations of modernity."[12]

Carole LaGrasse observes that appropriate road construction to civilize a country rather than exploit it involves improving convenience of *exchange:*

> Feeder roads radiating from market centers serve exploitation. The natural pattern of progressive, civilizing development is an intricate network of back roads or footpaths. In my community (in upstate New York) we actually have fewer miles of passable Town and County highways than we did before the massive highway building program of the past thirty years. As the area is pictured at the State and County level more and more as a tourist-drawing area, intratown services are allowed to decline, and communication within the township atrophies.[13]

Perhaps the most notorious illustration of the deleterious effects of road construction on indigenous populations is the building of the trans-Amazon highway in Brazil, an episode which should remind us that the extermination of entire populations is by no means a thing of the past. The building of this highway in order to permit the exploitation of the Amazon's mineral and timber resources, plus the ecologically disastrous clearing of the forest for cattle ranching and agricultural settlement, has had an almost totally destructive effect on the natives of the area, as their lands are seized and they themselves are destroyed by design (massacres, poisoning) of those who covet their land, by diseases newly introduced by the invaders brought by the road, and by the demoralization of their culture by proletarianization, alcohol, and prostitution.

Now the World Bank is financing a federal highway and colonization scheme in northwest Brazil which, Indian defense organizations in that country claim, would result in the extermination or marginalization of thirty indigenous communities inhabiting the area. These peoples have already been decimated by the incursions of "civilization" into their homeland; they have been herded onto tiny and resource-poor reserves incapable of supporting them while the territory that they originally occupied has been given away to ranchers settling in the area. The planned road would be for the benefit of the ranchers.[14] (The experience of an anthropologist as a World Bank consultant on this project is given in Chapter 12.)

The building of roads has political as well as economic significance. Roads are a necessary, even if not sufficient, condition for centralized power relations, as McCall reminds us. They are essential for the penetration of agricultural extension agents, and for the extension of clinics and schools sponsored by the central government. They also are important for the mobility of the police, the army, and the tax collectors. "In many UDCs [underdeveloped countries] police and paramilitary operate a sizeable proportion of national vehicles."[15]

While the World Bank's formal procedures do not permit it to cite these benefits as a rationale for transportation lending (they must produce predictions of economic benefit), there is considerable evidence that such considerations loom large in the minds of the borrowing government, and that in many cases the Bank is aware of and sympathetic to these aims. In a textbook devoted specifically to the economic analysis of Bank projects we find this passage, in which the goals of capturing the economic surplus of undeveloped areas and that of administrative control are closely interlinked:

First, the mission noted that by enlarging, surfacing and rehabilitating its highway networks, the government was trying to integrate the country into a more effective economic, social, and administrative unit. The government was not only seeking to increase output and productivity in both agriculture and manufacturing and to improve distribution; it was also aiming to transform areas of subsistence agriculture into cash agriculture and to open fertile but uncultivated areas to settlement. It also wanted to give Ethiopian producers better and cheaper access to markets at home and abroad by reducing transportation costs. Experience with the two highway programs previously financed by the Bank suggested that important developmental consequences would flow from the Third Highway Program. The earlier programs had induced a shift from subsistence farming to cash crops in certain regions by stimulating interregional and farm-to-market trade. They had also opened new areas for the production of coffee, the main export crop, and of the food grains, oilseed and pulses needed in the home market. They had lowered the operating costs of trucks and buses and, as a result, the expenses of transport generally. Finally, they had extended the reach and increased the efficiency of governmental administration, including education and agricultural extension services, by making personal travel possible on a larger scale than previously.[16]

A nonofficial observer of Ethiopian society has painted a grimmer picture of what highway construction has meant to poor people in the remoter areas of that country:

> The only way for a peasant to escape [confiscation of his land for nonpayment of taxes] is to possess an official, written receipt showing that he has paid land tax (since 1968 agricultural income tax). The more remote areas in southern Ethiopia have been brought closer to Addis Ababa and Government machinery through highway construction programs undertaken after World War II. The peasants and pastoralists which have inhabited these areas for generations have of course no receipts to show for the taxes paid. Much of their land has therefore been officially classified as "Government land" and the inhabitants reduced to tenants or driven away.[17]

Nevertheless, the same writer found that a road project under construction in another part of Ethiopia was "welcomed by all" even though "given the present social and economic structure ... the road might open up the area for the same kind of agricultural development seen in Sheboka: the entry of tractors and harvesters into the fertile lands and the exit of redundant tenants."[18] As McCall admits, "It would be partisan to argue that all impacts are purely exploitative. There are clearly real gains for certain sections of the population, and probably some benefits reach even the most oppressed." But he then cites a study made for the World Bank of one of its road projects in the Yemen Arab Republic. The authors

> received complaints such as: "only merchants and government officials will benefit." Moreover, 75 percent of the people not expecting any benefits lived within 1.5 kilometers of existing roads. Dunant et al. commented "[They are] already experienced ... and know that the situation did not improve since road construction."[19]

Investment in roads in Turkey in the 1950s had very similar effects to those in Ethiopia: the roads permitted the landed elites

to import tractors and harvesters and to expel their now redundant tenants. Since the tractors had created technological
unemployment but did nothing to increase overall crop yields,
"the peasants simply used the new roads to leave rural areas.
The major effect of investing in tractors and roads was to increase the number of unemployed and expand the urban slums."[20]
Roads, by facilitating the extraction of the agricultural surplus
from the penetrated areas, introduce the pressures which destroy
subsistence agriculture. By permitting the influx of manufactured
consumer goods, they made domestic household industries
unviable. High transport costs function as natural barriers
(analogous to customs barriers) protecting local industry. The
introduction of any type of transport which reduces these costs
destroys this natural protection. Those who control the crops
that are shipped out toward the cities are also able to purchase
cheap manufactured goods from the cities "and to dispense with
the high-priced products produced by the village weavers and
other craftsmen, who are thus forced to seek urban employment
or remain persistently unemployed."[21]

The few benefits that previously isolated peoples may gain
from the lowering of transport costs—quicker access to hospitals, cheaper manufactured goods, etc.—are outweighed by the
less visible but far more powerful forces that penetrate the areas
with the new roads, depriving many of these people (who may or
may not have been "poor" before the coming of the road) of their
livelihoods. Yet the World Bank, in its zeal to count the benefits
of its projects to poor people, indulges in fatuous generaliza-
tions such as the following (about the reconstruction of the
Longitudinal Highway in Chile, described as the "backbone of
the country's road network"):

> About three-quarters of Chile's rural poor and about 40% of its
> urban poor live in the areas directly influenced by the project and
> will benefit from this operation. Nearly half of these poor people
> are members of small farm families who depend upon the highway
> for their access to the rest of the economy.[22]

The "benefits" to the poor people of Chile will depend almost
entirely on the character of that economy and of the government

that controls and promotes the road traffic, and in present-day Chile that government will not benefit the poor.

The class bias of one road project is clearly apparent in the Bank's account of its negotiations with Mexico pursuant to a second loan for a toll highway project in 1965. The example is all the more illuminating as we are also given a glimpse of the Bank's role in influencing the design and execution of the project. In the first place, the highway itself was designed exclusively for the use of those who own modern forms of transport and can afford to pay for the privilege of traveling rapidly over a limited-access road built to the highest design specifications. This highway could not accommodate local traffic and formed a positive hindrance to it. Experience on the first Bank-sponsored toll highway project in Mexico had revealed a greater-than-expected pressure to provide underpasses and overpasses to satisfy local vehicle, pedestrian, and animal traffic, a source of irritation to the Bank because it fouled up their cost-benefit analysis, by delaying completion of construction and raising costs. The Bank missions' solution to this problem was to insist that "for the proposed project only those under and overpasses basic to it (those at existing roads and interchanges) should be included in the project being financed by the Bank. Any other overpasses should be financed entirely by Caminos [the Mexican toll highway authority]."[23]

Another source of delay in the Mexican toll highway project, and thus of frustration for the Bank, were the procedures required for acquiring right-of-way through *ejidos*, the communally owned areas established as a result of the agrarian reform program following the 1910 revolution. *Ejido* lands, complained the Bank, had been made virtually inalienable to protect the poor rural families that farmed them. These rights, the Bank felt, should not be allowed to delay construction of the new toll road, and therefore "the mission obtained assurances that the Ministry was revising its procedures so as to facilitate early acquisition of the rights-of-way, including those through *ejido* areas."[24]

A final point of difference concerned not the transport needs of poor farmers nor the rights of *ejido* landholding, but the capabilities of the Mexican construction industry, as against the rights of giant international construction firms to obtain large contracts for this project. Again the complaint was that Mexican practice had caused the project to suffer "delays."

> It was the general policy of the Mexican government not to encourage the creation of large domestic construction firms or the presence of large foreign ones. This policy, a legacy of the Revolution with its distrust of the big and the foreign, was carried out not only by letting contracts for relatively short segments of road, but also by dividing the works into separate contracts for earthworks, structures (bridges) and pavement. Largely as a result of this practice, very few foreign firms submitted bids, although international competitive bidding had been agreed upon as the method of letting these contracts; and all the contracts were let to Mexican firms.[25]

Although the Bank stated that the Mexican construction industry was on the whole "efficient and well-managed," some firms had encountered difficulties in obtaining materials and skilled labor or in using machinery and equipment "efficiently." The Bank claimed, rather improbably, that these difficulties were attributable to the size of the firms. The Bank insisted that for the new loan, the minimum contract size be set at the equivalent of $2 million to attract foreign bids. Also, "the mission suggested that the Ministry study ways in which future contracts could be increased in size and scope to get around some of the problems experienced during construction of the first toll project, and the Ministry agreed to do so."[26] It should be added that the Bank now claims to be reversing this process, and is studying ways in which contracts for road-building can be broken down into smaller packages, to encourage local contractors. If they are sincere in this, it represents a radical reversal from earlier policy, which was deliberately designed to favor international firms (see Chapter 1). Most probably it is only a token program.

Before we leave the transportation sector, one further point should be noted. As in the other sectors for which it lends, the Bank does not content itself with financing projects, but uses specific projects as a means to influence country-wide planning in that particular sector. The Bank has sponsored numerous studies of the "transportation sector" in the countries to which it lends, and on the basis either of these studies or of other consid-

erations, sets conditions for its loans that affect the future investment policies for the sector and its financing. A major question
here has been the respective roles of highways and railways in
future transportation investment. In the early years (the 1950s),
lending to railways, either for new lines or the rehabilitation of
older lines, amounted to twice that for highways. After 1960 this
situation was reversed and now road building comprises by far
the largest element in the sector.[27] This emphasis on road building, in the Third World as in the developed countries, amounts
to a substantial subsidy to the motor transport industry. It is,
after all, absolutely necessary to have roads constructed for
automobiles before Volkswagens, Toyotas, and Hondas can be
sold in a country. This emphasis has also created a strong and
virtually irreversible demand for motor fuels, which in most
Third World countries must still be imported.

The extent of Bank influence in planning in the transport
sector is illustrated by the case of Brazil. A year after the coup in
1964, which brought to power a procapitalist, proforeign investment government, the Bank helped finance an extensive transportation survey which greatly influenced transport investment
over the next four years. In this critical period it was decided to
"open up" the Amazon basin to corporate exploitation by constructing major roads and ports through the area.

> Furthermore, Brazil in two memoranda of understanding that were
> worked out with the World Bank in 1965 and 1967 agreed to
> undertake certain policy actions in the transport field, the most
> important being to limit highway construction until master plans
> had been completed, to close certain uneconomic railway lines, to
> cease building certain new lines, and to rationalize port operations
> and investments. Although the assurances given were not always
> carried through in full, the Bank has been able, in connection with
> the subsequent loans and a persistent dialogue, to have a good
> deal of influence on railway, highway, and port administration
> in Brazil.[28]

Where the Bank has made loans for railway rehabilitation, it
has typically exerted pressure for the "rationalization" of rail
charges for goods and passengers. The pressure has usually been
in the direction of raising rates and thus allowing the railway

authority to operate on an autonomous financial and managerial footing. Occasionally, however, the Bank criticizes some rates as being too high and "attracting competition from trucking." The railroad and port tariffs of the East African Federation, for example, "were designed so that any losses from hauling and handling freight deemed essential to development would be made good by profits from hauling freight that was deemed capable of paying all the traffic could bear." The latter category included high-value manufactures, petroleum products, and less-than-carload lots. "The Mission noted that the Administration was aware of the need to correct its tariffs by reducing charges for higher-rated goods and raising those on lower-rated goods."[29]

Electrical Power

Electrical power is a commodity that is produced (generation), transported (transmission), and sold wholesale and retail (distribution). It has, of course, peculiar features that mask its general resemblance to other commodities: for one, it cannot be transported by truck or train or sold over the counter to its retail customers; also, it is almost always a public utility, subject to government regulation if not directly owned and controlled by a public authority. For another, electric power is not only a commodity in itself but an essential input into most kinds of modern productive enterprise, thus falling under the definition of "infrastructure."

The financing of electric power projects was one of the first types of lending from the Bank to Third World nations; and for many years it remained the largest sector. At the end of fiscal year 1980 it represented, cumulatively, the second largest sector, after agriculture and rural development, with over $14 billion, or 21 percent of the total funds lent by the Bank for all purposes throughout its history.

Electrical power projects have been considered particularly suitable for Bank lending because they are heavily capital intensive, requiring expensive imported equipment produced mostly by the developed countries. As an "old-style" Bank project, this sector has been vulnerable to the deserved charges that its benefits go only to the already wealthy and powerful, whether in their function as owners of factories and mines or as the wealthier class of urban residents who can afford to pay for household electrical connections as well as the appliances powered by electricity. An early power loan to South Africa, for example, purported to relieve acute power shortages on the Rand, which contained many important mining and industrial centers; while another to Swaziland in the same period (at that time still a British colony) was intended to meet the power requirements of a mine operated by British and South African capital, the Swaziland Iron Ore Development Company. (The ore was to be sold to Japanese steel mills).[30] More recently, a 1978 power loan to Colombia (IBRD No. 1583-0) will serve a nickel mine owned by Hanna and Billiton (Shell Oil).[31]

Under certain circumstances electric power can even be exported from the Third World to the rich countries, i.e., when cheap power is embodied in an industrial process that would be prohibitively expensive elsewhere. The clearest examples of this process occur in the aluminum smelting industry, which consumes such large amounts of electricity that "a difference of 1 mill (.1¢ per kilowatt) in power costs adds some $16–18 per ton to the cost of ingot metal."[32] For this reason cheap hydroelectric power has been a preferred energy source; over 50 percent of the world's aluminum is currently produced from hydroelectric power.[33] In recent years the big aluminum companies have sought to utilize hydroelectric projects in Latin America and Africa, which as a rule are built by a public authority, financed by international loans (both public and private), and which contract out electricity for smelters at extremely cheap rates, well below what other users have to pay (where there are other users). The case of the Volta River Authority of Ghana, and its Akosombo Dam, which provides electricity at scandalously low rates to Kaiser Aluminum, is detailed in Chapter 9. A similar case, though in this case not in a Third World country, is that of the 1966 loan to Iceland's Burfell Falls power project. In that case the borrower was the National Power Company (Landsvirkjun), which agreed to contract most of the power of the project to Icelandic Aluminium Company, Ltd., a wholly owned subsidiary of Alusuisse, the Switzerland-based aluminum multinational. In Cameroun, a smelter is operated by Pechiney Ugine Kuhlmann with participation of the International Finance Company. Reynolds Metals owns half of a smelter in Venezuela powered by the Bank-financed Guri Dam. And the government of Guyana has approached Alcan, the largest aluminum producer in the world, as a potential customer for electricity from a hydro dam they hope the World Bank will finance. (The dam is opposed by the supporters of an indigenous Indian community that would be wiped out by the project, as well as by the government of Venezuela, which shares the watershed with Guyana.)

Although the needs of the consumers of the electricity seem to be the necessary and sufficient condition for World Bank support of the expansion of electrical capacity, it is worth recalling that in Latin America, where the Bank has made the bulk of its electrical power loans, the industry was established by private, foreign investors and controlled by U.S., Canadian, and European-based corporations. At the time the Bank began its lending to Latin America, these private, foreign power companies were increasingly under siege from nationalists advocating expropriation and national operation of this strategically sensitive sector, and by governments intent on regulating the prices charged to their citizens. Throughout its history of lending for power development the Bank has consistently harped on the necessity of charging rates to customers which would enable electric companies or authorities to operate in a financially viable manner. (Except, of course, when a multinational aluminum company with good political connections is the customer, as in the Valco project of Ghana.) While one must be sympathetic to the Bank's argument that those who do not enjoy the use of electricity should not be made to subsidize those who do, it is revealing to discover that its insistence on "economic" rates, as well as its first loans to the sector, redounded to the benefit of foreign, private owners.

A man who was a participating World Bank official at the time of which he writes recalls:

The first request to the World Bank for substantial funds to be used in Latin America came in 1947, when a loan was sought to expand Brazil's electric-power facilities and increase the capacity of its telephone exchanges. The loan request was favorably received, not because it was essential to Brazil's economic development, but because the applicant was the Brazilian Light and Traction Company of Montreal, a private and moreover a foreign company. The Bank negotiated with the company even before it consulted the Brazilian government, which was to guarantee the credit.[34]

This company, nicknamed The Light, remained a favored borrower of the Bank through the fifties and the early sixties—the years preceding the rightist coup of 1964. Table 3.1, taken from Judith Tendler's *Electric Power in Brazil*,[35] shows that The Light received the lion's share of all World Bank loans to Brazil in this period; this one company receiving 45 percent of all power loans and 41 percent of loans to all sectors. But even this understates the case. As Tendler shows in her text, The Light originally held 50.6 percent of the preferred stock of Furnas, the public company listed at the bottom of the chart, used it as its wholesale source of power supply, and vigorously promoted the interests of Furnas both with the Brazilian government and the World Bank. If the Furnas loan is combined with those to The Light, they amount to fully 73 percent of all power loans to Brazil before 1964, and 66 percent of *all* loans to that country.

It is also amply demonstrated in Tendler's text (though she interprets the situation quite differently) that The Light was able to guide the government into the type of investment in public power which would be complementary to and supportive of The Light's financial interest, rather than competitive with it. The Light's most lucrative business was in the retail distribution of electricity in the major cities of Rio de Janeiro and São Paulo. The government, on the other hand, found its niche in financing and running new generating facilities that comprised the most capital-intensive side of the industry and had a slow pay-off, and that sold a good part of their power to The Light, which distributed it.

By agreeing to mix its own generation with state supplies . . . the Light was not restricting access to any future distribution market it might want to seek. It could even look upon the government power as a way of shoring up its position rather than threatening it.

The Light, for example, instead of opposing the state-sponsored Furnas Plant, promoted it in order to reap the greatest possible benefit from its construction. Furnas planned initially to sell all of its power in a simple and profitable arrangement to São Paulo Light. The Light, in return, took a stock-holding participation in Furnas and championed the state company's cause at the World Bank. As a result, the Bank granted a $73 million loan to Furnas in 1958, at a time when it was making a point of not lending to Brazil because, among other reasons, of inflationary policies.[36]

Throughout this (precoup) period The Light carried on a running battle with the Brazilian government over policy regarding the rates it was allowed to charge. The World Bank consistently sided with the private company, insisting on the need to allow a sufficient return on capital. (The issue is rather technical, pivoting on the capital base used in calculations of allowable return, which had been eroded in Brazil and other Latin American countries by inflation. It appears from Tendler's account, too, that The Light was not really suffering, as a variety of "additionals" or surcharges were permitted to make up the deficiency in the basic rate policy.) If its leverage was not too successful, this is probably due to fact that The Light was more eager to continue receiving loans (of which it was the major beneficiary, as we have seen) than to press the issue of rates.

The Light came increasingly under nationalistic fire in the early 1960s, and (as in the case of Hanna Mining, see Chapter 6) faced a serious threat of nationalization. The World Bank did not make any loans at all to Brazil from June 1959 until after the military coup of 1964, which reversed most of the previous antiforeign-investment policies of the precoup period. The new military government was also quick to grant the foreign-owned Light the new rate structure that it had long desired. This was one step in a whole complex of policies that provided the precondition for the resumption of U.S. and World Bank aid to Brazil.

In 1969 the company (which had previously dropped the "Traction" from its full name of Brazilian Traction, Light, and

Table 3.1
International Bank for Reconstruction and Development:
Loans to Brazil (1952–1963)

Sector	Amount ($1,000,000)		Year
Railroads	$ 12.5		1952
Roads	3.0		1953
Railroads	12.5		1953
Electric power	264.1		1949–1962
The Light		75.0	1949
The Light		15.0	1951
The Light		18.8	1954
The Light		11.6	1959
CHESF[a]		15.0	1950
CEEE[b]		25.0	1952
CEMIG		7.3	1953
USELPA		10.0	1953
USELPA		13.4	1958
Furnas		73.0	1958
Grand total	292.1		

		Percent of power loans	Percent of total loans
Total to electric power	264.1	100.0	90.0
Total to the Light	120.4	45.0	41.0

Source: Judith Tendler, *Electric Power in Brazil* (Cambridge, Mass.: Harvard University Press, 1968), Table 7.1, p. 227; based on information from IBRD, *Eighteenth Annual Report, 1962–1963*, pp. 57–58.
   a. Companhia Hidrelétrica do São Francisco.
   b. Comissão Estadual de Energia Elétrica do Rio Grande do Sul.
   c. Subsequently canceled.

Power), took a new name, Brascan. It was under this name that the company reached an amicable agreement with the Brazilian government in 1976 providing for the sale of the company's property to the government for a large cash sum, which Brascan then tried to use to purchase Woolworth's, the huge U.S. variety store chain. Brascan also retained a 60 percent interest in a tin

mining corporation, Mineraçao Jacunda, which holds a concession in the Brazilian state of Rondonia, where the tin deposits
are reputed to be the largest in the world.

There are some suggestive parallels in the case of Bank lending to the Mexican electrical power industry in the same period.
In this case as well as in Brazil, a foreign, private power company, Mexican Light and Power Company (Mexlight) was a loan
beneficiary, although not such a predominant one as was The
Light in Brazil. Also in this case (as in much of the rest of Latin
America) the issue of rates was a sore spot between the foreign
company and a somewhat nationalistic government. The World
Bank sided with the private company, and made it clear in 1958
that any new loans to the Mexican power sector would be "contingent on the complete overhaul of the rate structure."[37]

The Mexican government, however, showed little willingness
to meet the companies' demands (American & Foreign Power
Company and Mexlight were the two major foreign companies)
and the eventual solution was (as in the case of Brazil, except
quite a bit earlier) the 1960 purchase by the government of the
companies' properties. As in Brazil, this nationalization was
an amicable business, perfectly satisfactory to the foreign companies; in fact Wionczek asserts that there is "more than circumstantial evidence to the effect that the initiative came not from the
state but from the foreign utilities themselves." The companies
had good reason to be satisfied with the settlement they received:

> There is no doubt that because of the difficult—if not hopeless—
> position of the companies in the late fifties the Mexican govern-
> ment could have arranged the transaction on much more favorable
> terms. Clearly it would have been possible to save many millions of
> dollars by putting the purchase offer on a take-it-or-leave-it basis;
> but such a saving might have been costly to Mexico in terms of
> future hostility on the part of foreign business interests. The Mexi-
> can state did not consider it advisable to provoke the enmity of two
> powerful foreign enterprises and was eager not to destroy its good
> relations with international public and private financial centers.
> . . . To the extent that Mexico's liberal attitude toward the com-
> panies helped to retain confidence in the country's political and
> economic future among foreign investors and in international fi-
> nancial circles, the price paid was well justified. Access to interna-

tional financing resources was now restored and the basis for future expansion of electric power facilities vital for Mexico's sutained economic growth was assured.[38]

One more condition remained, besides the satisfaction of the bought-out foreign companies, before World Bank loans could be resumed: the rate issue. The nationalization of the electrical companies allowed the government to do for itself what it could not permit the private companies to do, namely, to increase the over-all level of rates. "When the rate changes were made public early in 1962 the spokesmen for business, labor, and consumers declared them just, necessary, and unavoidable. Such protests as occurred were narrowly based and short-lived."[39]

The upward readjustment of rates reopened the door to World Bank loans; an enormous ($130 million) loan was extended less than half a year after the new rate schedules were put into effect.[40]

This raises an interesting question about the policy of the Bank and the direction of its pressures, for throughout its history its preference for private investment in the electric power industry, while discernible in such cases as those mentioned above, has not been pressed to the breaking point; while its insistence on a viable level of rates has remained a constant theme, even though its definition of what constitutes a viable level has undergone some modification. If there is political significance to the Bank's policies in this case, it will have to be sought at a deeper level than that of crude preference for private versus public enterprise. From the beginning the Bank has lent to both public and private entities in the power sector, and often to both within the same country. If the Bank had hoped to preserve private control of the power industry in Latin America, it has not been successful; and it has not ceased to lend because of its lack of success.

Whether dealing with private companies or with public ones, however, it has insisted on the necessity of "rationalizing" the level of rates. This issue cannot be separated from its insistence on the "autonomy" of public enterprises to which it lends, for "the financial autonomy of an enterprise, whether public or private, has been considered as conducive to its administrative autonomy, and the Bank has always favored a maximum degree of administrative independence for entities engaged in commercial operations."[41]

The Bank's preference for autonomous agencies has been analyzed by several commentators.[42] Perhaps the best critique is that of A. Fatouros, who summarizes the reasons for the Bank's preference as follows:

> The ability to act "in a businesslike manner" is probably the argument most frequently made. Several more specific arguments may be understood as subsumed under it: First, the avoidance of restrictive civil service procedures and regulations concerning personnel, supply and modes of operation. Second, the freedom to employ local, or quite often expatriate, high-level personnel, without complying with normal civil service rules, and to retain such personnel regardless of changes in the administration in power. Third, avoidance of partisan political pressures concerning general and specific policies and methods of operation. Fourth, ability to keep separate accounts and thus be able easily to determine the extent to which the project is self-supporting and to avoid covert subsidization of other activities. Finally, special reasons may exist for establishing an independent agency, for example, where cooperation of more than one state is involved (e.g., the East African Common Services Authority.)[43]

The emphasis on financial autonomy is basic to the aim of freedom from political control; an agency which has to return regularly to the legislature for budget appropriations will necessarily be subject to political scrutiny and control, while one which can generate its own revenues for operation and expansion can literally run amok and the government will need to take extraordinary means to stop it.

The Bank, as we have previously mentioned, proffers the plausible and sympathetic argument that people who do not benefit from a service (e.g., electricity) should not be asked to subsidize, through the tax structure, those who do enjoy it. This argument, however, should be seen in context. The Bank does not fret because the same tax system may be asked to bear the burden of compensation to nationalized foreign companies, as in the case of Brascan and the two companies operating in Mexico. Nor should we take literally its distaste for subsidies, for it actually insists that the government subsidize many of these same, so-called autonomous agencies including electrical power authorities, by subscribing to their equity or making interest-free loans as a sort of dowry. In Colombia, the Bank once curiously insisted on earmarking proceeds of a tax on *liquor* for the benefit of the power utility.[44] It is not government subsidy that the Bank really objects to, but political control.

But as Fatouros stresses:

> The fundamental point is that "political control" is not necessarily undesirable. It is at best simplistic to consider all manifestations of political—as contradistinguished from economic—concerns by the government as improper. . . . "Good" or "bad" management is not the only issue; there are policy choices to be made—and they should normally be made by those who are politically responsible. It is neither possible nor always desirable to separate clearly political and nonpolitical government functions. Radically divorcing certain matters, such as the operation of public utilities, from the political decision-making process is itself a political act, which has definite political consequences—whatever the Bank's or the host government's original intentions.[45]

In addition to the overall *level* of utility rates, the Bank has also concerned itself (though it would appear to be to a lesser degree) with the *structure* of rates, that is, the way in which costs are apportioned among various categories of users. In a casebook on project analysis, John King argued that differential tariffs should be supplied to various categories of electricity consumers. As he explains, "the costs of supplying electricity differ from one class of consumers to another. . . . Supplying electricity to rural areas tends to be very much more expensive than supplying urban areas, and the costs of supplying one kwh. to a residential consumer, even in the city, are far greater than those for one kwh. delivered to an aluminum smelter." He concludes that the Bank's position on the matter is that normally "the tariff should recover the full cost of supplying each main class of consumers as a whole."[46]

Several points could be made about this statement; the first is that this is the Bank's attempt to justify charging much lower rates to aluminum smelters than to other electricity users (which actually happened in the case of Ghana's Volta River project and Iceland's Burfell Falls project). Another is that it is not immediately self-evident how consumers should be classified for rate purposes: all industrial users vs. all residential, for example, or residential users divided into small vs. large consumers, or into even finer categories? A third point, mentioned by the Bank's semiofficial historians, is more important: this interest in the structure of utility rates and indeed in their level, they remark,

> raises delicate questions concerning the degree to which it is justifiable for the Bank to intervene in domestic economic affairs. If a country is to increase its savings rate, whether this is to be accomplished through higher utility rates, taxation, or some other policy might be considered the country's own decision to make. Again, if it is agreed that rates should be high enough to cover costs, it might, perhaps, be left to domestic authorities to determine how the overall costs should be divided between residential and industrial users.[47]

Yet a fourth point that might be mentioned is that the Bank has lately softened its position on this point, and as its public relations now emphasizes aid to the "poor" it is now popular to speak of "cross-subsidization" by one class of customers of another in public projects. This concept is neither new nor original with the Bank; it was long practiced, probably for political reasons, by many Latin American utility companies and indeed was the reason for the Bank's earlier attempts to insist that each class pay its own way.

Though the propriety of such interference in the sovereign rights of borrowing nations has been persistently questioned, the Bank has, by and large, prevailed on the issue of rates. Mason and Asher suggest that the rate conditions attached to power loans represent "the most deliberate, persistent, and successful attempts by the Bank/IDA to use the leverage of project lending to bring about significant changes in the borrower's policies" and that rate policies in Latin America and southern Asia have been "revolutionized, partly as a result of Bank influence."[48] And the victims of these rate rises have often been the poor, despite Bank attempts to represent all electricity users as relatively privileged. In Latin American cities, for example, where nearly all households have electricity connections, the rate increases decreed by the Bank have meant real hardship for working-class residential households, and have often been an issue in urban strikes and riots, e.g., the riots in Bogotá, Colombia, in January 1969.[49] It should be remembered that the Bank's sister institution, the International Monetary Fund, also frequently insists on rises in public utility charges in order to reduce or end public subsidies to the utilities, and that the IMF programs have also frequently occasioned riots—hardly an upper-class mode of protest. It should also be remembered that the Bank has tolerated, if not approved, the virtual public subsidy of the massive amounts of power consumed by Kaiser's aluminum smelter in Ghana, as the rates charged to Kaiser by the Bank-financed Volta River Authority are not only much lower than those to other classes of consumers but not sufficient to cover the costs of the project.

But we have still not arrived at the heart of the puzzle as to why the Bank is so insistent on public utilities (and other types of government-owned organizations) operating as autonomous entities on "businesslike lines." I have said that the issue of electric power does not represent a simple case of preference for private over public ownership. This may simply be because the private power companies themselves had no interest in keeping a foothold in a sector in which they were encountering considerable difficulties. The evidence for this is the enthusiasm with which they greeted, and some say planned, their liquidation to their respective governments, as in Mexico and Brazil. Miguel Wionczek cites a leading U.S. utility journal as editorializing, "For many years the handwriting has been on the wall for foreign operators of electric power and other utilities in Latin America. It is believed in many quarters that in due time about all electric power supply will be government-owned and operated south of the Rio Grande and as far as Punta Arenas."[50]

But insofar as public ownership was intruding into an arena that had once been a private preserve, still contained some privately owned companies, and had in any case great importance for businesses operating in the area, we may still ask why the Bank did not cavil at supporting public ownership of electrical (and other) utilities but insisted, with a curious fanaticism, on their operating *as if they were privately owned companies.* Since the Bank's loans are in any case (and every case) secured by government guarantee, why did they care so strongly that the utilities be independently operated and provided with sufficient means of securing revenue to guarantee that independence? I will suggest two reasons.

First, it appears that in most if not all cases in which these autonomous authorities are created or reorganized, the Bank insists that the private sector be well represented on its governing board. We find, for example, in Colombia, that the Bank requested "in order to avoid local political influence in Bogotá . . . the representatives of the Municipal Council be reduced to a minority and that *at least four out of the seven* seats be occupied by representatives of private banks and business interests."[51] It would be impossible to improve on Fatouros' commentary:

> It is by no means self-evident that the sway of special interests over the Empresas Publicas de Medellin was eliminated by removing it from direct control of the municipality and placing it under a seven-member board of directors, four of whom were "selected by the mayor from nominations made by banks and business groups." However intrinsically defective, the political machinery in less developed countries is often more responsive to public needs than the business or civil service elites.[52]

I would also hypothesize that there is another fundamental reason for the Bank to insist on the "businesslike" operation of autonomous public agencies. If publicly owned undertakings are to be run exactly along capitalist lines, they can thus be effectively prevented from presenting any effective competition to private enterprise—either in the economic or the ideological sense. If publicly owned electrical utilities must charge residential consumers just as much or more than the private foreign-owned utilities, these consumers will see that they get no benefit from nationalization. (Conversely, if governments were permitted to freely decide, through the political process, that the proceeds from one revenue-earning operation may be distributed to another purpose, there is no telling where the idea of redistribution might lead.) Enterprises that are run along businesslike lines will not permit their employees to have a say in the management, nor will their payrolls be available for experiments in different methods of rewarding work from those the capitalists deem "efficient." In short, if businessmen, or those who have learned to think like them, keep firm charge of public enterprises, they will not only serve the private sector more effectively but there will be no danger that they can become a pole of attraction by reason of working out new responses to the demands of their customers, clients, and workers.

In the beginning these thoughts were probably quite conscious: a subsidized public enterprise will be unfair competition for the private sector. It has by now become such firmly established practice that its original motivation remains only at a subconscious level. But I suggest that this is the real, political agenda behind the insistence on autonomous agencies.

Rural Electrification

The extension of electricity to rural areas is considered by some to be a way of providing service to the poor, but when examined closely this turns out to be another example of the geographical fallacy: not everything which happens in an area where many people are poor is necessarily going to benefit the poor. (To its credit, the World Bank policy paper *Rural Electrification* makes no such claim.) Indeed, as with most innovations, the introduction of electricity into a region with an inequitable social structure will tend to reinforce and even worsen that inequality.

The critics of rural electrification make three major points:

First, rural poor people cannot afford the costs of electricity in their homes, and have other needs that are much more urgent. In a "model" cooperative in the Philippines, financed by USAID,

only 6,000 of the 20,000 families in the service area were electrified as of 1975, eight years after the project was launched. This is not surprising, given the initial first year cost of $28.32 (consisting of a $20 connection fee plus a yearly minimum fee of $8.32). Adding the cost of household end-uses, electrification constitutes an extremely prohibitive expense for the rural laborer or tenant-farmer who typically has an income of only $241 per year.[53]

In Pakistan,

The percentage of households with electrical connections, in the twenty-five sample villages, varied from 12% in the Peshwar region to 39% in the Rawalpindi area, with a national average of only 24%.[54]

Similarly, in India, a governmental working group on energy policy

found that hardly 10 to 12 percent of households in the 2,300,000 all over the country which are officially classified as "electrified" use electricity. The reason is altogether simple: the electrification of rural households requires the installation of main metres and other equipment along with internal wiring which calls for an investment of between Rs 500 and 800 per household at the very least. Obviously, the overwhelming majority of the rural population, consisting of agricultural labourers, small peasants and tenants, rural artisans, etc. is in no position to make this investment.[55]

And according to Douglas Smith,

rural electrification goes first to the wealthier regions (often suburbs!), then the wealthier villages within those regions, and finally to the wealthy few households, farms, and businesses within these villages. Whether it be Karnataka State of India where installation, connection and appliance costs exceed the average per capita income, Nicaragua where "only on the largest, most heavily capitalized farms and ranches in the three cooperative areas was electricity used for production or processing purposes," or Colombia where the poor are explicit about their inability to use electricity because of lack of access to funds, the situation is similar. Rural electrification reinforces existing inequities in wealth, and it is often used as a reward to loyal regions and politicians for that very reason.[56]

The second criticism of rural electrification is that in the absence of any other significant social change, the changes it makes possible in the production processes will benefit only the already wealthy capitalist farmers, and in some cases will actually reduce employment opportunities. In the Philippines, those sectors of agriculture that consume significant amounts of electricity export most of their products.[57] Electric power for irrigation pumps will benefit those who own the land and can afford the pumps (see Chapter 8). The introduction of electrically powered rice hullers has had a drastic impact on the employment opportunities for poor women in Indonesia and Bangladesh who used to earn a living hulling rice by hand for others. It is estimated that 1.7 million women in Bangladesh lose their livelihood this way every year.[58]

The final point made about rural electrification by its critics is that, like road building, it goes hand in hand with counter-insurgency. "Both projects are directly useful to the military. Road building is essential to large-scale military transportation; electrification is needed to provide security lighting in rural outposts and towns." In the Philippines, crash electrification programs have taken place in Lanao del Sur, Samar, and the Bicol region—all strongholds of the Moro Front or the New People's Army, armed opponents of the government.[59]

5
Industry

> Rapid industrialization is a primary goal of
> virtually all developing countries and will be
> achieved one way or another. What is at stake is
> whether it will be predominantly private or gov-
> ernmental in ownership and control. What we
> are suggesting, therefore, is that external assis-
> tance agencies (which are themselves public
> entities) would be well advised to adopt what-
> ever policies consistent with the productive use
> of their resources are required for the promotion
> of a predominantly private industrial sector, in-
> cluding willingness to work with and provide
> financing for public as well as private interme-
> diate credit institutions and other governmental
> agencies dedicated to fostering rapid private in-
> dustrial growth.
> —R. W. Adler and Raymond F. Mikesell,
> *Public External Financing of Development
> Banks in Developing Countries*

For most people, industrialization is what "development" is
all about. Ever since Britain's industrial revolution, it has been
the industrial structure of production that has been the most
reliable indicator of developed nations as contrasted with the
undeveloped. A steel mill, a petrochemical plant—these are the
tangible symbols that a nation has entered the modern world.

And in truth it *is* industry that holds the promise of human
liberation from backbreaking toil. By combining capital equip-

116

ment with alternative sources of energy, commodities can be produced more cheaply (meaning with less expenditure of human time and muscle) than was possible by handicrafts. Yet the promise of liberation is not being fulfilled. In many of the so-called underdeveloped countries factories have been implanted; some of these countries contain entire cities and regions of factories—which provide employment to only a small fraction of the workforce but otherwise make no noticeable dent in the poverty of the many, perhaps even increasing that poverty in indirect ways.

Two major themes will be developed in this chapter. The first concerns public subsidies for private profit, which is nowhere better illustrated than in the "World Bank model" for national development banks. The second is the Bank's effort to foster a local capitalist class, even in countries where to begin with there was really none to speak of; and to make sure that where this local capitalist class does exist, that it will grow in alliance with international capital and not in opposition to it. For industry, being the focus of the most profound hopes for autonomous development, has naturally been the focus for nationalistic efforts to develop an economic structure that will provide an alternative to the penetration of multinational business and the foreign acquisition of local natural resources. Therefore, it is necessary for the proponents and representatives of international capital to accede to the demands for industrialization in the countries of the Third World, while ensuring that this development will proceed in directions which are congruent with the profit designs of multinational business, and do not challenge its power.

There is some difficulty in specifying the amounts involved in World Bank lending to industry, because of the peculiarities of the Bank's definitions. In the first place, figures for mining are included in industrial sector totals. But these figures exclude industrial loans and equity participations through the International Finance Corporation (IFC), which lends without government guarantee and only to private corporations; they also exclude lending for infrastructure or electric power projects, which are in some cases integrally bound up with an industrial operation. This leads to the rather anomalous situation that when the Bank lent funds for a bauxite mine in Guinea providing the raw material for aluminum to a consortium of North American and European corporations, and when it financed a smelter in Brazil for another consortium, these were counted as industrial loans. But when it financed a thermal power plant in Iceland for an Alusuisse smelter, or a hydroelectric dam in Ghana for a Kaiser smelter, these were not counted as industry loans.

With these caveats, the figures for Bank lending to industry, cumulative from its founding in 1945 through June 30, 1981, are as follows. The total sum lent is $13.7 billion, or less than 15 percent of total Bank lending. Of this total more than half (55 percent) was lent to development finance companies for on-lending (mostly, though not exclusively, for industrial projects) while 45 percent went to large, directly financed projects. The two largest types, by far, in the latter category are fertilizers, with 41 percent of all directly financed projects; and iron and steel, with 19 percent.

The relatively modest share of total lending is not due to any inherent unwillingness on the part of the Bank to finance industrial development. It is not even due to its doctrine, held during the Bank's early years, that industrial development is best undertaken by private enterprise and not by the state, since through IFC and national development banks the World Bank does lend to private industry. It is rather, I would suggest, that there is simply not that much potential for profitable and economic investment in Third World industry, if Bank guidelines are followed. The Bank's refusal to sanction protective barriers against international capitalist penetration, whether these barriers are of a socialist or national capitalist variety, leaves very few opportunities for profitable investment in peripheral countries, and in fact results in the bankruptcy and denationalization of many of their existing industries.

More important than the amounts involved is the fact that even where a considerable degree of industrialization has taken place in Third World nations, this industrial growth has brought not cheaper goods, higher employment, and a better life for the masses of the people, but rather the opposite: worsening distribution of income, increasing class polarization, and a deteriorating balance of payments situation, which accumulates a growing debt burden. The paradox that precisely those Third World countries that are the most successful "industrializers" are also the most heavily indebted, with import bills which chronically exceed their export gains, has been noted by myself and others.[1] The reasons for this cannot be fully explored in this chapter, nor fully explained by the activities of the World Bank, but we can find some clues.

The World Bank has not, until recently, had a sophisticated theory or model of industrial development; friendly critics Mason and Asher have chided the institution for devoting less attention in this respect to industry than to other sectors such as transportation, electric power, education, and agriculture. "The relatively ad hoc character of industrial financing is striking," they remarked in their 1971 evaluation.[2] Two key principles can be identified as guiding Bank decision-making in this sector, however, and indeed the relative lack of theory is undoubtably due to one of these principles. During its early years (Mason and Asher identify it with the Black administration, 1949–1962), the Bank assumed that industrialization was primarily the business of the private sector, and presumably investment decisions were therefore best left to the entrepreneurs with no need for a Bank philosophy. This did not mean they would not lend to private industrialists; for example, the private steel industries of both Japan and India were built with considerable help from the World Bank in the 1950s.

The Bank had a problem, however, since the private sector proved unwilling to subject itself and its books and contracts to the public scrutiny involved in applying for the government guarantee required for a World Bank loan, and the Bank had to devise some new institutional strategies to surmount this obstacle. The International Finance Corporation, a sibling of the International Bank for Reconstruction and Development (IBRD) which made loans that did not involve nor even permit government guarantees, was formed precisely to overcome this barrier to financing the industrial private sector. Similarly, financial intermediaries—national development banks and development finance companies—were founded or reorganized to serve as conduits of World Bank money to private sector enterprises. The Bank's insistence on private ownership or management went so far that, until 1968, it refused to lend to publicly owned development banks, insisting that control of such banks be vested in private hands even though public funding was essential for their survival.[3]

There has been a gradual softening in policy, the key changes taking place in the 1960s, so that today the Bank lends both to public sector industries and to publicly controlled development banks. This has not been due to any weakening of support for the private sector ("above everything else," said William S. Gaud, who was brought in to head the IFC when McNamara took over the presidency of the Bank, "we are trying to show that private enterprise works,"[4]) but rather to the growing realization that the private sector could more effectively be served by co-opting the public sector for that purpose. The IFC's *Annual Report* for 1980 gives the game away:

> [IFC]'s principal tasks are to provide and bring together financing, technical assistance, and management needed to develop productive investment in its developing member countries whether they be private, mixed, or, *where they are channels for assistance to the private sector*, government enterprises. . . ." (Emphasis added)

A comparison of provisions and conditions for World Bank loans to industry projects indicates that its position on government enterprise had not changed much between 1955 and 1979. In the earlier year, a Bank mission investigating a possible loan to a steel company in Colombia recommended that as a condition of the loan the government divest itself as quickly as possible of the 79.6 percent of the shares which it then controlled, and arrange for the transfer of the shares to private hands. The government complied, transferring its shares to a trustee bank before the year was over, and by 1962, seven years later, the ownership relation had been reversed and 79 percent of shares were in private hands.[5]

Nearly a quarter of a century later, on March 7, 1979, the World Bank signed a loan agreement of $98 million with a Brazilian corporation, Valesul Aluminum, providing for the building of a smelter. On the date of the loan signature, Valesul's stock was held as follows:

	percent
Companhia do Vale do Rio Doce (a state-owned industrial and mining corporation)	60.9459
Shell Brazil (Subsidiary of Royal Dutch-Shell)	35.0000
Reynolds International, Inc. (the U.S. aluminum company)	4.0541

In a shareholders agreement signed in conjunction with the loan papers, the government corporation was required to agree to reduce its stockholding in Valesul Aluminum from its currently held 61 percent to between 40 and 49 percent, i.e., to reduce its majority holding to a minority, by selling shares to private Brazilian investors.[6] This maneuver left Shell with the controlling interest in Valesul Aluminum.

Despite this direct link with the old policy that profitable industries should be privately owned, there has, as noted, been a definite shift toward flexibility in the treatment of publicly owned corporations; even some of the Bank-sponsored development banks are now permitted to invest up to 25 percent of their resources in public sector enterprises.[7] Along with this shift, however, the incoming McNamara administration signaled that another change in policy toward industrial investment was in the works. McNamara and Gaud, the man he brought in from AID, the U.S. foreign aid administration, criticized past Bank and IFC policy for its ad hoc, laissez-faire nature and indicated that they planned to shape things up and put industrial lending on a more systematic footing. The chief target of their attack was the protectionist policies of governments trying to build up a national industry with the aid of high tariffs and, even worse from the Bank's point of view, direct controls.

In an in-house interview for *Finance and Development,* Gaud emphasized:

> [I]f you are going to develop the industrial sector sensibly, you have to do it in accordance with an overall strategy of development. . . . One (of the things that have to be done) is making studies of the industrial sector in the developing countries, helping them figure out what their development priorities are in relation to their overall development requirements, giving them advice and policy

122   Cheryl Payer

guidance on what they should or should not be doing to encourage the growth of the private sector. Others include pointing out the relationship between such things as exchange rate, tariff policies, tax policies and licensing policies of one kind or another, to the development of a strong industrial sector and to industrial growth.[8]

McNamara went on the attack in his address to the Board of Governors of the Bank at the 1969 annual meeting in Washington. His address (according to a summary published in *Finance and Development*)

was critical of some of the policies followed by developing countries to promote industrialization. Local industries were all too often encouraged at the expense of agriculture, which had to remain the foundation of their economies. While industrialization required initial inducements, these could be justified only if, in the long run, they led to the emergence of efficient industries. The excessive and indiscriminate protection of import-substitution industries perpetuated inefficiency and hampered the effort to increase export earnings. The result was industrial sectors that produced too wide a range of items on a far less than optimum scale. . . . The rationalization of such unsound economic structures was bound to be a painful process resisted by vested interests. The Bank was establishing an Industrial Projects Department for the purpose of expanding lending to industry, and to advise developing countries in this critical field of investment.[9]

The chief tool grasped by the Bank in its new, more critical approach to industrial financing was the Economic Rate of Return (ERR). The old-style appraisals had concentrated on the Financial Rate of Return (FRR) to enterprises, in general approving projects that appraisal showed were likely to make a profit under the prevailing conditions in the country in which they were built. This was now judged to be insufficient; it was not the rate of return to the financed enterprise that should be the test of efficiency, but the rate of return to the economy. If an enterprise was profitable only thanks to subsidies from the government or high prices to customers thanks to import controls or high tariffs, the Bank's new philosophy decreed that it did not deserve to survive. Although put this way the policy sounds rational and even "socialistic," in practice it is used to keep national borders open to the penetration of multinational capital.

A seminar paper used for classes in the Bank's Economic Development Institute, where officials and economists from the Bank's Third World member countries are indoctrinated with the Bank's version of sound economics, is enlightening. This particular paper purported to advise officials from Bank-sponsored national development banks on the proper way to conduct an analysis of industrial projects applying for loans.

> In the industrial field, the real choice is between domestic production and imports. If a product can be imported at a cost lower than that of domestic production, then *prima facie* it may not be worth producing at home. The question then is: How to compare domestic costs with import costs particularly when domestic prices are out of line with international prices due to certain economic policies. In this case, the simplest procedure is to express all domestic costs in terms of international prices; since the comparison is in terms of an *identical* measure or yard-stick, it becomes a valid comparison.[10]

But the ERR was more than just a tool for deciding which enterprises could receive Bank financing; it was a technocrats' weapon with which protectionist policies could be attacked.

> If a project satisfied the economic criteria but is not financially sound, the top management has a good *specific* case to induce the government to modify its tax-subsidy policies so as to make the project financially sound. . . .
> [If the efficiency] test is not met as the cost of a domestic input is higher than its import c.i.f. price, the top management has a good specific suggestion to make to the government with regard to the relaxation of import control on this input. . . .
> Thus, these three criteria help the top management not only in its own decision making but also for persuading the government to make specific changes in policies in terms of a language that policy makers are likely to understand. . . .
> Such calculations of the shadow exchange rate would help the government policy makers also in modifying their exchange rate policies and/or trade policies relating to import control, tariffs and subsidies.[11]

Thus, at the same time the Bank was permitting more flexibility in the *ownership* criterion for projects and for develoment banks that it would fund, it was moving to tighten up the appraisal criteria both for the projects it financed directly and for the subprojects that it funded through its local intermediaries. The Industrial Projects department set up by McNamara produced a sector working paper in 1972 which repeated the criticisms of past Bank lending in the sector and of the policies followed by its borrowers:

> Import substitution has been the key characteristic of Bank Group operations in manufacturing, just as it has been the dominant industrial strategy in the developing world. An issue confronting the Bank Group now is whether it can make a contribution towards promoting an outward orientation of industry in the developing countries—in other words, whether it can help them achieve a more efficient and internationally competitive manufacturing sector.[12]

Only one other policy statement on lending to industry has been issued since the 1972 working paper, a sector policy paper on development finance companies, published in April 1976. This essay reiterates the emphasis on Economic Rate of Return analysis even while admitting that a study done on projects financed before 1969 showed little real difference between FRR and ERR, a result described as "surprising, given that in almost all the countries studied there was thought to be a fairly aggressive import substitution, protection-based industry development strategy."[13] Nevertheless, the study concluded that "the need to apply rigorous ERR analysis is greatest in those countries where there are wide discrepancies between domestic and international prices,"[14] a tautology since the *only* point of the ERR exercise is to utilize international rather than domestic prices in the analysis.

Of the industrial projects financed directly by the Bank, the published cumulative totals through FY 1981 show that most of the money went to fertilizer and iron and steel production (41 percent and 19 percent respectively of all directly financed projects).[15] The heavy emphasis on fertilizer production has been even more marked in recent years: in FY 1979, 70 percent of all industrial project lending was for fertilizer mining projects or industrial complexes, though this extremely high figure may be atypical.

The International Finance Corporation

Although the Bank is quite happy to lend to private entrepreneurs when a government guarantee can be secured for the loan, and may even insist on a govenment selling its controlling interest to private investors (as in the case of Colombia's steel plant and Brazil's aluminum smelter described above), the International Finance Corporation is the specialized organ of the World Bank with specific responsibility for aiding the private sector. Although the IFC has lent to locally owned enterprise and to wholly owned subsidiaries of foreign multinationals, its real preference is to arrange marriages of local and foreign capital—joint ventures. In fact, it is clear that the promotion of this alliance, and the mobilization of government support for it, is one of the chief objectives of overall Bank policy. The Bank has been wiser than some of the multinational corporations in seeing that the future of international capital in nationalistic Third World societies could be best served if the local capitalist class were guided into partnership rather than rivalry with the international giants. The IFC was explicit about the reasons for this in its 1969 annual report:

> Of the 31 principal development enterprises in which IFC has been associated in the past three years, 19—or 61 percent—were, from their outset, joint venture multinational companies. By its emphasis on this form of development enterprises the Corporation is an influence in the capital exporting countries for continuing the trend toward acceptance of the multinational company as the way to do business in developing countries. While there have been, and there will be, exceptions dictated by individual needs of particular projects, the joint venture, multinational company will continue to be the development enterprise into which IFC typically puts its resources.[16]

The IFC is generally omitted from discussions of World Bank policy because, although a member of the World Bank Group, it is a more separate organization than the IDA. The semiofficial history of the Bank by Mason and Asher tends to emphasize, even to exaggerate, the separate nature of the Corporation: "Very few projects have been suggested to the IFC by a Bank mission.

And in general, the staff of the Bank and IDA are uninterested in the activities of the IFC."[17] Be that as it may, the case for considering the IFC as an integral part of World Bank operations is a strong one. The IFC was formed in 1956, partly because the World Bank was unable to lend to private firms without government guarantees and wished to create an organization that could do so, partly to fend off agitation in the UN for a more radical type of development fund.[18] When originally incorporated the Corporation had only its authorized capital to deploy, and was permitted to make only loans. By 1961 the Articles of Agreement were amended to permit purchase of shares by the IFC, up to 25 percent of total equity. The potential scope of the IFC was also widened considerably in 1966, when the Bank extended a line of credit to it, although at the time the credit was not utilized because its top administrator wished to keep some independence from the Bank. In 1969 a $100 million loan from the Bank was taken up, and from that date through December 30, 1980, the Bank had lent the IFC a total of $550 million. During the 1960s the IFC not only carried out its own loan program but was assigned the responsibility of evaluating all industry, mining, and development finance company projects for the Bank as well. After McNamara took over the Bank presidency, these functions were shifted back to the Bank proper, while at the same time McNamara and Gaud, his man in the IFC, set about expanding IFC operations while aligning its work more closely to general Bank policy.

The IFC is mandated to aid private enterprise not only by making investments in privately sponsored projects, but by selling participations out of its own holdings to private investors, both local and foreign. Foreign commercial banks are the most important purchasers of IFC assets, and each annual report lists those that have bought participations in a given year. This is an important way in which IFC revolves its relatively small capital in order to augment the number of projects in which it is involved. Representatives of major international banks also constitute an "international advisory council" for IFC: Deutsche Bank, Banque de Paris et des Pays-bas, the Bank of Tokyo, Ltd., S. G. Warburg & Co., and Brown

Brothers Harriman were listed in FY 1980 as represented on the advisory council.[19]

I have already noted IFC's preference for financing joint ventures, associating foreign with domestic partners. In the early years of the Corporation's existence some of the foreign beneficiaries of this funding included Siemens (Brazil), Wm. Underwood (producing deviled ham in Venezuela), American Metal Climax (Mexico), Freeport International (Tunisia), Pan Am Airways and Intercontinental Hotels (tourism projects in Kenya and Columbia), Charter Consolidated Mines (Mauritania), BOAC (tourism in Jamaica), and Pechiney Ugine Kuhlmann (aluminum in Greece).[20] Up to 1974 each annual IFC report scrupulously listed the sources of all equity and loan capital for all projects, so it was easy to identify the foreign sponsors. After that year the information supplied has been more vague, but the report for 1979 affirms that "in most ventures, 57 percent, there was some element of foreign participation," and the names of several of the companies receiving investments that year reveal their foreign parentage, i.e., Volvo do Brasil, Pechiney-Ugine (Cameroon), and the Zaire Gulf Oil Company.[21] It is clear that whatever industrial investment the IFC is sponsoring, it is in conformity with the design of international capital and not a challenge to it. Whenever the Corporation finances a project it must be satisfied "that there are appropriate arrangements for repatriation of the investment and earnings of IFC and of any foreign partners who may be involved in the venture."[22] The 1979 Annual Report stated:

> In all of its activities the Corporation works to raise investor confidence. In addition to providing technical and financial assistance, the Corporation may, as an international institution, help facilitate the process by which investors and governments can arrive at mutually satisfactory agreements.
>
> The Corporation seeks to encourage the flow of private capital through the establishment or expansion of local capital markets and financial institutions. It also provides technical assistance to member governments in support of their efforts to create investment conditions which will encourage productive and beneficial domestic and foreign investment.[23]

National Development Banks

A discussion of the IFC cannot be separated from consideration of the national development banks which it promotes and funds with the Bank proper; the financial intermediaries are not only "projects" of the two but are designed on the same pattern as the IFC, entities that operate on a national scale as IFC operates internationally. Of the cumulative total World Bank and IDA industry financing through FY 1981, 56 percent was channeled through national development banks while only 44 percent funded projects directly. To understand the full scope of the Bank group's support of private enterprise, including its lobbying for changes in governmental policy and its mobilization of public resources in borrowing countries for the support of private enterprise, it is essential to understand the role of these development banks.

Development banks and development finance companies (DFCs) are corporations designed to furnish medium- and long-term finance to development projects, primarily in the manufacturing sector, although mining, agribusiness, and tourism also receive support. There are hundreds, if not thousands of such entities throughout the Third World (a 1972 survey found over ninety in Africa alone[24]), but only a handful, typically no more than one or two in a country, are recognized by the World Bank as their type of development bank (Table 5.1 gives a list of the banks so recognized as of June 30, 1975). Making matters more confusing is the fact that for legal and administrative reasons large amounts of World Bank and IDA project money may be channeled through development banks (such as Brazil's BNDE and Mexico's Nacional Financiera), which are not on this list.

What are the characteristics of "World Bank-type" development banks? First, they represent perfectly the principle of public support and funding for private enterprise. Not only do the banks fund primarily privately owned businesses, but until 1968 the development banks themselves had to be privately controlled to receive Bank and IFC support;[25] the Bank had consistently refused loans to government-controlled corporations, or insisted on their reorganization into privately controlled entities (as in

Tunisia and Morocco) as a condition of its assistance.[26] After 1969, in a change which parallels the shift in policy on lending to public sector industry, the Bank widened its options to allow financing of publicly owned finance companies, so long as these served the private sector and their management remained insulated from "political pressures," that is, the corporation was managed virtually as if it were a private institution. The Bank itself explains that this policy change was made because the old model was simply not applicable in many countries, which presented a barrier to Bank operations:

> In these countries, the model was not compatible with the wishes of the government to develop public sector institutions, or the factors necessary to bring forth private capital for an endeavour were not present, or the functions to be carried out were such that a market level of profitability could not be achieved without undue subsidies.[27]
>
> It was in recognition of these and other factors that the Bank modified its policy at the end of fiscal 1968 to enable it to consider lending to *government-owned or controlled DFC's serving the private sector.* Subsequently, it was agreed that the Bank would also assist DFCs providing finance to government-owned enterprises if this appeared appropriate in the circumstances, and if sound rules for making decisions were applied in financing such public enterprises.[28] (Emphasis added)

Despite this change in policy, the bulk of lending by Bank-supported DFCs has continued to go to the private sector: 95 percent of the total through FY 1975 and an estimated 85 to 90 percent for the next five-year period.[29] The new ability to lend to government-controlled DFCs however, resulted in a rapid expansion of the Bank's activities, whereas the potential for lending to private banks had been largely saturated by the time of the policy change. "While 32 new DFC borrowers were added to the Bank's books in the fiscal 1969-75 period, only seven of these were privately controlled. This low ratio reflected not the Bank's preference *per se* for government-controlled DFCs but rather a relative exhaustion of the opportunities for lending to private DFCs."[30]

Despite this emphasis on private *control* and operation for the

Table 5.1
DFCs Associated with the World Bank
(June 30, 1975)

Country	Name	Acronym
Eastern and Western Africa		
Botswana	Botswana Development Corporation	BDC
Ethiopia	Agricultural and Industrial Development Bank	AIDB
Ivory Coast	Banque Ivoirienne de Développement Industriel	BIDI
Ivory Coast	Crédit de la Côte d'Ivoire	CCI
Kenya	Industrial Development Bank	IDB
Liberia	The Liberian Bank for Development and Investment	LBDI
Mauritius	Development Bank of Mauritius	DBM
Nigeria	Nigerian Industrial Development Bank	NIDB
Senegal	Société Financière Sénégalaise pour le Developpement Industriel et Touristique	SOFISEDIT
Sudan	Industrial Bank of Sudan	IBS
Tanzania	Tanzania Investment Bank	TIB
Zaire	Société Financière de Développement	SOFIDE
Regional	East African Development Bank	EADB
	SIFIDA Investment Co. S.A.	SIFIDA
East Asia and Pacific		
China, Rep. of	China Development Corporation	CDC
Indonesia	Bank Pembangunan Indonesia	BAPINDO
Indonesia	P.T. Private Development Finance Company of Indonesia	PDFCI
Korea, Rep. of	Korea Development Bank	KDB
Korea, Rep. of	Korea Development Finance Corporation	KDFC
Malaysia	Malaysian Industrial Development Finance Berhad	MIDF
Philippines	Development Bank of the Philippines	DBP
Philippines	Private Development Corporation of the Philippines	PDCP
Singapore	Development Bank of Singapore	DBS
Thailand	The Industrial Finance Corporation Thailand	IFCT
South Asia		
India	Industrial Credit and Investment Corporation of India	ICICI
India	Industrial Development Bank of India	IDBI
Pakistan	Industrial Development Bank of Pakistan	IDBP
Pakistan	National Development Finance Corporation	NDFC
Pakistan	Pakistan Industrial Credit and Investment Corporation	PICIC
Sri Lanka	Development Finance Corporation of Ceylon	DFCC

Country	Name	Acronym
Europe, Middle East, and North Africa		
Afghanistan	Industrial Development Bank of Afghanistan	IDBA
Algeria	Banque Algérienne de Développement	BAD
Austria	Öesterreichische Investitionskredit Aktiengesellschaft	IVK
Cyprus	Cyprus Development Bank	CDB
Egypt	Bank of Alexandria	BOA
Finland	Teollistamisrahasto Oy - Industrialization Fund of Finland	IFF
Greece	National Investment Bank for Industrial Development	NIBID
Iran	Industrial Credit Bank	ICB
Iran	Industrial and Mining Development Bank of Iran	IMDBI
Ireland	The Industrial Credit Co.	ICC
Israel	Industrial Development Bank of Israel	IDBI
Morocco	Banque Nationale pour le Développement Economique	BNDE
Morocco	Crédit Immobilier et Hôtelier	CIH
Spain	Banco del Desarrollo Económico Español	BANDESCO
Tunisia	Banque de Développement Economique de Tunisie (formerly SNI)	BDET
Turkey	State Investment Bank (Devlet Yatirim Bankasi)	SIB (DYB)
Turkey	Türkiye Sinai Kalkinma Bankasi	TSKB
Yugoslavia	Privredna Banka Sarajevo	PBS
Yugoslavia	Ivesticiona Banka Titograd	IBT
Yugoslavia	Stopanska Banka Skopje	SBS
Yugoslavia	Kosovska Banka Pristina	KBP
Latin America and the Caribbean		
Bolivia	Banco Industrial	BISA
Brazil	Banco do Nordeste do Brasil	BNB
Colombia	Corporación Financiera de Caldas	Caldas
Colombia	Corporación Financiera Colombiana	Colombiana
Colombia	Corporación Financiera Nacional	Nacional
Colombia	Corporación Financiera del Norte	Norte
Colombia	Corporación Financiera del Valle	Valle
Colombia	Corporación Financiera Popular	CFP
Ecuador	Comisión de Valores - Corporación Financiera Nacional	CV-CFN
Ecuador	Ecuatoriana de Desarrollo Compañia Financiera	COFIEC
Mexico	Fondo de Equipamiento Industrial	FONEI
Trinidad and Tobago	Trinidad and Tobago Development Finance Company	TTDFC
Regional	ADELA Investment Company	ADELA

Source: World Bank, *Development Finance Companies*, sector policy paper, April 1976.

benefit of private enterprise, the World Bank-type development banks are *and always have been* heavily dependent on public funds, both national and international. In the first place, many of the institutions it assists would not be able to exist without World Bank support. In Joseph Kane's study of development banks, for which the sample consisted entirely of institutions associated with the World Bank, foreign funds provided over half of financial resources (51.8 percent) and this, he maintains, understates the true position because it does not include the line-of-credit availability from the World Bank and other foreign sources.[31] And the World Bank is the key to these foreign funds, even when they are supplied by private banks and other sources:

> A strong case can be made that the private foreign capital flows to the banks precisely because the foreign public sector has demonstrated confidence in the government and in the bank's management by investing its own funds after a thorough evaluation. Of the 19 banks with foreign equity funds, less than half had such funds prior to the funding by the World Bank group.[32]

The World Bank's model of privately controlled companies actually resulted in the creation of "hybrid institutions in which the Bank, foreign investors (usually international commercial banks), the government, and domestic investors (usually financial intermediaries and/or manufacturing enterprises or business associations) joined forces" in the Bank's own words.[33] The equity structure of one such bank, Industrial Development Bank of Afghanistan (IDBA), looked like this:[34]

Local capital		*in percent*
(60 percent)	Pashtany Tejaraty Bank	15.0
	Bank Millie Group	15.0
	Chamber of Commerce	10.4
	Cement Factory, Jabul Saraj	4.2
	small investors	15.4
Foreign capital		
(40 percent)	Chase Manhattan	7.5
	IFC	7.5
	Citibank	7.5
	Industrial Bank of Japan	7.5
	National Westminster Bank	7.5
	Credit Lyonnaise	2.5

A World Bank publication gives the information that the government controls 15 percent of the financing of the IDBA.[35]

All sources seem to agree that foreign commercial banks do not invest in development banks in the hopes of earning profits directly. Rather, the investment is made to generate "good will" for the primary business activities of those banks in the country and to keep tabs on business activity and investment prospects.[36] The IFC and the commercial banks do not just invest funds in the national development banks; they occupy key positions on the executive boards and are thus in a position not only to inform themselves about business activity but to influence its direction. Although Chase International Investment Corporation and Lazard Frères each owns only 8.9 percent of the Ivory Coast's Banque Ivorienne de Développment Industriel (BIDI), they were the actual promoters of the bank and occupy two out of five seats on the executive committee.[37] Seven of the twelve directors of the Nigerian Industrial Development Bank, Ltd. were foreigners in 1969, some representing the World Bank and IFC and others different foreign shareholders.[38] And while IFC may legally be forced to eschew a "management role" in the enterprises in which it invests, it is happy not only to sit on their boards but also to loan its personnel to these banks—in fact the Bank's definition of "competent management" (which is practically synonymous with foreign management in many countries) is always a condition of Bank support.[39] The author of one essay in a World Bank book on development banks, E. T. Kuiper, is described as an "IFC consultant" who "has been chief executive of the Industrial Bank of Indonesia, the Pakistan Industrial Credit and Investment Corporation, the Development Bank of Ethiopia, and Malaysian Industrial Development Finance Ltd."[40] It is safe to assume that these representatives of public and private international capital in controlling positions will not be inclined to lend to enterprises which challenge their own institutions' interests in that nation.

Some governments have a policy that national development finance institutions shall be at least majority owned by local shareholders (government and private). Before the Bank's 1969 change of policy, of course, the institutions also had to be majority privately owned to receive Bank support. It is amusing to note that IFC equity investments were permitted to count as local shareholding for the first condition and as private for the second, although of course the IFC is a public, international institution. The rationale for this form of Orwellian newspeak is that the IFC's hope and intent is eventually to sell off its shares to private investors, and such shares can be reserved for domestic investors when so required.

The structure of domestic capitalism varies widely in the countries in which the Bank and IFC operate, however. In some countries, including the major Latin American nations, India, and Pakistan, there existed a vigorous class of domestic entrepreneurs ready to seek and receive IFC and development bank aid and even to control their local development finance institutions. Colombia probably provides the extreme case: there the Bank is associated with no less than six private *financieras*, mostly regionally based, most of which are owned by local commercial banks and other groups such as the coffee and sugar planters.[41] At the other extreme, in much of black Africa and many smaller countries, the IFC has to represent *potential* domestic private capital, join with government equity, and hope that it can *create* a local investing class through its eventual sale of shares.

The last but certainly not least of the partners in the development bank cocktail is the government of the operating country, and its role is key. Governments support these banks in a number of ways, the most important being the supply of funds. This is obvious, of course, in a government-owned development bank, but in the private banks sponsored by the IBRD, government funds provide a peculiar and specific form of support to private profit.

In most of the countries in which the World Bank aided private development banks, it insisted that the governments contribute a form of finance known as quasi equity. Another example of newspeak, this was not equity at all but a long-term, low-interest loan that carried no ownership or control function. To understand the importance of this one must know something about the difference between loan and equity capital. In the usual corporate structure of finance, the owners of an enterprise put up the equity capital and receive in return *shares*, which carry not only voting rights in the annual meeting but the right to share in the profits of the enterprise in the form of dividends. The rest of the capital is raised through loans, at an interest rate that is *less* than the hoped for return on all invested capital. If business is good and profits are high, shareholders receive a higher return on their investment than the creditors (bond-holders) of the firm, who are essentially subsidizing the rate of profit because they are receiving less than the average return to capital and the shareholders are receiving more. The bondhold-ers have more security, however, because if profits are less than anticipated, the bite is taken out of the shareholders' dividends while the bondholders and other creditors are guaranteed their contractual rate of interest. If the enterprise fails, the share-holders' capital is applied to guarantee the repayment of loans taken out by the enterprise.

The proportion of borrowed money to share capital is expressed as the loan-equity ratio. It is in the interest of the *shareholders* to have as high a ratio as possible (also called leverage) because in normal times their dividends will be higher in proportion to the amount of lower cost borrowed money employed by the firm. Con-versely, it is in the interest of *lenders* to see that the loan-equity ratio does not climb too high, because this would mean that their money would not be adequately secured by the equity capital. The tug-of-war between the two interests generally keeps the ratio with-in reasonable bounds for any firm that uses both kinds of funds.

Now, the quasi equity supplied by national governments to World Bank-style development finance companies has the magi-cal quality of providing both high leverage to the shareholders and security to the creditors. The World Bank and the IFC, representing themselves and other creditors, insist that their associated banks maintain a quite conservative debt-equity ratio of 3:1 so that loans will be properly secured. The governmental loan, however, is counted not as a loan but as equity in this ratio! Ideally, the World Bank suggests that the government chip in 150 percent the amount of the share capital (in actual cases the ratio may be even higher), giving the following "model" propor-tions of real equity, quasi equity, and loan capital:[42]

share capital	100 units
subordinated loan (quasi equity)	150 units
total "equity"	250 units
borrowing power (3 times "equity")	750 units
total capital	1,000 units

Thus "the potential ratio of real debt to equity, which reflects the actual leverage on shareholders' equity, is on the order of 9:1."[43] To complete the picture, these loans not only provide security for the loan capital of the bank, but for the shareholders' equity as well: "if the company goes into liquidation, the share capital ranks either ahead of, or pari passu with, the subordinated funds."[44] In other words, if anyone gets left holding the bag, it will be the government, as lowest debtor on the entire capital totem pole.

For most of the private banks it has supported, the World Bank has insisted on government subsidy in this form of a large subordinated, interest-free loan; indeed, in all but a few cases (Colombia, Greece, Spain, and Venezuela are named as exceptions)[45] "without the provision of quasi equity capital, i.e., loans granted on terms far more favorable than those granted under market conditions, it is virtually impossible for a private development bank to come into being."[46]

In addition to the subordinated capital that it provides directly, the local government is essential to raising international capital, in a nicely dialectical relationship: having put up its own money, at World Bank insistence, the government then supplies its sovereign guarantee as the condition for obtaining World Bank loans. James Kane remarks of the World Bank-funded institutions in his sample of development banks:

> When the direct funding, debt or equity, provided by government is added to what government intermediation obtains in the form of external funds, then some 82 percent of all funds available to the sample banks in the sample period involves the active cooperation of the public sector. This is all the more impressive when one recalls that of the thirty-one sample banks, fifteen are privately owned and thirteen are of mixed ownership.[47]

Governments are also expected to provide special legal and tax breaks for the development banks domiciled on their territory. In one documented case, that of the BIDI on the Ivory Coast, a special covenant guarantees permission to sell shares abroad without restriction; the right to repatriate all investments, equity or loan; the transfer of all profits from the Bank's capital yield; and the transfer of all income of non-Ivorian personnel of the Bank. The BIDI was also exempted from certain types of taxes for five years of operation, and from other taxes for ten years.[48]

The most exhaustive summary of the "government connection" comes from a World Bank source:

All but two of the twenty-five privately or predominantly privately owned development companies with which the World Bank family is associated are under obligation to their respective governments or its agencies for important assistance in one form or another. Nineteen of these companies have public funds in their share capital, ranging from 4 percent to 44 percent. Fourteen have received loans on favorable terms, with long terms and grace periods, bearing little or no interest, and ranking equal or subordinate to share capital. The amount of the loans varies from two thirds to seven [!] times the original share capital.

Twenty of the twenty-five companies depend on loans from the government or its agencies or on discounting facilities with central banks for most or some of their local currency resources. Nineteen of them, which have received World Bank loans, have obtained government guarantees to cover the loans. Governments have also guaranteed loans by foreign governments to some of the companies. In many cases, the proportion of their funds derived independently of the government is small indeed, relative to total resources.

Governments have supplied two of these companies with funds to manage for investment or reinvestment purposes, the amount ranging as high as 38 percent of the total portfolio of one company. In another, the ratio reached 50 percent until recently, when most of it was converted to a subordinated loan. One company also draws upon a public fund created for the special purpose of making equity investments for increasing domestic participation in enterprise.

Governments have made it possible for several companies to obtain technical assistance free of cost or at reduced cost from friendly governments and international agencies. Eleven companies enjoy favorable tax treatment, either as a concession to each one individually or to development finance companies generally;

four companies are completely exempt from taxes on income earned and dividends paid.[49]

With all these privileges, the writer asks, "are these institutions really private?"[50]

Like the World Bank and the IFC, the development finance companies which they sponsor are expected to promote the alliance of domestic and foreign capital.

Although the technical problems involved in quantifying the amounts would probably make such an exercise impractical, impressionistic evidence affirms that foreign corporations and joint ventures are among the major beneficiaries of Bank-style development banks, and in some countries where private capital is especially weak they may be virtually the only beneficiaries. The Industrial and Mining Development Bank of Iran (IMDBI), for example, was sponsored by the Chase International Investment Corporation and Lazard Frères (who also sponsored the Ivory Coast's BIDI), two large banking corporations whose commercial interests in Iran under the shah were enormous. Chase and Lazard guided the organization of IMDBI according to policies suggested by the World Bank, and during the first five years of operation management was in the hands of non-Iranians. According to Joseph Kane, many of the firms aided were "new industries to Iran, introduced in cooperation with foreign industrial firms" as a result of contacts made by external shareholders.[51]

Until 1972, IMDBI's foreign exchange resources came exclusively from the World Bank, but in that year a change in legislation permitted the Iranian government to guarantee borrowings from foreign commercial banks. The last World Bank loan to IMDBI was made in 1974, at which point the rise in the price in oil allowed Iran to dispense with World Bank financial aid. In 1975 Business International compiled this impressive list of foreign companies participating in joint ventures financed by IMDBI:[52]

United States: Cabot, Gould, Harris, Westinghouse
United Kingdom: English Electric, British Leyland, Lucas
Japan: Nippon Electric, Kanebo Silk, Toshiba, Yamaha
Germany: Bosch, Daimler-Benz, Bayer, Hoechst, Mahle, Oscram, Siemens

Switzerland: Schindler
Sweden: Volvo, SKF
Holland: Phillips
France: Motobecane, Compteur de France
Belgium: Glaverbel.

The IMDBI did not escape the climate of corruption in the shah's Iran. The World Bank's last project appraisal admitted that about 25 percent of its total commitments (to 1974) were made to firms partly or wholly owned by directors of the Board of IMDBI, but excused this fact by asserting that these firms were in general efficiently managed.[53] But after Iranian assets in U.S. banks were frozen by President Carter in November 1979, after the revolution deposing the shah and the seizure of the U.S. embassy and hostages, Iranian investigators discovered that the IMDBI had been used to funnel some $570 million to the shah, his family, and institutions under their control. This was apparently facilitated by the presence of a high official of the Pahlavi foundation on the IMDBI's board of directors, from 1963 onward.[54]

BIDI did not have many African customers in 1971: "the national sector of the Ivorian economy received only a relatively small amount of promotion by BIDI and this was achieved through enterprises with public shareholding. The credit volume in respect of Ivorian private enterprise is insignificant, since private enterprise in the Ivory Coast is practically non-existent."[55] An evaluation of the Nigerian Industrial Development Bank (NIDB) concluded: "Judging from its operations and profitability NIDB is a successful undertaking. But the paradox of its case is that most of the beneficiaries from its financial disbursements had been foreign owned companies incorporated in Nigeria."[56] Borrowers of foreign currency from the Industrial Credit and Investment Corporation of India, Ltd. (ICICI) included not only some of the wealthiest local bourgeoisie (Tata Iron & Steel Company, also recipient of a World Bank loan in 1956) but also Hindustan Lever.[57]

The conspicuous position of foreign enterprise as beneficiaries of "national" development banks sponsored by the World Bank has led to protests. "Noting that much of the resources of private development companies is used to assist foreign-sponsored businesses, governments sometimes feel it desirable to ask the companies to interest themselves in supporting domestic entrepreneurs."[58]

Dorothea Mezger concluded her study of BIDI with the following observations:

> Without doubt BIDI is the most efficient development financing institution in the Francophone area south of the Sahara. . . . However, the question arises—efficient for whom? At present, the Bank is in the hands of mainly foreign capital owners, its borrowing of foreign origin, and its clients are largely non-Ivorians. As a result, the income, employment, and growth effects of BIDI's investments revert for the most part to the capital exporting countries, as is mostly the case with development aid. Moreover, the profits from BIDI's financing operations flow principally to non-Ivorians who in this way accumulate capital, whereas the Ivorians participate only minimally.[59]

The Bank-sponsored development finance companies are not financing *national* development, but foreign penetration of national territory.

But the finance companies' aid to foreign enterprise is not limited to finance. As the Bank's sector policy paper admits, "Individual DFC's usually account for a relatively small share of the total financing of new industrial investment (normally less than 10 percent . . . a much more significant determinant of success in developing the subsectors they finance is whether basic policies are conducive to the rational development of those subsectors."[60] Therefore, DFCs are coached on how to lobby the government for changes in policy and legislation that will favor the private sector or (in line with the new lending policy) will encourage government-owned enterprises to operate as if they were private sector institutions.

How does the Bank expect these "privately managed" development banks (which, as we have seen, are heavily dependent on government funds and guarantees) to comport themselves vis-à-vis the nation's policymakers? One Bank functionary produced what rings almost like a credo as a model of what such a bank should do:[61]

It welcomes opportunities to advise the government on economic and industrial policy, serving on government committees when invited but avoiding responsibility for public planning.

It equips itself adequately through study and research to act as a responsible representative of the private sector, and scrupulously avoids giving the impression that it is an arm of the government.

It uses its contacts with government agencies to the best advantage, for itself and for its clients.

It gives all due information to the government, but jealously protects from exposure to public bodies the information given in confidence by its clients.

We have already seen how the Bank's Economic Development Institute trains development bank officials to employ Economic Rate of Return analysis and to use this technique to criticize pricing and exchange rate policies that vary from world market levels. The lobbying function of development banks can encompass broad national issues affecting basic legislation on corporations and securities markets[62] or it can negotiate specific permits, licenses, and concessions for its clients.[63]

Thus, in exchange for essential financial support, a government finds itself with an institution that it cannot control because its "private" nature is supposed to insulate it from political interference, but that will lobby the government vigorously for legislation and policy changes which give more favorable conditions for private and for foreign investment. While it is not my intent to justify every type of government interference with the economy, it is clear that a government that honestly wished to set some autonomous criteria of rational investment, for example, the locally controlled production of basic goods needed by the masses, would be condemned by the Bank's standards of market rationality for "improper political interference" in the operations of the DFC.

The Fertilizer Industry in India

Following its decision in the mid-1960s to increase lending for agriculture, the World Bank grew increasingly interested in supporting the fertilizer industry. The emphasis on fertilizer-intensive development of Third World agriculture came at a time when the fertilizer market in the developed capitalist countries was glutted, and the fertilizer corporations (some of which were subsidiaries of petroleum corporations) greeted the new aid emphasis warmly. Industry organizations of the advanced nations set up a World Fertilizer Federation "to give aid to the less-developed nations in setting up programs on fertilizer uses."[64] The U.S. aid agency, AID, proposed that demonstration plots be organized as an "AID-industry cooperative effort which . . . would permit millions of farmers to see—with their own eyes—what fertilizers, properly used, can do for their future."[65] Just as the U.S. government had promoted domestic fertilizer use through its county agent network in the 1940s, so now, through AID and the World Bank, an unbelievably vast market beckoned in which fertilizer use would be promoted through demonstration or (as I will argue in Chapter 8) where needed, compulsion.

This market was much too large to be satisfied by the export surplus of the advanced countries, and the producing corporations explored the feasibility of building plants closer to the new markets. India was the biggest of these potential markets, but the fertilizer industry in that country was one in which, by policy decision, the public sector was reserved the leading role. Conveniently for the aid donors, India was at that time (1965–1966) suffering an acute foreign-exchange crisis and a famine in Bihar which sharply emphasized its dependence on foreign aid. With the leverage afforded by this crisis, the World Bank and the U.S. government successfully forced the Indian government to give the foreign fertilizer companies the incentives they demanded in order to invest: majority control of all projects in which they invest, monopoly rights over marketing in their assigned zones, freedom from price controls, and freedom to import their own feedstocks rather than using domestic naptha.[66] Amoco India, Inc., for example, a subsidiary of Standard Oil (Indiana), built the $70 million Madras Fertilizer Ltd. in partnership with the government, but it obtained the right "during the first seven years of its operation, to distribute its products through its own marketing organization and without price controls."[67]

By the 1970s the price of building a "world-scale" fertilizer plant ran into the hundreds of millions of dollars. Access to means of financing this large capital outlay is one of the major elements in deciding to establish this industry, and in general host governments are expected to provide a major part of the financing and equity capital, which can be borrowed from the World Bank. With such heavy capital costs involved, the profit to private industry has shifted to the supply of capital equipment and technology to Third World plants rather than the retail supply of fertilizers to farmers.

Usha Menon, in a study of recently built fertilizer plants in India, charges that while the World Bank gives lip service to the importance of "transfer of technology," in practice its lending methods prevent real transfer. His evidence comes from a comparison of the import content in three recently built fertilizer plants of comparable technology, all (this time) in the public sector, of which two were financed by the World Bank. Menon found that the projects built with World Bank aid, Nangal and Sindri, had at least a 25 percent higher foreign exchange content than the similar plant constructed at Haldia. This is all the more remarkable because "the plant at Haldia was built with suppliers' credit and bilateral loans which are considered as 'tied-aid' and which are at least 30 percent more expensive than normal loans."[68] He hypothesizes that the reason for this discrepancy lies in the World Bank's control over selection of the general contractor for building the plants.

> The World Bank exercises its control over the transfer of technology not only by its release of loan finances, but also by its control over the appointment of project managers, its ability to bypass government controls and, above all, the appointment of general contractors for the plant. The importance of choosing the main contractor is reflected in the fact that the plant at Haldia with the Planning and Development Division of FCI (Fertilizer Corporation of India) as the main contractor, was able to achieve a much lower foreign exchange content despite the fact that it had to use the much costlier "tied aid" while entering into separate agreements with various technology suppliers. At Nangal and Sindri the German contractor Uhde had complete control over the import of equipment.[69]

It is known from reliable sources, he adds, that the World Bank "desired" the FCI to conduct negotiations with Uhde. Menon also reports that the World Bank frequently objects to Indian bidders, even though their technical competence was satisfactory to the Indian contractor and their bids were priced lower than those of the foreign parties.

Petrochemicals in Brazil: The Copesul Project

In May 1978 the Bank made an $85 million loan to Companhia Petroquimica do Sul (Copesul), guaranteed by the government of Brazil for part of the estimated $836 million financing of a petrochemical complex near Porto Alegre in the Brazilian state of Rio Grande do Sul. As the Bank had never before financed a project in the field of petrochemicals, this loan cannot be called typical of its industrial lending policy, but it is of considerable interest nevertheless. Brazil is one of the most industrially advanced and politically sophisticated of Third World countries and the sector involves very advanced technology, which is to be transferred to Brazil in the course of the project, so it is probably not unfair to take this case to explore the limits that can be achieved under the so-called new international division of labor.

The complex, or "pole," will be the third of its type constructed in Brazil. The first was constructed near São Paulo, the country's industrial capital, in the early 1970s, and the second was located at Bahia in the depressed northeast. Each complex shares the same basic pattern. One core plant produces the basic petrochemical raw materials, primarily ethylene and propylene, from petroleum feedstocks—in this case naptha—from a nearby refinery. These products are then utilized by "second generation" plants to manufacture intermediate chemical products (low-density polyethylene, high-density polyethylene, polyvinyl chloride, polypropylene, polystyrene, etc.), which are then transformed by "third generation" plants into the familiar articles of industrial and household use made of plastics, artificial rubber, and artificial fibers. The first and second stages *must* be closely integrated, since the first-generation products are gases that have no alternative uses and cannot be stored or transported long distances.[70]

In all three of the Brazilian petrochemical "poles" the state oil company Petrobras has built and controlled the core, or first generation plant. In the Porto Alegre project the Petrobras subsidiary Petroquisa will hold 51 percent of the equity of Copesul, the corporation that will own and operate the core plant. The remaining 49 percent is to be held by FIBASE, a subsidiary of the government-owned Banco Nacional de Desenvolvimento Economico (BNDE). The core plant will thus be 100 percent government capital. The second generation or "downstream" plants (of which seven are projected) will be the realm of the private sector (with an admixture of some public capital). The pattern was set by the government when the second, Bahia, complex was built; it "incorporates a tripartite ownership scheme, whereby the raw materials center ... is fully owned by state-owned enterprises (with Petroquisa as the majority shareholder), while the equity of the downstream companies is divided between private Brazilian enterprises, Petroquisa representing state enterprise, and private foreign capital, which usually provides the know-how."[71] The effect of this tripartite formula is to ensure that each second generation plant will be controlled by two-thirds private capital (foreign and domestic) and at the same time two-thirds Brazilian capital (private and state).

Peter Evans has described the significance of the role played by the state corporation in running the core project at Bahia:

> In the eyes of its partners, the role of Petroquisa took many forms. Petroquisa's participation gave them confidence that the other private partners would not give up in the face of difficulties, leaving them without complementary plants and others to share the overhead.... Petroquisa also took the major responsibility for the parts of the project that were most likely to take losses in the early stages. Electrical generators, water supplies, the central cracking unit itself, had to be ready when the downstream plants began to reach completion, otherwise they would not be able to operate at all. Yet until all the downstream plants were operating at close to

full capacity the central facilities were likely to lose money.... Having Copene take charge of the central facilities meant that no individual private investor had to shoulder these risks.[72]

The World Bank saw the set-up for "its" project, Copesul, in essentially the same terms:

> By financing the Project, the Bank would also encourage the private sponsors of the downstream units to start implementing their projects which are on a later schedule. It would substantially reduce the main risk—uncertainty about timely availability of COPESUL's products—perceived by them for the successful implementation of the entire project.[73]

By taking part in the riskier first stage of what is really an inseparable project, the Bank was acting in a manner directly in line with its traditional infrastructure loans. Just as an aluminum smelter and the hydroelectric project that will supply its enormous need for power must be built together, with close coordination (one cannot survive technically, one cannot survive economically, without the other) but the infrastructure is often financed by government while the more profitable end remains under private control, so the core raw materials plant in these complexes is somewhat artificially separated, financially, from the whole for which it functions as infrastructure. As at Bahia, a mix of local state, local private, and foreign private capital was encouraged. Three-way participation may not be an absolute requirement: it was also reported that Exxon's petrochemical affiliate, Esso Chemical, was considering building a wholly owned synthethic butyl rubber plant. Copesul's second generation plants are listed in Table 5.2.[74]

A word should be said about the role of the International Finance Corporation. Although the IBRD was making its first loan in the field, the IFC is a veteran investor in Brazilian petrochemicals, with investments in the core plant and three of the second generation plants of the São Paulo complex and one in the Bahia complex. According to the Bank's appraisal document:

> In the Third Complex, IFC's efforts are being directed to assure adequate off-take capacity to coincide with COPESUL's commissioning. IFC has met with the sponsors of every second-generation

Table 5.2
Copesul's Second Generation Plants

Name of Plant	Cost	Production (in tons per year)
Poliofinas—Sul	$110 million	115,000 low-density poly-ethylene
Petroquisa (28.1%)		
National Distillers (U.S.) (28.1%)		
Unipar (incl. Hanna Mining) (23.7%)		
International Finance Corporation (15%)		
(of which 5% sold off to Bank of America)		
Polisul	$73 million	60,000 high-density poly-ethylene
Hoechst (Germany) (40%)		
Ipiranga (40%)		
Petroquisa (20%)		
Politeno-Sul	$91 million	100,000 low-density poly-ethylene
Politeno		
Sumitomo (Japan)		
Petroquisa		
APLUB (retirement fund)		
Vinisul	$170 million	150,000 monovinylchloride and polyvinylchloride
Mitsui/Toatsu (Japan)		
Petroquisa		
Olvibra		
Montepio de Familia Militar		
PPH	$75 million	50,000 polypropylene
Hercules (U.S.) (40%)		
Petroquisa (20%)		
Petropar		

Other projects still in the formation stage are listed as:
$100 million plant to produce 125,000 tons of styrene and 50,000 tons of propane oxide per year
  Ociteno
  Halcon
  Petroquisa
A plant to make 60,000 tons of polystyrene
  Proquigel
  APLUB retirement fund
  Petroquisa
Synthetic butyl rubber plant to produce 80,000 tons per year
  Petroflex (Petroquisa subsidiary)
  Maciel
  Gus Livonious

unit. . . . [In addition to the Poliolefinas investment] active discussions are being held with the sponsors of two of the next most
advanced downstream units, with a view to possible IFC investments in early FY 79. Because of their importance to COPESUL and
to the Complex, the Bank and IFC are collaborating closely to help
timely start-up of the downstream units.[75]

This suggests that the IFC's role is to fill gaps in capitalization
when appropriate private investors cannot be found. The appraisal also hints that the Bank might consider a second loan to
cover foreign-exchange needs of the second generation plants.

Government support of the downstream plants does not stop
with the assumption of the start-up risks of the core plant. The
government-owned development bank, BNDE, is committed to
supplying local currency debt financing both to the core plant
($201 millon at 1977 prices) and to the downstream projects
($292 million) in addition to the equity participation of its sub-
sidiary, FIBASE, giving the parent organization a total commitment of $642 million. It is responsible for virtually all of the local
currency debt financing for both the private and the public
sector organizations.

The Copesul project has been celebrated as one of the most
successful bargains for transfer of technology to a Third World
country. According to F. C. Sercovich:

> The third world-scale ethylene plant in Brazil (R.G. de Sul) entails
> a major effort not just at substituting domestic for foreign hardware
> and detail engineering services, as well as making maximum use of
> Brazilian technical skills. It also involves an attempt at fully ap-
> propriating, both in technical and legal terms, all assets and skills
> related to state-of-the-art process know-how, process design engi-
> neering, and R & D [research and development] in the ethylene field.
>
> It is convenient to emphasize that what is at stake here is not just
> a mere procedural change. It is a radical departure from previous
> approaches as regards large industrial undertakings by state-owned
> enterprises. A new strategic approach to foreign technology ab-
> sorption, adaptation, and domestic development is involved.[76]

The Brazilian government, through Petrobras, aimed at technological self-sufficiency in petrochemical technology and
demanded, in negotiations for the engineering contract for

Copesul, that the firm supplying the technology should also train Brazilians to a point where they would be able to make their own innovations and refinements as well as keep up with international technological development. Out of four foreign firms that submitted bids, the contract went to the only one that was willing to meet Brazil's demands for technology sharing: Technip, a state-owned French engineering firm, in association with a Dutch firm, KTI.[77]

Sercovich's study, while praising the unprecedented technological bargain closed by the Brazilians, gives some clues as to why Technip was willing to accede to it. The first is that the petrochemical industry is reaching a state of maturity in the industrialized countries, with signs of market saturation apparent as early as 1973.[78] By mid-1976, when Copesul invited tenders for the design and engineering of its plant, the worldwide decline in investment in petrochemical plants made the Brazilian contract "a very tempting step forward in the framework of a declining market."[79] And while Sercovich predicts, for a few Third World nations with Brazil in the lead, "the chance to develop autonomous, specialized, organized, and complementary R&D and process design engineering capabilities" leading to "an active and, eventually successful entry into the world market for chemical process plant, a market so far completely in the hands of advanced industrial country-based multinational engineering enterprises,"[80] he admits that the Brazilians "have no certainty whatsoever that during the course of the next 10 years, Technip-KTI's technology will remain competitive in the world market."[81]

Sercovich also remarks that Technip is just one member of a "family" of French enterprises, mostly state owned but including some privately owned, whose main interest is product exports, and that the engineering services provided by Technip are the "locomotive," pulling much larger product sales along after it:

> Technip itself estimates that between 2 and 3 percent of all French capital goods exports are a result of the "locomotive effect" produced by Technip's contracts abroad. As French engineering contractors use to say, "deux heures d'ingenierie vendues a l'etranger rapportent dix heures de travail a l'industrie francaise." (Two

engineering man-hours sold abroad create a demand of ten man-hours to the French industry.)[82]

The Bank appraisal reports that French suppliers are expected to win about U.S. $25 million in orders from Copesul, out of a total of $35 million imports not financed by World Bank and Inter-American Development Bank loans. A syndicate of French banks (the same ones which own 8 percent of Technip's equity) have offered "a tied credit line with attractive terms."[83]

There is no available evidence that the World Bank had anything to do with the technology transfer agreement concluded between Technip and Brazil—whether or not that agreement will in the end prove to be as advantageous for Brazil as Sercovich predicts. The contract with Technip had been signed before the World Bank loan was made, and was taken into account in the appraisal. And even if Brazil masters ethylene production technology, it appears that technological processes for the *downstream* plants will either remain in the hands of the (foreign) technology suppliers or will be purchased at a high price. The recently published memoirs of a high official of Hoechst, one of the downstream technology suppliers, reported that Hoechst had held long negotiations with Petroquisa

> to establish whether, and under what conditions, Hoechst technology . . . can be contributed. . . . We made this contribution conditional on our obtaining its selling rights for Hoechst do Brazil [sic] and we prevailed after long negotiation. When these plants go into operation in the early eighties, Hoechst will also be a factor in the plastics business of Brazil.[84]

The Brazilian Petroleum Institute has complained that the technical assistance fees on these projects are excessive, a group of seven projects with fixed investment costs of about $380 million entailing technical assistance and know-how fees of $25 million. "Besides the amount paid out for services, which weighs heavily on the Brazilian balance-of-payments deficit, a major complaint is that for each new project the technology must be imported."[85]

It was the intent of the Brazilian government in promoting the "triple alliance" of state, foreign, and local private investors that technology be transferred from the foreign to the local private partner. They are having obvious difficulties in finding appropriate local partners, however, and the participants in some approved projects

> obviously have no potential for making use of petrochemical technology. The Formosa Plastica shoe company and the Motepio de Familia Militar fund, once possible participants in the Petroflex venture, are two cases in point. APLUB, another retirement fund based in the state and active in two Basic Complex projects, is a third. Others, such as a Rio Grande do Sul company involved in soybean oil processing, are borderline cases.[86]

The insistence on local equity partnership, even when in the form of pension funds, however, is consistent with the World Bank's worldwide strategy of promoting and nurturing the local bourgeoisie *in association with* and not in competition with foreign capital. Another manifestation of this is the inconspicuous clause in the Bank's project appraisal that "private downstream companies may at any time purchase shares from FIBASE," the 49 percent minority partner in Copesul, if the project becomes profitable enough to make such participation attractive.[87]

One final point is worth making. According to the Bank's project appraisal report, petrochemical prices within Brazil are highly subsidized and imports penalized through high tariffs and an import deposit system, "raising the cost of some imported petrochemicals up to 150-200 percent of international prices."[88] Prices for the industry are controlled by the government according to a formula based on cost of production, allowing efficient producers a 23.8 percent before tax (16 percent after tax) return on investment.[89]

Unlike its usual practice, however, the Bank expressed no hint of disapproval of this protectionist policy and the price controls, on the contrary, assuming their continuation as a condition of the financial viability of the project (para. 8.03) and the downstream private companies. In the section detailing agreements reached between the Bank and the concerned parties as a condition for extending the loan, it is stated that the Brazilian government pledged that it will

> not take, or permit to be taken, any action with regard to the prices of the products of (a) the Borrower (COPESUL) which would preclude the Borrower, operating efficiently, from covering all its costs, servicing its debt, and earning a reasonable return on investment, and (b) the downstream companies which would preclude these companies, operating efficiently, from earning a reasonable return on investment.[90]

The Brazilian government was also obliged to commit itself to making a special study of petrochemical pricing policy and furnish it to the Bank for comments (para. 4.23). It is not clear what reforms the Bank might be driving at, but most probably a rise in the administered prices is desired, as capital costs of the new complex and the second (Bahia) complex are much higher than the first (São Paulo) pole on which pricing policy had been based, and with three structures in operation prices would have to be reconciled somehow.

It is not clear just why the Bank is taking no steps to dismantle protectionism in this case (the assurance of prices guaranteeing a "reasonable rate of return" is in any case fairly common in Bank agreements). It is my hypothesis that Brazil's economic leadership is simply too strong, sophisticated, and self-confident to give up policies it considers important, and that in any case the World Bank had no power to prevent the building of the third petrochemical pole as other funds would have been found; therefore it had not much leverage in this case. Whether this will continue to be true, now that private international banks are unwilling to bankroll Brazil's development by further growth in its foreign debt, remains to be seen. If a debt rescheduling, complete with IMF stabilization program, is imminent for Brazil, we will probably see radical changes in its protectionist policy since Bank-Fund leverage will then be much greater.

Structural Adjustment Loans

In recent years the Bank has become even more aggressive in pressing for industrial restructuring in selected borrowing countries. The tool with which this restructuring is to be achieved is structural adjustment lending, begun only in early 1980. Structural adjustment loans are program loans: quick-disbursing injections of untied credit that can be used for almost any type of import (or for the repayment of foreign debts falling due). The Bank has, of course, made a number of both open and disguised "program loans" before 1980, in forms which included "reconstruction" loans extended after wars or other catastrophes, "sector loans" for which the range of permissible imports was only broadly specified, and local cost financing, which smuggled in a proportion of free foreign exchange into loans that were nominally earmarked for specific projects. As the Bank put it:

> Although lending for structural adjustment is a new form of Bank assistance, such assistance is a natural evolution in the traditional program assistance that has always been (and continues to be) a part of the Bank's lending operations. Previous program lending, however, has generally been designed to meet the immediate consequences of crises. . . . As a result, the programs supported were concentrated on measures dealing with immediate difficulties rather than on finding solutions to a country's underlying, long-term structural problems. Structural adjustment lending, on the other hand, envisages the probability of multiyear programs being worked out and supported by a succession of loans. Because such lending will be developed with long-term objectives in mind, it is expected to have more enduring effects than the crisis-oriented operations that were characteristic of the Bank's program lending in the past.[91]

The structural adjustment loans are in essence an attempt to combine large quantities of untied aid, which will be urgently needed in the looming debt crises of the 1980s, with an unprecedented degree of meddling in the formulation of industrial sector policy. As these loans can be disbursed much more quickly than ordinary project loans, they may also be a method devised to postpone the day when net capital flows to a given country become negative (as discussed in Chapter 1) and thus preserve the Bank's leverage in that country.

In exchange for this fountain of money, the recipient country will be expected to carry out important reforms in its economy, of a type consistent with Bank demands through the years. The most important of these demands, unsurprisingly, is that protectionist structures—tariffs, controls, subsidies to local businesses, etc., be dismantled. Another important element is the expansion of incentives to business for export production. A number of observers have noted the close similarity to IMF balance of payments loans and the attendant conditionality; like them the Bank structural adjustment loans will be disbursed in tranches (phased drawings) and can be suspended if the country does not comply with agreements it has made to change its policies. "These loans do go to the heart of the political management of an economy," S. Shahid Husain, a regional vice president of the World Bank, said in a recent interview. "We will have to approach them with humility."[92]

The twin goals of balance of payments support (which usually also implies support for the specific government in power in the borrowing country) and the leverage on industrial policies may not be perfectly compatible, however. The fate of the first two structural adjustment loans made by the Bank is not encouraging. A $200 million loan to Turkey in March 1980 was described as not much more than a pure bailout; Bank officials intimated that Turkey was not seriously expected to deliver internal reforms "for the duration at least." And Kenya, recipient of the second loan, practically disqualified itself for the second tranche by violating conditions set for disbursement of the loan.[93]

The Philippines received a structural adjustment loan, also for $200 million, in September 1980. This loan is supposed to be contingent on the government's liberalizing its foreign trade laws and tariffs along the lines suggested by a report published by the Bank four months earlier, *Philippines: Industrial Development Strategy and Policies*. Although it is admitted that under the protectionist regime, Philippine manufacturing industry had grown "to the point that it has become a major factor in the development of the Philippines," and "compares well in relative size with other countries in a similar stage of development," the Bank's mission nevertheless urged upon the government a free trade regime which amounts to a suicidal undertaking. While a good part of the protected industry will be destroyed by the dismantling of protectionism, the country is urged to reorient its investment incentives toward labor-intensive export production.

There are a number of problems with this prescription. The first is that such a strategy depends on very low remuneration to labor, and is thus a prescription for perpetuating poverty. The Bank notes, *with approval*, that "Philippine wages have declined significantly relative to those in competing and customer countries; at present wages are one-half to one-third of those in Korea and Hong Kong, while productivity in many export firms compares favorably with that in these countries."[94] At the same time, Bank consultant Bela Balassa was advising the Korean government to prevent any further rises in real wages there, as that country's attempt at export-led growth was threatened by the improvement in the income shares of workers![95] The strategy of labor-intensive exports inevitably plays off one low-income country against another, and any gains that labor wrests for itself from a temporarily successful application of this strategy will carry the seeds of its own negation by pricing goods out of the market.

The other problem with this policy is the growing wave of protectionism in the wealthier countries that are the intended customers of these exports. As Walden Bello and John Kelly have noted:

> In the space of a few years, thirty-two major restrictions were slapped on Philippine products by ten countries. Textile exports, which were regarded by the Bank and the Government as the "locomotive" of its strategy of encouraging "nontraditional" light-manufactured exports, have been especially hard hit, forcing the IMF to concede that "export promotion has become particularly difficult in the present climate of uncertainty as well as trade restrictions faced by Philippine exporters." Export-led industrialization, it became clear, merely deepened the Philippines' chronic dependency as an agricultural-export economy.[96]

The 1980 World Bank report acknowledged that "the quotas imposed on imports of Philippine garments by the U.S., Australia, the EEC, and Canada will effect [sic] industry exports. In past years, such quotas have not been a severely limiting factor, but, as the exports expand, their pressure will become more severe."[97] But its response is merely that the textile industry must try harder, that "to minimize the effects of the quotas, the industry must be able to diversify and upgrade its product lines, so as to have the flexibility to shift production to lines unaffected by quotas."[98]

One of the specific recommendations of the Bank, in the Philippines and elsewhere, is that the government supply infrastructure, in the form of industrial parks, and incentives, in the form of tax exemptions and holidays, to foreign enterprises that wish to exploit the country's cheap labor. The new but already classic form of supplying all these incentives in a single package is the Free Trade Zone, or Export Processing Zone (several of which, in various countries, have been supported by Bank and IDA loans.) These extraterritorial industrial estates offer the foreign investor infrastructure and utilities (factory buildings, workers' dormitories, electricity, water and sewage, telephone and telex) in a location convenient to sea or airports; large tax exemptions, including the duty-free import of raw materials and intermediate goods; and exemption from labor regulations in force in the host country, amounting to the suspension of most of the rights of workers. In exchange, these countries get employment, remunerated at only 10-20 percent the level of comparable work in the developed countries, chiefly for teenage girls who are cheaper and considered more docile workers. Because of this preference for a category of worker that has not previously been employed for wages there is no overall impact on the level of unemployment. There is no creation of transferable skills or transfer of technology. Because of the low level of wages and salaries, foreign currency receipts are low, and must be set against the expenses incurred by the host government in providing the facilities; because of tax exemptions, income from this source is negligible. Competition among countries to attract foreign investment ensures that they will not be able to raise their share of benefits over time. Investment by the foreign corporation is low, as the project site and infrastructure are already provided, making it easy for the corporation to relocate in a few years to benefit from cheaper labor elsewhere.[99] It is difficult to see what a host country stands to gain from the establishment of a Free Trade Zone.

But the World Bank makes it clear that it is not satisfied with the establishment of these extraterritorial enclaves; its real goal is to extend throughout the territory of the country the privileges accorded to foreign migratory enterprise in such zones; to make the entire country a Free Trade Zone.[100] It is hardly surprising that a secret World Bank memorandum on the Philippines warned that "the World Bank's *imprimatur* on the industrial program runs the risk of drawing criticism of the Bank as the servant of multinational corporations and particularly of U.S. economic imperialism."[101] It is, however, really nothing new, but rather the intensification of a campaign *against* national industry which the Bank and the IMF have been waging, in the Philippines and other countries, for a long time.[102]

6
Mining

And so it was that "Botswana's" new copper-
nickel mine came to be financed by a South
African mining group, using a Finnish smelting
process and an American refinery in Louisiana.
The mine output was sold to guaranteed buyers
in West Germany. Perhaps it is pertinent to ask
just what contribution this operation will make
to Botswana's economic development?
—Greg Lanning, *Africa Undermined*

In its Annual Report for 1978, the World Bank announced a
policy decision that had been maturing for several years. The
announcement had nothing to say about relieving absolute or
relative poverty, for good reason: the beneficiaries of the increase
in lending for energy development and for nonfuel minerals
would be some of the world's largest multinational corporations
and the consumers of the industrialized world.

"A continuing supply of both nonfuel minerals and sources of
energy is critical to the health of the world economy," the
statement on nonfuel minerals began. However, it added:

> The views of developing countries and private foreign investors on
> how to exploit mineral resources have tended, in recent years, to
> diverge rather than come together . . . foreign mining companies
> and investors have hesitated to commit large funds to mining
> ventures located in countries that appear politically unstable or
> where there is a serious risk that the terms of investment agree-
> ments may be changed by the host government.

Here, as in other types of lending since its foundation, the Bank saw its role as that of the "safe bridge" for foreign capital.

> International financial institutions—the World Bank, IDA, and IFC, together with the regional development banks—can help bridge the difference between producing countries and foreign mining concerns by providing an international "presence" in mining ventures. Agreements governing projects in which one of the international financial institutions is an active partner are more likely to be regarded as fair by all parties and, therefore, to endure. In this way, foreign investment—particularly risk capital—should become more readily available for mineral production in the developing countries than it has been in the past.[1]

The Bank's words in fact understated the problem. There has been a revolution in mining finance in Third World countries in the past quarter-century (or less). This revolution has two aspects: the technical and the political. Technically, the problem is that the richest and most accessible sources of ores have all been used up or appropriated. In the past, a mining corporation would develop a mine by a series of investments, starting modestly and financing successive expansions out of returns from the original mine. This was all the easier as host government demands for revenues were generally quite modest and profits were high. With the exhaustion of these rich ore bodies, however, it became necessary to penetrate into remoter regions and/or develop less rich sources of ores. The techniques were developed to make this possible, but they are very expensive (particularly the infrastructure costs in remote areas); it can easily cost something like $500 million to develop a "greenfield" mine today.

At the same time, host governments have grown less complacent about allowing foreign corporations to export their nonrenewable mineral wealth. There is an almost universal demand for higher tax revenues from foreign mining projects; and there have been a long series of nationalizations of such projects, climaxed by the hostile expropriation of the giant copper companies Anaconda and Kennecott in Chile by Allende's Popular Unity government in 1971.

The upshot is that foreign corporations are now required to invest vast sums of money to develop new mines in politically volatile climates where they cannot even be sure an agreement will last until the mine comes into production. The corporations have naturally responded with new defensive strategies which amount to a revolution in mine finance. The new style comprises the following elements:

—joint venture and consortium arrangements, often involving a large number of companies of different nationalities, in contrast to the exclusive mine ownership of the past;
—heavy reliance on debt finance (usually 50 percent and higher) rather than equity finance, implying a heavy burden of fixed interest charges and lower taxable profits;
—involvement of foreign commercial banks and customers for the mine products as financiers of the projects;
—participation of export credit agencies of industrial countries and international financial institutions, primarily the World Bank, as sources of finance but also as political insurance;
—participation of the host government in a range of roles from the provision of infrastructure, to minority or majority equity ownership, to a fully owned, nationalized industry.[2]

Bank Finance for Corporate-Owned Mines

While the Bank's decision to finance petroleum and other energy projects represented a real change of policy, the Bank had been financing infrastructure for mining projects (as well as occasional lending for the mine itself) since at least 1959, when an aerial tramway was constructed in Gabon to transport manganese, a key ingredient in steel-making, from a mine whose largest stockholder was U.S. Steel. The following year it made a loan to Mauritania (the first to that country) for infrastructure serving an iron-ore mining consortium, MIFERMA, composed primarily of European steel producers, with French government and private capital enjoying a dominant role:

	percent
RIM (Mauritanian government)	5.0
BRGM (French government)	23.9
DNEL (French private capital)	14.5
Rothschild (French private capital)	15.3
British Steel (government capital)	19.0
Finsider (Italian steel; government capital)	15.2
German steel industry	5.0

MIFERMA is a good example of the new type of mine finance, with the participating steel companies taking virtually all the output of the mine through reserved production or shareholders' options.[3]

Similarly, the first Bank investment (1968) in another West African country, Guinea, was for infrastructure for another huge consortium mine, this time to exploit the rich Boké deposit of bauxite for the shareholders' aluminum manufacture. The Cie. des Bauxites de Guinée (CBG) is owned 49 percent by the Guinean government and 51 percent by the users' consortium, Halco. Halco's ownership is divided as follows:

	percent
Aluminum Co. of America (Alcoa, U.S.)	27
Alcan Aluminium Ltd. (Canada)	27
Harvey Aluminum (now Martin Marietta Corp., U.S.)	20
Pechiney Ugine Kuhlmann (France)	10
Vereinigte Aluminium Werke AG (Germany)	10
Montecatini-Edison (Italy)	6

Boké is the world's largest, richest bauxite mine, and the region in which it is located is host to more than a billion tons of bauxite.[4] A loan to Botswana in 1971 built infrastructure for the Selebi-Pikwe copper-nickel mine, of which the chief shareholders are American Metal Climax (AMAX) and Anglo-American of South Africa, both major mining conglomerates.

Back in the Americas, the Bank's first loan to the Dominican Republic, in 1969, was for infrastructure to support development of a nickel mine operated by a subsidiary of the Canadian multinational Falconbridge, the second largest nickel producer in the world. Meanwhile the IFC, the Bank's private-enterprise subsidiary, was investing in a nickel mine in Guatemala (Exmibal) operated by International Nickel Company (INCO), the world's largest producer of nickel.

In Brazil, the Bank helped finance a joint venture of Alcoa and Hanna Mining in aluminum production utilizing the bauxite deposits of Pocos de Caldos, Minas Gerais. The joint venture, Alcominas, has recently changed its name to Alcoa Aluminio. Another Hanna mining project in Brazil, MBR, about which more will be said below, also benefited from infrastructure financed by a Bank loan. In 1979 Valesul, an aluminum smelter located in Brazil, received $98 million as a Bank loan; it is owned by Companhia Vale de Rio Doce (CVRD), the giant Brazilian raw materials corporation, and subsidiaries of Royal Dutch Shell (UK/Netherlands) and Reynolds Metal Inc., the U.S. aluminum producer. As mentioned in Chapter 5, one condition for this Bank loan was that CVRD divest itself of its majority stockholding in Valesul to Brazilian private capital, leaving the Shell sibsidiary as the largest stockholder.

Most recently the Bank has lent $80 million to a nickel project in Colombia operated by Cerro Matoso, S.A. This corporation is owned by an agency of the Colombian government, a subsidiary of Hanna Mining Company, and Billiton Overseas, Ltd., a member of the Royal Dutch Shell Group. Hanna is to provide technical support and Billiton will assure marketing of the metal.

The Bank's affiliate, the IFC, has also made a number of investments in the mining sector. In addition to the nickel mine in Guatemala mentioned previously, the IFC has helped to finance copper mines in Chile (Mantos Blancos and Minera Sagasca, the latter a subsidiary of Continental Copper and Steel), in Peru (Cuajone), and in Mauritania (Somima, partially owned by Charter Consolidated and Penarroya); an iron ore mine in Mexico (Minera del Norte); a nickel mining and refining project in Brazil (Codemin, of the Hochschild group); and an alumina/aluminum project of Pechiney Ugine Kuhlmann in Greece. One IFC project deserving special mention is Mineracao Rio do Norte, S.A., a huge bauxite mining project in Brazil's Amazon region owned by CVRD (40 percent), Alcan (Canada, 19 percent), Cia. Brasileira de Aluminio (10 percent), Aardal of Sunndal Verk (Sweden),

Norsk Hydro (Norway), the National Institute of Industry of Spain, Reynolds Aluminum (U.S.), Rio Tinto Zinc (Britain), and Mineracao Rio Xingu (Brazil), all with 5 percent.

What is the significance of World Bank participation in these mining projects? Why would a private mining corporation seek, or accept, IBRD or IFC participation? There are several reasons. The first, of course, is money. Although the Bank typically finances only a fraction of total project costs, this can be significant if the loan is made to the government of the country that has taken responsibility for the infrastructure. Radetzski and Zorn remark of the Amax/Anglo-American project in Botswana: "Clearly, Selebi-Pikwe would not have been developed unless international agency financing had been available; infrastructure costs alone were one-third of the total estimated project cost."[5]

In previous years the infrastructure (ports, railways, and other means for transporting the minerals to ports, housing, shops, and clinics for the workers, power plants, etc.) typically would have been financed by the corporation itself; these investments are integrally bound up with the life of the mine, most having no value apart from its production. Today many of these costs can be socialized. Most of the IBRD loans mentioned above are made to the government, with only a few directly to the corporations.

The Botswana Case

The history of Selebi-Pikwe suggests that the government has been left holding the bag. Botswana, its mineral wealth aside, is one of the poorest countries in Africa. It borders on South Africa and is considered to be in the South African sphere of influence. There have been attempts to diminish South African control, however, and the concession for the Selebi-Pikwe deposits was originally given to Roan Selection Trust (RST), despite the interest of South Africa's giant Anglo-American corporation, the dominant mining conglomerate in Southern Africa. The U.S. corporation AMAX bought into RST's Botswana subsidiary, Botrest, when it went public in order to raise funds to prove the extent of the nickel-copper deposit. When Botswana approached the World Bank for financing for infrastructure for the mining development, the Bank required the mining companies to guarantee the loan, a condition which caused Botrest so much difficulty that it was forced to allow Anglo-American to become an equal participant with AMAX and to share in the management and technical control of the project.[6]

The project has had very serious financial troubles in its early years, for two reasons: copper and nickel prices have been much lower than projected, and severe technical problems were encountered in processing the ores.

The tax agreement between the government of Botswana and the mining company exploiting the Selebi-Pikwe deposits, Bamangwato Concessions Ltd. (BCL, owned by AMAX and Anglo-American) is now being renegotiated for the fourth time. Originally a royalty was fixed at 7.5 percent of the operating profits, or a minimum of $750,000 per year, but this payment was suspended in 1978, after the corporation had experienced technical and price difficulties. The rest of the tax provisions have been described as "well designed to meet the needs of the mining companies."

> The corporation tax was raised from 30 percent to 40 percent at the express demand of BCL, which wanted to get the maximum kickback under the double taxation agreements between Botswana, the UK and the United States. Under double taxation agreements, taxes paid in Botswana are offset against taxes in the UK and the United States. This reduced the tax liability of the parent company in its home country; and since Botswana's tax authorities are less experienced than those in the U.S., it is likely to be easier to manipulate the accounts so as to minimize *total* tax payments. *But the most important feature of the tax arrangements is that all capital expenditure is repaid before income tax becomes fully payable.* So the full tax return to the Botswana government will not begin for ten years.[7]

In addition, the government can levy tax on company profits only after the royalty has been deducted. Interest charges on the outstanding loans ($60 million, or half the cost of the mine, supplied by a consortium of West German banks) are also de-

ductible and represent more of the mine's surplus which escapes Botswana tax. And corporation dividends are freely re-
mittable to shareholders outside Botswana in their respective
currencies. The government has no say in the dividend policy of
the corporations, because although it has two directors on the
board of BCL, which operates the mine, it has no stake in Botrest,
which owns 85 percent of BCL.[8]

MIFERMA in Mauritania

The iron ore in Mauritania has also disappointed expectations. A World Bank official who has been closely involved with
Bank missions to Mauritania expressed his own opinion about
the project as follows:

> The Miferma project was originally regarded as the key to the
> future economic development of the country that would enable it
> to accelerate the pace of very slow progress that its otherwise
> limited resources made possible. It was to bring the age of indus-
> trialization to Mauritania, while providing budgetary surpluses
> that would make the country self-supporting, as well as able to
> finance an investment program. *In fact its influence on the economy
> has been slight, while it has not lived up to expectations in pro-
> viding revenues to the state budget.*[9] (Emphasis added)

The conventions on taxation, described as "unfair" by one
source, and the extensive sovereignty granted to the company
were signed by French ministers in the Mauritanian government
before the colony became independent. (Two other Bank loans
to mining projects in Africa, the Gabon manganese project and a
potash mine in the People's Republic of the Congo, were similarly signed before independence and negotiated under colonial
rule.) "These laws were not questioned by Mauritania until
1973, until which time they had insured the security of invested
and repatriated capital."[10] As in the Botswana case, MIFERMA's
profits fell far short of projections "because of a combination of
rising costs and reduced international prices of iron ore."[11] It has
to be remembered in this context that most or all of MIFERMA's

production was regularly purchased at a discount from the "regular" price by the steel mills, which owned more than 50 percent of its shares,[12] so what they lost as shareholders they would gain as customers. It was, again, the government that was left holding the bag.

In fact, what the government got out of this project with "new-style" financing was just an old-fashioned enclave project—a city in the desert and a railroad leading to the ocean. A breakdown of published MIFERMA accounts showing categories of income retained in the country against those sent abroad in the year 1969, when the mine accounted for 30 percent of Mauritania's GDP and three-fourths of its exports, showed the following:[13]

Local income: (28 percent)	taxes	16.8 percent
	other (including salaries for 4500 local people)	11.3 percent
		28.0 percent
Sent abroad: (72 percent)	material inputs	38.4 percent
	foreign salaries (800 persons)	9.4 percent
	profit repatriated	24.1 percent
		72.0 percent

Even these accounts overstate the value to the local economy, for as Samir Amin points out, practically all the income distributed locally to employees evaporates in imports; and tax receipts "do not . . . make possible more than a very slight improvement in the local public financing capacity, particularly in view of the *heavy recurrent charges necessitated by work on the infrastructure directly serving the mining economy*"[14] (emphasis added).

The Mauritanian government (after some internal upheavals) succeeded in renegotiating the terms of its colonial-era agreement with MIFERMA in 1973. It is of interest to recall that in the original loan agreement (249FR, March 17, 1960), disbursement of the loan could be suspended under the following circumstances (among many others):

Republic of Mauritania shall have taken any action for the dissolution or disestablishment of the Borrower or for the suspension of its operations, or a substantial part thereof; ... Any action for the amendment, suspension, or termination of the Mining Concession, the Tax Status, the Establishment Convention, the Port Convention, the Railway Convention, the Installation and Operating Convention, the Technical Assistance Agreement, the Commercial Agreement, and the Financial Agreement.

Of course, by the time a new agreement was negotiated (1973) disbursements under the original loan had long ceased (1964). And, as the ore had been taken from Mauritania for ten years under the old agreement, the original mine was rapidly being depleted. In 1979 a new Bank loan was made to Mauritania for opening two new iron ore pits, to gradually replace the first one. This time no European equity capital was involved in the operation (though five Arab states or entities were) but the French, the Japanese, and the European Investment Bank are all represented as creditors and, it may be presumed, as customers for the mines' output.[15]

It should be noted in passing that both the Selebi-Pikwe project in Botswana and the MIFERMA project in Mauritania experienced strikes by miners (in 1975 and 1968 respectively). In both cases the strikes were severely repressed by the government and the mining companies acting in concert.[16]

A Political Insurance Policy

World Bank money is not just money, however; it is an insurance policy. As suggested by the Bank's statement quoted at the beginning of this chapter, the Bank is consciously performing the role of guaranteeing the stability of the foreign corporation's investment. This role is recognized, and appreciated, by the mining industry. Raymond Mikesell remarks that there is a general belief that governments are less likely to default on loans in which international agencies have participated.[17] Another recent study of mining legislation concurs: "The financing offered by the World Bank is generally not viewed as just another source, rather the Bank's participation lends more importantly a degree of stability and legitimation to any project."[18] An examination of Bank-supported mining projects in two politically volatile Latin American countries—the Dominican Republic and Brazil—illustrates just how important such insurance might be.

Falcondo in the Dominican Republic

Falconbridge of Canada, the world's second largest producer of nickel, acquired rights to nickel-bearing laterite ores in the Domincan Republic in 1956. INCO, Falconbridge's rival and the world's largest nickel producer, gave up the properties when (according to an INCO executive) Dominican dictator Trujillo demanded "too big a bribe."[19] Trujillo's depredations were so gross that he was deposed and assassinated in 1961. The five years that followed did not provide a stable environment for investment by a foreign corporation in the nation's nonrenewable resources. The radical reformist party of Juan Bosch, the Partido Revolucionario Dominicano (PRD), swept to victory in elections held in 1962 on a program that included the prohibition of large landholdings, restrictions on foreign ownership of land, and profit sharing for workers. Bosch was overthrown by a military coup, with U.S. aid and encouragement, in 1963. At this point Falcondo, the local Falconbridge subsidiary, acquired additional mining concessions and announced its intention of constructing a $78 million refinery. However, "in view of the company's desperate need for markets in North America at this period, the announcement appears to have been designed to shore up the shaky Cabral government rather than reveal any serious spending intentions."[20] Continuing instability and economic decline led to another coup in 1965, and when it appeared that Bosch's PRD supporters might win the ensuing civil war, U.S. President Lyndon Johnson sent 20,000 marines into the country. The invasion, originally justified to protect North American lives, resulted in the installation of a pro-U.S. government under a former Trujillo crony, Joaquin Balaguer, in 1966.

One year later, Superior Oil, a Texas company with political and financial links to Lyndon Johnson, bought control of Falconbridge and immediately proceeded with plans to expand its Dominican nickel operation. "The Texas Nexus provided the basis for arranging financing, vital political influence in Washington, and insurance from the U.S. Overseas Private Investment Corporation [OPIC]."[21] ARMCO Steel was brought in as a partner for 17.5 percent of the equity. As a bona fide U.S. company, it would enable Falcondo to qualify for OPIC insurance against "war, insurrection, revolution, expropriation, or currency inconvertibility, any or all of which were possibilities not to be overlooked in the Dominican Republic."[22] Falconbridge holds 65.7 percent of the common stock and the Dominican government has 9.5 percent, with the small remainder held by other parties.

A remarkable feature of Falcondo's financing is the extremely high ratio of debt-to-equity finance. Only $15 million, or less than 8 percent of the project's $195 million cost, was put up by the shareholders. The bulk of the financing was provided in long-term securities from three U.S. insurance companies; First National City Bank and the Canadian Imperial Bank of Commerce provided short-term revolving credits, and $25 million came from the World Bank.[23] This high level of debt financing has three major consequences: interest payments take a very high share of total operating expenses; the return to equity (shareholders') capital is extremely high (in the first year of full production return to equity was 93 percent; in the slump of the mid-1970s Falcondo was the only member of the Falconbridge empire returning a profit) and tax returns to the host country are modest, because although the rate of profit is high, the absolute amount is smaller, since only profits, not interest payments, are taxed. But the debt structure must also be seen in political perspective. It minimized the financial commitment of the shareholders in a country with massive potential for political upheaval, and it spread the risk among several of the most powerful financial interests in the United States. The World Bank participation was as much a part of that strategy as was the OPIC insurance agreement.

The concession negotiated with the Dominican government was "highly favorable" to the corporation, according to a critical study: 33 percent taxation on profits, accelerated depreciation, no import duties, and exemptions from some of the foreign exchange regulations. The Dominican mining laws were virtually written by the Falcondo general manager, by his own claim.[24]

The Dominican government is also effectively shut out of two crucial aspects of Falcondo's operations: marketing and production technology. Falcondo is required by contract to sell its total production to Falconbridge at a price set by the parent firm, and it must pay Falconbridge a fee for this "service." The sale proceeds are deposited with the First National City Bank of New York as trustee, which holds and divides up this income in secrecy.

> Thus, the Dominican government is ignorant of and effectively eliminated from the management of this money, and has little control over how it is manipulated. Under such an arrangement, this immense pool of funds can be easily seized and impounded should the Falcondo complex ever be threatened with nationalization.[25]

Similarly, the technology used by Falcondo to exploit the Dominican laterite ores is top secret and totally controlled by Falconbridge. "Falcondo's ace-in-the-hole against nationalization, whatever turn Dominican politics may take, is to maintain a monopoly of essential knowledge about the production process."[26] The present government is not unhappy about these exclusions, however; it knows that as long as it complies with Falcondo's wishes, the company constitutes *its* insurance policy; i.e., if a more nationalistic movement tried to gain power, North American interests in Falcondo as well as other corporations in the country (notably Gulf and Western, the sugar company), would make a repeat of the 1965 invasion probable.

The benefits of the mining operations to the people of the Dominican Republic are minor. Only 1900 local jobs were created by the investment of $195 million at a time when national unemployment was estimated at 400,000. Labor problems began in the construction stage, before the mine even began production; and (as in Botswana and Mauritania) the strike was ruthlessly broken by the government and Falcondo acting in close concert. Of the taxes that are collected by the state from the company, a good proportion will be devoted to maintaining the present government in power and to maintain labor peace. An oversized and well-paid police and military apparatus employs between 30,000 and 40,000 people and consumes 30 to 35 percent of the government budget.[27]

Hanna Mining in Brazil

The Hanna Mining Company of Cleveland is a participant in at least four World Bank-aided mining projects in Latin America: MBR (iron ore) and Alcominas (aluminum) in Brazil; EXMIBAL, INCO's Guatemalan nickel subsidiary with IFC financing; and the Cerro Matoso nickel mine in Colombia. It is also part-owner of several World Bank and IFC-aided petrochemical projects in Brazil. The first, and still most controversial, of these projects was the one involving the iron ore deposits of Aguas Claras, since Hanna's interests were closely affected by the volatile Brazilian politics of the early 1960s—and eventually rescued by the military coup of April 1964.

In 1956 Hanna purchased controlling interest in a British gold mining company operating in Brazil called St. John D'el Rey. Hanna's interests were not in the modest gold operations, but in the potential iron ore deposits in St. John's concession area in the Aguas Claras region of Minas Gerais. However, two years earlier Brazil had promulgated a nationalistic mineral code, reaffirming a principle first stated twenty years earlier, that exploitation of Brazil's subsoil minerals could be carried on only by Brazilians, or by firms that were organized and registered in Brazil. The code was not retroactive, and St. John had obtained its concession in the early nineteenth century. Hanna organized a Brazilian subsidiary of St. John and began to pressure the Brazilian government for rights to export ore from Aguas Claras. The legal situation was sufficiently ambiguous that Hanna could maintain it was complying with the letter of the law, while its nationalistic opponents maintained that it was certainly violating the spirit. Hanna's rights became an emotional political issue, and President Joao Goulart issued an expropriation decree in 1962. Hanna appealed, and the matter was still in the courts when Goulart was ousted and killed in a military coup.[28]

The story of how the nationalism and radicalism of Brazilian governments in the early 1960s was radically reversed by the coup is told in chapter 7 of my book *The Debt Trap*. The role of the World Bank and its attitudes toward the successive governments is eloquently revealed in its cumulative statement of loans: no new loans were approved for Brazil between June 1959 and February 1965, even though Brazil is the largest borrower of all from the IBRD.

"For Hanna, the revolt which overthrew Goulart . . . arrived like a last minute rescue by the First Cavalry," according to *Fortune*.[29] John J. McCloy, the first president of the World Bank, was at that time serving as Hanna's counsel in Brazil. It was McCloy who escorted U.S. Ambassador Lincoln Gordon a few weeks after the coup to the office of President Castelo Branco, Goulart's successor, to ask for a restoration of the concessions as one condition for receiving U.S. financial aid.[30] The deed was done quickly. On Christmas Eve, 1964, Castelo Branco promulgated a presidential decree which (a) reversed the Goulart administration trend toward a government mineral monopoly by endorsing private development of Brazil's iron ore reserves; and (b) approved Hanna's plan to build loading facilities at Sepetiba Bay, an undeveloped deepwater harbor sixty miles south of Rio, and to construct a railway cutoff from the government-owned railway to the bay. On June 15, 1966, a reconstituted Federal Court of Appeals handed down a decision favoring Hanna's right to exploit the iron ore deposits.

In the late 1960s, Hanna joined with one of Brazil's largest holding companies, Cia. Auxiliar de Empresas de Mineracao (CAEMI), and with Japan's Nippon Steel to form a new iron-ore company called Mineracoes Brasileiras Reunidas (MBR). Hanna also formed a joint venture with Alcoa, Alcominas, to enter the Brazilian bauxite sector. In January 1968 the World Bank made a $22 million loan to Alcominas. In August 1971 it made a $50 million loan to MBR to finance the port development and railway extension necessary to export their iron-ore production. It is to be wondered whether George Humphreys, the head of Hanna Mining and one-time U.S. secretary of the treasury (thus ex officio U.S. governor of the IMF and World Bank) has been the reason Hanna has had such a repeated and fruitful partnership with the Bank. There can be no question that the coup, supported strongly by the United States, the IMF, and the World Bank, has had a great deal to do with Hanna's successfully expanding empire in Brazil.

Other instances are less clear. One can only raise the question, for example, as to whether the World Bank consciously aided Alcan to retain some claim to the rich bauxite deposts of Guinea, which once seemed irretrievably lost. In the 1920s a French subsidiary of Alcan (Boké) was granted exploration rights for a 2800-square-mile area in what was then the French colony. In 1955 drilling disclosed that the Sangaredi plateau within this concession was nothing less than the largest, richest single bauxite deposit known in the world. Alcan entered into a long-term agreement to mine the bauxite with the Federation of French West Africa, at that time still under firm French control, and began laying a railway from the coast to the mine site.

When the French colonies gained indepedence in 1961, however, Guinea was the radical breakaway, the only one of the colonies to refuse further close association with the former French masters. The Alcan mining agreement was a victim of this breakaway. "The new nation's leadership was determined that the country would own part of any future mining operation and a substantial portion of any supporting infrastructure, such as port and railroad facilities, as well as the major townsite. Alcan departed temporarily from the scene."[31]

In 1963 the Guinean government made an agreement with Halco Mining Co., a wholly owned subsidiary of Harvey Aluminum, Inc., which resulted in the formation of Cie. des Bauxites de Guinée (CBG), owned 51 percent by Halco and 49 percent by the Republic of Guinea, to exploit the Sangaredi deposit. The government then applied to the World Bank for a loan to finance the mining project's infrastructure.

World Bank studies showed that the proposed rate of mining— 1 million metric tons per year (mtpy)—was "patently insufficient to pay back the huge capital investment needed; 6 million mtpy was a more realistic target. But this was more bauxite than Harvey could possibly use."[32]

Harvey then approached other major aluminum producers "which had been waiting for the other shoe to drop." When the reorganization was finished, Harvey had only 20 percent of Halco and both Alcan and Alcoa, the industry giants, each had 27 percent. French, German, and Italian aluminum companies each had a smaller share of the company.

Perhaps the large scale of the mine really was an economic imperative, but the authors of a study of the French aluminum giant, Pechiney Ugine Kuhlmann (owner of a 10 percent slice of Halco) find this alliance among rivals worthy of ironic comment. Pechiney's chief executive officer explained back in 1968 that cooperation was made necessary by the "dimension which is suitable for new installations in order that they may be competitive." But, his critics ask, "competitive in comparison to whom? To the other aluminum groups? That is, to the same ones with whom one is cooperating for prospecting, extraction, or production? Polite rivals and fickle partners who get together in order to be competitive among themselves!"[33]

Another Latin American nickel project, this one a joint venture of Hanna Mining (again!) and INCO, the world's largest producer of nickel, encountered stiff nationalist opposition in Guatemala. The nickel deposits, near Lake Izabal, were discovered by Hanna, which then invited INCO in as a partner in their subsidiary named EXMIBAL. One of the first obstacles to be overcome was the lively guerrilla activity in the region where the deposits were located; the Guatemalan government put the rebellion down with a pacification campaign that left 3,000 Guatemalans killed.[34]

Since this was Guatemala's first world-scale mining operation, the nation had no mining code—which left EXMIBAL the opportunity to write its own. The taxation provisions were generous: the company was exempted from taxation completely for the first five years, and paid only partial taxes for the next five. Furthermore, it claimed that some 85 percent of its operations were not "mining," but "transformation industry" and thus entitled to more lenient taxation. The company also sought and received large-scale exemption from exchange control laws—exemptions justified on the grounds that they were needed to guarantee repayment of the foreign loans obtained for the project.

A storm of nationalist opposition broke when it was revealed that the government was virtually allowing EXMIBAL to write its own ticket—and then adopting the terms as the law of the land under constitutionally dubious procedures. The climax of the struggle came in the fall and winter of 1970–1971. Two members of an ad hoc commission protesting EXMIBAL's concession, Julio Camey-Herrera and Adolfo Mijangos, were assassinated.

> The suppression of public discussion of the EXMIBAL contract—as well as of many other controversial policies—was completed when Arana imposed a state of siege in November 1970 suspending all political and constitutional rights, imposing a nationwide curfew, and establishing formal censorship of the press.[35]

In February 1971 the government announced that it had concluded an agreement with EXMIBAL.

The government refused, however, to guarantee EXMIBAL's investment, which would have been required for a direct World Bank loan or for insurance by OPIC. EXMIBAL then invited the International Finance Corporation, which had been created for just such situations, to become its financial coordinator. It was reportedly on IFC advice that the proposed scale of investment was reduced from $270 to $120 million. A package of external loans was put together that provided most of the finance. The presence of the IFC was needed, however, not so much because it had superior expertise in mine finance, as because the presence of this arm of the World Bank would provide an implicit guarantee that the power of the Bank and of its backers would stand behind the investments of the other private parties.

Mining Legislation and Taxation Codes

The World Bank has not published a sector policy paper on mining, though one was approved in 1973 "not for public distribution" and was excerpted in *Report* (March-April 1974). A full-length book on the topic was published by the Bank, however, in 1977, coincident with the announcement of increased lending by the Bank in both the energy and nonfuel minerals sectors. Chapters 5 and 6 of this book, entitled The Mining Industry and the Developing Countries, are of interest to us, since they deal with the policy of governments in which mineral deposits are located.[36]

The book's authors recognize that there is a powerful trend today toward the nationalization of mines and their operation by state-owned companies. While this trend is accepted, the advice of the authors is to keep the functions of state-owned companies modest, essentially limited to the production of the ore. The state-owned company should be autonomous, i.e., insulated as far as possible from the political process. The importance of using expatriates and foreign management teams is underlined, and the authors indicate a preference for joint venture operations "where the partner, often with minority interest, is assigned full management responsibility."[37] Nationalized mining companies are warned against the perils of trying to market their own produce, and the value of collaborating with foreign sales agencies is stressed. Independent technological development is also discouraged; it is suggested that setting up a national research and development facility is uneconomic.[38]

The importance of mining legislation safeguarding foreign investors' rights is emphasized: "Without a mining law, no mining right can be established; without a right who would venture to risk his capital?" The foreign investor must be saved "needless delays" in obtaining the necessary permits, as in one case where it is claimed a corporation had to acquire approvals and agreements from nine different ministries and agencies.[39]

It is suggested that income taxes should be the preferred form of taxation, an issue the significance of which will be discussed later. Governments are, in general, warned of the adverse consequences of trying to increase their share of mining revenues: "further investment may be discouraged and revenue to the host country be reduced over the long term."[40]

Finally, these World Bank authors propose what they seem to consider an ideal tax system. I had some trouble believing I was reading this passage correctly. Bluntly, their suggestion amounts to allowing the investor to recoup all expenditures plus the "minimum return the management required a project to show before it decided to invest" *before any income tax at all is applied*. This is done by permitting *instant* depreciation of the investment and carrying any oustanding loss forward to the following year, increased by the percentage equivalent to the discounted cash flow return the mine is allowed to earn free of tax. After the corporation had recouped all its expenditure plus the desired rate of return, subsequent profits would be taxed at a "standard" rate. This would be pure gravy for the corporations, while (the authors admit) "the system does . . . have the major disadvantage that while the revenues accruing to the state may be greater over the long term, they are received at a later stage in the development of the mine. Consequently the tax rate must be higher to reach the same present value."[41]

This system is not really a tax at all but a postponement of tax, and would be combined with an income or profits tax. The corporations prefer this tax (or nontax) for obvious reasons; not only are they excused from paying taxes in the years before a mine begins producing, but they obtain higher rates of return when prices are low for the mine product. Their advocates argue that host countries should like the tax because "it will invariably be in the interest of the Government to ensure that reserves in a given deposit, deemed to be economically recoverable in the absence of taxation, should not be left in the ground as a result of onerous fiscal provisions."[42] One must quarrel with this reasoning; there is no reason on earth why a government should not leave its nonrenewable resources in the ground until it is ready to develop them itself, or at the least, until a better bargain can be struck. And it is certain that no corporation would accept such a deal if the terms were reversed and the government were allowed to recoup *its* desired return out of the first years of production before the company could collect a penny.

Loans to State-Owned Mines

The issue of mining taxation can be exmained in the light of Bank advice in connection with an actual series of loans to the

Bolivian mining sector: IDA Credit #455 (1974); IBRD Loans #1290 (1976) and #1331 (1976). These loans belong to a category which, unlike the projects previously discussed, are not made for single mines owned or controlled by a foreign corporation. The loans in question here have been made to the national governments of states that are rich in mineral deposits (Bolivia, Peru, Chile, Zaire, Burma) and that have at least partially nationalized the existing large mines within their borders. The intent of loans in this category seems to be not merely to increase production and exports, important though this objective may be to the health of the industrialized countries and their corporations; but to (a) ensure that the state-owned corporations complement the international *status quo* rather than challenge it; (b) encourage further mineral development to be undertaken by the private sector, by means of the favorable codes and taxation policies outlined above; and (c) finance risky exploration activities that private investors are no longer willing to undertake. In the case of Bolivia, the last two objectives are promoted.

The first IDA credit to Bolivia's mining sector, approved on January 15, 1974, contained a section which provided that "effective no later than June 30, 1974, or such other date as the Borrower and the Association shall otherwise agree, the Borrower shall promulgate a new Mining Code."[43] I could not determine what changes were required in such a short time, but in any event they were not the last word. The credit also provided funds for a comprehensive study on taxation and the mining structure in Bolivia to be carried out by the Harvard Institute for International Development. The Harvard report recommended introducing a corporate income tax.[44]

In 1978 a team of authors associated with the Harvard Institute for International Development (presumably the same team that did the IDA-financed study) published the book *Taxation and Mining: Nonfuel Minerals in Bolivia and Other Countries*.[45] In this book three authors describe what they call a general trend in the taxation of mineral enterprises from the old system based on royalties, collected on a basis proportional to the volume or value of minerals mined and exported, to the modern system of a corporate income tax. They do not say who was behind this general shift, implying rather that it is a kind of irresistible Zeitgeist. They do give an explanation as to *why* it has happened, from which we can make some inferences:

> The general shift from heavy reliance on royalties to income taxes was based on sound reasons. The average revenue that could be obtained from an income tax was higher than that which could be expected from royalties. The shift of risk away from the entrepreneur, implicit in the change to income taxation, enabled him to accept a higher expected rate of taxation. Moreover, the income tax was usually creditable against a foreign investor's tax in his home country. And the income tax gave the desired incentive for the rational exploitation of marginal ores.[46]

Now, aside from the vague promise that "average revenue" could be expected to be higher under an income tax, most of these reasons—shift of risk away from the entrepreneur, tax credits in the home country, and "incentive"—favor chiefly the foreign corporation. And if we look at the Bank's confidential appraisal report for its third mining sector loan we see that the claim that "average" government revenues will be higher under an income tax system is probably untrue in Bolivia's case; at least the mining companies are complaining that current taxes are too high:

> Mining companies are not subject to income taxation but rather to a *regalia* and export tax which together constitute 90 percent of tax revenues from the sector. Both taxes are levied upon the gross sales value of concentrates and result in *a substantially higher tax burden for Bolivian tin mining firms than experienced by their competitors in Malaysia, Thailand, and Indonesia, where taxes are at least partly based on income.* High effective rates of taxation directly increase the production costs which for tin, Bolivia's major export, already exceed comparable costs in other producing countries.
>
> Bolivia's present tax system materially inhibits mineral production, investment, and development, because taxation on gross sales revenue, rather than on corporate income, discourages exploitation of those deposits that are not high grade and discourages investments in new capacity.[47] (Emphasis added)

We may begin to suspect that the higher "average revenues" in the long term are predicated on the assumption that if tax *rates* are *lowered*, more investment will be encouraged and the government will get more revenue in the long run because more mines are taking more resources out of the country. We may remark that, again, no corporation would accept the argument that it should lower its profit expectations so that it will be welcome in more countries, and thus increase its gross receipts; every corporate accountant knows that it's not the size of gross income, but the rate of return on equity which counts. For a country the goal should be the proportion of benefits that remain in the country, rather than a (hypothetically) greater gross income sometime in the indefinite future, at the cost of immediate resource depletion.

We also begin to realize who is really behind the wholesale shift from royalties to income taxes. The Harvard team recommended that the Bolivians also make this shift, and devised a two-part program for them. Political and economic realities forced the realization that there were very good reasons, aside from any question of potential levels of income under the competing systems, why the Bolivians wanted to stick with a royalties system: "the (royalty) is relatively simple to enforce while more rational taxes may lend themselves better to tax evasion."[48]

This is an understatement. The income tax depends on the use, by the corporation, of modern methods of accounting, which the corporate system has itself created and of which it has the most sophisticated command. The amounts of minerals exported, and the value of the exports, can be determined relatively easily, even given the widespread practice of transfer pricing. An income tax, on the other hand, gives a multinational corporation full scope for the exercise of accounting chicanery and the application of arbitrary prices not just for the transfer of goods, but for technology, salaries, and a wide range of services. Fred Goff, in the previously cited article on EXMIBAL, spells out some of these implications:

> Since taxes are figured on profits, it is in the interest of EXMIBAL's backers to make their money off operating costs, where possible, rather than profits. And inflated costs which EXMIBAL's backers can allocate to members of their financial interest group represent earnings at the expense of the Guatemalan government. INCO's

long-term contracts for EXMIBAL's management and technical sales and services give it wide latitude for juggling the books and allocating costs.[49]

When it is recalled that a high percentage of development costs of mines is now financed by debt finance (interest on which goes to expenses, rather than profits) it becomes clear just why income taxes are the preferred form these days and *by whom they are preferred.*

It is clear also that the introduction of income taxes in Bolivia is for the benefit of the multinationals and not the domestic private mining sector, for the latter were so ill-equipped with modern accounting methodology it was necessary for the Harvard group to propose a two-stage transition:

> (i) a tax on presumed income, taking regular and systematic account of actual cost developments, combined with a low-rate levy ("production royalty") to stabilize fiscal revenue; (ii) once this system is well established, a change-over to a net profits tax, *at least for firms in a position to eventually meet the accounting requirements of corporate taxation.* Application of a net profits tax thus might be limited to COMIBOL [the state-owned mining organization] and 25–30 private firms which account for about 80% of mining output. *Producers unable to prepare proper accounts would continue to be taxed on a presumed income basis.*[50]

In 1976 the government of Bolivia requested design of a standard accounting system for the mining industry from the Canadian International Development Association (CIDA).[51]

The purpose of IBRD Loan 1331 was to finance a new government exploration fund in Bolivia. The proposed exploration fund, it is explained, is necessary in order to assume the risks that private investors are no longer willing to take.

> International mining companies . . . are increasingly reluctant to undertake exploration in developing countries for reasons of perceived political risk, as well as possible inadequate financial gains. The large amount of investment and the long time span entailed (between 6–12 years) before any return can be realized make companies less willing to invest in countries where they perceive either political instability or host country goals incompatible with foreign private mining interests.[52]

The Bank therefore recommended that the government establish a mineral exploration fund to socialize the risk. The National Mineral Exploration Fund (FNEM) would be incorporated as an autonomous "public development enterprise" in order to minimize political interference in fund operations. The terms of the loans which will be extended to mining entrepreneurs by the fund are not only totally risk-free but carry substantial tax advantages:

> The attractiveness of FNEM exploration credits relate to their con- tingent nature and tax concessions granted by the Government to FNEM creditors [sic]. Repayment of the exploration credit is con- tingent on the identification and delineation of an economic ore deposit, and payments are only due when the ore deposit is ac- tually being mined. In addition to the major risk-bearing of the Fund, the Government granted in July 1978, to all mining com- panies repaying (then and in the future) FNEM credits, tax exemp- tions allowing 60% of the royalty payments to FNEM to be deducti- ble from the Government "regalia." Assuming an 8% p.a. royalty payment on mine output value, the royalty is then decreased by 4.8% to an effective rate of 3.2% of that value.[53]

It should be remembered that while the Bank is urging these subsidies and tax concessions to private mining companies in order to make Bolivia's conditions competitive with those in other countries, the concessions made by Bolivia will in turn put pressure on its competitors to match terms by themselves pro- viding more subsidies and concessions. It is clear that far from playing the role in which it fancies itself as "honest broker," guaranteeing a fair deal to all parties, the Bank is actively com- bating the efforts of Third World governments to retain a higher share of the value of their nonrenewable mineral resources.

To end this discussion of Bolivia: while the evidence is only circumstantial, the Bank's economic memorandum on Bolivia (1978) notes that there have been two recent changes in govern- ment mining policy favorable to private mining in recent years. "Until recently, sizeable proportions of potentially mineralized areas were declared fiscal reserves by the Government, thus precluding private exploration activities. . . . The authorities have, in the meantime, decided to open these areas to both national and foreign companies."[54] Was the decision a condition of Bank lending? Also, it is stated that in the past, fear of nationalization had inhibited the growth of the privately owned medium-sized mines. "However, a privately owned industrial Bank (BISA) has financed an increased number of mining ventures since 1974."[55] That was the year in which the Bank made its first loan in the mining sector; and its second loan was made to BISA.

Lending to State-Owned Mines

Of the other countries which have received World Bank loans for their state-owned mining sector, the least that can be said is that none display any hostility toward the foreign mining firms which were nationalized. In Chile the copper development corporation, CODELCO, received no Bank loans until after the junta assassinated Allende and took power; now the current regime is busily opening its mining sector to new foreign investment. A World Bank loan in 1976 provided for the expansion of production from CODELCO's mines and for the reorganization of CODELCO itself, the better to facilitate foreign investment in the copper sector. Anaconda, the biggest loser in the Allende nationalization, has taken its handsome compensation payment from the junta and is planning the most ambitious new copper mining project in Chile. Other American companies, such as Exxon, Superior Oil, St. Joe, Foote Minerals, and Marvis are staking claims as well. A key provision of Chile's new mining code mandates that compensation for any future nationalization must equal the total value of the deposit. And despite government denials, rumor persists that even CODELCO itself, operator of the mines nationalized by Allende's government, will soon be denationalized.[56]

In Peru a loan was made (also in 1976) to Centromin, the state corporation which now runs the nationalized Cerro de Pasco mine. This nationalization was carried out, according to Dorothea Mezger, at the request of the parent Cerro Corporation—because the mine and its facilities were aging, no more tax write-offs were possible, and the company preferred to invest in new projects. Cerro now owns 22.5 percent of the new Cuajone project in Peru, in which the International Finance Corporation also is an investor.[57]

In Zaire, Gécamines, the state corporation now running the former Union Minière properties, received a World Bank loan for expansion of copper and cobalt production in 1975. Union Minière's sister corporation, Société Générale des Minerais, is still marketing the produce of the mines, for a fat fee of which at least 85 percent is supposed to represent compensation.[58] The Bank apparently stipulated in its loan to Gécamines that the company cease making payments to the government for general budget purposes, "thereby reducing the contribution of the minerals sector to general economic development."[59] The stipulation does not seem to have stopped corruption, however; newspaper reports claim that $20 million or more per month of Gécamines' average $120 million production disappears into the pockets of government leaders.[60]

One more World Bank connection with the mining sector should be noted. In the Zaire nationalization, as also in the case of nationalization of the copper mines of Zambia, the agreements were deposited with the Bank-sponsored International Center for the Settlement of Investment Disputes (ICSID). The Latin American countries have all refused to join ICSID. The purpose of this institution is to ensure the foreign investor that the host country government will not be able to exercise its sovereignty by unilaterally changing the agreements or by adjudicating disputes in its own courts. It is also, of course, one more strand in the tightly reinforced and interconnected network of obligations that the Bank has helped to build for the protection of the international investor and an expression of distrust for the national judiciary of its Third World members.[61]

7

Oil and Gas

For the first thirty-two years of its existence, the World Bank refused to extend loans to member countries for the purpose of oil and gas exploration or production. As the Bank explained at the end of this era, this was due to two reasons: first,

> before 1973, petroleum production in most developing countries was uneconomic at prevailing international prices, and supplies from low-cost sources, mainly in the Middle East, were increasingly abundant; on the other hand, where the economic justification was not in doubt, private finance was readily available.[1]

Outside observers, however, had a somewhat different way of expressing it. Michael Tanzer, an independent consultant on oil, asserts that before 1973, the Bank "had mechanically followed the interests of the oil companies."[2]

> [B]ecause the companies had low-cost crude oil available from Venezuela and the Middle East, they had no incentive to explore for oil within the oil-importing underdeveloped countries. As a rule, if they evinced any sign of interest in indigenous oil exploration, it was for the purpose of blocking the governments of the countries from undertaking such exploration themselves. In line with this, the international oil companies used the power of their home governments and their influence in world organizations such as the International Monetary Fund and the World Bank to pressure the governments of the oil-importing underdeveloped countries not to use public funds to undertake indigenous oil exploration.
>
> The nominal argument used by these "aid-giving" foreign institutions was that "aid money" should not be diverted to oil exploration (or building government refineries) because the international oil companies had the vast pools of capital and experience

needed for this task. The fact that, as these sophisticated foreign agencies knew so well, the international oil companies had little incentive to explore for oil, despite their capabilities, was ignored. The real aim of these foreign agencies was to support the international oil companies in their profit-making activities.[3]

The oil companies, in brief, told the Bank to stay out of their territory and the Bank complied. At the same time the Bank was—consciously or unconsciously—vigorously promoting a type of development through its lending policies, which required an intensive use of oil in preference to other types of energy.

Promotion of Oil Dependence

It is a remarkable coincidence that in every major sector of lending the Bank has systematically favored the type of project that required oil or gas, either as a fuel or as a feedstock. For example:

—in transportation, the Bank policy shifted away from lending predominantly for railroads (as it did in the 1950s) to devoting the most substantial part of its funds to highway construction in the 1960s.[4] This of course favored the use of private cars, trucks, and buses, which not only required high investment in private capital but a continuous supply of motor fuels. In 1980 the Bank was forced to acknowledge that "coastal shipping, river and rail systems are several times as energy efficient as road vehicles when used as heavily loaded bulk carriers . . . in many developing countries transport systems are energy intensive and are largely dependent on imported oil."[5] It did not admit its own role in this evolution, however, which came about not only through its project lending but through its influence on national transportation planning in many of the borrowing countries.

—in electrical power generation, Bank policy shifted in a parallel fashion from its early preference for hydro projects to favoring thermal power plants, most of them fueled by oil. This shift was justified by new "advances" in cost-benefit analysis that stressed the high cost of capital and showed more favorable returns on investment for thermal plants. Thermal plants did have a modest initial cost but required a permanent source of fuel, which in most cases had to be imported. The Bank's 1980 energy study reported that in that year developing countries would use nearly 1.5 million barrels of oil per day (it is presumably meant per year), at a cost of around U.S. $16 billion, to generate electric power.[6]

—fertilizer plants, which utilize hydrocarbons as feedstock, have been the favored form of industrial development. In fiscal year 1979, 58 percent of total funds for individually financed industrial projects were committed for fertilizer plants. This percentage does not include phosphate and potash mines, which were also financed as industrial projects.

—in agriculture, the use of commercial fertilizers, primarily nitrogen-bearing products based on oil and gas feedstocks, has of course been an essential part of the entire modernization strategy, whether the fertilizers are or can be locally produced or have to be imported. Agricultural strategy also requires the use of petroleum-based pesticides and in many cases an increased degree of mechanization of agricultural processes.

I am not arguing that there was a sinister plot on the part of the Bank to drive its member countries into a life-or-death dependence on the oil companies. The strategy could be, and was, defended by the most reasonable tenets of international comparative advantage (don't produce your own at high cost when you can import it much more cheaply) and the Bank's borrowers were certainly not the only countries that were seduced into a heavy dependence on "cheap" oil imports—Europe and Japan being the prime cases of this syndrome. But whether there was a sinister plot or no,[7] that is exactly what happened. The upshot is that the oil companies have, in the words of oil economist Peter Odell, "something of a stranglehold over many of the countries in which they operate." Even in the era of cheap oil, moreover, many underdeveloped countries were paying much higher prices than world price levels or the cost of delivery would justify, prices that were due entirely to the oligopoly powers of the oil companies.[8]

The World Bank was in the years before 1973 *both* refusing to finance domestic exploration and production *and* systematically encouraging higher usage of imported oil. Whether there was a plot is not really the point: this sort of reversal can happen at any time a country is dependent on outside sources (or markets), as is inevitable with an "outward-oriented" development policy.

The Politics Behind the New Direction

After the precipitous oil price increases following 1973, the Bank began an internal re-evaluation of its refusal to lend in the fuel sector. For one thing, the higher international prices made it difficult to maintain that domestic production would be "un-economic" in comparison to imports for many potential pro-ducers. For another, the correspondingly precipitous rise in the deficits and debt burdens of many of the Bank's borrowers threatened the financial viability of the countries themselves and, in case of a major failure to meet debt obligations, a crisis in the international financial system itself.

We can obtain some insight into the process that led to the reversal of the Bank's previous policy from an unpublished paper prepared by a Bank official for a workshop on mining legislation.[9] Although the Bank had previously made loans for minerals development, the decision to begin lending for oil and gas development was closely associated with a decision to ex-pand minerals lending. According to this paper, the Bank's studies on increased involvement in the mineral resources sector, which had been initiated at the request of interested developing countries, were "intensified . . . when the U.S. Government, through then Treasury Secretary Simon, asked the World Bank to review the U.S. proposal about the establishment of an 'Inter-national Resources Bank,'"a proposal first floated by Secretary of State Kissinger at an UNCTAD meeting in Nairobi in May 1976 which had received little support from other governments.

According to this account, the U.S. proposal had originated in

the U.S. Government's awareness of increasing tensions between developing and developed countries in the natural resources field, which tensions were thought to lead to a decrease in the developed countries' mining and petroleum investment in the developing world and therefore ultimately to a decrease rather than an increase in worldwide mineral production. As one of the U.S. papers on the proposal put it, "the central purpose of the IRB is to correct a situation in which the pattern of foreign, primarily private resource investment seems to have been distorted because of a deterioration in the climate for such investments, causing commercially viable projects [in developing countries] to be deferred or dropped in favor of an investment in less economically justifiable projects in developed countries.[10]

The World Bank accepted the assignment to review the proposal, asking three questions: first, whether the problem did indeed exist; second, whether the IRB could be expected to resolve the problem; and third, "if the IRB could not be expected to be a workable cure, what other solutions to the problem there might be." Their answer to the first question was yes, there was definitely a problem of insufficient exploration and investment in the developing countries. The answer to the second question was, however, no, the Bank deemed the IRB proposal to be insufficient and unrealistic, closely resembling a failed proposal in the early 1970s to establish an international investment insurance agency.

This left the third question, and the Bank proposed a broadened role for itself as the preferable solution. It was found that the Bank could play two important roles:

[F]irstly, to provide some sort of "international presence" in helping to bridge the differences between host governments and foreign mining companies, the expectation being that this "presence" would lead to fairer and more lasting agreements for the exploration of mineral reserves in the developing countries and that it also might help to attract the foreign investment (particularly risk capital) necessary in order to increase mineral exploration and production in these countries; and secondly, to provide developing countries with the advice and assistance they would need to draw up and implement comprehensive plans for the development of their mineral resources.[11]

It was quite clear from the beginning that the Bank's new direction in energy lending was not intended to be a challenge or competition to the established international oil companies, but was meant to be an economic and political "presence" that would overcome their reluctance to invest in potentially unfriendly environments.

The Bank officially announced its new policy of lending for oil and gas production in July 1977, shortly after the communiqué of the London "economic summit" meeting in May, attended by the heads of government of the United States, Great Britain, West Germany, France, Italy, Japan, and Canada, issued an invitation for such a step:

> The oil-importing countries have special problems in paying for the energy supplies needed to sustain their economic development program. They require additional help in expanding their domestic energy production and to this end we hope the World Bank, as its resources grow, will give special emphasis to projects that serve this purpose.[12]

Two points were particularly stressed as the Bank announced its new policy direction. One was that the Bank would finance only a small portion of the financial needs of the sector.

> Most of the funds will have to come from foreign investors and the producing nations; international financial institutions such as the Bank would need to contribute only so much as to permit them to assume the responsibility for appraising and supervising projects and helping producing nations marshal the total funds required. . . . Token loans would be sufficient to ensure an adequate international presence in projects with a high potential for profit; in other cases, a substantially larger share of project financing by the Bank might be required.[13]

The other important point was that the Bank was planning to finance mainly oil and gas *production* rather than *exploration*. "Because financing of exploration activities is an area best left to risk capital, the Bank's role in this area would be a minor one, at the margins, and only in special cases: for geological, geochemical, and geophysical reconnaissance, and for better appraisal of promising discoveries."[14]

The Exploration Dilemma

But herein lay a problem. The production of oil and gas is expensive, but not in relation to the payoff; it is not risky. While oil companies might appreciate an "international presence" to protect their investment against nationalization, there is no powerful reason why the host countries would have to borrow from the Bank, rather than from other commercial sources, at the production stage; nor is their any reason why they should feel compelled to give foreign oil companies a share of production, profits, and control once oil had already been discovered.

On the other hand, oil exploration could not, because of the very real risk involved, be justified on cost-benefit grounds normally used to justify Bank project lending. In an attempt to straddle this contradiction, the Bank came up with two formulas that would give it a "presence" (and thus an implicit stick to use against governments tempted to renege on commitments to companies made before the resources were discovered) at the exploration stage without commiting any money.

> One of the main reasons why mining and oil companies did seem to increasingly shy away from exploration activities in developing countries was their fear—justified or not—that once a discovery was made the host country might become tempted to unilaterally change the rules of the game. For this reason, oil and mining companies have at times indicated to the World Bank that a World Bank presence in the project already at the exploration stage might go a long way in quieting these fears. Another action the World Bank could take, it was therefore decided, would be to try to get involved in mining and hydrocarbon projects at an earlier stage than it historically has been doing, i.e. before a discovery was made. Various ways of such an early involvement were studied and, in principle, approved.[15]

One of these ways was for the World Bank to make a token loan to the host country to assist it in financing a small portion of exploration activities jointly with the foreign sponsor, on condition that the foreign sponsor would repay the World Bank loan in case the exploration activities were unsuccessful.

The second approach involved a Bank presence at the exploration stage linked to lending for production if the exploration proved successful:

> The World Bank would participate in the negotiations between the foreign investor and the host country government, either by sitting down with them at the negotiation table or by providing comments from time to time on the draft contractual documents about the government's and the investor's rights and obligations regarding exploration and eventual production, as and when these documents were being negotiated between the parties. If the World Bank was satisfied with the fairness of the arrangements, it could then, at the request of the host country government, confirm to both parties concerned that if a discovery were made, and if the World Bank's normal lending criteria were met, the World Bank would consider a request by the host country to assist in financing production or related infrastructure facilities.[16]

The second arrangement was the one utilized in the agreement between Gulf Oil Corporation and Pakistan, which the Bank announced in a November 28, 1978, press release. Under terms of this agreement, Gulf agreed to pay 85 percent of the costs of drilling up to eight exploratory oil wells, with Pakistan paying the remaining 15 percent. If commercial discoveries resulted, they would be developed on a 50-50 basis. Royalties and taxes, it was announced, would be not less than 50 percent nor more than 55 percent of yearly net profits. (It was not specified whether the company or the country would decide whether a given discovery was "commercial" or not.) The World Bank announced that it would consider providing financing, and helping to arrange other financing, if production resulted from the exploration project.

"Although the bank will provide no cash unless oil is discovered," a news story in *Business Week* remarked of the deal, "exploration would not have begun unless the World Bank's role had been nailed down."

> Efrain Friedmann, assistant director of the bank's energy department, sees the bank providing the aura of confidence needed to draw private lenders and equity investors into the project. There is little chance of default on a World Bank loan, since doing so would

virtually destroy the credit of the borrowing nation. The participation of the bank in the three-way partnership provides Gulf with assurance against any breach of contract by Pakistan. World Bank participation in such deals is "absolutely critical" says Friedmann, and its effect can "save years in getting a project launched."[17]

This interpretation was confirmed by a Gulf executive in a later interview:

"Considering all the explosive difficulties there, we would not be involved were it not for the World Bank's participation," said Herbert Hansen, Gulf's Houston-based vice president in charge of government agreements.

The World Bank has agreed to help finance the cost of production facilities if oil is found; it already has $3 billion invested in non-oil projects in Pakistan which, according to Mr. Hansen, represent another "substantial presence, mitigating against political risk" and is "reassuring."[18]

At the same time the Gulf-Pakistan agreement was being negotiated, however, the Bank was also moving on another front. It was becoming clear that the Bank's hope in 1977 that relatively modest Bank financing would attract a much larger flow of investment from private sources was too sanguine. Although Gulf Oil professed itself pleased with the program, it was apparently the only enthusiastic major oil company and the Pakistan deal remained the only specimen of its genre. It was also evident that lack of interest by the international oil companies was not necessarily due to lack of oil. In fact (despite the world Bank's pre-1973 complacency that the companies were developing oil wherever it was commercially attractive), vast areas in the' underdeveloped countries had apparently never been properly surveyed. The Bank's own studies showed that "since comparatively large areas of the developing countries remained unmapped, there was a higher probability of successful exploration in developing countries."[19]

The adequacy of past and current levels of exploration is a highly debatable subject as a result of differing evaluations made by specialists and potential investors of geological prospects, expected costs, and to some extent, of political risk. A study made for the Bank suggests that in most non-OPEC countries recent and near-term exploration levels are likely to be inadquate for their potential requirements, let alone their current needs.

Only 10 out of these 70 countries are found to be adequately explored, and 38 inadequately. Of the 23 countries that are judged to have high or very high prospects of finding viable petroleum resources only 7 have been explored adequately, 6 have been explored moderately, and the rest inadequately.[20]

If the Bank stopped to ask why the international oil companies were not interested in exploring for undiscovered oil even in this era of high prices, they did not come up with the obvious answer: that the companies might not wish to expand supply and possibly bring prices down again.

And with company incentives for finding oil severely limited, even with the political risk covered by the Bank, few companies (apart from Gulf, in a special position because of its own inadequate crude supplies[21]) were willing to take on the financial risks of exploration. As one oil executive told *Business Week*, "It is a very good way for the bank to go, but neither the country nor the bank wants to take the exploration risk. Who pays for my dry hole in Madagascar? That is still the oil company's problem."[22]

The Abortive "Revolving Fund"

The next attempt of the World Bank to respond to this problem was to promote a proposal for a "revolving fund" for oil exploration, to be funded by contributions by OECD (Organization for Economic Cooperation and Development) and OPEC (Organization of Petroleum Exporting Countries) member countries. The Government Accounting Office (GAO) report from which the following account is taken did not specify the mechanics of the Fund's operations, but presumably it would have resembled the United Nations Revolving Fund for Natural Resources Exploration[23] and a minerals exploration fund financed by the Bank in Bolivia in that loans for exploration would be repayable only if exploration is successful and results in production, in which case the borrower would repay a percentage of the market value of the production over a specified span of years. Such a plan would in fact have resolved the problem of exploration risk (providing that the odds were judged accurately enough to ensure replenishment of the fund in good time) for the host countries. It might, however, have made the privately owned oil companies seem dispensable. As an Exxon executive explained to the *New York Times:*

> If you had the bank supporting a national oil company with 7 percent money, it would take out of the picture the established oil companies, which have to require a larger return. . . . If a field looks good, let us do it ourselves—that's what's bad about the bank loans for exploration.[24]

Perhaps for that reason it was rebuffed by the United States government when a Bank official proposed that it be considered by the 1978 Economic Summit meeting in Bonn. Although Canada and France endorsed the concept, the U.S. delegation objected on several grounds:

—The evidence was not conclusive that lack of capital was the primary constraint on energy exploration in LDC's [less developed countries].
—U.S. officials did not think that high risk exploration was an appropriate use of public funds.
—Because the Congress was showing considerable reluctance to meet normal U.S. financial contributions to the World Bank, U.S. officials did not think it would be wise to imply that the United States was prepared to commit additional funds to the Bank—even for energy purposes.[25]

The communiqué of the conference ignored the revolving fund proposal, but suggested "that the World Bank explore ways in which its activities in this field can be made increasingly responsive to the needs of the developing countries, and to examine whether new approaches, particularly to financing hydrocarbon exploration, would be useful."[26] According to the GAO report, the Bank's proposal had aroused "consternation" within the U.S. departments of energy, state, and the treasury. One worry was that official funds, practically on a grant basis, "would be very attractive, and their availability might hold back any trend,

for example, toward improved host government-company relations. *LDC governments might also be reluctant to compromise
on private contract terms if alternative financing were available. . . ."*[27](Emphasis added)

Finance for Exploration

U.S. opposition caused the Bank staff to drop the revolving
fund proposal and propose instead that the Bank itself bite the
bullet and agree to finance some oil and gas exploration projects.
On January 17, 1979, citing the mandate given by the Bonn
summit meeting, the Bank announced that its Executive Board
had approved a program of expanded assistance for oil and gas
production that could also include exploration. One new item
on the agenda was national energy planning, for which the Bank
would provide financing for expatriate consultants to help in
devising national plans and policies for the energy sector, and in
creating or strengthening a national energy authority. It may be
assumed that the experts financed for this purpose will not be
advocates of national energy autonomy.

Assistance for exploration would include (a) survey work,
financed with technical assistance loans and credits, and (b) exploratory drilling. Of the latter, the press release stated:

> The Bank is willing to help and advise member governments *and
> foreign collaborators* in concluding agreements for petroleum ex-
> ploration and production. . . . The Bank would consider making
> loans (or credits) to member governments of oil-importing devel-
> oping countries to cover their share of exploration costs underta-
> ken *in association with a foreign enterprise. In countries where
> foreign investors are unwilling to invest capital* in petroleum ex-
> ploration, the Bank would be prepared to consider lending to cover
> costs of exploration done by an exploration company under a
> service contract.[28] (Emphasis added)

The large oil companies for the most part expressed approval of
this program; indeed some of them had been involved in shaping it. The Bank had consulted with about twenty companies in

the year preceding the announcement.[29] Treasury Department officials told the GAO researchers that they did not solicit oil company views specifically on the new Bank policy or the defunct revolving fund proposal, but "over the years had been in fairly constant dialogue with oil company officials concerning U.S. energy policy."[30]

Gulf Oil, said a spokesperson, had been involved in the evolution of the present Bank program for three or four years. They felt that World Bank participation at the exploration stage was "a good idea to protect private capital from host governments unilaterally changing the rules after such projects begin to pay off."

> The Gulf spokesman said that after seeing news reports on the World Bank's consideration to finance oil and gas development projects, he called the Bank and discussed the concept with Bank staff and suggested that Gulf would like to participate in a trial project. The Bank agreed and from this came an agreement with the Bank and the Government of Pakistan for oil development and production. Since then Gulf has worked out a similar deal with Zaire and the Bank's International Finance Corporation. . . .
>
> He said that Gulf officials have had discussions with the Bank staff during development of the current program, as well as with officials of the Department of State and of the Treasury. He said that Gulf is in favor of the current program and is not concerned with the downscaling of the program from a separate fund of $500 million [for, among other reasons] *the necessary ingredient in a risky project is the Bank's presence and influence rather than its money.*[31] (Emphasis added)

A Mobil spokesperson told the GAO researchers that "World Bank staff contacted him directly and later visited Mobil headquarters in New York to specifically discuss the World Bank's potential role in stimulating oil exploration in LDCs." He said there was a "tremendous contrast of viewpoints" on the new World Bank role: "even within Mobil there are many who think it is a good idea and many who think it is not."[35] The only vocal opponent of the scheme was Exxon, the largest and richest of international corporations. Despite vigorous lobbying at the Bank, the departments of state, the treasury, and energy, and the Central Intelligence Agency, Exxon was unable to prevent the adoption of the proposal.[33] It finally took the step of sending a last-ditch letter to Secretary of the Treasury Michael Blumenthal, two days before public announcement of the Bank's expanded energy lending program, expressing its concern that the risk of exploration projects make them "ill-suited" to Bank lending and worrying that poor countries where oil exploration was unsuccessful "would be called on to pay the cost of such exploration anyway." Exxon's real concern, however, appeared to be that such a program would preempt industry control: "Finally, were the Bank to offer to make loan financing available for exploration in a particular country, it should do so only after ensuring the acreage involved had been offered to industry on reasonable terms."

Blumenthal's reply to C. C. Garvin, Jr., Exxon's chairman of the board, came weeks after the Bank policy had been announced and stood firm in its support for the program. He added reassuringly, however, that

> the Bank's primary role in this area, as in others, is that of a catalyst, facilitating increased private capital flows and maximizing the total effort. . . . the Bank hopes through facilitating survey work to encourage widespread dissemination of geological data both to reduce risks and to enlarge the possibilities for private bidding and participation in energy exploration and development.[34]

Exxon received no support from the other oil majors. Standard of Indiana, although professing neutrality on the merits of the World Bank plan, strongly dissociated itself from the position taken by Exxon in the letter to Blumenthal and reported it was actively looking for an opportunity to work with the Bank on a project to test the new program.[35]

Within a few months even Exxon was backtracking from its originally hostile position, claiming that the Garvin letter stemmed from a "misunderstanding" about the plan's intent and fear that it would replace companies, although Exxon still did not plan to participate.[36]

The previously quoted Exxon executive, now on loan from the corporation to the World Bank's energy section, explained the change of heart: "We think it's great if they want to help countries gather data, or lend them money for geologic survey work so they can evaluate their potential better. We only take exception to lending for exploratory drilling to generally inexperienced national oil companies."[37]

Other companies were enthusiastically backing the plan, and a new corporation was formed with the expressed intent of serving as a broker bringing together governments, companies, and the World Bank. Known as the International Energy Development Corporation, this had as shareholders Volvo of Sweden (now diversifying into oil exploration), Sulpetro, Ltd., a Canadian oil and gas company, the Kuwait Petroleum Corporation, and AZL Resources, a Phoenix-based agribusiness corporation. The chief executive officer of the new corporation is Maurice Strong, AZL's chairman and a former head of the Canadian national oil and gas corporation.[38]

The Bank's Role: An Evaluation

How we should evaluate the World Bank's role vis-à-vis foreign companies and host countries? The Bank itself claims to be playing the role of honest broker.

> Since the new policy about World Bank assistance for exploration was introduced just over one year ago [the first, 1977, decision is meant here—C.P.], there has been one case where draft petroleum exploration agreements between a member government and a foreign investor were submitted to the World Bank for comments and where—we like to think—these documents were subsequently substantially improved in the interest of the host country as a result of the comments made by the World Bank.[39]

The Bank's assistance to geological surveys can enhance the bargaining power of the host government:

> Accurate geological information is particularly valuable in negotiations between governments and private investors who are seeking to acquire exploration rights. A host country that can provide detailed geological information, when it opens an area for bids, increases the competition for exploration rights. . . .[40]

The Bank also intends to help build a "knowledgeable negotiating agency," the absence of which "may lead the government to ask for terms that do not offer a reasonable incentive to the investor or, on the contrary, to accept terms that are too favorable to the latter."[41]

It should be clear, however, that if the foreign oil companies have not heretofore been interested in exploring for oil and gas in this category of country, the Bank's advice must inevitably be concerned mainly with enhancing the conditions offered to the companies. A sampling of recent press releases announcing loans or credits for survey and exploration work seem to confirm this hypothesis:

> The Government of Somalia attaches high priority to the development of domestic hydrocarbon resources and wishes to attract foreign companies to undertake petroleum exploration. . . . [Consultants funded under the project will] assist in updating the legal framework and devising a strategy for promoting the country's petroleum potential and negotiating with petroleum companies. . . . As a result of this project it is expected that onshore tracts in Somalia will be ready to be offered for exploration by competitive bidding to companies by about mid-1981.[42]

> The $90 million Bank-financed project will . . . help the Bureau . . . develop leads which could attract foreign investments.[43]

> The project will support the government's efforts to discover petroleum by encouraging foreign oil companies to explore the most promising offshore areas of Honduras. . . . It also covers . . . consultant services to review the country's petroleum pricing and taxation system. . . .[44]

> The project is expected to improve knowledge of the productive potential of the hydrocarbon sector which will also help attract private investment for petroleum exploration and production.[45]

> Technical assistance will be provided for . . . promotion for exploration of the more promising areas with petroleum potential to foreign oil companies. It is expected that up to four blocks will be ready to be offered to oil companies as early as 1982.[46]

> Technical assistance will also be provided to strengthen the capacity of Turkey's General Directorate of Petroleum Affairs (GDPA) to attract foreign oil companies to explore for oil in Turkey.[47]

Consistent with the government's policy of encouraging cooperation between public and private ventures, a number of international oil companies have been granted concessions to explore for oil and gas in the Gulf of Thailand.[48]

According to the Bank's assistant director for energy, Efrain Friedmann, if the Bank hears complaints from private oil companies about the legislation or financial incentives in a particular country, it may hire consultants to talk with officials in that country about improving their energy laws.[49] (And also charge the consultants' fees to the proceeds of the energy loan, which the borrowing country has to pay back.)

This approach seems to be bearing fruit already. In Madagascar, which broke off exploration contracts with foreign oil companies in 1975 and nationalized Caltex and Exxon facilities the following year, a request for a Bank mission to review geological and drilling data led to a new exploration law that has attracted ten foreign bidders.[50] Turkey received a petroleum sector loan in November 1980 after liberalizing incentives for foreign investors in oil earlier in the year.[51]

Egypt, recipient of three World Bank oil and gas loans, has also liberalized terms for gas exploration by foreign companies. Brazil, Argentina, and Peru, all of which have received Bank loans for the energy sector, have concurrently opened exploration up to private investors.

In the 1960s the World Bank refused India's pleas for oil exploration financing. In the early 1970s, going it alone, the Indian Oil and Natural Gas Commission (ONGC) hired their own technology for offshore exploration, and discovered the enormously successful Bombay High fields. The World Bank has extended two loans for the development of Bombay High, one, its first-ever for oil or gas production, in 1977, and the second, a "jumbo" loan of $400 million in December 1980. The second loan coincided with a very controversial policy reversal—an open-door policy toward international oil companies that completely overturned the previous emphasis on self-reliance. Critics of the policy point out that the government has chosen to weaken the Oil and Natural Gas Commission, which had proved its expertise in independent exploration and production.[52] According to the Bank's project appraisal for the second loan:

> Another area where the Bank can now assist GOI [Government of India] and ONGC relates to oil exploration. Until recently GOI's policy regarding foreign oil companies has been hesitant, and not encouraging to the oil industry. The Government has recently announced a major policy change in this regard, and intends to enter into oil exploration agreements with foreign oil companies. The Bank is now providing assistance in this respect, in particular regarding (i) Government approach to negotiations with foreign oil companies; (ii) contractual matters (model contracts); and (iii) monitoring (probably by ONGC) of the oil companies' exploration and development activities after permits have been awarded.[53]

There is hardly room for doubt that the World Bank's jumbo loan was extended on condition that the country invite foreign investors in rather than spend the funds beefing up ONGC's independent capabilities.

It should be clear that every dollar spent by the host country (some of which are financed by the World Bank) reduces by that much the "risk" capital that has to be spent by any company subsequently coming on the scene. It is only logical that the country should be able to negotiate better terms at that stage, having financed the riskiest part of the business itself. What needs to be asked is, why does the host country need foreign participation (on an equity basis) at all, having established prospects good enough to attract it? Oil consultant Tanzer maintains that they don't. "Overall, I think the method of preferred choice is for countries themselves to put up their own capital, take the risks, hire the technology. Then, if they find oil, they control it and have the power to decide how to exploit it, including leaving it in the ground, producing it at a slower rate."[54] By contrast, under the World Bank program the host countries take over some if not all of the risk, but surrender at least part of the profits and control over the oil to the companies after the presence of oil is established. In the oil sector, as in many others, the Bank forces borrowing governments to finance the low-return, high-risk element of investment, leaving the rewards to the foreign corporations.

In truth, the underdeveloped countries are in an extremely difficult position. Despite Tanzer's optimism, few of them are today in a position to raise the large sums of risk capital involved, given their already heavy overhang of indebtedness, and particularly in the smaller countries the odds may be heavily against finding any oil at all. The abortive "revolving-fund" plan that the World Bank proposed, only to have it shot down by the U.S. government, might have been a good solution to the problem *if* it were administered as a tool to promote national financial independence, and not (as the existing Bank program) as a shotgun to force Third World countries into marriage with the international oil companies. It would appear that such an idea is at least as utopian in today's world as the suggestion that each country should go it alone. Even the much more conservative plan for vastly expanded energy lending through an "energy affiliate" of the World Bank, proposed by McNamara in August 1980 and supported by the Carter administration, has been vetoed by the Reagan administration.[55]

The Proposed Energy Affiliate

The Reagan administration's justification for rejecting the proposed $25 billion energy affiliate is contained in a Treasury Department report issued on July 28, 1981.[56] This report purported to examine the Bank's past lending to the oil and gas sector in order to ascertain whether it had been preempting private equity investment. Specific projects and categories of projects were examined as to whether their effect on private investment had been positive, negative, or neutral.

Exploration promotion projects, in which governments are advised on how to attract private investment in exploration, were approved as they "could be expected to generally support private investor interest." Infrastructure projects such as a gas pipeline in Thailand were deemed to be an appropriate field for bank financing and to have a favorable or neutral impact on foreign investment. The "Letter of Cooperation" strategy used by Gulf Oil in Pakistan was regarded as "particularly promising" for companies who seek involvement in order to serve as an implicit political guarantee, but it was pointed out that this had involved as yet no actual loan.

Special praise was reserved for Bank conditionality, which could be used to change host government policies adverse to foreign investment, including unwillingness to release promising acreage to exploration.

> To increase foreign private investment in oil and gas development reduction in average host government tax rates or other policy changes (such as depreciation, accelerated cost, recovery, etc.) having a similar effect would be beneficial. Here, the "neutral" stance of the Bank can play an important role. As a multilateral "development advisor" it can help LDC's revise their incentive structure to encourage investment. . . .[57] (Quotation marks in original)

"Highly significant policy changes" in terms of overcoming political opposition to private, foreign involvement in energy development have already taken place in Argentina, Brazil, and India, the report noted approvingly. It was suggested, however, that the acreage which India opened up for foreign investment in 1980 was not the most attractive and that further Bank leverage might be needed to pry open the most promising areas (such as the Godavari Basin) "by conditioning Bank financing on the host government's agreement to allow private companies to share in such exploration (and subsequent development)."[58]

The Treasury report took issue, however, with most Bank loans for exploration drilling and some loans for production of proven fields. Exploration financing, it complained, may have the effect of making private capital superfluous.

> Exploratory drilling has traditionally been financed from private equity capital put at risk; this is the price private companies pay for access to potential oil reserves. Once this cost has been incurred and substantial resources delineated, national oil companies have little incentive to turn to private foreign companies to share in the profits from exploiting such discoveries.[59]

And production loans for proven reserves could obtain credit on commercial terms. The loans to India, with an estimated rate of return of 70 to 100 percent, are cited as an example.

Increased Bank lending offers LDC governments much lower cost alternative financing—which serves to encourage the expansion of state oil and gas companies at the expense of private capital and may result in hardened contract terms where private companies are involved.[60]

There remains a core of disagreement between the Reagan administration, representing the interests of the oil majors, and the World Bank, increasingly concerned with the balance of payments impact of massive oil imports on its already heavily indebted borrowers. The disagreement focuses on the need and desire of Third World countries with heavy oil import needs for their own production capacity. The Treasury report admits that such countries, which are not likely to be good sources for export oil, are not attractive to private investment.

> In some cases, foreign investment may be less attractive in countries with large oil import needs and (concomitant) balance of payments problems. It appears that large integrated companies primarily interested in assuring crude supplies for downstream operations are particularly affected. Even smaller companies may be marginally more reluctant to invest in heavily oil import dependent countries such as Turkey because continuing balance of payments problems may result in difficulties in converting local currency earnings for remittance. A similar problem arises with discoveries of reserves of non-associated gas. . . . oil companies find it difficult to attain an adequate and reliable return on development of gas solely for LDC domestic consumption.[61]

But from the viewpoint of the country concerned, such small fields might play an important role in relieving balance of payments constraints, and the Bank is not yet ready to give in to the oil companies on this point.

A May 26, 1981, memorandum from the Bank's Energy Department director to an executive director points up the conflict:

> It is inevitable that national and corporate interests sometimes diverge: a country is concerned with the immediate impact that even a small discovery would have on the economy, while a foreign investor determines project priorities in the context of a worldwide network of producing, refining, and marketing units. Furthermore, while the rapid oil price increases in recent years have made exploration more profitable across the board, companies naturally

focus their initial interest on producing areas and large structures. They may, in time, turn to higher risk areas or small structures, but most LDCs, crippled by huge import bills cannot afford the wait until they reach the top of the companies' priority list.[62]

Mendaciously the Treasury report interprets this memorandum as meaning that the Bank is willing to supply financing even where private sector funds might be available, whereas it is clear that private companies are not interested in the areas in question, and are taking the dog-in-the-manger position that the Bank should not be allowed to finance such projects even though they themselves are not interested.

For all its efforts to propitiate the oil companies in devising its energy development programs, a gulf remains between the interests of the oil companies and those of the international banks who are (belatedly) becoming alarmed at the prospects for servicing of their massive Third World lending. Commercial bankers contacted by the magazine *Multinational Monitor* ridiculed the Treasury's assertion that the World Bank displaces private capital lending, and indicated that they found the Bank's energy lending to be a positive advantage to their interests.[63] At the end of 1981 there was speculation that the Bank, with the support of its European members, would plow ahead with the plans for its energy affiliate and hope that the United States would eventually come around. The opposition of the OPEC countries to the creation of the affiliate (because they object to developed country control of the organization) will probably kill any such ideas, however.[64]

8
Agriculture and Rural Development

Exporters can best make certain of supplies
by encouraging cultivators to borrow on the
security of their crops; importers of western
goods can sell more if the cultivators enjoy easy
credit; and the more that cultivators borrow the
greater is the profit of western banks which supply the fluid capital essential to the working of
modern economic machinery. Thus exporters,
importers, and bankers all gain by the entangle-
ment of the cultivator in debt, and, however
much they deplore the consequences, they must
as men of business work on business lines.
—J. S. Furnivall, *Colonial Policy and Practice*

The problem of rural poverty in the Third World is severe.
Millions of men and women farm tiny parcels of poor or ex-
hausted soils inadequate to support them at a decent level.
Millions more work as tenants, paying a large proportion of their
produce to nonworking landowners, or as laborers who have no
land of their own to farm and must sell their labor for a pittance
on a daily or seasonal basis. Still more millions have been driven
to seek a precarious existence in city slums because they find no
possibility of supporting life in the countryside.

The cartel of international development institutions led by the
World Bank proposes agricultural "modernization" as the only
possible solution to this spectacle of misery. Massive transfers of
capital, in the form of fertilizers, pesticides, earth-moving equipment, construction materials, and expensive foreign consultants,

will enable the soils of the Third World to grow more. And if the distribution of this produce is so unequal that it is itself a cause of poverty, as is generally recognized, then this "arsenal" of modern inputs and techniques will be aimed more precisely at "target" groups of the rural poor, thus enabling them to emulate their well-to-do neighbors by becoming modern on a miniature scale.

Posing as champions of the small farmer, the World Bank and most other bilateral and multilateral "development" agencies are in fact a major part of the problem of rural poverty. As this chapter will demonstrate, the real purpose of their policies and projects is not the abolition of poverty or even the improvement of the lives of poor people, but the appropriation of their land for production to serve the markets of North America, Western Europe, Japan, and the elites of their own capital cities. The new wrinkle of this modernization strategy is the appreciation by the international development policymakers that it may be more efficient, even in capitalist terms, to allow small farmers to remain on their land—as supervised, unfree labor—than to run large farms and plantations with a hired labor force.

Peasants will be forced to "develop" despite themselves, with little choice in the matter. But even while this new strategy is applied sporadically, large numbers of peasants are being evicted from their lands in the name of development—not just for the creation of new and larger farms, but for the building of dams, roads, tourist complexes, and mines (all financed by the world Bank and its affiliates), which continue to swallow small peasant holdings and send their proprietors into city slums. And those farmers who are allowed to remain will be virtual development peons—controlled by coercive, manipulative, and all too often ignorant developers so that they will deliver their surplus: in the form of produce to multinational traders, in the form of payments to the international corporations who sell farm machinery, chemicals, and management services, and in the form of taxes to their national elites.

Bank Lending in Support of Agribusiness

Lending that was specifically intended for agricultural development took a minor place in the Bank's program during its first fifteen years. Over the period FY 1948–63, Bank lending to agriculture amounted to only $628 million, or 8.5 percent of its total lending. Most of this money went for dams and irrigation systems. If agriculture was relatively unimportant in Bank thinking, however, the impact of its projects was not minor in the areas which the Bank "aided." Furthermore, some loans that were not considered "agricultural" have in fact contributed essential infrastructure to the agribusiness sector. A case in point is the development of large estates on irrigated land in northwest Mexico.

The northwest of Mexico contains unusually flat and fertile riverine land in a zone of mild temperatures. A modest amount of irrigated and riverine land was developed for commercial crops such as sugar cane in the early half of this century (and in the process the indigenous inhabitants, the Yaquis, were massacred, enslaved, and driven off their lands). But in the 1950s, with World Bank loans assisting the construction of major new dams and the extension of modern irrigation systems, the agriculture of the northwest took a great leap forward. Between 1952 and 1958 the total area under irrigation in that region more than doubled. A new class of private owners, more modern than the old hacendados, acquired the most desirable of the newly opened lands; although limited by law to 100-hectare holdings, they could amass much larger estates by nominally assigning land titles to various family members. The politically weak small peasants, whether on private plots or communal (*ejido*) holdings, were excluded from the distribution of the new lands and left with inadequate holdings of inferior lands. Some of the *ejido* lands have since been abandoned because salinization from poorly maintained irrigation works has destroyed the fertility of the soil; other lands have been rented out to private farmers because the ejidatarios could not make a living for their families on the amounts of land they held (most of the ejidatarios were estimated to have less than ten hectares apiece).

It was not just the dams and irrigation works financed by the World Bank which made possible the development of large commercial agriculture in northwest Mexico. Without efficient transportation networks and power supplies, the agriculture of the northwest could never have developed into a large-scale export enterprise. Therefore World Bank loans were allocated to hydroelectric power projects serving the area, and to the rehabilitation of an old railway, the Pacifico, which runs north and south along the coast from Guadalajara to Nogales, Arizona— the gateway to the U.S. market for the cotton, rice, fruit, and vegetables grown on the irrigated estates. And when inadequate drainage threatened to make the entire irrigation program self-defeating, the World Bank poured new loans into the search for a solution.[1]

The social problems spawned by this "integrated regional development" have proved to be a time bomb for Mexico, and for its northern neighbor. Some of the impoverished peasants have migrated to Mexico's cities to become the urban poor. Many, possibly millions, have become legal and illegal immigrants in the United States. But despite this massive export of humans, enough poor peasants remain in the Mexican northwest to threaten the tenure of the agribusiness interests with populist expropriation.

New Directions in the 1960s

In 1963, prompted by the U.S. government,[2] the Bank decided to increase its support for agriculture and to diversify its lending into technical services, rural road construction, processing industries, storage, marketing, forestry, and fishing. By the end of the 1960s the share of agriculture in total lending rose to almost 19 percent.

In 1964 the International Finance Corporation (IFC), a member of the World Bank Group specifically mandated to finance private enterprise, began to acquire shares in privately owned companies, including agribusiness ventures. Between 1964 and 1976, the IFC committed $46 million in the form of loans and equity to "large and generally corporate enterprises which manage the production and/or processing of agricultural goods for domestic consumption or for export."

The agribusiness recipients of this capital through 1976 are listed in Table 8.1 on pages 212 and 213.

What neither the table nor the accompanying article reveal is that many of these agribusiness entities are subsidiaries and affiliates of large foreign corporations. Bud Senegal, for example, which received three commitments, was until 1976 an affiliate of the California corporation Bud Antle, Inc. In Senegal Bud produced vegetables flown to the affluent European market and, in the off season, livestock feed.[3] (See Chapter 9.) Similarly, "Hellenic Food Industries" is a subsidiary of Del Monte, which operates in an area of Greece where the World Bank has financed irrigation facilities. The Iran-California Corporation, which was organized to exploit dam and irrigation facilities the World Bank built in Iran, is run by the Trans World Agricultural Development Corporation of California, in which the Bank of America held a substantial interest. The same year that the Guatemalan flour milling concern received the first IFC agribusiness credit, 1959, it began an affiliation with General Mills, which continues to the present. The Venezuelan deviled ham factory is a subsidiary of William Underwood Co. of Boston; Protinal of Venezuela, which has received two commitments, is affiliated with Pillsbury; the Ethiopian sugar estate has a Dutch parent company; the tea company in Rwanda has an unnamed "private U.S. sponsor." Private banks that share in the financing of these projects include the Northwest International Bank of New York, Chase Manhattan, Bank of America (in Morocco as well as Iran), and unspecified British and Spanish banks. And these are just the names that could be gleaned from IFC annual reports as each loan commitment was made; there are doubtless more which are not named.

Through supporting these enterprises, this World Bank affiliate is actually financing a *regressive* land reform because the corporations benefiting from these loans often use them for the purpose of acquiring the necessary land by buying out smaller agriculturalists. As the Bank explains in its public relations organ, *Finance and Development*:

Table 8.1
IFC Commitments in the Agribusiness Sector

Fiscal Year	Country	Project	Description
1959	Guatemala	Industria Harinera Guatemalteca, S.A.	Flour milling
1959	Chile	Fideos y Alimentos Carozzi, S.A.	Pasta manufacturing
1960	Colombia	Industrias Alimenticias Noel, S.A.	Manufacturing of pasta, crackers
1960	Tanzania	Kilombero Sugar Company, Ltd.	Sugar
1961	Venezuela	Diablitos Venezolanos, C.A.	Production of deviled ham
1964	Tanzania	Kilombero Sugar Company, Ltd.	Sugar (2nd commitment)
1964	Chile	Fideos y Alimentos Carozzi, S.A.	Pasta (2nd commitment)
1965	Colombia	Industrias Alimenticias Noel, S.A.	Pasta (2nd commitment)
1965	Colombia	Almacenes Generales de Depósito Santa Fé, S.A. "ALMAVIVA"	Grain storage
1966	Morocco	Compañia Industrial del Lukus	Tomato and pepper cannery
1966	Colombia	Industria Ganadera Colombiana, S.A.	Cattle fattening
1968	Ethiopia	HVA—Metahara, S.C.	Sugar estate and mill
1969	Venezuela	Protinal, C.A.	Animal feed mixing, storage and distribution

1972	Senegal	Bud Senegal, S.A.	Vegetable growing
1973	Venezuela	Protinal, C.A.	Animal feed mixing (2nd commitment)
1973	Iran	Iran California Company	Commercial farming
1974	Senegal	Bud Senegal, S.A.	Vegetables (2nd commitment)
1974	Nigeria	Lafiagi Sugar Estate	Sugar
1974	Philippines	RFM Corporation	Manufacturer of various foods
1975	Greece	Hellenic Food Industries, S.A.	Tomato canning
1976	Philippines	Philagro Edible Oils, Inc.	Copra oil processing
1976	Senegal	Bud Senegal, S.A.	Vegetables (3rd commitment)
1976	Rwanda	Société d'Investissement Rwandaise du Thé, S.A.R.L.	Tea processing
1976	Ecuador	Sociedad Agícola e Industrial San Carlos, S.A.	Sugar
1976	Nicaragua	Propiedades Azucareras de Nicaragua, Limitada	Estate sugar growing and milling

Source: John W. Lowe, "The IFC and the Agribusiness Sector," *Finance and Development* (March 1977): 26.
Investments correspond to those designated under "Food and Food Processing," in the IFC's Annual Reports. See the Annual Reports for amounts. Projects are listed by commitment; in some cases disbursements have not been made. Fiscal year ends June 30.

The financing of large land acquisitions, conceptually speaking, involves the refinancing of the holding of an asset (land) by one group as opposed to another. The basic question is which owners, in terms of general policy, are the more desirable ones. The answer should be: those that will develop the land most effectively. The assemblage of large tracts of land for agribusiness projects can greatly increase agricultural productivity and allow large economies of scale in agricultural production.[4]

The article admits to some embarrassment because some of the land acquired by the "very large schemes" that they have financed is in fact not developed but held for capital appreciation; in fact this may (as in the case of cattle-grazing projects) contribute more to the profitability of the project than the sale of fat cattle. This would seem indeed to be a glaring case of land transfer that is not being productively used.

Bank Lending to Livestock

"Lending for livestock operations continues to be the single most important type of credit activity," the Bank's sector policy paper on agricultural credit reported in 1975. Livestock loans constituted nearly one-third of all Bank credit projects at that date, and in Latin America the figure was extremely high—70 percent. Between 1959 and 1973, the World Bank authorized a total of sixty-three loan projects with a beef component, involving $839.2 million and $1,004 million more of local funding. For 1974–1980 the Bank planned seventy additional loan projects "with a beef component," involving $1.4 billion, of which 63 percent was to go to Latin America and the Caribbean.[5] Of twelve agriculture/rural development loans made in Central America to the end of April 1978, three were exclusively for beef production and six more contained large components for livestock raising.[6]

The purpose of these loans was not to increase local consumption of animal protein, but to supply the affluent North American market for utility grade beef used in hamburgers and frankfurters. Livestock promotion is perhaps the most socially detrimental form of agriculture; Ernest Feder has charged that "increased beef cattle and meat production in the third world represents a far greater direct, immediate and long-range danger to nutrition ... than the green revolution, and an enormous additional threat to the survival of the peasantry."[7] And Beverly Keene asks:

> Why beef cattle for export, and not rice and beans and other basic foods so essential to a hungry people? Why beef cattle, so extensive in its use of land, the scarce resource in Central America, and with so little demand for labor when millions are seeking employment? As in its other operations, the interest of the World Bank in promoting livestock in Central America does not seem compatible with a desire to confront the conditions and structures which produce hunger and poverty.[8]

The expansion of cattle ranching inevitably favors the rich and powerful over the poor and defenseless, as peasants and indigenous groups are forced off their land to allow its conversion to pasture, and crop lands are diverted from the production of human nourishment to that of cattle fodder. Where ranch expansion does not directly displace subsistence agriculture it requires the destruction of forests, which is hastening the ecological deterioration of agricultural land in Central America at an alarming rate (see Chapter 10).

By the Bank's own admission, most of its livestock loans go toward the development of large-scale commercial ranches.[9] One Paraguayan rancher, the owner of 17,300 acres, borrowed $48,000 under an IDA program in 1966.[10] Both Feder and Keene dispute the Bank's claim, in a few of its programs, that it is aiding "small" ranchers. Feder discovered that while FIRA (the Mexican agency that rediscounts livestock credits for commercial banks under the World Bank program) "has repeatedly pretended that it is financing mainly the ejidatarios and other smallholders," its own statistics do not support this claim. In one ranching community in the state of Veracruz, Feder estimates that about three-fourths of the funds went to the rich.[11] And Keene found that in Honduras and Costa Rica, "what the Bank calls 'small' is not always so small," since many of the beneficiaries are among the 12 percent of ranches that comprise more than 100 hectares.[12]

The "Green Revolution"

A new phase of Bank lending to agriculture began in 1969, when it financed a project in India for the production of seed of high-yielding varieties of food grains, a key component of the green revolution. The green revolution, which was prematurely hailed as the solution to the world food problem, brought in its wake new types of agribusiness interest in Third World agriculture. The new varieties of wheat and rice, hailed as "miracle" seeds, needed heavy inputs of fertilizers, herbicides, insecticides, and farm machinery for their success. Indeed, the point of the entire seed-selection process was the development of a strain that would most efficiently convert energy in the form of chemical fertilizers into energy in the plant grain, without counterproductive side effects such as "lodging," in which a tall, slender stalk is unable to support the weight of the fertilizer-swollen grain. The Bank provided and continues to provide funds for agricultural credit, which are re-lent through a variety of national institutions (commercial banks, development banks, special crop and project authorities, cooperatives, and even private traders and merchants) and which must be spent on such purchased inputs for the production process. The supply of credit and the conditions on which credit is supplied serve to introduce the farmer to purchased commercial inputs and in fact to enforce the use of such inputs.

As a result of Bank support to India's green revolution, "India's progress toward achieving economic self-sufficiency in food grains within the space of a few short years has done much to highlight . . . the so-called 'second-generation' problems of the green revolution."[13] This euphemism refers to the fact that despite increased production achieved in some countries in some years by the application of fertilizer and imported technology to high-response varieties of seeds, problems of food distribution, land distribution, and even the security of yields have worsened in precisely the areas of greatest success. Even if India does produce enough food now to feed all its people, all the people are clearly not getting enough food. Many small farmers have lost their land, and tenants and sharecroppers their rights to share the produce of the land they till, because the enhanced productivity and value of land have tempted large landowners to acquire more land and switch to systems of hired rather than tenant labor. And the ecological and genetic effects of the new seeds have meant that whole areas have been vulnerable to blight, or rodent attack, or insufficiency of water supply.[14]

The semiofficial history of the Bank gives several examples of agricultural loans that have had the effect of worsening the distribution of land and income in the borrowing country: "a remarkably successful IDA credit" that helped finance tubewells and pumping plants in West Pakistan and a $27 million loan for agricultural credit, also to Pakistan, benefited only large farmers.[15] Similarly, in Colombia "medium- and large-scale producers appear to have been the principal beneficiaries of the agricultural and industrial credits the Bank Group helped to make possible."[16] Irrigation in Mexico and livestock loans in other Latin American countries had the same effect.[17] "In Colombia, Ethiopia, and Pakistan, the new technology financed by loans contributed to the displacement of tenants. This was due to the lack of supporting changes in the institutional structure, especially land tenure."[18] Rather than changing or dismantling the type of lending program that has such effects, however, the Bank chose to *add* yet another type of program to its expanding repertory: rural development, in which the emphasis is supposed to be on reaching the "small farmer."

The Attack on Self-Provisioning Peasantries

There are still large areas of the world where the farming population participates in the cash economy only marginally, growing the bulk of their own food needs in small plots on which a large variety of plants are grown intercropped, or herding animals that supply protein foods and a small surplus for trade. Such areas are found in fairly wide regions of Africa and Oceania, with smaller pockets in relatively remote parts of Latin America and Asia peopled mainly by cultural minorities. The income of such people is low in cash terms, but this does not necessarily mean that they are deprived of basic necessities, or consider themselves poor and in need of "development."

For example, the Kalinga and Bontoc peoples of Mountain Province in the Philippines are regarded by most of their countrypeople as backward and primitive. But they consider themselves to be

> among the most prosperous and secure in a country where many agricultural workers live a marginal existence. There are no absentee landlords here, as the land is held communally and is not regarded as anyone's private property. The people grow enough food to support themselves and still have enough left over to earn the cash necessary to purchase tools and housing materials.[19]

These peoples are in the news because their self-sufficient way of life is threatened by a planned dam project, which will inundate their spectacular steep hand-built rice terraces in order to produce electric power for mines and for urban residents. Sophisticated enough to discover the plans intended to relocate them, to organize national coalitions of support and international publicity, the Kalingas and Bontocs have vowed to wage guerrilla war if necessary to prevent the building of the dam, for which the World Bank is financing a large downstream irrigation component. Other minority groups in the southern Philippines are preparing campaigns of resistance to similar plans to build dams for electric power on their own lands.

Even more revealing than this example are the comments in a World Bank country report on the native farmers of Papua New Guinea (PNG):

> A characteristic of PNG's subsistence agriculture is its relative richness: over much of the country nature's bounty produces enough to eat with relatively little expenditure of effort. The root crops that dominate subsistence farming are "plant and wait" crops, requiring little disciplined cultivation. . . . Until enough subsistence

farmers have their traditional life styles changed by the growth of new consumption wants, this labor constraint may make it difficult to introduce new crops.[20]

To be sure, not all self-provisioning farmers exist in such a happy state of primitive affluence. Most, it may be surmised, work long hard seasons on poor and difficult soils—in large part because the better lands have already been appropriated for commercial agriculture. It must be stressed that they are not isolated from markets linking them to the national, and even the international, economy. Some part of their crops they may have to sell in order to pay taxes and rent; otherwise they participate voluntarily in these markets on a relatively small scale, trading for the few outside amenities that they need or fancy—metal tools, China teapots, plastic shoes, cloth—while still relying on their own plots to provide the bulk of their diets. They are not dependent on the market for the near totality of their sustenance, as "modern" people are.

While it is not claimed that their situation is idyllic, these are by no means the most severely disadvantaged inhabitants of the Third World. But, in the current language of the World Bank, self-provisioning agriculture is called "subsistence" farming and falsely equated with poverty (as in "level of subsistence"). When poverty is defined in terms of money income, such farmers are automatically included because cash income and expenditures are low. But in a poor country, a self-provisioning farm family with an annual cash income of only a hundred dollars a year may well be leading a more comfortable and healthy life than a family in a North American slum with a cash income of several thousand dollars.

A pointed example is provided by Cynthia Hewitt de Alcantara's account of a Yaqui community in northwest Mexico, which was engulfed by an irrigation project in the 1950s. The community, Potam, was inhabited by members of the Yaqui tribe who had returned to their homeland after a diaspora had scattered them throughout Mexico and the southern United States. They were not ignorant of the modern world; most had worked in it, under unfavorable conditions; all of the members of the community spoke Spanish and a few knew English as well.

Deliberately choosing to build a self-sufficient unit that would supply as many of their needs as possible, they needed money for only a few purchased items, such as clothing, coffee, and sugar. The money which they earned through sales of produce, handicrafts, and occasional work for Mexican farmers "never seemed to exceed 700 pesos a year for any family and was generally much less."[21]

The construction of the Alvaro Obregón dam made the Yaqui system of subsistence agriculture unviable by depriving them of their water supply, and in order to survive they were forced to join the system of irrigated cultivation administered by the government. But "the purpose of the commission was much broader than simply remedying an acute shortage of water in a subsistence farming area. Government representatives were equally intent upon utilizing the occasion of the construction of irrigation works as the entering wedge of a programme to commercialize Yaqui agriculture."[22] A mandatory, capital-intensive agricultural technology was introduced, and heavy indebtedness was the result.

> Deprived of the possibility of living from the produce of subsistence plots, inhabitants of indigenous communities along the Yaqui river could no longer survive without money. . . . A typical annual farm income per family during the 1950s thus oscillated around 3,000 to 4,000 pesos. This was four to five times the amount of money required by a Yaqui household in the 1940s but innumerable needs formerly met without money had to be covered by it. Observers of the time, including Yaquis, agreed that it was absolutely insufficient: the anthropologist Martinez Matiella reported that "very few Yaquis do not long for the time when . . . they produced subsistence crops, and they insist that they had corn and beans for the whole year, with money left over for clothing."[23]

Hewitt concluded, emphatically, that there is "no necessary correlation between monetary income and basic wellbeing."[24]

The Destruction of Subsistence Farming

World Bank policy statements make it clear that the real aim of its smallholder programs is the destruction of what is left of so-called subsistence production and the integration of all agricultural lands into the commercial sector through the production of a "marketable surplus" of cash crops, for the domestic market or for export.

"Rural Development," states the sector policy paper with that name, "is concerned with the modernization and monetization of rural society, and with its *transition from traditional isolation to integration with the national economy*"[25] which in turn is closely integrated with the international economy. It aims at "greater interaction between the modern and traditional sectors, especially in the form of increased trade in farm produce and in technical inputs and services."[26] Agricultural credit, according to another sector policy paper, is especially important to small farmers "if they are to produce a marketable surplus and thereby contribute to the development process."[27] "The Bank will continue to support special project authorities, such as those created in limited areas of Africa, *as instruments to draw farmers from subsistence to commercial agriculture.*"[28] The Bank's director of Agriculture and Rural Development stated the purpose baldly when he wrote, "The traditional, small-farm sector would have to become the producer of an agricultural surplus rather than the provider of surplus labor, as it had been in the past."[29]

This incessant emphasis on drawing poor people into the market economy evades the question as to whether these people are really in need of this kind of help, and whether they wish to be dragged into a dependence on the market. But from the Bank's point of view it is explicable, probably even inevitable. The "poorest of the poor" in its member countries are the victims either of landlordism, or of the already accomplished "modernization" of agriculture in the most accessible areas (or both). They have either migrated from the rural areas to the cities, and thus ceased to be a rural problem, or form the rural labor force, whose continued degradation is essential to the profitability of commercial agriculture, or they deliver the surplus they produce to their landlords. For the first group the Bank will build water spigots in urban slums. For the second the Bank will do nothing, because it is allied with the commercial farmers. Although the Bank talks a lot about creating employment, it is never suggested that this should be to such an extent as to raise the average of real wages throughout the society; on the contrary, Bank policy strives to keep wages low, in order to keep prices "competitive" on the world market. The third group can be helped only by reforms of the tenure system, which the Bank timidly endorses in a very general way, if the landlords are the traditional sort and not modernizing agricultural entrepreneurs.

Wherever landlords are prevalent, however, they typically have strong ties with both the local and national government. If the Bank made a serious attempt, in a specific country, to use its leverage to insist on some sort of land reform, it could find itself unwelcome in that country; landlords do not willingly commit suicide as a class, even in return for development aid. And if the Bank goes ahead with a poverty-oriented project in a landlord-dominated district, its activities will be tolerated by the local elites only so long as they can be effectively subverted or co-opted.

The attack on self-provisioning communities, on the other hand, will receive the wholehearted support of the borrowing government, which shares the Bank's hope that these citizens, until now relatively unproductive from the point of view of the national economy, will contribute their surplus to exports, to urban markets, and to the government directly in taxes. There will be no objections from the elites, and overcoming the resistance of the target population becomes a fascinating sociological challenge.

For the small farmers *do* resist—sometimes actively, as the Kalingas and Bontocs are threatening in the Philippines—but far more often passively, through a lack of interest in the improvements that development experts are eager to thrust upon them. It might even be said that the problem of how to motivate peasants to "modernize" is the chief burden of agricultural development literature.[30] This traditionalism would be self-defeating if the proffered development truly promised a better life for all. It is more likely that in most cases the small farmer takes a close look at what is offered, weighs it against his or her present situation, and finds it wanting.

Commercial farming means risks, additional to the natural phenomena that are intrinsic risks of farming anywhere:[31] the risks of market prices that fluctuate according to happenings in other parts of the globe, of input prices that may not be commensurate with the increased output, of increased vulnerability to pests when uniform genetic stock is used, and so forth. The Bank has two answers to this problem: first, to assert that agricultural change depends on farmers accepting "the risk associated with increasing their output";[32] second, to manipulate the variables so as to conceal from the farmers the real extent of the risk. Price guarantees and input subsidies are the most common form of this manipulation. If such measures could effectively insulate the small farmer against risk, there would be nothing to criticize here, but such policies cannot be sustained by governments over the long run, especially governments short of capital, and once the farmers are effectively hooked into the market the subsidies may be withdrawn.[33] In theory the World Bank opposes subsidies; in practice they encourage them in order to draw farmers into greater participation in the cash market. Is it any wonder that farmers who are urged to accept the risk of cash farming see a gamble in which a few may win, but the majority are likely to lose what they have?

Persuasion and Coercion: How the Projects Work

The World Bank, in promoting commercial farming and the integration of the small farmer into the world market, is following in the footsteps of colonial governments that devised a variety of policies to make their colonies pay the costs of their own imperialist rule. In Africa, for example (where the process happened most recently), they tried to draw peasant agriculturalists into commercial agriculture from the inception of colonial rule. When peasants could not be enticed into the market with the bait of imported consumer goods, less voluntary methods, such as forced cultivation, corvee labor, and money taxes, were imposed. Some of the World Bank methods do not differ all that much from forced cultivation, as we shall see from a survey of types of Bank projects aimed at the small farmer.

There are two basic types of agricultural projects, no matter who finances them. In colonial Africa, these two types were called the "transformation" approach and the "improvement" approach. The idea behind the transformation approach is that conservative peasants must be uprooted from their customary institutions and placed in a transformed setting in order to revolutionize their production practices. The main lever is control over land tenure, and the coercive aspects of this method are obvious.

The Transformation Approach: Settlement Projects

Settlement projects employ the transformation approach. A site is selected which agricultural experts believe can be cultivated more intensively than it is being cultivated. The land is then acquired by the government through its powers of eminent domain, and the people who have been cultivating or pasturing animals or hunting on that land are evicted or fenced out of the area to be developed. "In most countries, although land taken for settlement may not actually appear to be in use, customary rights of use are usually claimed over it. This is particularly the case in Africa where many settlement schemes have given rise to permanent conflict between customary and statutory rights."[34] If the evicted farmers are identifiable and have established rights to the soil, they may be "compensated" by the offer of a place in the new settlement scheme.[35] The rest, and those who do not want to be turned into settlers, are simply out of luck. The potential for ethnic conflicts is high when settlers taken from one part of the country are moved into an area previously occupied by a different group.[36]

Ideally, settlers should be chosen for their proficiency in farming, but this is hard to measure—particularly for the most needy who would have lost the land they had been farming. In most cases the places seem to have been distributed as political favors, or for paramilitary purposes.[37]

Let us now follow the fate of the farmer who was evicted from the settlement area and given a place in the new project, assuming this time that the project is well planned and has a chance of success on its own terms. The new settlers are under the strict supervision of the project authority, which has built the necessary roads, irrigation works, central buildings, and has staked out the individual plots. The farmer is instructed what crops to plant, supplied with the seeds, fertilizer, and pesticides that the experts have prescribed, and strictly supervised to make sure the planting, weeding, and harvesting are done at the right time and in the approved manner. At harvest the crop will be delivered to the project authority, and the farmer will be paid an amount calculated from prices set by the project management, less the cost of inputs and an amount for the amortization of the capital cost of the settlement infrastructure. Costs of management will also be deducted. Depending on the project, the farmer may receive title to his plot when and if the investment costs are finally paid off. For the most part, however, the land is leased to the settlers, and anyone who refuses to follow the directives of the project management may lose his lease.[38] In such projects modernization is strictly enforced.

It is not coincidental that the Bank's new interest in the productive potential of the small farmer comes just at the time when large agribusiness firms are realizing that their future lies not in the direct ownership of vast tracts of land, but in control over production through contracts with producer-suppliers (and, at the other end, control over markets). Direct ownership of land ties up large amounts of capital, exposes the owner to the risks endemic in agricultural production, requires the control of a concentrated, often unionized, labor force, and runs the risk of nationalization.[39] Supervised smallholder production, on the other hand, throws much of the risk onto the farmer, and is a cheaper way to obtain the labor of an entire family.[40]

Smallholders and plantation crops

This is best illustrated by a particular type of settlement project, the "outgrower" schemes associated with "nucleus estates."[41] Certain crops that in the past were grown only on plantations, because tight control of cultivation practices and speedy delivery to the processing plant were imperative, are now grown by

226 Cheryl Payer

smallholders clustered around a smaller plantation and processing plant run by a company that provides technical supervision, inputs, and processing for the outgrowers, who have to sell
their crops through the company. By 1975 the Bank had supported tea projects in Indonesia, Kenya, Mauritania, and Uganda,
rubber in Indonesia and Malaysia, cocoa in the Ivory Coast, and
oil palm in Nigeria.[42] The extension and supervision functions
are performed by private companies with the technical expertise
required—the same companies that also have an interest in the
purchasing and marketing of the commodity.[43]

A subsidiary of Michelin, for example, is managing a new
rubber outgrower project in the Ivory Coast. And Nicola Swainson's research has shown how the smallholder tea project in
Kenya, begun under the colonial government, was controlled
and utilized by Brooke Bond Liebig, the giant British tea multinational.[44] In many projects, however, the real control is difficult to
trace because private capital is associated with partial government ownership, as in the Ivory Coast, where the two corporations managing the palm oil industry (which has received seven
World Bank loans), Palmivoire and Palmindustrie, are 60 percent and 27.6 percent privately owned, respectively. In addition
to the outgrower projects, direct loans to traditional plantations
are still made; for example, the May 1978 loan for the rehabilitation of oil palm production in Zaire, in which some 70 percent of
the benefits will go to Unilever's estate. Smallholder participation in this scheme is planned in the future.[45]

The Bank and the nomads

Settlement plans affecting nomadic pastoralists in the Sahel
and certain regions of the Middle East are a special case. Here the
Bank, and most other development specialists as well, are playing the old game of blaming the victims. Transhumant herders
have for centuries been making rational use of the sparsely
watered grasslands bordering deserts that cannot support cultivated crops. They move their herds (camels, cattle, sheep, goats)
from place to place as water and grass supplies ebb and flow
with the seasons. By all accounts they are proud people and

tenacious of their way of life, though poor in consumer goods for which they have limited use. They supplement the protein foods their beasts supply with grain bartered from settled farmers, exchange manure for grazing land, and earn cash income by occasional work for the farmers and the sale of animals. Some were at one time owners and landlords of settled farming areas, which gave them insurance against the climatic hazards of transhumant life.[46]

These people became victims of development as the formation of national borders under colonial rule and the introduction of rigid patterns of property ownership cut them off from the richer extremities of the lands they had grazed.[47] Expensive and ill-designed deep well development projects compounded the problem by concentrating herds around wells that overgrazed the surrounding grasslands.[48]

The governments of the countries containing the nomads are generally hostile, considering them nuisances and parasites because they are difficult to control and to tax.[49] For this reason there have been a number of efforts to resettle nomads as cultivators.[50] It is also widely believed that many nomad deaths in the drought of the early 1970s can be blamed on the lack of interest of governments in aiding them—extending even, some suggest, to rulers welcoming the deaths because they could clear the way for agribusiness development in those areas.[51]

The development experts of the World Bank are not so crude, and their analyses of the nomad problem have a superficial plausibility. But their proposals to solve the problem have nothing to do with the well-being of the nomads individually and threaten to wipe them out as a culture, as well as possibly preparing new ecological disasters for the area. The World Bank claims to be worried about overgrazing of the land. This is a real problem, not denied by anyone. But the Bank experts imply that the reason for overgrazing is the ignorance of the herders and their irrational economic practices, such as unwillingness to sell their stock and consequent overpopulation and pressures on available grazing. The truth is, however, that the nomads overgraze their pastures for the same reason that subsistence farmers exhaust their soils and poor people cut down ecologically essential forest stands (all conservation problems with which the Bank claims to be deeply concerned): because they are desperately poor, and even though they know it is bad for the soil, or grassland, they have no choice if they want to survive. As commercial farming and forestry take over the best land and forest resources, shutting out the masses of the population and reserving the fruits of these resources for wealthy owners, the poor cultivators and herders have no option but to exploit their meager resources beyond the limits of a stable system.

The Bank, however, says nothing against the commercial ranches and farms that are fencing the nomads out of their traditional pastures, just as it says nothing against the large farms that have been formed by the evictions of smallholders and tenants, or the commercial logging firms that have despoiled huge areas on every continent. Instead, they blame the victims, who overwork the land because they do not have enough of it, not because they do not know any better.

According to Gavin Williams, there is a close connection between commercial ranching and controlled grazing projects. In Kenya and Botswana, for example, they form a package. The "enclosure" of land for commercial ranching creates or intensifies the grazing problem for pastoralists (and farmers who combine cattle-keeping with settled agriculture). So they get "communal, controlled grazing" schemes, the government gets commercial projects with a high "take-off" and export revenues, the rich get profits from commercial ranching, and the poor lose a large share of the commons and control of what remains.[52]

The Bank's prescription for the overgrazing of nomad land exposes the fact that its concern is for the land and its potential produce, not for the people. The experts have no new techniques that could make Sahelian grasslands more productive. The only solution they can propose for overgrazing is "controlled grazing" (known and practiced by the nomads for centuries, so long as they had access to enough land) by which the Bank means destocking. Grazing areas are to be delimited and "grazing permits" issued for a carefully controlled number of stock only. This would force the herders either to sell all their stock in excess of the permitted number, or to take them further afield, to land that is even poorer and more arid, which they will then have to overgraze until famine provides the final solution.[53] Destocking a grazing area means depopulation, since family herds are probably already as small as they can be and still provide subsistence; at least one Bank publication admits this frankly:

> Destocking means reducing the human population in this region as well. Stock raising is capital intensive rather than labor intensive; it is most productive when undertaken on a large scale. There are already more Masai living on the range than can be supported by stock raising. . . . *Range development must eventually involve relocation of a majority of the population and, hence, a disruption of tribal life.*[54] (Emphasis added)

Nothing is said about where these people can go when they lose their rights to herd their stock.

The fad for turning nomads into settled farmers is now waning, as enlightened opinion comprehends that the Sahel is too fragile for cultivation and that pasture is the most rational use of the land, even by modern commercial standards. But the nomads have their own ecology and economy, which is rational for them but is foreign to international capitalist standards. Therefore the development experts decree that they must either become commercial ranchers, or make way for those who will.

The prejudice against the nomads' way of life was stated crudely in a report of a committee of governments of the Sahel region:

> These populations represent a heavy social, economic and political drain for their countries. . . . They don't take care of anything, refuse to do manual labor, evade taxes, sell their animals only reluctantly, and therefore do not contribute as much to the economic life of the country as we have a right to expect from them. . . . Their diet is a luxury and a waste, for they get more than 50% of their caloric needs from animal products. Nowadays, to consume more cheese and milk than cereals is a luxury . . . and to pay more for cereals than the meat they sell is an economic absurdity that prevents any possible integration with a market economy.[55]

But the viewpoint expressed is not really different from that in a superficially sympathetic and enlightened World Bank report:

Development of cattle production is also constrained by traditional management practices and attitudes to cattle—regarded as a store of wealth and as conferring prestige rather than as a means of production—among the nomadic herdsmen responsible for most of Nigeria's beef production. These practices are a *rational response to a harsh environment*, given the knowledge and conditions of the period in which they have developed, but today they are leading to *deterioration of the land resource* and are designed for *survival rather than productivity. New pressures on resources and new demands for beef* make these practices and attitudes inappropriate. They are, however, deep-rooted and difficult to change at the pace necessary to match demand. The approach to livestock development must therefore not only seek to accelerate change among traditional producers (including research into how this can best be promoted) but must also explore ways of introducing modern, commercial production techniques, probably utilizing *a new group of settled stock farmers.*[56] (Emphasis added)

As this paragraph incidentally reveals, the Bank is probably putting more research into finding out how to persuade the nomads to destock than it is into discovering what the people themselves feel their needs to be. The Bank's philosophy on livestock populations is in fact almost indentical to their views on human population control, at least where poor people and their stock are concerned: "If there were less of you (your cattle), you (they) would be fatter." Understandably, the pastoralists reject this negative reasoning, and some are resisting violently.[57] Grazing restrictions are probably impossible to enforce in areas of extensive transhumance, but the attempt may well lead to war. What the Bank and its clients, the large commercial ranchers and meatpackers,[58] really mean when they give this advice is, "If there were less of you and your cattle, you would require fewer of the resources we want to exploit, and there would be less of you to covet the lands we have already appropriated." A powerless group that has not been able to defend its own territory is not likely to gain more power by limiting its numbers. Nomads do not, in fact, have a very high birth rate, and previous reports of a "population explosion" of livestock in the Sahel may have been based on faulty analysis of census statistics.[59]

Area Development Projects

The other type of approach to rural development has been called the "improvement" approach. In this method rural society is not picked up bodily and turned around as in settlement projects, but is rather taken *in situ*, accepting the existing land tenure situation. Peasants are to be persuaded by rural development agents to adopt the modern inputs and new crops that will enable them to produce a larger surplus for the market. While some country-wide projects are funded (which typically involve the strengthening of some government body in the agriculture sector), the more usual Bank project concentrates on a comparatively small area, which is then saturated with extension agents and credit for the recommended inputs. In the now fashionable "integrated rural development projects," roads, marketing facilities, water supplies, and electricity may be included. Schools and clinics may also form part of the package, but the Bank finances only the physical building (which benefits local contractors, but is probably the least important element in warm countries where shelters can be constructed cheaply), and it is arguable that the main function of these components is to provide the sugar coating to render the entire project palatable and facilitate the experts' entree: everyone wants schools and clinics, even if they aren't sure about commercial agriculture.

This approach would at least seem to be less coercive than the settlement schemes, but there are many problems. Some of these problems will thwart the Bank's intention of transforming traditional agriculture; but others ensure that insofar as agriculture is transformed, the problem of poverty will worsen for most people in the area.

Supervised credit: how profitable for the peasant?

For one, the small farmer may have little choice in the matter. Credit is often extended to groupings of peasants in cooperatives whose primary function seems to be mutual responsibility for the repayment of loans. A close investigation of some of these credit groupings might reveal that adherence is not a strictly voluntary matter (more research is needed on the constitution of such groups). Once a farmer agrees to participate in a credit program, the conditions attached to the loan are nearly as stringent as those enforced in settlement projects. Use of prescribed inputs is enforced by the delivery of credit in the form of already purchased fertilizers, seeds, machinery, and so on, rather than cash. Participation in insurance programs may be mandatory; delivery of crops to the project authority or a government purchasing agency is usually required. Sowing, spraying, and harvesting practices are specified. The price of inputs and services are charged to the peasants' accounts, so that they have no real opportunity to make their own cost-benefit calculations before discovering that the sums have been deducted from the payment due on delivery of the harvest. Insurance programs for crop losses may be denied if the farmer has not strictly followed the instructions of the extension agents and the credit-issuing bank; non-repayment of credits can be legally punished by taking over the farmer's land (by the bank or the peasants' credit organization).[60]

All these strictures were found in the Bank-financed Papaloapan Basin Project (Mexico) studied by Hannes Lorenzen, who found also that the peasants reacted with a variety of measures of passive resistance: disinterest in meetings called to explain technical measures, diversion and resale of the inputs supplied in kind, even bribery of the supervisors charged with enforcing the cultivation practices; and finally, the withdrawal into subsistence farming with which they were familiar. Lorenzen concluded: "That which the engineers unanimously characterize as 'stubborn, backward, and immoral' is actually simple economic behavior: If the technology is profitable I will use it, but when its costs exceed my earnings I must refuse to pay for it."[61]

"Building on the best"

Another problem, pointed out by many critics, is that the areas selected for projects tend to be those that are best provided with land and water resources in the first place—the strategy of "building on the best," which is typical of capitalist development. To the natural advantages of the chosen area are added the massive insertion of extension advice and monetary credit, creating an area which is not just advantaged, but "pampered." There is typically a high ratio of extension agents to farmers in Bank project areas.[62] The effect, if the project is successful, will be to sharpen regional inequalities in the country.[63]

Worse than this is the problem within the selected area itself. We can identify two varieties here: the inequality existing when the Bank project begins, and that which the project itself will create. The first type of inequality is not caused by the Bank, but it is not challenged by the Bank, either. Although here and there in the Bank literature we find some timid admissions that elites may have some interest in preventing the emancipation of their clients, the predominant official view is that rich and poor coexist peacefully within rural society and that both small and large farmers can profit from the adoption of modern techniques proportionally to their ownership of land (a hefty source of inequality to begin with). This assumption allows the Bank to count as poor "beneficiaries" of its projects everyone who lives within the targeted area, regardless of the actual effects of the project. According to the Bank's director of Agriculture and Rural Development, Montague Yudelman:

> Area development projects . . . are for the purpose of developing large areas, which are chosen because per capita incomes are below average and the rating by social indicators is low. The underlying assumption of the area approach, which is typified by the introduction of infrastructure and rural services, is that most of the benefits (though not all) will go to the target group. In the main, most people who live in areas in which average incomes are low and which are generally deprived of social infrastructure tend to be poor themselves.[64]

This is circular logic, and willfully blind politics. But in this way the poor to be "helped" by a given program can thus be impressively represented in numerical terms, even though a much smaller number of wealthier residents will get a larger share of the benefits. As the sector policy paper admits:

> It is notable that rural development schemes usually do not aim to provide benefits exclusively to the rural poor. . . . Often the rural development objective is subordinate to the objective of increasing

agricultural output (or marketed output). Even where this is not the case, a program aimed at providing service or extension to the small farmer will rarely exclude the medium-sized farmer, if by including him sizable increases in output can be achieved.[65]

The Bank refuses to recognize that the poor are connected to the wealthy by bonds of exploitation, seeing instead only their physical proximity.

In most cases . . . the poor are found living alongside the prosperous. They sometimes suffer from limited access to natural resources. But more frequently they suffer because they have little access to technology and services, and because the institutions which would sustain a higher level of productivity are lacking.[66]

The Bank even tries to make a virtue of necessity, and admits more willingness to propitiate than to challenge "vested interests [who] ensure that the poor are denied access to the inputs, services, and organizations which would allow them to increase their productivity."

In many countries, avoiding opposition from powerful and influential sections of the rural community is essential if the program is not to be subverted from within. . . . Thus, in cases where economic and social inequality is initially great, it is normally optimistic to expect that more than 50% of the project benefits can be directed toward the target groups; often the percentage will be considerably less.[67]

A close look at the Bank's own estimates and admissions thus reveals that they are doing considerably less to "help" the poor than their frontline publicity would suggest. But the problem is even worse, as some case studies show. Bangladesh is a country that contains a large number of the "absolute poor" about whom McNamara speaks so eloquently, and it is a large recipient of soft-term International Development Association (IDA) loans from the Bank. Half of World Bank project loans to Bangladesh (one-quarter of total loans) are for agriculture and rural development.

Two Americans who lived for several months in a Bangladesh village have described the local effect of an irrigation project which was designed to benefit both large and small farmers.

Project aid reached our village in the form of a deep tubewell, one of 3,000 installed in northwestern Bangladesh in an IDA project. The tubewell, designed to produce enough water to irrigate 60 acres of land, is a valuable asset, for with irrigation farmers can grow an extra rice crop during the dry winter season. Irrigation also insures the regular spring and monsoon season crops against drought, and allows earlier plantings which reduce the risk of flood damage.[68]

In theory the tubewells were supposed to be purchased and used by twenty-five to fifty farmers grouped into cooperatives formed for this purpose. "But in reality, the tubewell in our village was considered the personal property of one man: Nafis, the biggest landlord of the area. The irrigation group, of which Nafis was supposedly the manager, was in fact no more than a few signatures he had collected on a scrap of paper."[69] Nafis got the $12,000 tubewell by virtue of his political influence, at a cost of less than $300 in bribes to local officials, and installed it on his own land, where he could irrigate thirty acres. This is only half the size of the area capacity of the tubewell, but the price Nafis planned to charge neighboring small farmers for use of the water is so high that the well will not be used to its full capacity. Nafis is the *only* beneficiary of the project in his village, and—if the tubewell succeeds in raising his income—he will probably use that income to purchase plots to add to his own, driving the previous owners into landlessness.

The Real Significance of "Program Loans"

World Bank officials may privately deplore the fact that the governments with and through which they must work are not committed to the cause of helping the rural poor, but their lament must be seen in perspective. Fully half of World Bank loans to Bangladesh are not project loans, but "commodity aid," in other words a program loan to the Bangladesh government that will collect the receipts from sales of the commodities imported under the loan. The purpose of program loans is simply to support and strengthen the recipient government, in this case a government intimately allied with local landlords such as Nafis. So, while gently deploring the subversion of its good intentions by local elites and the lack of government interest in rural reform, the Bank is one of the most important forces ensuring the survival of that government and those rural elites.

Where distribution of income and power in rural areas is grossly unequal, the story is always the same. In Ethiopia (before the revolution of 1974), a fertilizer distribution project was designed explicitly to reach small farmers. But in its third year of operation [1973] "the project covered some 14,000 peasant households out of which approximately 70% or 9,800 were tenant families. Instead of reaching these, the project has given service to a small number [194 in 1973] of landowning peasants, among whom a considerable part belonged to the relatively wealthy stratum."[70] In Guatemala the Bank solved the problem of reaching "small farmers" by defining them as anyone with less than 45 hectares of land (108 acres)—a category which encompasses 97 percent of all Guatemalan farmers. Half of the funds would go to "small farmers" thus defined, while the other half would go to "medium" and "larger" farms in the top 3 percent.[71]

"I don't care what country you take," an agricultural specialist with wide experience in Latin America told me, "if you follow World Bank money down through the distributing institutions, it's all going to the wrong people."

The Genesis of Inequality

In a situation of pre-existing inequality the rural elites will prevent their clients from utilizing credit if they cannot find ways of appropriating the benefits themselves. In areas where rural class differentiations are not yet large, Bank methods pose a different problem: that of encouraging and intensifying class differentiation into a layer of landlords or labor-hiring small farmers on the one hand and expropriated landless laborers on the other.

In area development programs, acceptance of the experts' advice is, in theory, voluntary. It is probably impossible for extension workers to reach all of the thousands of small plots included in an area development program, even if the ratio of extension workers to farmers is much more favorable than in the rest of the country. And, for good or bad reasons, not all the farmers in an area will be receptive to the experts' advice. But there will be in most societies a small minority of rural entrepreneurs who foresee an advantage for themselves in becoming the pioneers of commercial agriculture. And, whether they are genuinely good and efficient farmers or simply well-connected local opportunists, it is inevitable that this small group of so-called progressive or master farmers will have the first claim on the attention of extension agents and credit from the banks.[72] The comfortable assumption of the Bank policymakers and the extension workers is that the success of these pioneers will have a demonstration effect which will persuade the laggards to adopt new methods.

What is happening, however, is that this small minority of farmers, insofar as they are successful, acquire more land from their less "progressive" and less fortunate neighbors, subsequently hiring the latter to do the work that becomes inconsistent with their social status as they become wealthier. This process, which has been well documented in many countries for the first years of the so-called green revolution, is now being extended into new, previously undeveloped areas cultivated by small farmers.[73]

In one of the great ironies of the development process, the Bank moves into areas where class differentiation is slight and a genuine possibility to help smallholders exists—and through its methods ensures that the undeveloped society will evolve the kind of social structure that renders any help to smallholders impossible; in fact may create absolute poverty where it did not previously exist, and possibly even wipe out smallholders as a class.

"Land Reform"—World Bank Style

Most of the areas of the world where self-provisioning agriculture survives and class differentiation is still embryonic are those where land is held under traditional forms of tenure, usually labeled "communal." In these societies every member has a right to a plot of land which he or she farms and from which the farmer can appropriate the produce, to consume or sell. Generally the plot may be inherited by the farmers' children (or sister's children, in matrilineal societies) but cannot be alienated to outsiders without the approval of the community. In one scholar's words, farmers in these societies "use" land, but they do not "hold" it in the Western legal sense, and their right to land may be revoked if it is not cultivated.[74]

This type of land use, found throughout Europe in medieval times and in most areas of the world at the time they were conquered by Europeans, now survives mainly in Africa and in small remote pockets of other continents. The colonial powers did not take a consistent attitude to this type of usufruct tenure in Africa; while in some areas they promoted the spread of Western-type freehold (usually accompanied by a disregard of women's rights to land of their own), in others they found it useful to preserve communal tenure as a means both to prevent the emergence of a prosperous rural bourgeoisie and to guarantee a minimum of food security at no cost to the colonial government.

It is revealing that the Bank, in its sector policy paper on *Land Reform*, cites as practically its only contribution to the change of land ownership patterns the financing of a program designed to replace communal tenure with individual ownership in a small African country. Malawi is a small, nominally independent, black-ruled country in southern Africa which was once Nyasaland, part of the Rhodesia federation. It is still a labor reserve for white-ruled southern Africa,[75] and under the effective control of British and South African capital. The Lilongwe Development Program in Malawi is one of the Bank's showcase rural development projects, supposedly intended to benefit the poor farmers of the area.

During the preparation of the Lilongwe project, the Bank

recognized that there was "an opportunity to change the existing land tenure pattern of customary right of usufruct. The need for change to a more secure and lasting tenure system was evident. . . . IDA credits are being used for the land survey (both topographical and cadastral), the provision of . . . staff, vehicles, equipment, and the construction of housing and land registry." More than 1 million acres are now included in the program.[76]

The Lilongwe project is not the first Bank-assisted program for the transformation of communal tenure into absolute private ownership. The Bank previously supported the colonial government of Kenya's project to establish individual tenure in the heart of the Kikuyu territory during the Mau Mau rebellion and the white-controlled Rhodesian government plan for the compulsory and comprehensive transformation of communal tenure in all the lands of that country "reserved" for blacks. In both cases the political ramifications were of great importance: the Kikuyu program was a transparent counterinsurgency measure, while the Rhodesian plan was designed in part to provide white industrialists with a captive labor force by denying migrant labor the right to return to land in the reserves.[77]

The "security" issue

The argument typically used to justify this revolution in land tenure is the assertion that land titles will give the cultivator security and thus encourage investment to improve the land. This is often linked to insensitivity to or hostility to women's rights to land use and/or matrilineal forms of succession, "the implication being that it is the husband, rather than the wife or her male kin who makes decisions concerning improvement of the land . . . and the assumption that a man will be more willing to improve the land if his own children are to succeed to it."[78] The consequences of this ideology for the welfare of women and children have been severe.[79]

A number of observers have challenged these assumptions, showing that individuals have in fact sufficient security of tenure under traditional systems to improve the land and to plant cash and tree crops; and that the African system not only provides security to all members of the community but also has more flexibility in allowing adjustment of population to available land through migration, the fallow system, etc.[80] A few have even made the point that the source of instability lay elsewhere:

> If there is any feeling of insecurity in his right of occupation it arises not so much in fear of interference by members of his own community but from the apprehension that the Government may, for its own purposes (such as the need of land for public use or for alienation to colonists), disturb him in the possession of his holding.[81]

The truth is that the registration of land to individual ownership *destroys* the security of traditional tenure forms, and African farmers were in general hostile to official attempts to change their tenure rights. "Apart from a handful of progressive individual farmers, there was no demand for change. . . . Cultivators as a whole would have resented advantages for a favored few and the latter were themselves anxious to avoid becoming objects of jealousy and suspicion."[82] As one legal expert noted drily, apropos the land registration law when it was first introduced in Malawi: "There is no surer way of depriving a peasant of his land than to give him a title to it which is as freely negotiable as a bank note."[83]

But the real objective was not stability for the proprietor, but its opposite, the creation of a market in land that would force more productive (by world standards) use of the land. The best explanation of how this mechanism operates was given by Montague Yudelman, now director of the World Bank's Department of Agriculture and Rural Development, in a 1964 book on the Bank-supported tenure reform in the black-reserve areas in Rhodesia:

> So long as land remains a free good there will be no cost factor to encourage greater productivity. Reliance will have to be placed on the usual "pull" factors—the desire for higher incomes, for example—to encourage more productive use of land. *Hitherto these pull factors have not been very effective in themselves.* It is possible that a "push" factor could be introduced by having a variable land tax graduated on the basis of land potential, but such a tax cannot be implemented without a clear definition of the size

and nature of holdings. . . . By and large, *it would seem that an effective "push" factor would come from the creation of an effective land market.*

If tribal land were converted into a negotiable asset, and if there existed a market for land that related its market value to its productive potential, the prices of different tracts of land might well differ sharply. Land that could provide a salable surplus would command higher prices than land that could not be used in this way. In these circumstances, an efficient market for land would bring about a circular action: better land would be higher priced because it could produce more, but because it was high priced *there would be pressure to use it to yield higher returns,* and so better land would have to be put to more productive use than poorer land. It can also be argued that once land had a price, it would have to yield an income comparable to that which could be realized from a comparable investment in fixed-interest securities. *This would preclude emphasis on subsistence production and would ultimately lead to specialization of production and commercialization of agriculture.*[43] (Emphasis added)

Yudelman (who was not employed by the Bank at the time he wrote this) was an enthusiastic supporter of the creation of land markets, although he knew that the benefit would not accrue to the laborer on the land: "The creation of a market for land will surely mean that there will be renter and *rentier* classes." Rather, the land market would economize on "scarce managerial ability" by allowing "progressive" producers to expand holdings "to the limits of his competence and financial resources," perhaps aided by special credit programs for able producers.[85]

The effect of a market in land is thus much the same as that achieved directly in settlement schemes: the subsistence farmer is forced to go commercial, producing crops for the cities and the world market, on pain of losing his or her land to those who are doing so. The fiat of the project authority is replaced here by government taxation policies and by the "impersonal" market mechanisms, which some people are better able to manipulate than others.

The question of credit

It may seem paradoxical to suggest that Third World agriculture needs *less* credit (particularly of the international kind) than it is presently receiving, not more, but in many countries peasant "beneficiaries" of World Bank programs have become overburdened by the debt attendant on such credit. In order to repay their cash debts the benefits, if any, of the increased productivity caused by the purchased inputs must be returned to the large international firms that supply the inputs. In the case of "outgrower" schemes the benefits go to the company purchasing the products produced cheaply by smallholder family labor.

Evidence is accumulating from many parts of the globe which shows that institutional credit for the purchase of "modern" inputs is impoverishing, rather than enriching, the smallest farmers. The examples that follow are taken either from areas which are directly objects of World Bank projects, or refer to national agricultural credit authorities which serve as intermediaries for Bank funds to small farmers.

In a tobacco-growing project in Rukwa region, Tanzania:

> After five months of very hard work that involved the whole family, including children, the average gross income per family came to T. Shs. 2,075 in 1973/74. Out of this was deducted 770 for the cost of inputs, 72 for society levy, and 116 for interest on capital leaving the poor peasant family with Shs. 1,117 [equivalent to 54 per month per adult worker]. There were complaints by the World bank that the Government had not fulfilled its obligations under the agreement to settle the required number of people in the area for tobacco growing. *People therefore had to be forced to move into the area, and to abandon their usual habitat.* As a result, a maize production area was converted into tobacco production for export.[86] (Emphasis added)

According to the head of a peasant association in an area being developed by the Société d'Amenagement et d'Exploitation des Terres du Delta du Fleuve Senegal, in Senegal:

> This first year, we grew four hectares, and we owed 174,000 francs for fertilizer and fuel; at that rate, if we have 20 hectares, we'll owe 500,000 francs [actually 870,000]. That's what we have against SAED. We don't reject SAED: we want to be free to say what we want to buy, and to keep our own accounts. We don't need much fertilizer because the soil is good. It's not old soil. SAED would say, take 20 sacks, 30 sacks—then we're in debt. We don't want that.[87]

In northern Nigeria,

> Wheat, tomatoes, maize, cotton are among the priority crops on these various projects. They are scheduled to be grown for sale, to go to town, to the flour mills, livestock feed factories, cotton ginneries. They are not intended for local consumption and they compete directly with the growing of staple foods. The consultants' theory that these farmers will be able to purchase their food needs is belied by the evidence of the last few years. . . .
>
> The net result of this imposition of intensive farming for the market, using new technology and growing new crops, is that farmers are being told to invest more money and labour in farming, give up other (often more reliable) occupations, take more risks in an already risky situation where drought, erratic rainfall, pests, poor project management, and a volatile market hardly make agriculture a predictable venture. In these circumstances where credit, extension advice, technology are necessarily concentrated on the wealthier, influential and larger farmers (as smaller farmers have not the resources needed to use them) it is not surprising that land is changing hands, and that many small farmers are either unable to participate or are being forced off the project land altogether.[88]

And in the Federal Land Development Authority (FELDA) settlement schemes in Malaysia;

> *Indebtedness:* Each settler family on acceptance of resettlement in the scheme was given an *imaginary loan* of $15,000 to $25,000. A certain number of acreage of land was allotted to each of the famil[ies] usually about 7 acres. This allottment is more or less on a temporary basis in the sense that if the land is neglected that family will be asked to leave the scheme to make way for another peasant family, without any form of compensation for the work already done on the land. Usually none of the plots are neglected, because being landless for generations, each peasant family is determined to take the land for keeps. Being landless and poor all their life, they accepted the *imaginary loan* without much complaint. According to this *imaginary loan* system, each family will be given a monthly allowance of $70.00 (and, measured by any standard, this is far below the poverty line). Out of the $70.00 they have to contribute 50 cents to "seedlings" and $1.00 to "cooperative society" in the scheme. Still the settlers remained and worked on the land without fuss because they were promised that when the

land became successful, they could earn at least $300 to $400 a month. With this earning, if realized, they could afford to give a decent life to their family, and there will be surplus for them to pay the *imaginary loan*. In time, they were promised further, the land will be theirs.

Permanent Debt: Bilut Valley Felda Scheme is the oldest scheme in Malaysia. No doubt, one of the most successful. A primary jungle has been transformed into a "virgin" rubber plantation. The virgin trees grown from good seedlings produce latex in good quantity and quality. Ordinarily, with that amount of latex produced, they could have easily earned $400 per month. But strange enough their income did not increase . . . (because) the government has limited their income to the amount of $70. Any income surpassing the $70 limit is automatically expropriated by the Felda under the pretext that the expropriate sum is used for the payment of the *imaginary loan*.

As a test case, a settler in the Bilut Valley, through mutual cooperation with others, raised enough money to pay off the *imaginary loan*. But Felda came with a bold answer that it is not prepared to accept the payment, neither would it give title of land to the settler concerned. Secondly, a settler in the Kampong Awah Felda Scheme paid his *debt* "religiously" for three years in succession only to be told by the Felda that his debt to Felda has increased to $18,000, i.e. an increase of $4,000 from the original imaginary loan.[89]

This account goes on to suggest that the real beneficiaries of the rapid increase over time in "development expenditures" per family and per acre in the FELDA schemes are big contractors allied with the ruling party. This brings us to a very important point. As Gavin Williams (and others) point out, "Rural development is big business, offering contracts and employment to construction and consultancy firms, international experts and bankers, fertiliser, chemical and seed manufacturers and distributors, officials, extension workers and even, for short periods of time, labourers."[90] The farmers, having no choice in the matter, are saddled with the bill for the inputs they have not been able to select for themselves. The potential of this captive market for the sellers of these wares is limited only by the amount of money which governments, in conjunction with aid institutions, can be persuaded to invest in the projects. In Rodolphe de Koninck's words:

The magnitude and lucrativeness of the market that green revolution peasants represent have been amply documented elsewhere. What deserve to be underlined here however are: firstly, the role played by the state in insuring the rapid development of this market through the provision of credit, extension services and infrastructure; secondly, the fact that this internal market is essentially controlled by foreign interests. . . . The green revolution peasants constitute a typical captive market. . . .[91]

It is then left to the state, through the project administration, to collect the money due from the farmers. If the Malaysian example is typical (and only a larger number of cases can suggest whether it is) the debt is of such a magnitude that it will never be paid off. This then becomes a legal lien justifying the extraction of all the farmer produces above the "allowance" left him by the state. Though no longer a "subsistence" farmer, he may be working at or below a "subsistence" wage.

The World Bank is in the business of lending money. Its officers gain promotion on the basis of how well they are able to fill the quota (they call it the "pipeline") for the area or country under their charge, in order to meet McNamara's massively expanding lending goals. As a result, they fund projects that are dubious by their own standards of cost-effectiveness, and lend large sums to projects that could have been funded at much less cost.[92] The result is projects which are top-heavy with money spent on overpriced inputs, including an army of expensive foreign consultants. The traditional moneylender seems benign in comparison.

9

Water Resources

Water is still regarded by most people as a "free" resource, yet in many areas of the earth there is less fresh, clean water than the existing populations could use, and the relative scarcity of this basic resource will become ever more important as polluting industries proliferate. "As energy has dominated discussions of resource use in the 1970s, so water shall in the 1980s. Everywhere water—a life necessity, has become a scarce resource," according to water consultant Douglas V. Smith.[1]

It is scarcely possible to enumerate all the many functions water performs that are critical to human life and to most of the activities included in the concept of "development." Fresh water is required domestically, for drinking, washing, and cooking. Arable land would be worthless without sufficient and timely water required by the growing crops. Fish, whether raised as a basic food, cash product, or for sport, require the proper watery habitat. Rivers are important avenues of transportation, especially for bulky, low-value goods such as logs and ores. Waterpower from dammed-up rivers is an important source of power needs, complementing energy produced by fossil fuels and nuclear power. Industries and mines, in addition to consuming hydroelectric power, use vast quantities of water directly as a solvent, for flushing away wastes, and for cooling. Many recreational activities center around bodies of water.

As these demands proliferate and multiply, conflicts over rights to use water also become more frequent and bitter. It is now a commonplace that the basic unit of analysis of water usage must be the entire drainage basin of a river system, since any activity in one part of the system has potential repercussions throughout the basin for users in other parts. Upstream water users can divert water for their own use (e.g., for irrigation), so that it is not available to downstream residents or industries that previously depended upon it. Or the upstream users may return the used water laden with physical, chemical, or radioactive pollutants (fertilizers, pesticides, industrial wastes, etc.). Or water used for cooling processes may be returned heated, so that fish and vegetation can no longer survive. Deforestation or poor cultivation practices in the upper reaches of the river basins will release soil to be washed down as silt. This silt will shorten the life of reservoirs built to produce hydropower, and the reservoirs may prevent the silt from fertilizing downstream farmlands that had previously depended upon it. Untreated sewage and pollutants can poison the domestic water supply of downstream users, causing sickness and death.

The power of downstream water consumers over upstream inhabitants is of a different type, but in many cases is no less devastating. In order to control the supply of water (to prevent flooding, to supply power or water for irrigation, etc.), the downstream users, who are typically in control of national governments, build dams and reservoirs that flood the homes and farms of communities which are less politically influential, depriving the inhabitants of their habitats and livelihoods. Downstream users may also enact laws that regulate farming and logging practices in the upper reaches of the watershed and enforce these laws against people who have no access to other resources.

All uses of water threaten, at least potentially, the rights of other users, in this complex and interdependent system. To those of us who were brought up on the fairy tale of the entirely beneficent "multipurpose project" (à la TVA), which provides flood control, electric power, irrigation, navigation, and recreation for the greatest good of the greatest number, it will be necessary to reorient our thinking to accommodate the fact that "it is a very unusual reservoir that brings nobody any harm."[2] Even the supposed benefits of multipurpose water projects conflict with one another: the best dam for flood control purposes is an empty one, the best one for hydroelectric power and irrigation purposes is a full one. But power generation requires the release of water on a schedule that responds to variation in the demand for power, and irrigation usage requires the release of water when it is needed at critical periods for plant growth. In the Tennessee Valley project, the conflict between the aims of power generation and flood control were difficult to reconcile; irrigation had to be excluded altogether because "if that also had to be kept in mind by the control engineers . . . their judgment and strength of mind would have been taxed still more severely."[3] The conflict between power and irrigation demands is spelled out by Richard Reidlinger, writing about northern India:

> [W]ater releases for generating electricity are determined on a day-to-day basis. The irrigation system can absorb some limited fluctuation in releases due to changes in demand for electricity. But if the magnitude of the fluctuations is greater than the system can absorb, unscheduled releases must either be made into the irrigation system or passed on downstream. In the latter case the water is lost for this irrigation system, although it may be used further down the river. In the former, the water is unexpected and thus has a low value to cultivators.[4]

A similar conflict is noted by John Waterbury for the Nile Valley.[5]

But all water users are not equal in the sight of the government that plans, builds, and finances water control projects. The allocation of water among competing uses and users is effected, when not by sheer force or money, by official bodies that are creatures of the most powerful corporate claimants on water, or heavily influenced by them. Reidlinger's account of northern India is also illuminating on this point:

> The extent to which irrigation is treated as a by-product of reservoir storage cannot be quantitatively estimated due to lack of data, but it should be substantial for several reasons. Demand for electricity by industrialists for their factories, and by wealthier farmers for their tubewells and machinery, is strong and growing. These groups have much influence and political power. In addition, a fertilizer factory established in the area when the Bhakra Dam electricity was surplus uses much power in electrolysis, although the opportunity cost of that power has increased substantially.[6]

Even when, as is increasingly the case, planners recognize that the entire river basin must be taken into account when planning water management policies, they remain concerned mainly with the needs of the corporations, the large farmers (in actual possession, or to be attracted by assured irrigation supplies), and the cities (meaning chiefly their business, industrial, and wealthier residential districts).

Nature does not charge fees for the use of water, but in order to divert water from the course nature lays out for it, human beings have to pay other human beings, for labor and machinery (past labor), sums of money that may be very large indeed. This is where the World Bank comes in. Though the Bank does not have a "water control projects" sector, in fact projects in nearly all of its sectors involve the control or the use of large quantities of water. Hydroelectric power is one of the largest objects of bank lending; irrigation, mining, industry, fisheries, and urban water supply and sewerage have all attracted large amounts of lending. Because water usage cuts across many sectors, the Bank has published no policy paper or working paper on water control, comparable to the ones it has produced for other types of projects. It was not until 1976 that an outside consultant was retained to make a survey of the Bank's water control projects and recommend a multisectoral approach to the problem. His unpublished report makes clear the scope of the Bank's influence on water control. "Water resource projects have always been a major portion of the Bank's program, estimated variously from 20 to 45 percent of the total, attaining over a billion dollar size in the latest (1975) complete calendar year."[7]

The report presents the following breakdown of the billion-dollar investment in 1975:[8]

	million $
Hydropower	154.0
Irrigation, flood control, fisheries, rural development	528.0
Water/sewage/urban sites and services, and tourism projects	7.0
Water supply and sewage disposal	240.0
Total	1,029.0

Until recently, the Bank has not considered water control

projects as interrelated, but has compartmentalized them in such sectors as electric power, agriculture, urban sites and services, and so on. Consequently, it lacks a publicly articulated policy on water control projects, though occasional published work refers to certain policy stands. For example, Robert Wade mentions the World Bank's insistence on the "Kota" method of irrigation in India, involving large-scale mechanical grading of irrigated areas, asserting that at least until 1974 the Bank insisted on "Kota or nothing," refusing to consider alternative forms of small-scale, less-intensive water control.[9] Other, more recent publications and private communications make it clear that this tradition has continued after 1974, in practice if not in theory.

The general lack of policy statements makes it necessary as well as desirable to look at the documented results of actual Bank water projects. The rest of the chapter will thus review two of the most common, and numerically and financially most important, types of projects: large dams and irrigation projects.

Dam Construction Projects

Big dams raise many troubling ecological issues: the diversion of water from downstream users, the disruption of flora, fauna, and fish habitats both upstream and downstream from the works, the spread of disease vectors, the accumulation of silt, and so on, but the starkest example of disregard for the rights of poor people derives from the displacement of those individuals who have lived and farmed the riverine lands that are permanently inundated by the reservoirs behind the big dams. This does not happen only in poor, Third World countries; it has happened and is still happening in the United States as well (for example, the Tellicoe dam in Tennessee). But in developed or underdeveloped countries, the victims of dam displacement are almost always the people who have no political clout, those who are still happily ensconced in a semisubsistence agriculture. In many cases that have been documented, they are pockets of "minority" cultures differing from the dominant ethnic or cultural group, for it is such peoples who have previously been driven into the remote hill country that is too inaccessible to attract land-grabbers from the lowlands. Their land has great use-value for the people who farm it, but little commercial value except as the site for a reservoir. The water typically is stored as a source of potential electric power, to be transmitted to the cities, industries, and factory farms of the lowlands. The class bias of most big dam and reservoir projects is glaringly apparent. The population to be displaced by the projects is regarded by the Bank (following the lead of the governments to which it is lending and the industries who will benefit from the project) as merely objects to be moved out of the way.[10]

Two large hydroelectric projects in Africa provide good examples of how the costs and benefits of such projects are distributed. One is the Kariba Dam, which was built between the territories of Northern Rhodesia and Southern Rhodesia, at the time joined in the Federation of Rhodesia and Nyasaland; now the territories belong to Zambia, to the north, and Zimbabwe, to the south. The other is the Volta River hydroelectric project in Ghana.

The Kariba project

The Kariba hydroelectric project, first funded by the World Bank in 1956, was its largest single project loan at that time. The reservoir created by the dam was the largest artificial lake in the world at the time it was built.[11] The frontier on which it was located has been one of the most sensitive in the southern Africa subcontinent, as the white-dominated federation was dissolved in 1963, followed by the independence of black-ruled Zambia on the northern bank of the Zambezi in 1964 and Ian Smith's Unilateral Declaration of Independence for white-ruled Rhodesia in 1965. The racial situation in the area made this now "international" project one with profound racial and class implications as well.

The project may originally have been intended as a means of cementing the unstable federation by making the northern territory dependent for electric power on the southern (controlling) member. It is alleged that technical considerations favored location of the project at another site, Kafue, located in the north, but the government of the federation preferred the location on the southern side of the Zambezi, where the power station was situated. "All the actual generation of power (took) place within the territory of Southern Rhodesia, giving the government of the latter an extremely powerful weapon to use against Zambia, if it were inclined to breach its obligations."[12]

The dam was designed for one purpose: the generation of electricity. The major beneficiaries of this purpose were the copper-mining corporations operating in Northern Rhodesia: the Anglo-American Corporation of South Africa, Ltd., under South African and British ownership, and Roan Selection Trust, controlled by American Metal Climax, Inc. (AMAX), which together accounted for virtually all the copper production in the territory. The needs of these two companies seem to have been the main impetus behind the entire project. "So urgent were demands of copper companies for more power that Rhodesia's hydroelectric board started to do preliminary work on the dam last year even before financial arrangements were made," reported the *Wall Street Journal*.[13] Secondarily, it was assumed that some power would be made available to existing and potential industrial centers in Southern Rhodesia.[14]

As Patrick McNally wryly observed, "To date, the major thing Zambia had received from the Kariba Dam and other World Bank loans was $55.6 million of debt assigned to it upon the dissolution of the Federation."[15] In an effort to free itself from dependence upon the power plant controlled by Ian Smith's government, the Zambian government sought and received *new* World Bank loans in 1970 and 1974 to build a power station on the *north* side of the Kariba Dam.

Who paid the costs for the building of the Kariba Dam and reservoir? The taxpayers of the nations that succeeded the Federation of Rhodesia, of course, and the hundreds of workers who died in accidents while working on the dam itself. But also the 56,000 people who inhabited the two sides of the Zambezi River that had to be flooded to form the reservoir, a cluster of ethnically and culturally related groups called Batonka on the Rhodesian side and Tonga on the Zambian side. With a subsistence culture described as "primitive" by the officials in charge of resettlement[16] they were powerless politically, thus fairly typical of victims of hydroelectric projects designed for mines and industries. Although these people were certainly poor and probably suffering from various diseases, the effects of the relocation program certainly made things worse rather than better. The Kariba Dam relocation is probably the best-studied example of mass relocation necessitated by a reservoir, since in 1956 Elizabeth Colson and Thayer Scudder initiated a program to monitor the physical and cultural affects on relocatees. (This study was continued through 1973, and their observations were published in a number of specialized and general publications.)

A 1975 article by Scudder summarizes the experience of his specialized research into relocation problems. "For the large majority of any population, compulsory relocation is a traumatic experience which causes multidimensional stress . . . it is hard to imagine a more dramatic way to illustrate impotence than to forcibly eject people from a preferred habitat against their will."[17] Some of the Tonga people did try to resist the relocation, and eight potential relocatees were killed in a violent confrontation with the resettlement authorities. The resistance failed, and a poorly planned relocation proceeded. Officials believed that there was sufficient land to relocate the people displaced by the dam. When the time for filling the reservoir approached, it became clear that this was not the case and "resettlement [became] a crash and tension-ridden program to move the people before inundation."[18] The various Tonga and Batonka groups, which had always communicated and intermarried with the cross-river groups, were resettled on land further away from the river, on both sides, disrupting the social unity of the community (another typical feature of relocations occasioned by the flooding of reservoirs).

Although regretting that precise statistical studies are not available, Thayer Scudder concludes:

> There is good reason to expect that the transition period is associated with a higher death rate and with an increased incidence of disease. Factors supporting this interpretation include higher

population densities in relocation areas, nutritional stress caused by inadequate food supplies, inadequate domestic water supplies and changes in the nature and incidence of disease.[19]

Population densities are higher because there is simply not enough land available in most countries to make it possible to compensate the relocatees with quantities and qualities equivalent to that of the riverine land from which they have been removed. People therefore have to be resettled in areas already occupied by other groups, who become indirectly victims of the resettlement through the increased crowding to which they are subjected. Ethnic hostilities between the "host" group and the newcomers are a common result. (Host reaction to the Tonga refugees seems to have been relatively mild—they objected to the Tonga's ritual drumming, an important part of the Tonga culture according to Thayer.)

Food supplies were inadquate during the transition period because people were advised not to plant crops that would have to be harvested after the planned move—which was then postponed several times. Relief supplies from the government were required, but the supplies provided were clearly inadequate. Shortages of food and water during the journey itself added to the intrinsic stress of the move.

Ironically, supplies of fresh uncontaminated water for domestic use are typically one of the most severe problems for resettled victims of water control projects. According to Scudder:

Reception areas frequently are waterless prior to relocation—one reason why they are not already densely populated. Racing against time, understaffed resettlement authorities first must choose (often on the basis of inadequate surveys of surface and ground water supplies) the type of water system to be installed. Then installation must be completed before resettlement and financial and organization arrangements made for ongoing maintenance and repair. Throughout this process the main risk-takers again are the relocatees.[20]

Even a rather self-congratulatory account by a Rhodesian official of the resettlement of the Batonka, on the southern side of the river, admitted that one of the biggest problems that scheme faced was the provision of water supplies.[21] Before resettlement, the Tonga and Batonka had taken the water they needed freely from the river.

The inadequate food and water certainly contributed to disease and death rates: the Colson-Scudder survey of Tonga resettlement reported some eighty deaths from an epidemic of bacillary dysentery, a disease spread by contaminated water and more dangerous in populations suffering protein deficiencies and generally inadequate nutrition. Another fifty-six women and children died of a mysterious disease now generally believed to be caused by a poisonous plant gathered by the women to supplement their inadequate food supplies.

Farming practices required in the zones of resettlement mean that the Tonga have been forced to work harder and longer on worse soils.

> The Valley Tonga were peculiarly vulnerable to the impact of resettlement because of their land-tenure system. At one blow they were faced with a reorganization also of their methods of land usage. The majority of the people have been settled in the hills where they have been allocated land which normally would be subject to shifting cultivation only. Since there is insufficient land in the hills to permit shifting cultivation, given the increased population now dependent upon it, new techniques will need to be introduced permitting a conservative type of agriculture based on rotation and possibly on the use of fertilizer. There is probably too little land to permit even of short-term fallowing, which is the only conservative measure at present known to the people. In their old areas they had permanent fields, but they had not needed to develop any techniques to maintain fertility.
>
> Even given the introduction of new techniques, it is doubtful if there is sufficient land in the resettlement areas to provide the whole of the population with adequate fields for subsistence purposes.[22]

Colson also noted that women's rights in land (the Tonga/Batonka were a matrilineal society) had been severely compromised by the resettlement, in which land was allocated to men with regard to the number of wives they had. The women "lost their old rights without an opportunity of immediately establishing new ones."

> Although land has been allocated to men with regard to the num-

ber of wives which they have, this does not mean that the wives have become the owners of such land. Since the husband has the responsibility for clearing the fields, the Valley Tonga concede him the right of ownership. Few women, except widows and divorcees, have had fields cleared for them by other men and only they can claim undisputed ownership. The rest hold land only at the pleasure of their husbands. If they seek a divorce or separation, they also vacate their fields. . . . [Tonga women] have lost in some measure their independence, and have in general become much more vulnerable to the demands of their husbands and their husbands' lineages.[23]

The Volta River project

While there are few clearer examples of who benefits from (indeed, who instigates) and who pays for development projects, Kariba is not the only such case. Another is Ghana's Volta River reservoir, dam, and power station. The story is very similar, though without the racial overtones of the Rhodesia-Zambia confrontation.

The costs and benefits of the Akosombo Dam on Ghana's Volta River are well-documented, thanks to David Hart's recently published history and evaluation of the project.[24] Hart has attempted an ex post cost-benefit evaluation of the type that a fully responsible funding agency should have attempted ex ante—but which in fact is rarely if ever done. In this he has included the important work of examining who profited from the benefits and who paid the cost. It is a highly instructive exercise.

The basic idea of the Volta River project, that of harnessing the energy of the Volta River to power a smelter that would process local resources of bauxite, dates back to 1915 when the territory of the Gold Coast was under British rule. A number of successive plans for the project were proposed, but all remained abortive until the late 1950s, when the Henry J. Kaiser Company was asked by the Ghanaian government (on the suggestion of President Eisenhower) to reassess a prior project evaluation. The reassessment report produced by Kaiser recommended a dam at Akosombo and an alumina plant and smelter at Tema, utilizing local bauxite deposits.

In 1959 five major U.S. aluminum companies—Kaiser, Alcan, Alcoa, Olin Mathieson, and Reynolds—formed the Volta Aluminum Co. Ltd. (VALCO) to explore their joint interests in the project. In the next two years Alcan, Alcoa, and Olin Mathieson withdrew from VALCO, leaving Kaiser with a 90 percent interest and Reynolds with 10 percent. By 1962 a complicated financing package had been put together in which a $196 million dam and power plant built by the Volta River Authority (VRA) would supply power to an aluminum smelter owned by VALCO (Kaiser and Reynolds). The dam and power plant would be financed one-half by the Ghanaian government and one-half by loans from the World Bank and UK and U.S. bilateral financing—loans which would be guaranteed by the Ghanaian government. (The U.S. government also financed $96 million out of the $128 million total cost of the VALCO smelter.) The Ghanaian government-financed VRA was to repay its loans with the proceeds received from the sale of electricity to VALCO and other customers.

Ghana's President Nkrumah wanted a showcase industrial project for his country which would utilize its complementary resources of bauxite and cheap electric power and promote other industries through the supply of power. It was also proposed to make an irrigation scheme part of the river development project. To Kaiser and Reynolds, however, the cheap electric power was the only attraction. The smelting of aluminum from the intermediate product, alumina, is so highly energy-intensive that the cost of electricity is the primary determinant of the cost of aluminum production; thus a substantially lower price means a higher profit margin. They were not interested in Ghanaian bauxite, and despite Kaiser's own initial evaluation recommending the use of local bauxite, it was subsequently agreed that the smelter should, initially, use imported alumina. The ostensible reason for this modification was to reduce the capital cost of the project, but in fact Kaiser had a surplus of alumina from its refineries elsewhere in the world. When the VALCO smelter began operations in 1967 it used alumina refined in Louisiana from Jamaican bauxite. It still does.

It is arguable that Ghana may be better off leaving its bauxite in the ground for the present rather than making a present of it to Kaiser. However, it is indisputable that Kaiser got what it wanted, extremely cheap aluminum. The original price agreed in the power contract for electricity sold to the smelter was 2.625 mills per kWh (kilowatt hour) ($.002625). David Hart suggests that we compare this with

(a) the average cost in the 1960s of industrial power used for primary metal production in the U.S.A. which was 7 mills per kWh;

(b) a quoted reasonable price for electricity for aluminum smelting up to 1970, of 4 to 4.5 mills/kWh;

(c) the price paid by Kaiser Aluminum in 1976 for coal-based electricity for its smelter at Ravenswood, West Virginia, which was 12 mills/kWh.[25]

According to Hart, the World Bank advised Ghana that VALCO's initial offer of 2.5 mills/kWh was too low, and mooted alternative figures of 3.0 and 3.5 mills kWh. The Bank also insisted that the agreed electricity price be fixed for thirty years only (sic!) instead of the fifty years proposed by VALCO, and criticized other aspects of Kaiser's proposal. Hart concludes, "Thus the World Bank seems to have been acting as a buffer between the Ghana government and the competitive commercial interests involved in the project."[26] The World Bank eventually participated in an agreement that fixed the price much lower than its suggested 3.0-3.5 mills, however, so its criticisms on that score had little effect because it was clearly not eager to press them.

The Bank apparently had no leverage over Kaiser, and because its lending was contingent on Ghana reaching a "satisfactory" agreement with VALCO, Ghana had none either.

As an anonymous but apparently knowledgeable source explains:

The World Bank initially hesitated to back such a clearly exploitive agreement but, faced with growing Soviet influence in Ghana and the possibility of working in the interests of US foreign policy, finally relented and agreed to underwrite the scheme. The rationalisation offered for this decision was that, contrary to all previous conceptions, the success of the scheme now depended not on the smelter load and its payments for power, but on the non-smelter demand. This was only one year after the Bank had indicated that ". . . at 2.5 mills, power revenues from the smelter alone would never be large enough to cover debt service."[27]

In a case study of the Volta River project used in a Bank textbook on project evaluation, it is explained that "the mission believed that in order to attract the aluminum industry the project would have to supply power for the smelter at a price which would be competitive with the prices at which the aluminum industry could obtain power in other parts of the world"—which that source gives as between 2.5 and 3.5 mills.[28]

The rate charged VALCO for electricity can be changed only with the agreement of the World Bank, a condition usually found in Bank loan agreements. If Ghana unilaterally changes the term of any of its agreements with Kaiser, the World Bank is entitled to demand immediate repayment of its loans. This sanction has even been extended to the terms of a 1978 loan for a new dam at Kpong—a dam made necessary because VALCO preempts such a large proportion (about 70 percent) of the nation's electric power that even the huge Akosombo plant is insufficient to supply Ghana's growing domestic and industrial demand as well as the VALCO block. The Kpong agreement provides that if the country moves to change any of its agreements with Kaiser, without World Bank approval, the Bank can call in all its Volta River project loans.[29] (Since Ghana could not pay off all loans immediately, the effect of this provision would be to legitimize a whole arsenal of punitive sanctions aimed at changing either the government policy or the government itself. But obviously the hope is that the provision will act as a powerful preventive measure.)

The price of 2.625 mills was to have remained in force for thirty years, but the rate has been raised several times by agreement (the World Bank does, after all, have an interest in the financial viability of the Volta River Authority, its creditor). After long, difficult negotiations between VALCO and the VRA, the rate was set at 3.25 mills in 1977, backdated to 1973. This was still a fantastic bargain to VALCO, even more so than the original considering the radical increase in petroleum energy costs since the early 1970s.[30] Hart's calculations show that in 1976, when VALCO accounted for 58 percent of the maximum demand on the VRA's system and 65 percent of the energy used, even at the 3.25 mills/kWh rate VALCO was not paying the cost price of generating the electricity it used.

The rate paid by VALCO can be compared with that charged other customers of electric power in Ghana. The Electricity Corporation of Ghana (ECG) distributes to most other consumers a "blend" of electricity bought from the VRA and that produced itself by diesel generation. The average rate paid by customers of the ECG in 1973 was 22 mills kWh. Twenty-five percent of electricity sold by ECG goes to commercial enterprises and for street lighting, 25 percent is sold to private residences, and 50 percent goes to special load customers who buy power at a cheaper rate. When VALCO paid 3.25 mills, the special load customers paid 13 mills, commercial lighting paid 83 mills, and the domestic supply rate was 22 mills. Even though the price paid by Kaiser (VALCO) in 1980 had risen to 4.8 mills/kWh, close to twice that in the original agreement, this obviously did nothing to remedy the imbalance in electric rates within Ghana. And, at a time when countries like Malaysia and Australia are mooting 15 mills/kWh as an appropriate rate for new smelters, the VRA obviously is still supplying a stunning bargain to Kaiser.[31]

The justification given for VALCO's low rate is that as a large baseload customer, taking a uniform quantity of power twenty-four hours a day, 365 days a year, it provides a constant demand at a low administrative cost (compared, for example with the costs of metering and billing small customers). VALCO's managing director, Ward Saunders, has been quoted to the effect that the rate paid is "reasonable" because "the VRA has low operating costs. We enabled the dam to be built, we enabled Ghana to get electricity. We provide the foreign exchange for Ghana to meet its debt payments on the dam."[32] But, of course, if VALCO were not in the picture, Ghana would not have had to build such a large dam. A much smaller hydro project would originally have sufficed for the country's electric power needs exclusive of VALCO's smelter, and as the country's power consumption has grown the other customers have not enjoyed the advantage of Akosombo's cheap electric power. In fact, 65 percent of Ghana's modern energy is supplied by imported petroleum, while VALCO reaps the lion's share of cheap hydroelectricity and does not even pay the generation costs.

> VALCO's high consumption of low-cost power has had serious repercussions on the rest of the Ghanaian economy. Many heavy industrialization projects remain at the drawing board stage because of shortage of power while the general shortage has meant the imminent importation of power from Ivory Coast until the next generation expansion scheme, at Kpong, becomes operational in 1981. But even this scheme, costing $300 million, will not satisfy demand. . . .[33]

The World Bank stipulated, in its loan agreement for the Volta River project, that the authority should charge a price for its electricity sufficient to cover operating and capital amortization costs—a fairly typical requirement in loans of this type. Yet "a World Bank official overseeing the Volta River Project freely admits Kaiser's electricity payments are so low that the stipulated rate of return is not even being met."[34]

The low cost of electricity to Kaiser means that other consumers of electricity are subsidizing Kaiser by paying higher than average prices for their electricity. *This was a deliberate part of the World Bank planning when the project was approved.* As the case study in the Bank's own textbook asserts, the low tariff for electricity to VALCO had to be subsidized by residential, commercial, and other industrial users, who were (in the original design) to be charged 15 mills—the same as would have to be charged with a steam plant that had been part of an alternative project design (presumably excluding VALCO's participation). The Bank's evaluation mission "also pointed out that since the smelter tariff had been definitely fixed, the profitability of the project would depend in large measure on the size of the non-smelter load and on the tariff to be charged to non-smelter consumers."[35]

Even if one is not obsessed by power elite theories, an interesting connection is noted here. When the original agreement with VALCO was signed in 1962, George Woods was chairman of the First Boston Corporation, an underwriting firm which had enjoyed a semiexclusive monopoly on the World Bank's borrowing in U.S. capital markets since 1951. In 1956 Woods had led a

World Bank mission to Pakistan that led to the establishment of a privately owned development bank in that country.[36] While in a position of close and influential contact with the Bank, Wood was simultaneously (from 1952 to 1963) a director of Kaiser Steel. He resigned this position when, in 1963, he became president of the World Bank, and on leaving the presidency in 1968 he became chairman of the Henry J. Kaiser Family Foundation.[37]

We can now compare the considerate treatment accorded to Kaiser's compelling corporate need for cheap power wih the fate of the 80,000 Ghanaians (over 1 percent of the country's population) who lived in the 8,500 square kilometers that were flooded by the lake created by Akosombo Dam. The displaced people were offered a choice between cash compensation and the offer of land and a house in exchange for what they were losing; about 10,000 of the total chose the cash compensation.

The working party planning resettlement adopted three guiding principles:

First, that resettlement should be used as an opportunity to enhance the social, economic and physical conditions of the people.

Second, that the agricultural system should be improved to enable the people to move from a subsistence to a cash economy.

Third, that the resettlements should be planned and located in a rational manner, so that the flood victims as well as others in the area of impact could derive maximum benefits from the changes involved.[38]

The evidence indicates that despite these fine principles, the majority of the displaced people found themselves worse off than they had been previously. For one thing, the housing provided proved to be not very suitable. A "core" house of only one room was provided, and the settlers were expected to build on the rest of the house themselves. In theory, the settlers were to have been given the materials necessary for house extension but in practice this did not occur, and the cost of obtaining the required materials was prohibitive for most of the people. According to Hart, "Planning restrictions were vigorously enforced compared with the normal Ghanaian attitude of laissez-faire, so that houses had to be completed in approved materials that were difficult to obtain."[39] Could this be for the benefit of the suppliers of the expensive "required materials"? I can think of no other reason. Even when fully built, the houses were smaller and more crowded than the houses that had been flooded. They were also colder at night and hotter during the day than the traditional mud and thatch houses.

In theory, dispossessed landowners were supposed to receive compensation for crops and buildings destroyed, but "a very clear and definite policy on this issue does not seem to have been formulated." Those who were resettled by the VRA were charged for their new houses (described above) and received compensation for their crops and buildings only if their value should exceed the stated value of a resettlement house, which was £330. "Since the value put on traditional houses was very low, this happened but rarely." As sociologist D. A. P. Butcher commented, "This was not in keeping with declared policy of compensating for crops in full and replacing flooded houses in kind." Those people who chose compensation in cash rather than in kind were paid as little as 2 cedis for a traditional house (roughly $2.34 at the time of inundation). Most of the compensation payments were long delayed, paid out five or more years after the move, and thus were of no help to the people during the period in which they had to establish themselves elsewhere.[40] (Imagine for a minute how Kaiser Aluminum would react to such a compensation policy, if its operations were ever to be taken over.)

Hart found that by the end of 1976, twelve years after filling of the lake began, no compensation at all had been paid to any of those whose land had been flooded. Payments made to owners of land acquired for the resettlement scheme have been so tardy that "it seems possible the task will never be finished. . . . Since the government has not properly compensated the 'host' farmers for their lost land they consider that they have not yet sold, and so the resettlement sites have been the venue for constant wrangles over who owns what area of land."[41]

It was planned that in order to "enable the people to move from a subsistence to a cash economy," agricultural schemes would be established analogous to those described in Chapter 8.

Land was to be allocated in small plots (totaling about five hectares) to individual farmers but mechanized cultivation was to be used across several plots.

> The farmers [were to be] responsible merely for weeding and harvesting their strips of field with the costs of the use of mechanized equipment being shared on an acreage basis. The VRA was to own the tractors, distribute and sell fertilizers and buy a significant quantity of the agricultural produce. In fact, it is easier to see the resettled farmers as agricultural laborers for the VRA than as individual farmers acting in mutual cooperation. Their position was probably worse than that of an agricultural laborer for the latter is not responsible for the success of the crop. The subordinate position of the resettled farmers is further confirmed when we realise that farmers were to be "assigned" to certain types of agriculture by the VRA. About 40 percent were to be arable farmers, 40 percent tree farmers, 15 percent livestock farmers and 5 percent pastoral farmers.[42]

This type of approach soon proved to be a failure, however, and the settlers had to be given free food relief under the UN Food and Agriculture Organization's (FAO) World Food Program. The VRA then stopped clearing land itself, and offered payment to the settlers in the form of food for manual land clearing. This project too has fallen far below expectations, and "at most of the resettlement sites sufficient land could only be found for a maximum allocation per farmer of just over one hectare which is insufficient for subsistence by either traditional or modern techniques."[43]

Such was the fate of some 80,000 people who happened to be living in an area needed to supply Kaiser Aluminum with cheap electricity. Why did the resettlement project fall so far short of its own objectives? Hart's conclusion is that "the necessary inputs of time, money and effort were just not made available in sufficient quantities. . . . In the view of those running the main aluminium and electricity project the resettlement scheme remained too much of a troublesome adjunct."[44] For one thing, the portion of Volta dam construction funds earmarked for resettlement (VRA funds) was limited to £3.5 million, the Ghanaian government being responsible for expenditures over that amount.

Though Hart does not speculate on the reason for this limitation, it clearly makes it easier for World Bank economists to come up with a favorable "rate of return" if the real costs of the program are underestimated and an arbitrary limit imposed.

In an attempt at a comprehensive assessment of the Volta River project, Hart surveyed other "side effects" of the building of the dam that received little attention when the project was designed. On the positive side, he found a largely unexpected side benefit in the development of a fishing industry on the Volta Lake. Although clam and creek fishing on the lower Volta were largely wiped out by the effects of the dam, the value of the catch in the Volta Lake far outweighs that loss. On the other hand, the health menace from the spread of schistosomiasis (bilharziasis) and onchocerciasis (river blindness) have been underestimated and the agency charged with combating the spread of these diseases has received very little funding. Chemical spraying with DDT and molluscicides has typically been used in programs supported by the FAO, the World Health Organization, and the Bank to control these diseases, but these poisons have powerful effects on other flora and fauna (the molluscicides, for example, killing off all snails and not just the disease vector of schistosomiasis, so that as soon as applications are stopped the "guilty" snail can renew its numbers along with the others). Hart's attempts to attach a monetary value to production lost because of this disease are, I believe, as misguided as the Bank's efforts in the same direction: in the first place, it has to be done with a host of questionable assumptions; in the second place, in areas with limited resources and disguised unemployment, the disease will mean a hardship for individuals but not necessarily a loss to the GNP; but most important, surely this is a moral issue and does not have to be made "real" by dressing it up in numbers.[45]

The proposed irrigation of the Accra Plains by water from the dam has never been implemented, which is just as well as it would have been extremely costly and "even more inappropriate than the resettlement agricultural scheme." The filling of the lake has cut off some farmers from their previous urban markets, and lake transport has not developed sufficiently to fill the gap.

The effects of large water projects are multifarious, and those who receive the benefits are not the same ones who pay the costs.

The Rise and Fall of Lake Lanao

The next example comes from the Philippines, where the World Bank has supported the National Power Corporation (NPC) with a series of seven loans totaling $208.3 million. While some of this money has gone for thermal generating equipment, most has been spent on hydroelectric power development in two areas: Northern Luzon, where power drawn from dams in the mountainous north of the project is transmitted to the cities and industries of the island's lowlands, including the capital, Manila; and Mindanao, where also the control of rivers in the highland areas provides power for industries and agribusiness in other parts of the island. Since the inevitable inundation of land areas and acquisition of land for right-of-way has been carried forward with little or no sympathy for the rights and needs of the people who have farmed the land for hundreds of years, a process aided and abetted by the high level of corruption and favoritism prevailing in the Philippines, the threatened people have begun to fight back. Local resistance to the plans of the NPC, of which the Chico River controversy is the best known but by no means unique,[46] have led to a state of virtual warfare. A disputed area of the Chico River project is under military occupation, and a leader of community resistance to the project was murdered in early 1980. On the large southern island of Mindanao, a number of employees and subcontractors of the NPC have been massacred by rebel groups as they tried to construct transmission lines and towers for the Agus River Hydroelectric Project in the province of Lanao del Sur. The national army and constabulary (PC) stationed in the area apparently have to devote at least half of their strength to providing security to NPC construction.[47]

Our focus in this section will be once more on a lake, but unlike the lakes created by dams on the Zambezi and Volta rivers, this lake is a natural one, and the people in question live around the lake. Lake Lanao, the second largest lake in the Philippines, lies in an upland setting of great natural beauty. The Maranao ("People of the Lake") practice the Muslim religion, and their colorful batik clothing and the distinctive architecture of their mosques set them off culturally from the "Christian" Filipinos who occupy the lowlands—and staff the national government and the National Power Corporation. To the visitor they seem gentle and friendly—a delightful people in a lovely landscape—but their land is crisscrossed by military patrols, shots ring out in the night, and poverty and anger provide recruits for rebel groups that sabotage, ambush, and murder. The poverty and the anger have deep roots, of course, and the story that Lindy Washburn calls "The Rise and Fall of Lake Lanao," a story of the manipulation of the water level of the lake by the downstream powers-that-be, gives some insight into the problem.

> As long as the Maranao have been a people, Ranao—the lake—has existed. To the lake they have bound their identity: in their own eyes and in the eyes of outsiders they are Maranao, people of the lake. On its shores they have established their villages and towns and built their mosques, with its water they purify themselves for prayer, in its wetlands they cultivate their rice, from its depths they gather fish, across its expanse they transport goods and people, from it they take water for drinking and cleaning.[48]

To the government in Manila and the National Power Corporation, however, Lake Lanao is the headwaters of the Agus River, a prime resource for the development of hydroelectric power to be used throughout the island of Mindanao. The power supplied will be used by such industries as the National Steel Corporation, the Kawasaki sintering plant, International Harvester, and USIPHIL, among others. A total of seven power plants are planned along the length of the Agus River.

What has this to do with the Maranao who live on the verge of Lake Lanao? The Agus River has always been the natural regulator of the lake: when the lake level is high, more water leaves the lake than when the level is low. The wide fluctuations that this causes in the volume of flow in the river are intolerable for purposes of power generation, which requires a steady flow. Therefore, if the power potential of the system is to be realized, Lake Lanao must be managed like an artificial reservoir: "the flow of the river must be stabilized at the expense of destabilizing the lake level."[49] In order to guarantee a uniform flow of water through the generation equipment, an intake regulation dam has been built at the outlet of Lake Lanao, which can potentially raise the surface level of the lake to 702 meters or reduce the surface level to 692 meters. (The dam was completed with Asian Development Bank financing and began functioning only in November 1977, although two World Bank loans, the Third Power Loan in 1962 and the Fourth Power Loan in 1967, had initiated the installation of "permanent control works at outlet of Lake Lanao for partial lake regulation.")[50]

This manipulation of the lake level has had drastic effects on the lives of the people who live beside the lake and depend on it for multiple essential functions. Their mosques are built on the water's edge to facilitate the daily ablutions required by their religion; a rise in the level of the lake would flood the mosques, while a fall would separate worshipers from the lake by many meters of muddy flats. The best agricultural land is the basak, the marshy flat land used for wet-rice agriculture, watered by the tributaries feeding into the lake from the mountains. Lowering the lake to a level that affects the water table will diminish the traditional productivity of the land, while raising the level of the lake would flood the basak area, also rendering it useless.[51] Wide fluctuations in the level of the lake would obviously have a drastic effect as well on the other source of the region's food, fishing, by destroying the habitat of some fish and permitting the rapid expansion of others. River transportation is also made difficult by shorelines that alternately overflow and recede from banks and docking facilities.

The year after the intake regulator began to function was the driest in five years. While a constant flow of water was delivered to generators downstream, the level of Lake Lanao declined from 701.78 meters in November 1977 to 699.97 meters in June 1978. It does not sound like much—less than two meters—but it is the lowest the lake has ever fallen in the memory of those who live beside it. In the summer of 1978 Lindy Washburn interviewed a number of the people who made their living from agriculture, fishing, and lake transport in and around Lake Lanao. Below are some of the comments these people made to her.[52]

Nearly everyone here is a fisherman or farmer. For the farmers it is also hard. Like me, I have a *basak* field. One side is on the lake and one side on the river. Because we had no rain, the river was very low. When the rain came, the ground soaked it up quickly, it ran out and went to the river. It did not stand in the field like last year, so I could not plant any rice. Last year I harvested almost twenty sacks. (P.4)

Our harvest is less now because of the dry season (or drought) and the amount eaten by the rats. For two years we have not harvested anything. The lake is very low, so the soil becomes cracked and hard. Before the water would come up to here (midcalf) but now it barely covers the ground. Because of this the rats are more numerous. They easily come into the fields and reproduce rapidly. (P.6)

There is a time (season, month) when the fish can be caught. But these days the catch is very small.... Ever since November 1977 until now I have been *minus P 50* each day. Before I caught worth fifty pesos every day, now most of the time I catch nothing. The reason for this is the lowering of the water. This construction they have made along the Agus River in Marawi draws the water away. (P.8)

There are many waterlilies which collect here, making it a good area for fish to come and lay their eggs. But when the water evaporates or becomes lower the rocks and weeds are exposed. The fish cannot come up to this area, so fewer reproduce. The fish in the lake are disappearing.

When I went out before with this spear gun, I could sometimes catch ninety pieces of the big tilapia in one day. Three pieces sold for ten pesos. Each day I would sell around sixty pesos' worth, then we would eat the rest. Today I usually catch zero. Sometimes one or two, but rarely that. I make two pesos in one day. (P.10)

It's difficult for us also in washing clothes and taking a bath, and in fetching our drinking water. At first we thought it didn't matter that the lake was lowered, as long as we could use a faucet for water. But now we have to pay a lot for the faucet—fifty or sixty pesos a month. At least the lake was free!

The problem is, we supply the water for the electricity and we get nothing from it: our electricity bills are high, our water bills are high. We supply, and in the end we are left with nothing. The National Power takes the electricity for factories in Iligan. We have no factories in Marawi. When we want to work for them, we go and apply for a job as laborers. Then they say they have openings for foreman only. So a foreman goes to apply, and they say their openings are for laborers only. It's all politics. . . . (P. 12)

In past harvests I would get three hundred sacks of rice from my land—it was good and fertile, well-watered. This year I am not sure if I will be able to get twenty sacks. Even twenty sacks I can't count on! The reason is not rats, it is because there is no water. There is no water in my fields. . . . Here in Taraka we have three main sources of income—farming, fishing, and launch operating. The launch operators have stopped, the fishermen can barely catch enough for their families and the farmers are as I have said. . . . (P. 16)

What recompense have the Maranao received for the strangulation of their means of livelihood? Very little. They have, after all, not been directly dispossessed from their land, like the victims of artificial lakes. Some, who own land on the lakeshore, have even had their land extended when the waters recede (conversely, if heavy rains come and the lake level allowed to rise in order to regulate the river, these same people will lose land to the lake). They have merely been deprived of less than two meters of water in the lake—which has had a devastating effect on their earnings. People who once made a decent living for their families are now striving desperately to feed them; many have had to emigrate to distant towns in search of work.

The Maranao have been treated with contempt by the NPC "developers." They were not informed in advance of the effects of lake regulation by those who were making the plans, nor allowed to suggest alterations and compromises that might have mitigated the effects of the project on their basic needs. A derisory compensation of 10,000 pesos ($1,350) was allocated to each municipality bordering the lake and its tributary rivers, and "it is strongly rumored that grateful public officials in the eligible municipalities seldom pass the benefits onto their constituents."[53] In the government's priorities, the need for hydroelectric power overrides the need of a powerless, heterodox people for a stable livelihood.

Irrigation Projects

Reservoirs, clearly, must displace people unless they are planned for already barren areas. But surely irrigation must be wholly beneficial? For irrigation is, by definition, the delivery of the right amounts of water at the right time for growing crops. It makes farming possible where it was not before, or it enables two crops to be grown in a year when natural rainfall permits only one; it delivers a secure water supply in regions where rainfall is capricious; it increases the productivity per unit area of land and thus the value of the land; it permits the cultivation of higher value crops; it (usually) increases labor inputs (and thus employment) on a given area. Surely this is a way in which small farmers can benefit from development, and the landless laborer as well?

So I thought when I began this part of my research. A survey of the literature on irrigation, and an investigation of a few Bank loans for dams and irrigation projects, has revealed a picture of benefits and beneficiaries that is considerably more complex than the above. And, it demonstrates once again that benefits from projects implemented in unequal societies will accrue disproportionately to the wealthy and powerful. There are several different ways to design irrigation projects, and each has its own pattern of effects on small farmers and the landless.

The most obvious detrimental effects are to be seen when the land to be irrigated is expropriated by fiat from its previous owners so that it can be allocated in large tracts to foreign-owned agribusiness, which will work the land with labor-saving modern, mechanized agricultural methods transplanted from the fields of California. (The detrimental effects on the poor are similar, of course, whether the agribusiness entrepreneur is local or foreign.) Two well-documented World Bank projects follow this pattern: one, the Dez Irrigation Project in Iran and the other the agribusiness activities of the Bud Corporation in Senegal.

The Dez River project

In 1960 the World Bank made a $42 million loan to Iran for a huge hydroelectric dam and pilot irrigation project on the Dez River in the western province of Khuzistan. The loan was made even though its staff appraisal had rejected the project: "[The Bank's] own calculations showed a thermal power plant (using flared gas) would have been more economic."[54] Puzzled as to why an oil-rich country would need a 6.6 megawatt hydroelectric generating facility, the Bank was intensely lobbied by David E. Lilienthal, former head of the TVA, and at the time head of a consulting firm, Development and Resources Corporation (D & R) financed by the banking firm of Lazard Frères. Bank president Eugene Black had put Lilienthal in touch with the Iranians "to see if the billion dollar program of development they have put under way can make use of us."[55]

Lilienthal, a water resources enthusiast thanks to his TVA years, found the suggestion of a dam at Dez irresistible. "Fate had a hand in it all," he enthused in his journal; "God must have intended that a dam be built in that great gorge."[56] Indignant at the Bank's rejection of the dam, Lilienthal hammered away at meeting after meeting with challenges to their engineers' reports. He and the Iranians wanted a grandiose project that would provide the shah, who was still trying to consolidate his hold on the country after the ouster of the nationalistic Mossadegh, with a tangible symbol of progress. Despite the negative noises from the Bank, Lilienthal and the Iranians began to build the dam anyway, gambling that they would be able to force the Bank's hand. Lilienthal was also fired by cold war considerations: the Soviets had offered help with the development of Iran's northern rivers, and the shah indicated that he would prefer that "the West" outperform them by financing the Dez River dam. "In the back of my mind," Lilienthal wrote,

> there is the strong feeling that, powerful as the Bank is, it could not permit itself to get into a life-and-death row with Iran at this particular juncture in human affairs. The political and military importance of that country has never been greater to the West; only a strong technical case against the Dez would be strong enough, it seems to me, to outweigh these other considerations.[57]

Lilienthal and the shah won; the Bank approved the project. A project appraisal textbook explained rather lamely that although Dez was judged to be the less economic method, "the Bank's freedom of choice had been considerably reduced by the investment already made by Iran of the equivalent of about $15 million in the dam and generating equipment."[58]

Lilienthal was not just interested in the dam, he was determined to promote development of the Khuzistan region à la TVA. In a country where scarcity of water was the chief constraint on agricultural expansion, irrigation was the obvious direction to take. Looking down on the flat land below the dam site, Lilienthal had another vision:

> The land is dark, almost black, bottom land. Our Dutch agricultural people [a firm subcontracting with D & R] say that on this land are "good farmers," quite a tribute, in a simple phrase that means much the same the world over: men who know how to deal with land and water and the forces of nature, with the things they have at hand. With the dam providing an assured water supply during periods of dry weather—such as now—a summer crop and a green cover once more are possible. I could just see what could happen when the irrigation works, after the Dez is built, begin to be filled with water.[59]

A pilot irrigation project to cover 20,000 hectares on the left bank of the Dez River south of Dezful was included in the Bank loan for the dam (which when dedicated was named Reza Shah Pahlavi Dam, after the shah). The pilot project suffered from a series of vicissitudes, however—first the opposition of the landlords in the area, who had originally agreed to make improvements and pay water charges; then the shah's land reform and the formation of the Khuzistan Water and Power Authority (KWPA) along the lines of an Iranian TVA. Peasant acceptance of new risks and new debts was not as high as hoped, and the idea of sweeping aside the peasants to make room for mechanized agribusiness took hold in both Iran and the World Bank.

In 1968 new legislation was passed. The Law Governing Establishment of Companies for the Development of Lands Downstream of Dams gave the Ministry of Energy the "authority to establish Agro-Industry Companies . . . for the purpose of maximum utilization of water resources and land irrigable from dams."[60] Now the World Bank jumped in with both feet. In 1969 it signed Loan 594 (Dez Irrigation Project—Stage I) for $30 million with the government of Iran. In the loan agreement the Bank bound Iran to close consultation on the uses of the water supplied under the project.

> Sect. 5.02(a): The Borrower shall not permit the water made available as a result of the project financed under the First Loan Agreement and as result of the Project financed under this Agreement to be utilized for any purposes other than those provided for in such Agreements, without the prior approval of the Bank.

> Sect. 5.14: No part of the area of the Project shall be developed by vertically-integrated commercial enterprises (agribusinesses) except to the extent that such development, including its scope and location, is consistent with the obligation of the borrower under Section 5.01(a) above and is in accordance with a schedule of implementation determined by agreement between the borrower and the Bank.

Lest readers take that last paragraph as hostile to agribusiness, it should be said that Section 5.01(a) requires only that "the Borrower shall carry out the Project with due diligence and efficiency and in conformity with sound agricultural engineering, economic and financial policies and practice." These clauses indicate, rather, that the World Bank was fully cognizant of, approving, and probably even controlling, the subsequent lease of large tracts of land to new corporations.

In the early 1970s several corporations were formed by some of the world's largest banks, farm equipment manufacturers, and Iranian capital to obtain leases to the rich valley land irrigated at Dez. In the majority of cases these were joint Iranian-foreign companies. Helmut Richards has compiled a list of these corporations, together with their holdings and their shareholders, as of 1973. This is reproduced on the facing page, with the percent ownership of each corporation.[61]

Despite the heavy foreign ownership of these projects, most of the capital was raised in Iran, primarily from the Agricultural Development Fund (ADFI), established in 1968. The ADFI ser-

Hashem Naraghi Agro-Industries of Iran and America (20,000 hectares)

Hashem Naraghi Development Co., Escalon, California	51
First National City Bank, New York	30
Iranians' Bank, Teheran	10
Three individual stockholders	9

The Iran-California Corporation (10,000 hectares)

Agricultural Development Fund of Iran (ADFI)	15
Khuzistan Water and Power Authority (KWPA)	5
Mr. K. Taleghani and Partners	10
Trans World Agricultural Development Corp.	30
Bank of America International Financial Corp.	20
John Deere Corp.	10
Dow Chemical Corp.	10

Iran Shellcott Co. (15,000 hectares)

Shell International, Ltd.	70.5
ADFI	15
Bank Omran (belongs to Pahlavi Foundation)	10
Mitchell Cotts (operating agents)	4.5

International Agricultural Corp. of Iran (17,000 hectares)

Chase Manhattan Bank	15
Bank Melli	5
Mitsui (Japan)	5
Ahwaz Sugar Beet Factory	15
ADFI	15
Diamond A Cattle (Roswell, New Mexico)	15
Hawaii Agronomics (operating agents)	15
KWPA	15

Dezkar (5,000 hectares)
    Shareholders: a group of retired generals

Dez Farm Corporation (17,000 hectares)
    Shareholders: former peasant farmers and landowners in the area of
    the Dez Irrigation project. Managed by the government.

viced only large farmers, as the minimum loan amount was one
million rials ($13,200).[62] And where did the ADFI get the money
to lend? From three World Bank loans, in 1970, 1972, and 1974,
for a total of $60.5 million (Loans 662-0, 821-0, and 1046-0).

And, in 1973 the International Finance Corporation (IFC), the Bank's private enterprise affiliate, invested $1.25 million in one of the agribusinesses, the Iran-California Corporation.[63]

No people had to be resettled when the Dez River dam was constructed (one of the reasons Lilienthal saw the divine hand in the project).[64] But what of the "good farmers" occupying the land leased to the corporations? They had to move away, off their old villages and into "new towns" out of the way of the modern agricultural operations, but close enough so they remain available as agricultural labor. In 1974 it was estimated that 17,000 people had been displaced to make way for corporate farming. What Richards has to say about the resettlement sounds like a scene from the Volta River dam resettlement. The displaced people were crowded into "modern" (but smaller) cinder block houses that are hotter in summer and colder in winter than their traditional mud houses. Communal taps and outside lavatories (one for twenty persons) are the only plumbing facilities.

In theory, landowners were compensated for the land taken over. But, according to a top executive of the Iran-California Corporation, "All the villagers got progessively in debt as Khuzistan modernized. So badly in debt that when KWPA came to buy their lands, the net gain of the villagers was almost nothing."[65] In any case, all of those who were forcibly relocated in the new cinder block towns were billed for their new houses, which pretty much wiped out any sums owing for their land.[66]

The final irony of this project is that the investments were not even profitable for the corporations. Some in fact may have invested not so much in the expectation of big profits as to curry favor with the shah's government to the benefit of other investments.[67] But these huge businesses with their California technology were not the "good farmers" praised by Lilienthal, "men who know how to deal with land and water and the forces of nature, with the things they have at hand," and most of the big foreign investors have withdrawn from the agribusiness companies. In a neat case of cannibalism, IFC-funded Iran-California (and two other companies) were taken over by the Bank-funded Agricultural Development Fund (now called Agricultural Development Bank).[68]

Bud-Senegal

A parallel example is that of the Bud Corporation of California, specialists in mechanized market-gardening of fruits and vegetables for the tables of citizens of the richer countries. In 1971, the Dutch subsidiary of the California firm, Bud Antle, proposed to establish a plantation in the Cap-Vert area of Senegal, which would supply off-season produce, shipped by sea and air, to the European market. When agreement was reached with the Senegalese government, in 1972, a local subsidiary was formed with majority foreign capital but a 48 percent participation of a government corporation. The new corporation was named Bud-Baobab, probably because the company had to uproot scores of magnificent baobab trees, some as much as twenty-five feet in diameter, with Caterpillar bulldozers.[69]

The Sengalese government agreed to expropriate the people occupying the 800 hectares that Bud had selected as the most convenient for vegetable growing; it also exempted the company from profit tax and from customs duties for a ten-year period. It provided as well a large part of the infrastructure for the plantation, particularly roads and irrigation.[70] The International Finance Corporation made two commitments to Bud's Senegal affiliate, in 1972 and 1974.

The water supplied to Bud was piped from Northern Senegal. As Claude Reboul has emphasized, the favoritism showed to Bud in this respect amounted to a virtual slap in the face to the Senegalese peasants and their need for water.[71]

Despite this tender treatment, Bud, like the agribusiness corporations in Iran, failed to turn a profit. They had trouble with their transport contracts and trouble with the water, which turned out to be too salty for their drip irrigation apparatus, but above all the yields achieved by their ultramodern methods of farming were laughable. As a trouble-shooting mission of experts concluded in 1978, "The promoters of Bud thought they could transplant American agricultural methods which they themselves had scarcely mastered into the completely different context of the Cap-Vert—and thus the lamentable yields."[72] By 1976 the deficits were so heavy that the private sponsors refused to put up more capital. The Senegalese government therefore put up the money itself (and IFC made its third investment in four years), became the majority shareholder with 61 percent of the stock, and named the company Bud-Senegal. The funds and efforts that the state poured into the company for the next three years brought yields to the point where Senegal became the leading exporter of off-season vegetables in Africa, but the financial problems were never solved, and in September 1979 the company went into liquidation. The chief result of the project, according to Christophe Batsch, has been to convince the "good farmers" of the surrounding area that the old methods of cultivation are best, even if their profits are skimmed off by merchants and transporters.[73]

The Senegal River project

But have the leaders of Senegal, and the World Bank, learned any lessons from this debacle? Claude Reboul remarks that just two months after the liquidation of Bud-Senegal, the first stone was laid for the Diama Dam on the Senegal River, part of the ambitious Bank-funded Senegal River project. The project involves Mauritania and Mali, in addition to Senegal, and is another exemplary case of water management tradeoffs, with an international twist. A second dam will be built upstream of Senegal, at Manatali in Mauritania, to provide electric power for Mali, and the entire river will be dredged annually to provide Mali with an outlet to the sea. The costs of these changes to the riverine farmers of Senegal will be disastrous, as the dam will put an end to the silt-bearing floods which have irrigated and fertilized the river banks that they cultivate. Claude Meillassoux asserts that the peasants are being deprived of the energy of the river so that the energy can be harnessed to furnish electricity to industries, and that the peasants should demand permanent compensation from the authorities in recompense for what they are losing forever.[74] The authorities, however, are putting in place their plans to "give" the peasants expensive irrigation works and to force them to grow rice for commercialization, rather than the millet and kitchen vegetables which they now grow on the river flood plain.[75]

Meillassoux points out as well that ecological studies underline the severity of the effects that the proposed works will have on the fish population, an important part of the local food supply, as well as other flora and fauna of the area, some already rare. But the most affected populations along the river bank have been told nothing about what to expect—about the end of the annual flooding, about changes in the number and species of fish. When questioned about ecological problems of the project (including the displacement of 10,000 herders when the lake behind the Manatali Dam is filled) the planning director of the Senegal River Valley Development Organization (in French, OMVS) replied complacently, conceding that herders and fishermen would be disrupted and that two species of fish would be eliminated. But, he countered, "environmental questions don't really have the same place in Africa as they do in Europe or the United States, because here people don't have enough to eat."[76] The fact that it is the herders, the fishers, and the peasants along the river flood plain that do not have enough to eat, and will have even less if the predicted effects of the dams are realized, is clear to other observers if not to Mr. Sheikh Bati. But, as the Bud-Senegal episode should have made clear, "the economic and social effects, like the ecological consequences, are for the most part dangerously unpredictable."[77]

Land speculation and irrigation

Even where there is no official resettlement policy, small farmers holding lands that are slated for irrigation may stand to lose them, through various ploys, to large farmers and land speculators. For one thing, officials and their associates who have advance knowledge of planned development can buy up property before the owners have found out that their land will increase in value in the future. This "natural" expropriation is facilitated by the fact that dams and flood protection embankments are usually built first, and irrigation channels last, in many water management projects. "In the interim period, farmers are deprived of both the flooding which sustains traditional agriculture and the irrigation water which might support modernized agriculture.'"[78] In the interval, the farmers may be forced to sell out to larger entrepreneurs, who can afford to bear the cost of a few years of reduced income in view of higher land values in the future.

Cynthia Hewitt de Alcantara gives a vivid example of one mechanism by which small farmers were separated from their property in the Mexican northwest:

> Some of the *colonos* in the settlement of Marte R. Gomez remember in the following way the process through which the majority of their fellows lost their land. Around 1953 it became known in Sonora that the large new irrigation canal (El Canal Alto) of the Alvaro Obregon Dam would pass near their property and make it immensely more valuable. Shortly thereafter, according to the recollections of the surviving *colonos*, the official bank began to delay their crop credit, and provide inferior or unusable wheat seed and fertilizers. Their expenses rose and they had several disastrous years. . . .
>
> In 1956, when water from the new canal had just reached the lands of Marte R. Gomez and permission to use the old wells of the farms had been revoked, the manager of the official bank called a meeting of all the *colonos* there. He said that clients of the bank owed it an impressive amount of money, and that they would either have to sell their land or rent it in order to repay their debts. This was apparently part of a programme ordered from Mexico City, in which the government foreclosed on all properties with outstanding debt to federal agencies. The majority of the *colonos* of the settlement sold their twenty hectares for between 400 and 700 pesos a hectare (when the market price was about 5,000 pesos a hectare) to two of the largest and most politically influential land-owners of the state.[79]

But there are, or course, some small farmers that do hang onto their land. There are even large irrigation schemes that specifically plan to settle small farmers on demarcated plots of land to be watered by the irrigation works. These plans are, of course, a variety of "settlement schemes" in which irrigation may be only one, though a major, component and thus the remarks on such schemes in Chapter 8 are relevant here. To illustrate, let us look at the Bank's Appraisal Report of the Rahad Irrigation Project in the Sudan, for which an IDA credit of $20 million was extended in 1975.

The Rahad project

The first thing to be noted is that, as in most settlement schemes, people were already living and farming the area in question. According to the Bank's report, a 1969 cadastral survey and farm census showed that some 16,000 households, of which some 14,800 worked small landholdings and 1,200 were landless families lived in the immediate vicinity of the project in an area of 319,000 feds (a fed is just over one acre).[80] They raised mostly sorghum, the staple food, and kept livestock that shared the sparse grazing with nomadic herds. The proposed irrigation project that would occupy nearly all of this area (300,000 feds), however, would support only 13,700 tenant families, or about 2,300 fewer people than already farmed the territory.[81] There would be no room for about 12 percent of the people who lived in the area *before* the project, except perhaps in secondary and tertiary occupations serving the tenant families who received land.

The farmers who were allowed to stay would be subjected to the rigid discipline of the management corporations (again, typical of all types of settlement schemes). It can hardly be put better than in the Bank's own appraisal:

The Rahad Corporation Act specified relationships between the Corporation and its tenants:—

   (a) The Corporation has power to reject applications from unsuitable persons, even if they held title or rights to land in the area;

   (b) The Corporation will provide inputs and services for, and would market cotton, groundnuts and any other cash crops which might be adopted in the future;

   (c) The Corporation will provide a full range of mechanized field operations, including land levelling, planting of crops and harvesting of groundnuts; and

   (d) The tenant will pay a fixed "Land and Water Charge" in lieu of a share of the proceeds of crop sales.

The tenancy agreement would be for an indefinite period but could be terminated only in case of default by the tenants: it would not be mortgagable or assignable. The agreement would provide that the tenant must grow approved crops only and follow the Corporation's approved rotation, initially: Cotton: groundnuts: cotton: groundnuts: cotton: fallow.[82]

As Martin E. Adams remarked in a review article, "large irrigation schemes have special problems emanating from their high costs. Financiers inevitably demand the imposition of authoritarian management to safeguard the flow of benefits from the outset." In the case of the Rahad project, "the total income accruing to government and the corporation will be designed to cover administration, overhead, and development costs, but *any variation in income due to prices and yields will be borne entirely by the tenant.*"[83] (Emphasis added) Worse than this, the fixed land and water charges were planned to rise as the tenant's productivity rose—meaning, apparently, that the risk of failure would be borne by the tenant but productivity gains would be appropriated by the corporation. The projection in the appraisal report predicted:

> At full development tenant's average gross income would have risen to £Sd 410 [$1,175 per family]. Project charges would be increased progressively to maintain net tenant incomes at about £Sd 200–240 (US $575–690), or two to three times the estimated present farm family income in the project area. However, since sorghum would not be included in the permitted rotation, tenant families would need to purchase staple foods at an estimated cost of £Sd 15 [$43] per year.[84]

Thus, again as in other settlement projects, the tenants would be, essentially, cheap salaried labor, but with a ceiling and not a floor placed on their earning power. For an income that, according to Bank calculations, was two or three times their present one, they would have lost all autonomy as cultivators, all chance to protect their own livelihood through subsistence cultivation. And, at full development, the corporation would appropriate fully half of their gross income for "services provided." It seems the real beneficiaries of this project will be the contractors, the consultants, and the government tax rolls.

The Question of Water Charges

The Bank has tried to insist that beneficiaries of irrigation projects be required to pay for the costs of the projects, either through direct water assessments or land taxes that would capture some part of the increased productivity. In practice the Bank has usually had to content itself with requiring that charges cover at least operation and maintenance, though ideally it would prefer that the capital costs be amortized as well. Bank studies have even proposed that the project authorities, or government, might aim at recapturing up to 100 percent of the increased productivity made possible by the water supplied.[85] It has also been suggested that water be auctioned to the highest bidder, in order to ensure that water goes where its marginal productivity will be highest.

While the last suggestion would surely ensure that the wealthiest and most powerful would be able to get all the water they need, at the expense of the poorer, one cannot make such a glib judgment on the general principle of recouping water costs from farmers. If the beneficiaries are large landowners, then patently they should not be subsidized at state expense. If they are small landowners, they may or may not be privileged relative to the national mean, and there is some reason to the argument that private persons should not be able to make windfall gains from publicly funded improvements. A correct policy must be decided, in short, in the context of the general conditions of power relations and equity within the society. In practice, given the types of government supported by the World Bank, it is likely to be the large landowners who are subsidized—even if rate covenants are insisted on by the Bank they are likely to be ignored—while the little guys are subjected to the regimentation and surplus appropriation apparent in the Rahad project.

It should be unnecessary at this point to stress the fact that heavy water charges, whether paid directly to a project authority or via taxation, perform the function of forcing producers more deeply into the market economy and precluding subsistence production that "merely" feeds the family and allows a few purchases. One finds scattered throughout Bank literature remarks to the effect that water rates and land taxes should be set "so as to provide an incentive to farmers ... to step up production."[86] The incentive here is not that of growing more so that one can earn more at the market—where conditions may in fact be very unfavorable for the farmer—but the incentive of growing more (or higher value crops) so one's land will not be taken away, one's lease canceled, as the penalty for nonpayment. Seen in this perspective, it does not matter so much whether water charges are collected from large farmers and landlords—they are already fully incorporated into the market system. It is only the small and powerless who may prefer to limit their dependence on the market, and thus have to be coerced to deliver their surplus. An expensive irrigation system provides both the reason and the excuse for this coercion.

The Bank has been criticized by many thoughtful observers in the water resources field for financing only huge, technically sophisticated, expensive projects and ignoring the cheaper, labor-intensive small-scale works constructed and maintained by local labor.[87] There is a good reason for this: the Bank is not set up to do anything else. The Bank's function is to push huge sums of money; inexpensive local systems should not need large amounts of foreign aid, and if local resources cannot be found to construct and maintain such waterworks, it must be asked what in the structure of the society is preventing such apparently productive use of resources.

Irrigation and Inequity

And finally there is the impact of irrigation in Asian societies in which the existing structure of landholdings predates the coming of irrigation, or in which existing works are to be rehabilitated, with no new project authority to skim off the surplus.

In such societies we find problems analogous to those discussed in relation to "area development projects." That is, the existing inequalities in wealth and political power will usually manage to skew all attempts at an equal distribution of benefits from irrigation. This problem has been elegantly summarized in an article by three water resource specialists who are openly concerned about the problems of equity posed by the distribution of this scarce resource. They point out that "inordinate influence" by the more powerful farmers can be exerted in three ways:

(1) when distributaries are improved or relocated so as to improve water deliveries to land owned by powerful irrigators; (2) the rules of water allocation are changed or ignored so as to allocate larger and more regular water supplies to more powerful irrigators; and (3) selective enforcement of rules exists such that the more influential farmers are given favorable treatment.[88]

Most large-scale canal irrigation systems are "planned to be egalitarian in that equal quantities of water are allocated per unit of irrigated land," though in fact this may be very unequal since those who have larger amounts of land will get more water. Empirical evidence suggests, they say, that water is often not equitably distributed with respect to land surfaces, particularly in times of water scarcity when there is not enough to go around. The authors identify two main sources of inequality. The first is geographical: farmers at the "head end" of the distributary canal have a more secure supply than those at the tail end, both because of inefficiencies in distribution (seepage and evaporation losses) and because irrigators further up the canal have the opportunity for illegal diversion of water to their own fields. The tail-end fields simply have to take what's left over.

The second source of inequity is political:

> Farmers with larger holdings and other forms of economic power frequently have more secure water supplies. The social status of individual irrigators, which is frequently related to their economic power, is also cited by many as an important factor influencing water security. . . . In the short run, those with greater economic power and social status may have an inordinate influence on the operation of irrigation systems. To illustrate, they may be able to influence the formulation and implementation of irrigation schedules so that their fields receive earlier, larger, and more assured deliveries of water. Further, if water-distribution regulations are broken, larger farmers may be able to secure more favorable resolutions to the charges assessed against them. In the longer run, those with more power and status may be able to influence decisions on the redesign of irrigation systems so that their fields become more satisfactorily served with water. In addition, those with more economic power may be able to buy land having more favorable access to irrigation than those with less power.[89]

To illustrate this general theory in more concrete terms, Anne Booth has made a careful study of irrigation in Indonesia, for which the Bank has made fifteen loans since 1968, totaling $732.6 million. Most of this money has gone for the rehabilitation of existing irrigation networks originally constructed by the Dutch colonial government. After six credits had been extended for irrigation rehabilitation (to 1975) it was realized that "in many cases only primary canals had been 'rehabilitated' together with the necessary structures (dams, watergates, etc.). The delays in completing the secondary and tertiary channels meant that the benefits of the rehabilitation had not resulted in higher yields for the farmer."[90] Therefore with its seventh loan the Bank turned its emphasis to the building of tertiary networks for the projects it had originally funded. But the construction of tertiary canals—the network that delivers the water to individual fields—and even more, the administration of the water distribution system once these canals are completed, depends on the quality, technical expertise, and dedication of local organizations that have to run these systems. And it is here that the inequality and pervasive corruption of Indonesian society and government seem to be thwarting the goal of efficient use of water.

Ideally, says Booth,

> the process of water management in gravity-flow irrigation systems involves constant attention from experienced supervisors down to tertiary level. Such supervisors must have the trust and confidence of individual cultivators because in times of relative water shortage they must decide which fields can receive sufficient water to grow the high yielding crops such as paddy, sugar cane, etc. and which fields must be deprived of water and therefore be obliged to cultivate less water-intensive crops.[91]

But in Indonesia the reality is quite different. Corruption is all-pervasive, and the irrigation system is not immune to this ill of the larger society. "The powerful position of the *pengamat* [irrigation overseer] naturally opens him to the temptation of taking bribes from farmers, to ensure that in times of scarcity their fields will be the favoured ones."[92] The Bank, recognizing the key role of village organization, is now pressing the Indonesian Department of Public Works to emphasize the formation of village-level water use organizations. "How successful this policy will be, given the difficulties outlined above, remains to be seen," Booth remarks with obvious skepticism. "Governments everywhere in Southeast Asia tend to be sensitive about potential rural subversion and are often reluctant to encourage farmers to join organizations for fear of infiltration by politically destabilising elements."[93]

> [T]hose villages in Central Java where water management was most efficient were ones characterised by relatively equal access to irrigated land, little absentee ownership and village leaders who enjoyed the trust and confidence of the people. The problem of water management cannot be divorced from the wider socio-economic problems facing agriculture in Java, among them unequal access to land, growing landlessness and increasing absentee ownership and ineffective administration at local and village levels.[94]

Booth also attempts to make some judgments about the allocation of benefits from these IDA and Bank irrigation investments. She points out that even if the system were working perfectly, it would benefit a small proportion of the owners of irrigated riceland (*sawah*), and country-wide, less than half the rural households own any sawah at all. The households benefited, poor though they may seem to the World Bank, are not by any means the worst off in Indonesia.

Since, as she pointed out, the water management system is not ideal, access to water depends de facto on "the ability of the operator to influence the decisions of local irrigation officials." This further narrows the group of beneficiaries to include two of the most powerful groups: the village officials who obtain the best irrigated land in the village as a prerequisite of office; and the officials who accept bribes for redistribution of water, thus realizing at least part of the benefits of improved productivity. Booth concludes,

> Given the present limited access to land, and irrigated land in particular among rural households, it appears likely that the irrigation infrastructure may aggravate existing income inequalities especially in those areas where pressures of population are greatest. This is hardly an argument for not undertaking such investment, but it does mean that some of the claims put forward for irrigation investment as a means of achieving "redistribution with growth" should be viewed with scepticism in the Indonesian context.[95]

10
Forestry and Tree Farming

As everyone knows, Smokey the Bear is a
symbol of the United States Forest Service. And
for almost a hundred years the United States
Forest Service had been the greatest landholder
in Chamisa County, although most of the land it
held had once not so very long ago belonged to
the people of Milagro. And, since the Forest
Service's management of its recently acquired
property tended to benefit Ladd Devine the
Third, big timber and mining companies, and
out-of-state hunters and tourists before it benefitted the poor people of Milagro, the poor
people of Milagro tended to look upon Smokey
the Bear as a kind of ursine Daddy Warbucks,
Adolf Hitler, colonialist Uncle Sam, and Ladd
Devine all rolled into one.
—John Nichols, *The Milagro Beanfield War*

As an example of the Bank's policy and practice with respect
to the allocation of scarce resources, this chapter will examine
its lending for forestry projects within the context of a worldwide crisis of forest depletion.

It is generally agreed that the progressive destruction of the
forests of the Third World constitutes a crisis of major proportions. A Bank publication estimates that although the forest area
in "developing countries" exceeds 1,000 million hectares, it is
being consumed at such a rate that it could disappear within
60 years.[1]

This is probably optimistic; an ecologist warns that

> at the most extreme, most lowland forests of the Philippines and Peninsular Malaysia are likely to have been logged over by 1985; much the same applies to West Africa. Little could remain of Central America's forests within another 10 years. Virtually all of Indonesia's lowland forests seem certain to have been exploited for timber by the year 2000; something similar could well hold good for Colombia and Peru, where, together with extensive areas of eastern Amazonia in Brazil, cattle ranching could claim large tracts of virgin forests.[2]

Of course, not all forests which are exploited for timber are doomed to disappear. In the tropical rain forest, for example, where population pressure is often relatively light, the loggers take out relatively few trees (though they often damage many others) and some kind of green cover speedily reasserts itself. But unless there is sound forest management, and appropriate sylvicultural measures are taken, the forest is permanently degraded from the standpoint of its usefulness to people. But management in tropical forests is a rarity, limited to one or two research plots or window-dressing operations on a very small scale.[3]

Where forests in the tropics are disappearing, their disappearance may be critical not only because humans consume wood directly in so many forms, including fuel, but because the forests play such an essential role in conserving and storing water. In the absence of forest cover, water runs off the surface of the earth, causing floods, carrying away tons of nutrient-laden topsoil, silting up riverbeds and reservoirs downstream. The consequences for a region's agricultural productivity can be devastating.

Blaming the Poor

If there is general agreement on the existence of a crisis, there is less agreement about the causes of this crisis. Here we find an interesting example of the World Bank's class bias, for the Bank puts the blame squarely on the shoulders of the poor.

> Humans are—out of perceived necessity—destroying the basis
> of their own livelihood as they violate the limits of natural sys-
> tems. Those most vulnerable to these trends are the poor of the
> world. Their search for the basic requirements of food and fuel
> often force them to hasten the destruction of their own productive
> environment.[4]

Overexploitation of existing wood fuel resources and the destruction of forests are caused by shifting or settled cultivators,
both the villains and the victims in the Bank's ideology. "Roughly
90 percent of annual wood consumption in developing countries is used for fuel."[5] "Increasing population pressure has
always been a major cause of forest depletion. . . . The expansion
of *encroachment* and shifting cultivation is the major cause of
forest depletion."[6]

Eric Eckholm in *Losing Ground* (one of only three books cited
as references for the sector policy paper) also puts the blame on
the poor, incidentally defending corporate exploitation in a very
misleading fashion:

> The two principal causes of deforestation today are *land clearing*
> *for agriculture and wood gathering for fuel*. A third cause is lumber
> harvesting for direct or industrial use, but, *as a source of deforesta-*
> *tion, this is far less significant on a global basis than the other two.*
> *Much of the world's timber and forest-products industry manages*
> *its available forests on a sustained-yield basis.* In some of the areas
> where timber concessionaires, local or foreign, are often less con-
> siderate of the future, such as in Southeast Asia and tropical Africa,
> the principal negative consequence is frequently not land denuda-
> tion—vegetation of some sort springs up quickly in the humid
> tropics—but rather the economic loss as the most valuable and
> usable species disappear.[7] (Emphasis added)

Eckholm is sensitive, however, to the inequities in distribution
of agricultural land which may lead to the clearing of forested
land not well suited for cultivation. He is eloquently sympathetic to the plight of the poor people who are destroying their
own habitat.

> People hungry for land are not apt to leave forest or pasturelands
> unplowed, regardless of what ecological soundness dictates. Farm-
> ers hungry for bread are not likely to defer production this year to

enhance soil quality for the next generation. Those with no other means than wood to cook their dinner cannot be expected to leave nearby trees unmolested even if they are labeled "reserved" by the government. And people brutalized by exploitive economic and social systems will probably not treat the land any more gently and respectfully than they are treated themselves.[8]

The Bank's policy paper mentions—in passing—that "tenure insecurity and exclusion of people from better land by inequitable patterns of land ownership"[9] is one of the causes leading to encroachment on forest areas. The "coordinating author" of the policy paper, Graham Donaldson, went even further in an interview: "In fact, the population need not press in on this marginal land if we were to organize our agricultural systems better. In short, it's not population growth that's the key, but rather the poverty element."[10]

But are the poor, in fact, the chief authors of the destruction of the forests? Experts not so close to the World Bank have made a very different diagnosis. For example, Jack Shepherd says in *The Forest Killers*, "cut and slash agriculture does pose a threat to the tropical forest. But a far more serious threat comes not from native populations in search of food and land, but from international cartels devouring timber."[11] Shepherd tells of literally millions of acres of concessions for logging operations obtained by companies such as Weyerhauser and Georgia-Pacific based in the United States, and Japanese companies (Sumitomo Forestry, Misui Busshan) in the Philippines, Indonesia, and Malaysia.

Norman Myers provides a more nuanced view, explaining that farmers usually invade forest lands that have first been opened up by commercial loggers who take only the most valuable species. He also gives more precise estimates of the proportional responsibility of the different types of forest exploiters.

Elimination of tropical moist forests stems primarily from the commercial logger/follow-on cultivator combinations, which is thought to be accounting . . . for 200,000 km² per year. The fuelwood cutter could well be responsbile for 25,000 km² per year, and the ranching entrepreneur (confined to Latin America) for 20,000 km². . . . These figures do not include other agents of forest destruction . . . who eliminate the forest for various reasons, but whose destructive impact is not on a scale to match the three main categories.[12]

Overcutting in Southeast Asia

Three Southeast Asian countries—the Philippines, Indonesia, and Malaysia—in recent years provided 66 percent of all world exports of hardwood, compared with 16 percent from other tropical countries and 18 percent from countries in the temperate zone.[13]

The Philippines was the first of these to be exploited for its timber resources. An FAO survey predicts that by 1990 at the latest all virgin forest designated for production purposes will have been cut over,[14] while according to World Bank estimates reforestation compensates for only 5 percent of the forest cut.[15]

American and Japanese capital is deeply implicated in the wood industry on the southern island of Mindanao, which produced 72 percent of the country's logs in 1977.

> Two companies are 100 percent American owned, *Findlay Millar* and *Weyerhauser.* Lianga Bay is 83 percent owned by the American firm Georgia Pacific Corp. Boise Cascade, also American, has 40 percent equity in *Zamboanga Wood Products. Agusan Wood* is a member of the Ayala group of companies, and thus has 40 percent of its holdings owned by Mitsubishi. *PICOP* is controlled by the Sorianos, who are Amerian citizens. *Nasipit* and *Philippine Wallboard* have both British and Amerian equity holdings. *Sta. Ines Melale* has Amerian and Japanese equity, while *ADECOR* has a tie-up with Mitsubishi.[16]

Banks such as Citibank, Bank of California, and Bank of Nova Scotia led syndicates lending funds to these industries.

In the past two or three years, the Philippine government has taken what pretend to be steps toward conservation and reforestation. In October 1978 President Marcos announced a ban on commercial logging operations in "the entire Ilocos region, Benguet and Mountain provinces, Central Luzon, the Metro Manila area, certain portions of the Bicol region, the Leyte provinces, Masbate, and the Lake Lanao watershed area." Curiously, notes the "Mindanao Report,"

> the logging ban has been concentrated in areas where minimal logging has been taking place. Loggers in Mindanao can still continue to destroy forested areas, and deplete the regions's natural

resources. Despite a massive reforestation program launched by the government President Marcos himself admitted that only 50 percent of loggers are complying with reforestation and forest protection directives.[17]

The World Bank remarked, in its project appraisal for the Pantabangan watershed project (to be discussed below) that "excellent legislation exists today to manage and control logging and grazing and to undertake reforestation. However, this legislation has rarely been enforced."[18] At the same time, the government promotes and encourages the expansion of the wood-based industries, and grants huge new concessions to private companies.[19] The absolute, as well as relative, share of the Philippines in world hardwoods exports is declining, however; the exhaustion of the nation's forests, and the government's attempts to ban the export of unprocessed logs to encourage the local processing industry, has impelled the international companies (and a number of Filipino companies that supply them) to move to the relatively unexploited Indonesia and Malaysia.

In 1975 the Malaysian government adopted a national forest policy "to conserve forest resources, to realize sustained yields from the productive forest, and to curb the export of logs in favor of increased exports of wood products."[20] How well such policies will be implemented and enforced remains to be seen, especially as under its 1963 constitution forestry is reserved to the states. The persistent overcutting of the last decades in Peninsular Malaysia means that local industry will run short of wood in twelve to thirteen years and will have to import logs, while Sarawak is following the path of severe overcutting already experienced in Peninsular Malaysia and Sabah. Weyerhauser officials in Sabah concede that in less than thirty years there will not be any commercially exploitable wood left in the jungles under their control.[21]

The large-scale exploitation of the huge hardwood forests of Indonesia's outer islands did not get underway until the economy was turned in the direction of export-oriented growth under World Bank guidance in the late 1960s. Timber exports, which amounted to only $10 million in 1966, had risen to $160 million in 1971, and approximately one-third of all foreign capital investment in the country at that time was in the timber industry. This investment was promoted by First National City Bank (Citibank), among others, which published a brochure in 1969 called *Indonesia: The Timber Industry.* This stated that

> it is not unlikely that Indonesia will replace the Philippines as the largest timber supplier in the Far East, particularly now that the Philippines must conserve its fast depleting forest reserves. Already more than 30 foreign firms, including American, Japanese, and Filipino interests have been granted rights to exploit a total area of about 5.6 million hectares of timber land in Indonesia. Japan, one of the world's largest users of logs in particular, has been gradually turning to Indonesia for log supplies as the Philippines has restricted log exports.

Citibank assured potential investors that they could expect tax exemptions, assured repatriation of profits, and an "appropriate" depreciation of fixed capital assets, as well as U.S. insurance to investors.[22]

In little more than a decade, the timber companies had denuded large areas of fine hardwood stands. According to a recent work on the Indonesian economy:

> The development of the timber industry has probably come in for more criticism than any other industry, with charges ranging from denuding the soil and absence of reafforestation, through coercion of small farmers to surrender land to logging interests, to speculative brokerage of timber concessions. But above all . . . policy in this industry has been marked by the assumption that the national economy can "take off" after a few decades of plundering the national heritage for re-investible funds.

There were horror stories of timber "mining" similar to that of Weyerhauser in Malaysia (Weyerhauser was also in Indonesia, with a 1 million acre concession that it plans to exploit completely before its concession expires in 1990.)[23] A Danish-French company in Riau was reported to have cleared out 20,000 hectares of a 70,000 hectare concession within two years. "Moreover, the huge profits to be made out of forestry were bound to excite the avarice and authoritarianism of the powerful local hierarchies . . . [whose] own short-term private capital accumulation was in direct conflict with the long-term ecological basis of mass livelihoods.''[24] It was reported that farmers in one area of East Kalimantan were ordered *not* to grow rice, the apparent reason being to force the farmers to offer their labor to the timber companies. In 1973, a report by the governor of South Kalimantan stated that ''if local residents attempted to continue their traditional rights of tree-felling to make homes they would be accused of being thieves.''[25]

It is clear that the international lumberjacks are going to follow the cut-and-run strategy wherever they can get away with it. They can be controlled only by governments who are willing and able to get tough in enforcing strict conservation measures. But if the ability of Third World governments is very far from what would be needed for effective enforcement, the more serious problem is that the will is lacking. The fact is that collaboration with the timber companies will bring more immediate returns, to governments and well-placed individuals, than the attention to the long-term ecological basis of mass livelihoods.

World Bank Policy

What, then, is the World Bank's prescription for remedying and reversing the destruction of the forests of the Third World?

The Bank's sector policy paper allows, obliquely, that uncontrolled commercial cutting occurs, but refuses to go as far as to admit that it is a big part of the problem of deforestation. The policy paper also notes:

> It is estimated that more than two-thirds of the natural closed forest area in developing countries is subject to no regulation or control. . . . The extraction of this resource, however, provides valuable foreign exchange that can provide potential benefits to a much larger population.[26]

And the commercial exploitation of the forests by private corporations is seen as an almost totally favorable proposition:

> Developing countries' exports of forest products rose from $1,500 million in 1970 to over $3,000 million in 1975. Future world

market demand for tropical hardwoods suggests that this trend will continue. The developing countries contain the world's main reserves of tropical hardwood; they have, therefore, a major advantage in this area.[27]

True to its general philosophy, the Bank looks forward to an even stronger demand from the rich markets for tropical lumber, even though most of the "foreign-exchange earnings" will be carried off by the private, usually foreign-owned companies doing the exploiting, and the rest will go to their local allies, not those who bear the environmental costs.

If few or no curbs are to be placed on the commercial exploitation of tropical forests, what then does the Bank prescribe to help solve the urgent problems of overcutting? First, the cost of reforestation is held to be a responsibility of the government, not of the corporations. This is for a reason exactly analogous to that for government spending on roads and electric power: it has to be done if the private sector is to continue to profit, but it's not profitable for the private sector to do it.

> Public ownership has been the historical norm, because the land has generally not been formally occupied (and, thus, never subject to private ownership or control). Forestry also involved long-term investment, where not all the benefits can be appropriated directly as in the form of wood, and is thus not generally attractive to private investors.[28]

Second, forestry programs should be devoted not so much to preserving the existing forests as to replanting lumbered-out areas with cash crops in the form of trees. The most valuable tropical hardwood species require between fifty and one hundred years to grow large enough to produce logs, and no corporation or even government, it would seem, has a time horizon that long. On the other hand, it takes only twenty-five to thirty-five years for softwood trees. Thus, according to the Bank's published country study of Malaysia, "many preferred species of temperate and tropical hardwoods can be regarded as virtually non-renewable resources" to be mined rather than cultivated.[29] What governments are to do in the forestry sector is to grow uniform stands of commercial tree varieties, to be harvested by private enterprise. This, of course, is exactly what the timber barons want.

In the tropical countries, fast-growing species of pine and eucalyptus are planted to produce short rotations. In most cases these plantations are not established on barren land, but on land that has recently been selectively cut, or clear-cut, by timber companies. In some cases the indigenous forest is cleared away for the plantation simply because the species that grow there are not commercially valuable (they may have value for the local populations, but this is commonly not taken into account in the evaluation of projects). It is clear that the ecological value of such plantation projects is, at best, neutral. In the case of small-holder tree-farming projects, trees which bear commercial crops (fruit, nuts, gum arabic), and pulpwood trees with an even faster rotation are prescribed.

Third, the Bank professes to desire an increased share of value-added for the exporting countries through more local processing of logs.

> Rather than developing the capability to process tropical hard-wood logs locally—and thereby reaping a major share of the potential economic benefits—many export unfinished logs only and very few have developed export-oriented, plantation-based wood industries. There is an urgent need to bring about a change in this situation. Securing more favorable terms of trade for the forest product exports of developing countries is a key issue.[30]
>
> In the field of large-scale wood processing, the Bank will assist major log-exporting countries to define appropriate policies for the development of their export trade in forest products. Special emphasis will be given to increasing local processing of manufactured products and maximizing value added. It will advise governments how to formulate incentives for the establishment of domestic manufacturing facilities.[31]

The issue of local processing is an ambiguous one. Frequently, the local processing is in the hands of the same concession-aires (transnational or local) that are guilty of overcutting, and it is they who get the profits. It is clear from the citations just given that it is seen by the Bank as a "sweetener" for even greater exports of wood products from poor to rich countries. But in practice, nations that have passed laws trying to enforce local processing have found themselves losing business to other countries which place no such restrictions on the export of logs (as the Philippines is losing markets to Indonesia and Malaysia).

The Bank likes to think of itself as an "honest broker" reconciling the interests of both its borrowers and the multinational corporations that want to exploit the borrowers' forests. But how, in practice, do they do this? Details of this type are usually closely guarded corporate secrets. In the forestry sector, as in practically every other, the Bank is intensely interested in the overall legal framework that sets the terms for the exploitation: its sector policy paper promises "assistance to governments in preparing or revising forest policies, laws, regulations, land use plans, and contracts allocating forest concessions, timber sales, and wood processing. . . ."[32] Yet in the few cases in which evidence allows us a glimpse at the type of advice the Bank gives to its borrowers, it seems as if the advantage it presses is all to the good of the multinationals. Let me give two examples, the only ones I have found save for some vague statements about "strengthening forestry institutions." Both come from unpublished policy appraisal documents.

The first example comes from the staff appraisal report for an $18 million loan to the Ivory Coast in June 1979 (sixteen months after publication of the sector policy paper). The project itself will be described in more detail later; for the moment I am concerned only with a comment in this paper on a quota system introduced by that nation in 1972 that attempted to increase its share in processing of the logs cut by requiring that 40 percent of the total cut be made available for local processing. The Bank's comment was:

> Enforcement of the 40 percent quota regulation is difficult and available data indicate that it is not always respected. . . . There are, however, sound reasons for not insisting too rigorously on the immediate in-country processing of the highest quality logs. There is a strong demand for these in Western Europe, where they are sold to a large number of highly sophisticated veneer and plywood producing industries with secure market outlets for their products. Quite apart from the difficulty of achieving rapid penetration into these markets, the installation and operation of such specialized machinery in a humid tropical environment impose additional

costs which render it difficult for such plants to compete effectively with industries more favorably located.[33]

Apparently the Bank's support for local processing extends only
so far as is deemed convenient by the foreign corporations extracting the logs.

The second example of Bank advice comes from the list of
agreements reached (i.e., leverage, or measures required by the
Bank as a condition for extending the loan) for a $12 million loan
to Jamaica, also in June 1979. In this case the Bank's pressure on
behalf of "the private sector" is apparent. In order to implement
this project, a new state-owned corporation, the Forest Industries
Development Company (FIDCO) was formed. It was specified
that four out of the twelve members of the board of directors
were to be from the private sector. Even more revealing, however, is this paragraph:

> Jamaican income-tax laws and regulations do not provide incen-
> tives for investment in forestry; revaluation is not permitted and
> loss carry-forwards are limited to five years. As well as penalizing
> FIDCO, present regulations would strongly discourage the private
> sector from investing in forestry. To provide equitable treatment
> for forestry investment, the government would confirm in the Plan
> of Action that it would study the income-tax regulations with a
> view towards forestry and discuss its study with the Bank by Dec.
> 31, 1981. The study would be part of its overall review of income-
> tax regulations.[34]

From these two examples it would seem that the Bank's view of
its role as an "honest broker" comes down mainly to making sure
that its borrowers meet the wishes of the corporations by providing more favorable laws and policies. It is not a stance that favors
the preservation of the rapidly dwindling tropical forests. It is,
however, consistent with the Bank's diagnosis of the problem as
caused by the uncontrolled "spontaneous" destruction of forests
for agricultural settlement and by poor people cutting down
wood for fuel. The problem of "spontaneous" agricultural settlements should presumably, in the Bank's view, be distinguished
from "controlled" settlement sponsored by corporations and
governments, much of which has been funded by the Bank. The

destruction of forests in Costa Rica and El Salvador, for example, has been attributed to the rapid spread of cattle ranching to provide beef for the North American market. The Bank has been heavily involved in financing beef ranching in Central America. The sector policy paper admits that the "most controversial" area of the Bank's current rural forestry activity is "the conversion of high tropical forests to areas of agricultural settlement, e.g., the Brazil settlement and Indonesian transmigration projects";[35] in other words, the destruction of forests for agriculture.

Whatever sympathetic noises the Bank makes in its policy paper on the plight of the poor people, it is clear that in its view the poor are the "forest killers," while the corporations are rational harvesters, providing income directly to only a few, it is admitted, but supplying foreign exchange to the whole society.

Many of the sectoral issues relating to these circumstances are *sociological.* Securing the cooperation of local people who are destroying the

> forests (shifting cultivators, nomadic pastoralists, and "squatters") presents formidable social problems. The measures required to ameliorate agricultural abuses are obvious—reduced stocking, voluntary migration, and resettlement in sedentary pursuits. Success in achieving these measures, however, can be both costly and politically unpopular. Further, resettlement is frequently impracticable because there is nowhere else to go.[36]

What, then, does the Bank mean when it says that over half the forestry projects in its projected lendings program are "people-oriented" rather than "industry-oriented"? It is time to examine a few specimens of these people-oriented projects, through the confidental project appraisal reports, to see what they involve. As it happens, the three projects on which I could get the most details are all quite different from one another. Two of the projects are in the Philippines; one a smallholder tree-farming project in Mindanao and the other a watershed protection project in northern Luzon. The third project is in the Ivory Coast.

Tree Farming for PICOP

The first case study is Loan 1506 to the Philippines ($8 million in December 1977). The Bank calls it a smallholder tree-farming project, but we might rename it "pulpwood for PICOP." It is a project which is *both* people-oriented and industry-oriented: the people are to work for the industry. A publication by the Food and Agriculture Organization (FAO), which prepared the project for Bank financing, gives this description of its essentials:

> 1. This project forms part of an on-going Agro-Forestry Develop-ment Plan initiated in the late sixties by the Paper Industries Corporation of the Philippines (PICOP) with the objectives of en-suring raw material supplies for its mill complex at Bislig Bay in Eastern Mindanao and improving the socio-economic conditions of smallholders in the area. . . .
>
> 2. Under the terms of the project, loans will be granted by the Development Bank of the Philippines (DBP) to some 1,300 small-holders in the Bislig Bay area to assist them in planting tree crops and in developing crop and/or livestock production. . . .
>
> 3. Smallholders will plant about 10,400 ha. of *Albizzia falcataria* over a seven-year period. Trees will be grown on an eight-year rotation. PICOP will provide the seedlings at cost and technical assistance in exchange for first rights to the mature pulpwood at the prevailing market price. . . .[37]

Who is PICOP? The FAO document describes it as "the sole domestic producer of newsprint and the major supplier of in-dustrial paper in the country." The government has granted it a "preferred and pioneer industry status under which the com-pany receives a number of incentives to development."[38]

What the FAO paper, and the glowing Bank descriptions of the project, do not tell us, is that PICOP was the fourteenth largest corporation in the Philippines in 1977, the year of the loan, with sales of P 800.8 million ($108 million). It was controlled by the Soriano family, one of the great oligarchic families of the Philip-pines who hold U.S. citizenship, and part-owned by the multi-national International Paper Company. With its Bislig Bay sub-sidiary, PICOP is the largest holder of concessions for forest exploitation in Mindanao, with a total concession area of 233,539 hectares. In the same year it received the World Bank loan (for it is clear PICOP was the actual beneficiary), it also received three syndicated foreign bank loans for a total of $80 million; syndicate leaders included Citicorp International, Bancom International, and Philippine Pacific Capital Corporation.[39]

The FAO paper makes it clear that it was PICOP who promoted the program of tree farming for the purpose of meeting its need for supplies of pulpwood.

> PICOP could advantageously meet 100 percent of its groundwood requirements from Albizzia, but insufficient supplies have limited PICOP's consumption of this species to only 15 percent of total requirements. In the late 1960s the Company launched its Agro-Forestry Development Plan. Under the plan a participating farmer devotes 20 percent of his land holding to food and livestock production and 80 percent to fast-growing pulpwood trees (mainly Albizzia) grown on an eight-year rotation.[40]

Farmers eligible for participation in the project would be those occupying a minimum of 5 hectares in the project area, that is, within a 100 km. radius of the PICOP mill at Bislig, "the maximum economic distance for extending technical assistance." Further, the FAO document notes, the farmer must sign an agreement contracting to market his production under the project to PICOP.

It may be true, as Bank publicity claims, that farmers can get rich growing these trees:

> Look at the history of the first Philippines smallholder tree farm project. This was a pilot program that tried to get farmers interested in accepting credit for growing *Albizzia falcata*, a fast-growing pulpwood species. The response was quite dramatic. The farmers took to it very quickly, and some of them made a lot of money from it. I remember visiting the project area about two years ago; we met one particular tree farmer who had made so much money out of the project that he had bought himself a school bus out of the proceeds. He had painted the name of his bus on the front: "Miss Albizzia Falcata." I think that must have been an encouraging indication to other farmers in the area that forestry can be a profitable business.[41]

Since the Albizzia do not produce income until the seventh

year after planting, the trees in question could not have been planted later than 1970, seven years before the World Bank loan was signed. Unless the Bank was involved in designing PICOP's original pilot project, it had nothing to do with this man's wealth at all, except to take it as encouragement for the expanded phase of the project. But if the planted area is to be expanded from 1,816 hectares in the pilot project to 10,400 hectares in the expanded project, it is possible that the "market price" could decline considerably when the expanded area is in full production. In any case, since all farmers have a marketing commitment to PICOP, it is obvious that the mill will be the main determinant of the market price that it will pay. Thanks to the Bank loan, and the "pioneer industry" status entailing privileges and monopolies granted by the Philippines government, this fourteenth-largest corporation in the Philippines will have 10,000 hectares of captive supplies for its mill, to be purchased at a price determined by itself. The project evaluation assumes sales for a 10-hectare plantation of P 2,048 ($276) ("constant value"—presumably that of the late 1970s when the project was evaluated) in the seventh year after planting, rising to a peak of P 6,212 ($838) in the fourteenth year and then leveling off to P 5,799 ($783).

I wrote to a local contact in Agusan del Sur, near the PICOP territory on the island of Mindanao, who has made a study of tree-farming projects in the area, to enquire about rumors I had heard that small farmers could not afford to wait eight years for payment for the trees and were selling out their woodlots to PICOP employees. This person confirmed that the smallholders constitute a captive supply for PICOP, as there are no major alternative uses for falcata (the common name for Albizzia falcataria):

> They are the only buyer and solely determine the price, whether the supply is big or small. The farmers are completely at the mercy of the company. . . . (But) the company is not completely at the mercy of the farmers, even if they were organized, which they are not. The farmers under contract with PICOP supply only a portion of the company's needs. They have their own industrial tree plantations . . . 33,000 hectares of man-made forests.

My source said that he did not know of farmers who had to sell out, and did not think it had happened on a large scale.

I rather think that small farmers were wise enough not to sign up in the first place, knowing very well that trees can't be eaten.

The complaints I heard are of another kind, that the price of falcata is low and does not increase over the years very much, that at the time the contract was signed the promised income looked very big, but is in fact much smaller due to inflation, that there are losses because PICOP is slow in collecting the trees which have been prepared for hauling.

What it comes down to is, that only farmers with enough land to sustain their families or people with a stable income from other sources can afford to plant falcata. M. D. Rebueno [author of an admiring article about the scheme in a Manila newspaper] admits as much when he says: "Yet agro-forestry is not the main business of farmers in the Bislig area. It is only their sideline." Indeed, only under-utilized lands can at some profit be planted to falcata. Small farmers . . . won't be able to hold out. If the World Bank claims to help small farmers, they make a claim they won't be able to substantiate. Only the better-off are given the chance to make a gain from their otherwise idle lands.[42]

The Pantabangan Watershed

My second case study, also from the Philippines, is a watershed management project, for which a $38 million loan was granted in July 1980. In this case the title of the project accurately represents the concern behind it. As the project appraisal document states, the impetus to the project came from concern over the fate of big projects in the lower reaches of the watershed:

> A total of approximately 1.4 million ha. of the denuded lands is located in watersheds or catchments which are *sources of water to important irrigation, power, and water supply dams. The potential threat to the economic life of these facilities* as a result of erosion and sedimentation has caused considerable concern to the Government.[43] (Emphasis added)

The government's ban on logging in 1978, mentioned above, was in fact for the purpose of controlling watershed erosion in watersheds serving a number of multipurpose dams, not for control of excesses of logging companies elsewhere. The appraisal admits that in the area covered by the project, excessive commercial logging was the cause of forest depletion, shifting cultivation affecting only 3 percent of the area of the watershed.[44] According to the Bank's appraisal, "The people living in these watersheds have moved there due to population pressure and scarcity of employment in the lowlands. They are extremely poor and survive on shifting hillside agriculture and occasional labor income from Government public works."[45] It's worse than that, but we have to get outside of Bank publications to find just how poor these people are, and, more important, why they are poor. The major part of this loan is going to the Pantabangan watershed, an area of 24,500 hectares serving the Pantabangan Dam, a multipurpose project for which the World Bank extended a $61 million loan in 1974. Two Mennonite church workers from the United States who visited Pantabangan in 1978 described what they found there:

> Pantabangan used to be a small community nestled in the Upper Pampanga River Valley just north of the Central Luzon Plains. Rice, vegetables, and other market crops, supplemented by a few small craft projects gave a better than average livelihood to this community of 14,000 people. But today, people weep when they look down from their resettlement area high above the dam site which swallowed their land and homes since 1974.
>
> Water from the dam brings second and third rice crop harvests each year in lands below the dam on the plain. But for the people of Pantabangan, this World Bank supported project has brought brokenness, the end of a secure village life and no hope for the future. Over 100 of the houses built by the government for the people have slid down from the hillside and been destroyed because the ecological balance developed over the centuries was destroyed. When the hard rains came, nothing was left to hold the loose clay in place.
>
> Land on the hillsides is poor for farming so many families walk up to 20 miles to distant hillsides where little fields of rice and vegetables are tended—far away from roads or markets. One or two children are left in the Pantabangan resettlement houses to attend school and to keep the house from being repossessed by government authorities. Relief rations come irregularly from the World Food Program. These once dignified people are also the objects of

other "welfare" projects, both public and private, but hope has gone out of life. Little wonder that the military had to be sent in to make sure that local people would *not* attend or disturb the glittering opening ceremonies of the dam, purportedly Asia's largest, about two years ago.

Before the project was started, people tried protesting through petitions, negotiations, and demonstrations. Twice they went to Manila in trucks and buses to protest at the presidential palace. Nothing happened. Now various training programs come and go, but without local industry, the only real jobs are tree planting for the government and a few jobs at the dam site. One resident wondered how this could be called development or modernization. He also wondered how the World Bank with its world wide staff in Washington could be so insensitive to the destiny of local people.

Compensation for their land has long since been used up. We asked one old man if he had any advice for the dozen or more other such projects now being planned or developed in the Philippines with foreign financing. He kicked the ground, looked out over the lake and in a voice of resignation said, "We are just little people. We have no say."[46]

Now these people who have been crowded onto the upper slopes of the watershed threaten further destruction because they are forced to farm on slopes unsuited to farming. The tree-planting jobs provided by the government under its reforestation program are not working as designed; the operations, "by offering employment only for planting are, in fact, providing the local population with an incentive to destroy the seedlings in order to get more employment," says the World Bank. "Any successful watershed management program would have to give the local population a stake in the survival of the trees."[47]

The World Bank's attempt to provide a solution to the problem of keeping the trees planted has two main thrusts. The first is to prohibit people from carrying out the type of land-use activities deemed destructive.

Field crop agriculture would be *restricted* to land of 5 percent or less average slope, unless the land is bench terraced. Existing benched vegetable producing areas in the Diayo and Canili watersheds would continue operating but any expansion would be *strictly controlled*. Grazing of family livestock belonging to local inhabitants would be *permitted in designated areas.* The number of animals would be *strictly controlled* and stall feeding would be encouraged.

Influx of population into the watershed would have to be *regulated* so that the total population does not exceed the capacity of the project to provide an adequate livelihood. With uncontrolled migration, people would overuse the land and defeat the purpose of the project. NIA would control the influx of people into the project area by a system of *registration* which would give priority for employment to the existing residents.[48] (Emphasis added)

Such control, it is recognized, would be extremely difficult (and "prohibitively expensive") to implement without the cooperation of the local population. The Bank's solution is to provide the inhabitants with a profit-sharing plan. Sustained full-time work for 4,710 people or 1,570 families is promised for 1985 (these figures apparently assume that three members of each family would be employed). This represents about one-fourth of total population in the watershed, if the figure given for 1975 population is extrapolated to include the 4.1 percent annual growth rate that it is said the area experienced between 1970 and 1975. (It's not clear how the people displaced by the reservoir fit into this figure.) Labor requirements are expected to peak to 6,780 people or 2,260 families by 1995, when according to the Bank's projections, labor demand would significantly outstrip supply. The shortage would be filled by immigration, presumably by an influx controlled by the registration authority mentioned above.

These favored residents of the watershed would receive not only a labor income (at a rate of $300 per year, or P 16 [$2.16] per day of work), but would be associated with the profits of the scheme.

Initially, a revenue sharing scheme would be adopted since the project is not expected to generate a profit [from the sale of tree products] till the eighth year of operation. A certain percentage or a fixed amount of gross revenues would be distributed to employees starting in the third year of operations. Such an early distribution of revenues is important to gain the confidence of the people in the area and to impress on them the personal advantages to be derived by making the project successful. . . . In addition to the individual incentive schemes outlined above, communal incentives would be provided by assigning a portion of the revenues or profits to the village for projects such as scholarships, communal water supplies, playgrounds, etc. to be chosen by communities in consultation with NIA [National Irrigation Authority, the implementing organization]. The size of communal incentives would depend on the forest protection and fire prevention performances of the various communities.[49]

It must be admitted that this is, if nothing else, a novel and ingenious plan for solving the problem of denuded watersheds. The whole plan would depend on an intensive public relations effort, utilizing "trained sociologists" to explain its working to the people whose cooperation is so essential.

It is of course impossible to say at this point, before the project has even begun and without personal knowledge of the community that it concerns, what the effects will be. Nevertheless, a few predictions may be hazarded.

—Jobs will be provided for a large number of people. In fact, it is likely that this is a make-work proposal thinly disguised as a profit-making project. I would predict that profits do not materialize, but if they do that they will be skimmed off by a corrupt bureaucracy and the rank-and-file employees will see little of them.

—The employees of the project will be set as police against the rest of the members of the community, for whom the rather vague communal incentives will be seen as a laughable motivation, if not an outright insult.

—The immigration and land-use controls will be subverted by corruption, and the watershed will continue to deteriorate. The Philippine government has never heretofore taken the livelihood of its poor people to heart, and a manipulative pretense of doing so in this case, in order to attain the real ends of the program—to preserve the downstream benefits of the dam and irrigation—will not be successful.

Forestry in the Ivory Coast

The third case study concerns a World Bank loan in June 1979 to the Ivory Coast. The Ivory Coast is, like the Philippines, a country whose stands of valuable hardwood species have attracted international timber companies; and like the Philippines also, it is predicted that "if present patterns persist, the Ivory Coast will lose virtually all its primary forest by 1985."[50]

As we have seen in other cases, the World Bank acknowledges the activities of the commercial timber companies without criticizing them. Timber exports by expatriate companies have been a major source of foreign exchange and of government revenues in the Ivory Coast. The Bank's appraisal report describes the pattern of logging:

> To date, exploitation of the high forest in the Ivory Coast has followed the historic pattern of selectively logging only a few species with high value on the export markets. . . .
> Without the program, it is doubtful that any of these areas could have been retained as productive natural forest. Previous logging activities had resulted in the extraction of the readily accessible, high quality exportable timber and, without Government's initiative in commencing the reforestation, all four sites would have been virtually valueless as sources of timber at least over the next 20 years.[51]

But, just as in the sector policy paper, it is not the big companies that are blamed for taking away the valuable species, but the spontaneous clearing activities of shifting cultivators, and the collection of firewood. It is briefly noted that cash crop plantations also contribute to the felling of the forests:

> There are plans for the development of the still largely unexploited, but potentially rich, southwestern part of the country where oil palm, coconut and rubber estates, with associated smallholdings, are already being established. This energetic pursuit of agricultural expansion and diversification has contributed to the rapid reduction of the country's forest reserves and their preservation is now a matter of major concern for both economic and environmental reasons.[52]

This type of clearing must be okay, because the Bank has made at least twelve loans to the Ivory Coast precisely for the development of oil palm, coconut, and rubber estates. It is the uncontrolled activities of the rural population that are pinpointed as the cause of ecological destruction:

> A major preoccupation has been the depletion of the country's high

forest resources by inadequately controlled exploitation and the infiltration of the rural population. New farms are quickly established in *forest areas rendered accessible by roads constructed for the extraction of timber.* . . . The most recent Government estimates indicate that the area of exploitable forest is being reduced at the rate of 0.5 million ha. a year due to *agricultural encroachment upon logged over areas.*

Where population pressure in the area is high, *farmers follow the loggers and cut and burn most of the remaining timber,* irrespective of its value.[53] (Emphasis added)

It would seem that the simplest way to stop deforestation, then, would be to stop the loggers from building roads that the agriculturalists can follow, but as the country's power structure has become dependent on the leavings of this commercial exploitation, this has never been seriously considered. It is also considered unrealistic to enforce a program of sustained-yield cutting, though lip service is paid to this goal: "While the rational exploitation of the natural forest in order to enhance its productivity . . . remains a long-term strategic objective, the means of achieving this increased production are unclear and past efforts have met with little success."[54] If the forests will be totally destroyed within five to ten years, of course, a long-term strategic goal of rational exploitation is nonsense. Clearly the problem is that no one in power is willing to give up the public and private income derived from letting the loggers have their way, but the Bank acts as if the problem is one of "trained manpower" and could be solved by providing technical assistance for the "strengthening of the existing Department of Studies and Programming"—a component of the project.

It should also be mentioned that the eventual total depletion of the most valuable slow-growing varieties of timber is implicitly viewed as positive by the Bank, since the exhaustion of these species will lead to higher prices for plantation-grown timber and species of secondary value—a factor on which the rate of return for this forestry project, among others, is dependent. Of course the same goal could be achieved *immediately* by strictly enforcing sustained-yield cutting rates—unless the timber companies had the opportunity to move on to other countries who would not control them so strictly. Such a policy would also preserve the natural forests—but let's not be politically unrealistic.

What the Bank and the goverment are planning to do is to establish plantations of fast-growing varieties of trees in four previously logged-over areas north of the capital. While these plantations would produce a commercial yield, the language of the appraisal report leaves no doubt that one of the major purposes of the project is to preempt the territory and keep the squatters out:

> The methods envisaged to reduce, and eventually to halt, the destruction of the forest for agricultural purposes would include measures to slow down the movements of population from the savannah areas towards the southern forests. . . .
>
> Although the four project areas are located within forest reserves, the land surrounding these reserves is heavily farmed and pressure on the remaining areas of high forest has been strong. *It is partly for strategic reasons that these concessions have been selected* for the first major program of reforestation. While plantations of any kind are respected as occupied land, the natural forest belongs by tradition to the people and can be acquired in many areas by the simple initiative of clearing the land and planting it with food crops.
>
> Without the program . . . it would be almost impossible to prevent infiltration by villagers intent on establishing food farms, and it is a legitimate assumption that, in less than 20 years, all the cultivable land would have been absorbed into the traditional pattern of shifting agriculture.[55]

The Ivory Coast project, so far as I am aware, is not called a "people-oriented" project, and yet it is clear from these excerpts that it is very much concerned with poor people—with preempting them, with fencing them out. Vague statements are made in the appraisal as to the need to encourage these people, by demonstration and education, to intensify and stabilize their agricultural holdings rather than continually cut down forests to establish their farms. Now it may well be that the common interest is best served by preserving the forests, and a more intensive agricultural system is necessary in order to achieve that goal and to allow the cultivators to improve their lives. But it is unlikely that people will believe in and cooperate with such a system so long as they see the foreign timber companies ripping off the forests in collaboration with their own elites, while they get no benefits from this exploitation. It is questionable as well whether the Ivory Coast government has the same incentive to improve the lives of its humble agriculturalists as it does to earn foreign exchange and tax revenues from timber and plantation crop exports. And it must be pointed out that the *target* rate for the reforestation program, which the Bank doubts can be achieved within the project period, is only 10,000 hectares per year, while the forests are being destroyed at a rate of 500,000 hectares per year. If indeed the bulk of forest destruction is caused by clearing for agriculture, the government will have to introduce improved agricultural techniques in a great hurry, which is unlikely.

Other Forestry Activities

These three examples may be supplemented by brief comments on Bank forestry activities in three other countries. The first two are the "social forestry" programs in Gujarat state, India and in South Korea, which are the only positive examples (along with the People's Republic of China) Eric Eckholm could find for his 1979 publication subtitled *Forestry for Human Needs*. Both programs were established about 1973, with the World Bank entering the picture to finance expansions of the programs after they were already underway (in South Korea in 1976; in Gujarat in 1980).

Both programs show fundamental similarities; in both cases the national or state government encourages local village institutions (in South Korea the specially created Village Forestry Associations; in Gujarat the village government, the *panchayat*) to utilize underused lands for village woodlots. In Korea private lands are appropriated, with the owner promised a 10 percent cut; in Gujarat the *panchayats* were asked to set aside the land (ownership status remains unclear in Eckholm's account). In both cases villagers would do the labor, with seedlings provided by the government, and would be responsible for protecting the growing trees, with some rights for gathering grass and fruits. Finally, when the trees reach maturity some would be sold locally as fuel (in Korea, "distributed among households"), with a commercial surplus from which proceeds would belong to the village association.

It would seem, from Eckholm's account, that both programs have been successful in achieving a considerable amount of replanting by the villagers; what is less clear is how much the villagers are really benefiting. Eckholm claims that "the benefits have been well distributed among the peasantry" in Korea, but he also cites evidence that the Village Forestry Associations are "in reality . . . top-down government controlled-organizations with compulsory membership and membership fees."[56] The village woodlot program is a component of the Saemaeul, or New Community Movement (NCM), of which another scholar has written:

> Another problem that somewhat tarnishes the NCM's image of glittering success is the dissatisfaction of the poorest (usually landless) village residents, who generally make up from 10% to 20% of all households in any given community. They complain that they have been persuaded to contribute labor for NCM projects out of all proportion to the benefits received, most of which accrue to middle level and wealthy farmers.[57]

Similarly, Eckholm believes that "new wealth is created on communal lands and is shared equitably among villagers" in Gujarat, and thereby "the absolute well-being of the poor will be improved." At least in Gujarat the poorer villagers were *paid* to do the work on the woodlots, but the proceeds from the harvest are split between the *panchayats* and the forest department. And Eckholm says himself that

> the use of the *panchayats* as the main filters through which village opinions are expressed and benefits are distributed is enough in itself to keep the program from rocking the socioeconomic boat; the tendency for these bodies to be dominated by economic elites and political factions is legendary.[58]

It requires a great leap of faith to conclude that benefits distributed through the *panchayats* are "shared equitably among villagers."

Three Indian scholars at the Indian Institute of Management in Bangalore have made a study of a social forestry project in Kolar district, Karnataka state, which is a candidate for expansion with World Bank funding. They found that the major impact of this project, and of others already being financed by the Bank in Gujarat and other states, was to encourage commercial tree-farming for urban markets on land that had previously been utilized for food crops. They concluded:

> The high sounding objectives of social forestry in general, and the World Bank project in particular, of serving the basic needs of the deprived rural population through a strategy of involving them in the management of forests raised on hitherto unutilised and uncultivated land are found to be inconsistent with the content of the project. Instead of special effort being directed at involving rural communities in raising and protecting useful species on common and waste land, the thrust, even in policy, is on providing incentives to farmers to transfer land from foodcrop production to farm forests. Instead of selection of species being made on the basis of criteria of appropriateness to the needs and purchasing power of the people, the species to which importance had been given, that is, Eucalyptus hybrid, is neither materially suited to be integrated in the life support systems of the rural community nor financially within their reach, given that there exists a better market for Eucalyptus away from rural areas. This trend of inappropriate choice of species seems to be the centre of political controversies around several other World Bank aided major forestry projects in other parts of the country. In the Himalayas the Chir Pine monoculture and the Tropical Pine in the Bastar region of Madhya Pradesh are viewed by the local people as an attack on their local life-support system. In the light of the project proposal, the empirical trends in shifts in land use as analysed in the present study are found to be a result of conscious policy orientation.[59]

The last example comes from Kenya, home of ecologist Norman Myers, who defends the World Bank's ecological consciousness:

> Among development banks, the greatest progress with environmental safeguards seems to have been accomplished by the World Bank. According to a comparative survey by the International Institute for Environment and Development, the Bank's position is

now "more sophisticated and comprehensive than that of any of the other development banks . . . and it is continuously evolving in a positive direction." In principle, the Bank is committed to a review, and where necessary to a restructuring, of every project that has a signficant environmental component. This screening process begins with an environmental reconnaissance when a project is first conceived, moves on to environmental monitoring during the phase of on-the-ground activity and winds up with an environmental post-audit.[60]

Two things might be said about this assessment. In the first place, the World Bank has no competition from the other development banks, as the latter are doing virtually nothing. The second is that there is an exceptionally cozy relationship between the World Bank and the International Institute for Environment and Development (IIED), which applauds its ideological consciousness so warmly. Robert S. McNamara sits on the IIED Council, and William Clark, who became IIED president in 1980, came to it from the World Bank, where he had been vice president for external affairs (which includes public relations). The IIED, which has a number of large corporate sponsors, has also received several grants from the World Bank. It would be surprising if such an organization were very critical of the Bank.

Moreover, in another passage, Myers seems rather dubious about the effectiveness of these procedures in the case of a program in Kenya with which he is personally familiar:

A World Bank study has reviewed the program, and looked at Nature Reserves in each of the two forests in question. . . . The Arabuko-Sokoke's Nature Reserve of 30 km² is to be supplemented with another Nature Reserve of 10 km², but the area at issue contains little red soil, the only known habitat of the threatened owl. Nevertheless, the World Bank considers that "Each of these areas (Nature Reserves) will be large enough to sustain on a viable basis their particular ecosystems." *The Bank's statement does not explain the basis for its evaluation, it does not define the "particular ecosystems," it does not say what is implied by "sustain on a viable basis," and it does not mention anything with regard to the dimensions and design of reserves.*[61] (Emphasis added)

Here again a great leap of faith is necessary to conclude that the Bank is sincere in its environmental assessments.

11
Urban "Shelter" Projects

> Historically, violence and civil upheaval are
> more common in cities than in the countryside.
> Frustrations that fester among the urban poor
> are readily exploited by political extremists. If
> cities do not begin to deal more constructively
> with poverty, poverty may well begin to deal
> more destructively with cities.
> —Robert S. McNamara, September 1, 1975

"Poverty-oriented" programs in urban areas, like their counter-
parts in the countryside, invariably have a political dimension.
In those democracies that survive in the Third World, slum areas
are recruiting grounds and strongholds of rival parties, and
government housing projects are spoils that can be used to win
and reward supporters (Jamaica is one example which comes to
mind). In the far greater number of nondemocracies, slum areas—
as the home of the disadvantaged and dispossessed—are always
potential foci of political opposition.

Urban renewal, the antecedent of today's "slum upgrading"
programs, has a long historical connection with counterinsurgency, dating back at least as far as Haussmann's design for
rebuilding Paris after the struggles of 1848 with "long, straight
broad streets, as though made to give full effect to the new
cannon and rifles."[1] And, although urban renewal usually is
motivated by the desire to raise and/or realize property values
(about which more will be said later), current newspaper stories
tell of whole urban areas that have been attacked and razed
specifically because they represent centers of heterodox politics.[2]

Paved streets, widened footpaths, and street lamps represent improved amenities for residents but also provide for easier pursuit of criminals and dissidents by government forces. The elaborate and detailed censuses and surveys required for any poverty-oriented project provide intelligence that can be used by the police as well as the construction teams and social workers; and these and the implementation of the public works provide cover for an army of government functionaries, not all of whom are interested in helping the poor. Although explicit awareness of this dimension is seldom acknowledged in Bank documents, Bank officials are certainly aware of it. A recent Bank publication entitled *Shelter* echoes McNamara's concern: "The daily contact between urban elites and low-income groups concentrated in urban areas where shelter is inadequate is potentially more explosive, politically and socially, than any problems of widely scattered rural settlements."[3]

Bank officials have admitted some perplexity on how to attack the problem of urban poverty, embodied as it is in poor people (most newly migrated from the rural areas) who have no assets to valorize. Hollis Chenery, the Bank's vice president for development policy, said in 1976:

> We have been somewhat encouraged by going into rural development several years ago, and we think we have identified an approach to rural development in which, by focusing on small productive units and strengthening their capability, we can make small farmers productive and also improve their incomes. That analogy has not been worked out in the urban field yet. . . . There is no clear analogy to the small farmer. The small businessman is one area, one type of activity, that we would like to know more about, but there is this large unstructured sector, the urban informal sector, about which very little is known.[4]

If the Bank itself shows little confidence that it knows the way to solve the basic problem of the urban poor—the need for a regular and adequate income—it has plowed ahead nevertheless with a set of programs for improving living conditions in slum areas and squatter developments. Before considering these directly, however, let us try for a moment our own analogy to the Bank's rural development process. I argued above that the Bank's rural development programs actually aim to appropriate the small farmer's resources of land and labor for the benefit of foreign capitalists and overseas consumers. Similar arguments were made in the chapters on forestry and on water resource control. If we were to draw an analogy from these situations to that of housing for the urban poor, it would look something like this: the most valuable resource possessed by the urban poor is the urban land on which they are squatting, which is valuable because of its location. The traditional form of urban renewal, in cities of the developed as well as underdeveloped countries, has been to appropriate those locational values by "urban renewal—people removal": the condemnation of low-income housing and/or the eviction of squatters to make way for commercial properties and luxury housing.

Stated this way, such an analogy would clearly be not just unfair but false. Although many of the governments it aids have clearly been guilty of such policies, the Bank has taken a stand against "people removal" in most of the urban infrastructure projects for which it lends directly. The sector policy paper called *Housing* (1975) obliquely condemned such practices as "counterproductive:"

> The most common such policy is a cycle of demolishing low income urban neighborhoods and using the land for other purposes. Refusal to accept existing low-quality housing as at least an intermediate solution to the housing problem is common. The consequence is a continuous process of construction of temporary dwellings which last until the government clears the land for other purposes or until they are washed away by tropical downpours. Thus, as the value of land close to the city center increases, squatters are forced to move toward the expanding periphery away from employment and other opportunities, never along the way having had the opportunity to build up equity in a house.[5]

The last line places a curious emphasis on property values, but Bank president McNamara took a more impassioned humanistic line in his address to the Board of Governors later the same year (the same speech from which the epigraph is quoted):

> The deprivation suffered by the poor is nowhere more visible than in the matter of housing. Even the most hardened and unsentimen-

tal observer from the developed world is shocked by the squalid slums and ramshackle shantytowns that ring the periphery of every major city. The favelas, the bustees, the bidonvilles have become almost the central symbol of the poverty that pervades two-thirds of the globe. It is the image that is seared into the memory of every visitor.

But there is one thing worse than living in a slum or a squatter settlement—and this is having one's slum or settlement bulldozed away by the government which has no shelter of any sort whatever to offer in its place. When that happens—and it happens often—there remains only the pavement itself, or some rocky hillside or parched plain, where the poor can once again begin to build out of packing crates and signboards and scraps of sheetmetal and cardboard a tiny hovel in which to house their families.

Squatter settlements by definition—and by city ordinance—are illegal. Even the word squatter itself is vaguely obscene, as if somehow being penniless, landless, and homeless were deliberate sins against the canons of proper etiquette. But it is not squatters that are obscene. It is the economic circumstances that make squatter settlements necessary that are obscene.

And, rhetoric aside, the evidence does indicate that the Bank presses its borrowing governments to minimize the relocation of housing in its urban upgrading projects. To this extent it must be applauded for opposing a particularly inhumane practice of bulldozing slums out of existence, even if this is done for practical as well as humanitarian reasons: "the consequential problems of a displaced populace that can neither afford nor find a place in the lower-density and more expensive replacement units are well recognized."[6]

The Bank's Policy Paper

It is necessary to take a closer look at what the Bank is doing to alleviate the urban housing problem before we can fairly evaluate its policy. An examination of the chief points made in the sector policy paper is appropriate here.

The first point to be made about the policy paper is that it reveals a tender concern for capitalist property values and a confidence that with better and/or less regulation, the market can do more than it is at present to solve the housing problems of the poor.

> Institutional controls generally arise from legal barriers and administrative controls erected to protect specific groups or interests. Zoning often prevents parcels from being allocated to their highest and best use [i.e., most remunerative or profitable—C.P.], either by imposing limited categories of use or by restricting unit density. . . . Minimum wage legislation and unionization have been blamed for limiting the flow of labor into the housing sector, raising unit costs. Rent controls discourage the expansion and maintenance of the housing stock. Institutional arrangements governing housing finance, such as interest rate ceilings and collateral requirements, may inhibit the mobilization of savings.[7]
>
> The attempt to prevent the capture of socially caused gains by private individuals and to offset the imperfections of housing markets by introducing rent controls has a long and unsuccessful history. . . . Because they limit returns on housing to less than market levels, rent controls inhibit additions to housing stock and lead to deterioration through lack of maintenance. Attempts to control the prices of public utilities or urban transport have had similar financial repercussions. In addition they distort the location decisions of households and firms.[8]
>
> The lack of mortgage funds frequently constrains housing. However, this is not so much a housing issue as a question of developing the financial sector. In most developing countries, to build a range of suitable intermediaries is the first task. But financial intermediation generally requires reforms in financial markets. The freeing of interest rate restrictions, measures to encourage competitition among banks, the ending of inappropriate banking practices, the promotion of life insurance companies and pension funds—all increase the availability of long-term credit, and hence, potentially, of finance for an efficient housing sector.[9]

Clearly, as in every other sector we have examined, lending for specific urban projects is to be used as a lever to influence sectoral and national policies on urban land use and financial institutions.

A second theme of the policy paper is the necessity of lowering the price of housing to a level that can be afforded by poor people. It is a logic akin to "don't raise the bridge, lower the water"—if we can't figure out how to guarantee an income that will cover the costs of basic needs, maybe we can devise a way of lowering the costs.

> To be effective, housing policies and programs have to be tailored to a country's income level and households' capacity to pay. Many housing programs have met with little success because they have attempted to meet housing "needs" rather than the effective demand for housing. In contrast to estimations of need according to arbitrary standards, effective demand is derived from a household's ability and willingness to pay for housing.[10]

A survey was made of existing public housing programs in six cities, and it was concluded (no doubt correctly) that the cheapest units were unaffordable for from 35 percent to 68 percent of urban residents, depending on the city studied. Bank researchers then ran a number of calculations to determine how public housing could be made affordable to larger sections of the population by reducing space per household, reducing the level of public services (i.e., shared rather than private water and sanitary facilities), and varying the distance from the city center (peripheral land is obviously cheaper than land in the center).[11] These calculations show that in the low-income countries, even the lowest standard of formal housing and services in the worst locations would be still out of reach of relatively large sectors of the population. From this the Bank concluded that it should not finance *housing* construction at all, rather, "squatter area upgrading programs and sites and services approaches, stressing low space standards and high proportions of self-help construction, appear to hold the most promise at present."[12] The Bank's policy is thus to lend for two main types of housing infrastructure projects (often combined in a single project), called "sites and services" and "slum (or squatter) upgrading": "In sites and services projects, land plots are leveled and furnished with access roads, drainage, water, sewage and electricity. Schools and health clinics have been provided in all projects; some also include refuse collection, fire protection services and other public facilities."[13]

The slum upgrading approach preserves most of the existing housing stock, with the exception of a few structures that may have to be demolished or moved to accommodate the extension of urban services at very basic levels (widened, paved, and/or drained streets and footpaths, piped water and sewage service, street lighting, community buildings, schools and clinics, etc.). Curiously, the policy paper states that "its most important contribution is to give the poor security of tenure."[14]

The Granting of Land Titles

By security of tenure the Bank does not mean merely the promise that the shantytowns will not be bulldozed out of existence by the government, but rather the actual granting of title—the transformation of squatters into legal property owners. And with the acknowledgment of the centrality of this element in most Bank projects for urban shelter, it becomes possible to reformulate the analogy with rural development projects. As we have seen, the granting of individual land tenure in areas where agricultural land had previously been under collective control created a land market that represented the *exact opposite of security of tenure* for those farmers who were not willing and able to adopt a market orientation—the land would quickly pass out of their hands for inability to pay the increased taxes, if for no other reason. Further, in most rural development projects we find that the supposed "beneficiaries" are actually a captive market for a package of "improvements," which often turn out to be far more expensive than they are worth to the participant. In this fashion surplus is extracted from the small farmer sector for the benefit of the national government and the merchants and suppliers who sell the required inputs and purchase the prescribed crops. Could something along these lines be happening in the urban infrastructure projects aimed at the urban poor?

According to the sector policy paper:

> Introducing an element of equity into urban landownership by giving squatters security of tenure is an urgent policy issue in most cities in developing countries, and one with high returns in terms of retained and improved housing stock, access to earning oppor-

tunities and consequent welfare. *However, the payment for an appropriate portion of the actual land value should be required in exchange for title to avoid excessive subsidies to only part of the poor.*[15] (Emphasis added)

In order to assign tenure to squatters, it will be necessary for the government to purchase land from its private owners, but "land within existing city limits is usually very costly."[16] The Bank hurries over this admitted difficulty to the happier conclusion that peripheral land can be acquired much more cheaply for *future* serviced sites. But most of the contested squatter areas are located *within* city limits, for reasons that the Bank recognizes, i.e., peripheral areas are too far away from employment opportunities and in many cases squatters who have been transported to newly built serviced sites on the periphery of cities have quickly moved back into the center to build another shantytown.

As Rod Burgess has warned in an article critical of the suggestion that all poor people need is title to the ground their home stands on:

> The intervention of the State through the large-scale purchase of urban land would have equally dramatic effects on land values. No matter what the policy, *it would increase the housing costs to those groups who would otherwise have avoided them.* The problem of legality in other words is fundamental to the issue of market valuation of land.[17] (Emphasis added)

There is also more than a hint in the sector policy paper that the "beneficiaries" of a land entitlement program would find themselves paying higher taxes in return for the improvement of their properties:

> The capture for social use of some of the gains, or "betterment," accruing to land and housing owners from public improvements is another important issue. By capturing betterment, society does not penalize a landowner for putting his land to productive use, but simply reduces any incentive to hold land for other than productive reasons.[18]

This curious, contorted reasoning may be compared with Montague Yudelman's rationale for individualizing land tenure in Rhodesia and taxing land according to its *potential* "highest and best use." While the policy paper admits that "in practice, valuation problems and erosion of the tax base through exemptions have limited the effectiveness of the taxes" (i.e., politically influential owners can shift the burden to the less powerful), such taxes are "increasingly called upon to provide revenues."

> Raising tax receipts from land can alleviate some of the burden of taxes on capital, stimulating the flow of investment and the development of financial institutions. Moreover, a program of public improvements financed by betterment levies or equipment charges tends to reduce uncertainty about the pattern of future urban growth, thereby encouraging private investors.[19]

It appears that while the poor will not be bulldozed off the land they are occupying, they may well find that land "improved" under their feet to the point where those who cannot afford to put it to "productive use" (whatever that means in the context of an urban shantytown), are evicted quietly by legal process.

Can the Poor Afford to Be Upgraded?

Is this assumption too Machiavellian? Remember, the quotations above come chiefly from the official position paper of the Bank, one which was approved as a policy statement by the Executive Board before its publication. The policy paper is confident that the poor will be able to afford the improvements it plans to finance; this would appear to be the basic aim of the elaborate calculations performed to decide what the poor can afford. A footnote to these calculations informs us that the assumption is that "poor families will spend 15% of their household budget on accommodation at a real interest rate of 10% [and that] 'affordability' means ability to purchase over time on these terms. . . ."[20]

This assumption may seem modest enough to someone living in New York City but it probably overestimates the ability of the poor to pay rent. A study of the King Phet slum area of Bangkok showed, for example, that average housing expenditure including utilities amounted to only 3.25 percent of average monthly income, and that even the lowest income households were paying less than 10 percent of their monthly income for housing services.[21]

The question remains whether this assumption, as well as the figures used by the Bank to derive data on income levels, bears any relation to reality. The Bank seems in any case confident that its approach is a realistic way of helping the poor.

> Financial arrangements for projects vary widely. The costs of water and other utilities are sometimes recovered through user charges, but more often are grouped with other charges in project rental payments. The experience of other organizations with projects of this type suggests that payment delinquencies are relatively low, and therefore manageable, when the projects are appropriately located, standards (and, therefore, costs) are commensurate with incomes, and management is efficient. There have been two modifications to the full cost recovery approach. It is accepted practice that costs of community facilities, such as schools and health clinics, typically financed out of general revenues, are not charged directly to project occupants. Secondly, if calculations of social costs and benefits so indicate, there may be implicit or explicit "subsidies" in the treatment of land in central locations where the target occupants are unable to afford such land at full market value. The occupants thereby gain security of tenure without full, and sometimes without any, payment. Beyond this, subsidies would generally be counterproductive because they would make it impossible to replicate the project on a broad scale.[22]

Thus, the Bank assumes that its target population (which, as will be discussed later, almost never includes the poorest 10 to 20 percent of a city's population) can afford the services it will finance, while Rod Burgess and I suspect that the "improvements," however desirable some of them may be, will eventuate in the collection of payments and taxes that are considerably higher than what the population is now paying, and that will be for many, if not most, more than they can afford. To settle this question we need empirical material, which seems to be not readily available. Few independent observers have published their findings on the Bank's urban poverty projects, and even fewer of these seem to have raised the relevant questions: How much, and to whom, were the project residents paying in rents before improvements; and how much are they/will they be paying for utilities, mortgages, and taxes after the project is completed? Will the increased costs be offset by expenses (such as high payments for fresh water previously carted in) that are no longer necessary? Will residents be able to meet the payments, and do they consider the improved services worth the added cost? And, what will happen to the area residents who are not eligible, or cannot afford, to become beneficiaries owning their own plot of land? It must be remembered that beneficiaries must themselves bear the full cost of building the house itself (loans for obtaining building materials are often provided) or improvements to structures already standing, in addition to project assessments; the Bank makes its projects "affordable" largely by leaving this part of the cost to be borne directly by the plot owner.

Direct evidence on these questions is available for only one relatively well-documented project, that of the Tondo Urban Foreshore Project in Manila, Philippines, which is the object of the following case study.

The Tondo Foreshore Project

The Tondo Foreshore of Manila is the largest and most conspicuous urban slum in the Philippines, a shantytown of more than 180,000 residents. It also has a large, well-organized, and militant coalition of squatters' groups, the Ugnayan Tondo.

In September 1972 President Ferdinand Marcos declared martial law in the Philippines, a move that guaranteed his perpetuation in office and allowed the government to crack down on all forms of opposition to its policies of a maximum open door to foreign investment.[23] Following the declaration of martial law, the World Bank drastically stepped up its lending program in the Philippines, probably at the instigation of the U.S. government, whose own aid program had been handicapped by attempts to reduce bilateral aid to human rights violators. The Bank and

IDA approved a total of $1.3 billion in loans for the Philippines for the five fiscal years 1974–1978, or approximately four times the $301 million funneled to the country from 1946 through 1973. By 1976, the Philippines had been designated a "country of concentration" by the Bank and was its eighth largest recipient of loans, up from thirteenth in 1973. While overall Bank lending rose by a factor of three from the early 1970s to fiscal year 1979, loans to the Philippines rose by a factor of *eleven* in the same period.[24]

At the same time the country's first lady, Imelda Marcos, began to take a strong interest in the "beautification" of Manila, a territory that it seemed she regarded almost as her private property. Her plans for beautification involved good old-style urban renewal, including total demolition of the Tondo squatter community and its removal to an adjoining new housing project built on landfill and/or remoter projects on the periphery of the city, to make way for modernized port facilities, widened highways, and an industrial park.

The government requested World Bank financing for the project; the Ugnayan Tondo responded with indignant and militant resistance, and thus the stage was set for a curious episode of three-cornered consultation and negotiation among the World Bank, the government, represented by the project authority it established to administer the program (Tondo Foreshore Development Authority), and the representatives of the area residents who would be most affected by the project. The following picture emerges of one set of these negotiations, in February 1975, as recorded in a set of minutes and records kept by the Tondo Ugnayan and made available to me by the Southeast Asia Resource Center in Berkeley, California.

Consultation with the community

At these meetings the World Bank representatives affirmed their agreement with the principle of "minimum relocation" demanded by the Tondo coalition, explicitly promising that it would not fund any project involving massive demolition. At the final meeting, the Bank promised the residents' representatives that every person would either be given title to his or her land or aided to move to a new location, that the total cost of all improvements would be less than what families were currently paying for purchased water supplies, and that prices would be reduced for individuals who could not afford the charges.

Yet, however sincere the mission members may have been in their assurances, signs of stress and tension that forebode future problems are discernible in this set of letters and minutes. The major tension lay in the relation of the Ugnayan to the Philippine government's executive agency, represented in these negotiations by a General Tobias. The Ugnayan demanded representation on the board of the Tondo Foreshore Development Authority (TFDA); the Bank representatives declared themsevles favorable in principle to the idea but "this should . . . be resolved by the people and the TFDA." General Tobias was of the opinion that "present conditions do not allow yet for peoples' representation in TFDA. . . . He added that there have been meetings and consultations with the people—hence, people have been involved in the planning process." Upon this a Tondo resident "expressed the fear that people's opinion would be asked but in the end, the TFDA will have the final say—just like the forthcoming referendum, people would be consulted, but it is the president who will finally decide." Tobias warned, "Even without financial assistance from the World Bank, the President intends to carry out the plans for the renewal of Tondo." He cautioned against any act that would make the World Bank mission think that the Tondo Foreshore people and the Project Team have been bogged down by conflict.

Shortly thereafter the Bank's head of mission told the meeting that "General Tobias and his team are the best representatives in expressing the Tondo Foreshore peoples' needs and aspirations," a sentiment the Ugnayan would hardly endorse.

The Bank mission was careful to emphasize that they could not tell the Philippine government what to do; they were guests of the Philippine government and, as the Philippines was a member of the World Bank, they were indirectly employees of the Philippine government. The difficulties inherent in this three-cornered cooperation were underlined when the most active leader of the Tondo residents' organization, Mrs. Trinidad Herrera, was detained by the police for alleged "distribution of materials advocating boycott of the referendum and circulating manifestos on torture of political detainees." Her detention prevented her from attending the last meeting scheduled for consultation with the Bank.

Despite its willingness to take part in consultations with project area residents and its professed sympathy for their standpoint, the mission head warned that it could not be bound by the preferences of the residents. "He said that there will always be alterations on projects, that plans evolved will eventually be different from that [sic] was originally presented. This will always happen because plans are evaluated according to the guidelines of the World Bank."

The February 1975 meetings found the Tondo residents' organization "extending their appreciation for the real, sincere efforts exerted by the World Bank in listening to the peoples' demands and aspirations." "The people of Tondo, and their friends and sympathizers are happy with the thought that they have a friend in the World Bank!" three members of the Ugnayan Executive Committee enthused in a letter to the Bank's chief of mission, promising to give the Bank team a very simple "sendoff" ceremony on the last days of consultation.

The referendum opposed by Trinidad Herrera passed easily, not a surprising result under martial law conditions. It established a metropolitan Manila government with powers that overrode those of the several separate municipalities. Imelda Marcos was soon appointed general manager of Metro Manila. Although Bank officials hardly subscribed to Mrs. Marcos' fatuous ideas for beautifying the city, they strongly supported the creation of the Metro Manila government and made it the chief object of their "institution-building" efforts with respect to their urban projects.

Within a year, the Tondo residents' confidence in World Bank assurances had been shattered. To be sure, the main commitment made in the 1975 consultations by the Bank has been fulfilled: massive demolition of residents' dwellings has not taken place. But the Bank's inevitably close association with

Imelda Marcos' office, and its failure to institute ongoing consultations with urban residents, destroyed most of the confidence engendered in the February 1975 meetings.

A vigorous protest was staged at the Habitat conference in Vancouver, B.C., in July 1976 when an international design competition for a housing project was won by a New Zealand architect who had never visited Manila. Exiled Filipinos and their sympathizers protested that Tondo residents had been systematically excluded from the planning of the project and judging of the competition. Five Tondo residents who had been invited by the World Council of Churches to attend the Habitat conference were prevented by the Philippine government from leaving the country. It was also revealed that the previous February when the World Bank suggested that Trinidad Herrera be permitted to join the jury selecting the winning design, the government ordered her arrest and she was forced into hiding, preventing her participation. UPI reported that 2000 people were arrested during a demonstration in Manila timed to coincide with the Habitat conference.

In addition to complaining of government repression, the Habitat protesters pointed out that the proposed housing would be too expensive for most Tondo residents. A statement presented in Vancouver by Ugnayan stated that the average Tondo resident can afford to spend only 10 percent of a P 371 monthly income for rent, while the prize-winning design, if built, would require rentals of P 70 to 100 per month.

> The problem, simply stated, is not that decent housing is too expensive, but that decent salaries are denied to workers, the same as decent incomes are denied to rural peasants—especially tenant farmers. The denial of decent wages and incomes is accomplished in various ways such as government hindrance of the trade union movement in the cities and of peasant unions in the countryside.[25]

The World Bank was not directly responsible for the controversial design competition at Habitat and privately agreed with the protesters that the rental levels were unrealistic. The disputed project was an Imelda Marcos brainchild, to be built on land immediately adjacent to the area of the Bank project and financed by the Philippine government. An internal Bank memorandum to brief President McNamara for a meeting with Mrs. Marcos stated: "It is our judgment that the Habitat project will in fact provide housing and a level of services not affordable by slum dwellers or squatters, but we have not expressed this view formally to the Government." The Bank could hardly avoid association with Mrs. Marcos' projects, however, because of its close cooperation with the Metro Manila government which she headed and its funding of a project in which she took a close if not very sympathetic interest. (The loan agreement was signed in Washington, by Mrs. Marcos and President McNamara, two days after Mrs. Marcos made a speech at the Habitat conference and denounced the demonstration.) The assumption on the part of the protesters that the Bank was behind it all was not, on the whole, unjust.

A more direct and embarrassing confrontation between the Bank and the proposed "beneficiaries" of its Tondo project followed four months later, when Manila hosted the annual meeting of the World Bank and the International Monetary Fund. In preparation for this meeting, Imelda Marcos decided to "beautify" the Tondo slum area by forcibly evicting an estimated 400 families, demolishing their homes, and (after a five-day delay during which the families lived on the street) carting them off to a desolate area on the outskirts of the city, three hours traveling time from their work on the Tondo docks. The demolitions permitted the widening of a road for the conference delegates' tour of the city.[26] High wooden fences were erected around all of the shanty areas visible from the road.

Embarrassed Bank officials tried to dissociate themselves from the demolitions, but refused requests for a meeting with Tondo representatives. One scheduled meeting with the Bank's action officer for the project was canceled at the last minute. "We thought it was politically inappropriate because it seemed the meeting was developing anti-martial law overtones," a Bank representative explained. The Tondo organizations demanded that the loan be canceled in a letter addressed to McNamara. "The martial law Government's concept of development, which is also identical to that of the World Bank, is diametrically opposed to ours," the letter from Ugnayan declared.[27]

The loan was not canceled. A second urban project, providing for 8,600 services sites in Dagat-Dagatan and similar programs in three regional cities, was signed in December 1978. A third urban loan, for $72 million, was signed in March 1980 (this one will extend the urban upgrading concept to other slum areas of Metro Manila), and future loans are contemplated in a continuing program of assistance to the urban sector. The Bank considers the Tondo project a success; both implicitly in its continuing program of lending, and explicitly in its public relations material. An article in *Report: News and Views from the World Bank* discusses the Tondo project at length as a vindication of Bank policies, affirming that the area has been brought to the "take-off" point, whatever that may mean in reference to a residential area.[28] The description of achievements under the first project is even rosier in the appraisal report for the third urban project loan:

> Land titles are now being issued, and beneficiaries have recently commenced their monthly payments. Costs are close to appraisal estimates. The upgraded area shows remarkable improvement from its previous condition. The vast majority of families have invested considerable personal capital in transforming their homes from shacks into attractive 2-and 3-storey dwellings within a period of six months, thereby providing opportunities for sub-letting and more efficient use of the land. Streets are paved and clean, and gardens are being planted. The earlier atmosphere of tension has disappeared. The open serviced sites at Tondo and nearby Dagat-Dagatan have been occupied and are being rapidly transformed into attractive dwellings through the residents' self-help. The achievement to date strongly validates the concept of issuing land titles and provision of basic services to stimulate community upgrading.[29]

This rosy picture is in strong contrast to the findings of a West German housing expert who made an independent investigation of the Bank's two urban projects in late 1979. Dieter Oberndorfer found a "lack or almost total absence of genuine cooperation and communication between the implementing authorities and the squatters. . . . The ignorance of the barangay officials can only be explained by a high degree of carelessness for the lot of the people affected by the various upgrading measures." One of the results of this "carelessness" was the implementation of plans that were too costly for the squatters to afford.

The Cost of Bank Projects

"Affordability" is a central point of Oberndorfer's critique. He found that on the basis of an *official* survey by the implementing agency of the project "it can be assumed that 28 percent of the households can definitely not afford the subsequent rentals to be paid for infrastructure improvement and land titles." However, he notes:

> The sample of the survey quoted has been based on highly un-realistic assumptions as to the income structure in Tondo fore-shore. . . . Taking into account that according to official statistics 38% of the Tondo Foreshore squatter population lives below the "non-starvation" level . . . it seems highly unprobable that these 38% of the population can pay the rents foreseen by NHA. The number of households which cannot afford the rental to be paid after reblocking has been completed must be even much higher. Looking at the data available on income distribution . . . and ex-penditure patterns . . . we assume that only 30–40% of the squatter households *can afford* to pay regularly the rents foreseen . . . this means that 60 to 70% cannot pay the rentals.[30]

The report notes that about two-thirds of the households have highly irregular sources of income, and "will have great dif-ficulties to pay their rents regularly on a monthly basis." Evic-tion is required after three months of nonpayment. Those who cannot afford the betterment of Tondo will be forced to move elsewhere, according to the Bank's plan.

And, it must be remembered, what has just been described is the *lower cost* program, which does not include any payment for housing. Most of the serviced sites in Dagat-Dagatan built for relocated squatters under the Bank program will be much more expensive. Official estimates, described in the West German report as "extremely unrealistic," show that 29 percent of re-locatees will not be capable of paying lease rents for the smallest

60 m² plots. Oberndorfer estimates that up to 60 or 70 percent will not be able to pay for the bigger and more costly plots.

Bank officials have responded publicly to the "leak" of the West German report only by charging that it "contains inaccuracies." But an internally circulated Bank response is reported to have admitted that

> the government's provision of shelter to the urban poor in Manila with which the Bank has been associated benefited fewer people than ultimately need assistance and cannot necessarily reach the very poorest segments of society . . . (because) a policy of housing subsidy for the poor which does not contain a repayment element, requiring comparable repayments among residents of a new or upgraded settlement would, we believe, eventually both be unworkable and socially deceptive in the communities to which it is directed.[31]

A Bank appraisal states that Tondo residents were spending an average of P 28 per month or less than 10 percent of income, on shelter in 1974. The Bank assumed, however, on the basis of "international experience," that families below the twenty-fifth percentile could afford to spend 18 percent of their income on rent. The reasoning is something of a parody of itself: essentially the Bank said that people can afford to pay more because they aren't paying very much now.

> [M]ost squatters, who constitute 70% of the total population, are not currently paying for land they occupy. Also, since this data shows only actual housing expenditures, it does not include imputed rents for those structures and lots that are owned individually, fully paid for, and occupied by the owner. Like most surveys of actual housing expenditure, this survey, therefore, tends to underestimate the percentage that families could spend on shelter, since it includes many families with no current shelter expenditures.[32]

Those with incomes below the fifteenth percentile are dismissed as transients and renters who "are expected to receive substantial indirect benefits," but who would be resettled in a cheaper site if they could not afford rents in Tondo after the improvements are made.[33]

The upgrading process in Tondo involved a procedure called "reblocking," or preparing a subdivision layout as a basis for providing road and path access, water and sewage lines, and other services, and establishing land tenure and individual plot boundaries. According to Bank sources, the Bank had argued for a minimal approach to reblocking that would leave most existing structures where they were and add new streets only to provide access to fire protection vehicles. Government project staff, however, argued for an upgrading process that would result in a more regular street and lot layout pattern and involve movement and realignment of structures within blocks. The issue was "depoliticized," according to the Bank, by leaving the decision among reblocking alternatives to each neighborhood concerned.

In practice, this solution allowed the government project officers to have their own way, reporting that residents were voting for the most radical, and expensive, reblocking scheme in each case, whereas it seems that in fact the *barangay* (ward) officials charged with conducting the "voting" did not themselves know that there were alternative, and cheaper, reblocking options. Residents, of course, did not know they had a choice in the matter. The Bank now admits that "many *barangay* chairmen were confused in the beginning stages of the project and in some cases pushed more expensive options over ones cheaper to *barangay* residents," but it claims that these intitial mistakes have now been largely corrected—now that it is too late to do anything about it. If the Bank was sincere in this respect, it certainly had an overly optimistic view of local democracy under martial law.

One more type of evidence—the project appraisals for the third urban project, approved in 1980—will shed some light on the Bank's own perception and justification of what it is doing.

A Third Urban Project

World Bank Report 2703a-PH, the staff appraisal report of a loan which will extend the Tondo and Dagat-Dagatan approach to some thirteen other slum areas in the Metro Manila area, reveals that about half of the land now occupied by squatter settlements that will be "upgraded" by the project is owned by private landlords; the rest is government land. The program provides for "acquisition, or expropriation where necessary, of squatter land from absentee landowners for resale to residents." (The landlords who are expropriated are, it is rumored, those opposed to the Marcos oligarchy.) The cost to the residents of this transaction will be mitigated by the fact that government land is "free" and costs to beneficiaries will be equalized between those squatting on what is now private and what is government land. As in the first Tondo project there will be an "upgrading" program in some slum areas—called zonal improvement program (ZIP)—and the provision of serviced sites in others. "On completion, improved ZIP sites will be transferred to respective local governments who will collect plot charges from project beneficiaries and . . . will assume responsibility to discharge debt incurred by NHA (National Housing Authority) under the ZIP program."[34] Affordability to beneficiaries is a principle design criterion. According to Bank data, "At an average of P 68 per month [project charges] would be affordable to families earning P 340 per month which is below the 10th percentile of the Metro Manila income curve."[35]

Examining these figures more closely, we note, first, that the figure of P 68 per month, the cheapest program in the package, lies *above* the range of P 20-60 that the Bank stated was previously being paid to private landlords (what, if anything, squatters on government land were paying and to whom is not known); for many people it would be far above their preproject rentals.

But the Bank assumes that these low-income residents can pay 20 percent of their income for rent, while the Ugnayan reported that they can afford only 10 percent, or about P 37 per month. According to the West German critique of the Tondo project, households at the fortieth percentile (i.e., those better off than 40 percent of the population) have to spend 78 percent of their income on food, which means that the percentage at lower income levels would be even higher—scarcely leaving P 68 per month for rent.

In short, the World Bank figures turn out to be highly unrealistic as a guide to "affordability" of the projects by the poorer slum residents. Here again, remember that we are discussing the *cheapest* option: monthly charges for serviced sites are estimated to start at P 92 per month and move upward to a point where they could be afforded only at the seventy-fifth percentile.[36]

The sites and services component will provide a bonanza to private developers, as the Bank has chosen to turn half of the plots over to them in order to "provide a comparative evaluation of the relative efficiencies of public and private developers." The private developers will receive considerable direct and indirect subsidies from the government, which will provide off-site infrastructure, community facilities, and a loan for up to 35 percent of construction financing. The government will also guarantee the availability of long-term mortgages through discounting to the secondary market.[37]

This component of the project will be administered by the Ministry of Human Settlements (MHS), headed by Imelda Marcos. The breathtaking scale of corruption in which the Marcos family and its government are involved illuminates the reality behind the Bank's statement that "the MHS has extensive contacts with private developers."[38] The private developers would build only the larger and more expensive lots, the cheapest having an estimated monthly rental of P 114 More than half the plots, however, would be considerably more expensive than these. It is difficult to see what this exercise could conceivably prove about the relative efficiency of public and private sectors.

It should be added that this project, like the previous ones in the urban sector, will involve the Bank deeply in the restructuring of urban government institutions. The most important of these is the transfer of considerable powers, including the power to levy and collect local revenues, from the existing cities and municipalities to the Metro Manila Commission headed by Mrs. Marcos. The rationale expressed for this transfer of powers is the disparity in provision of services, collection of local revenues, and fiscal performance among the various units, but one certain consequence will be to decrease local control over services and taxation. The World Bank clearly intends that this reorganization will improve the collection of tax revenues, which definitely will be required if the costs of the Bank project are to

be recovered, i.e., all costs not recovered directly from beneficiaries will have to be financed by local governments. Increased
tax collections will be facilitated by the Bank project itself, as

> based on the properties of the Tondo Foreshore area, the value of
> properties would increase significantly when the structures are
> upgraded. The areas improved through the project would be reas-
> sessed for property tax purposes, and the resulting additional
> revenues are expected to greatly exceed the increased operation
> and maintenance cost.

The Bank maintains that these tax payments will, nevertheless,
represent only a small burden to the households, in the order of
P 4 per month.[39]

"Affordability," Property Values, and the Poor

The project is thus justified in cost-benefit terms through
the anticipated appreciation of property values. Although it is
necessary to be cautious in accepting the Bank's own rate-of-
return estimates, which are usually manipulated to justify a
project that may have been chosen for quite other reasons (see
Chapter 3), it is worth noting that the Tondo project is cited as
proof that a high rate of return can be achieved in this way. Of the
urban upgrading program, the appraisal predicts that "the metropolitan tax base would be expanded by bringing a significant
amount of blighted land into the urban economy. Based on
increases in property values, a 42% economic rate of return is
now estimated. This high rate of return is consistent with that
now experienced in Tondo (40–50% IRR)."[40] For the sites and
services component, "an economic rate of return of 26 percent is
anticipated, based on appreciation of property values."[41]

Thus there is considerable evidence for the hypothesis that
despite the absence of bulldozers, the effect of Bank projects is to
realize the potential value of urban property at the expense of the
really poor, who will almost certainly be driven out of newly
upgraded areas by economic pressure. We also have some evi-

dence that this is not merely the effect but probably the *intent* of Bank planners.

The mayor of another Philippine city, Cagayan de Oro, traveled to Washington in September 1981 in order to confront the Bank with the problems of his city's slum improvement program agreed to by his predecessor. An investigation by Mayor Aquilino Pimentel discovered that 3,000 squatters in the Cagayan de Oro slums, now paying between P 5 and P 20 per month for housing, will be expected to pay P 120–150 per month once the World Bank project has improved their lots. Pimentel found that most had not even been informed by the World Bank that there would be any increase in monthly payments. The mayor also protested that over half the project cost was to come out of the city's budget, which he and his city council felt would be better spent on schools, hospitals, and social services. He therefore requested that the city's financial responsibility for the project be terminated.

At the Bank, officials expressed amazement at the cost figures Pimentel quoted for their own project, and at the fact that squatters had no idea what they would be charged for the improved sites. They nevertheless threatened that if the mayor withdrew from the project, he might find it difficult to obtain World Bank funding for other projects. Pimentel told the Bank to keep its money, and the meeting broke up on an angry note.[42]

Evidence from other projects is still scanty, but something similar is happening in Lusaka, Zambia, an urban area where land is neither scarce nor expensive and where conditions are quite different from those in Manila. An American Friends Service Committee field officer who conducted a survey of consumer expenditures in a housing area undergoing Bank-style "upgrading" found that a minority of families in the area could not afford even the minimal cost of upgrading:

> To the extent that service charges and loan repayments are enforced, these households will either have to sell their homes and move to a compound that has not been upgraded or they will have to change their priorities. It is quite possible that nutrition will suffer in this period of rising costs.[43]

The housing project, he believed,

has made a large and positive contribution to the welfare of the majority of the people who live in what used to be called the "shanty compounds" of Lusaka . . . but even the best project has its limitations. . . . The reason why so many people have settled in squatter areas in the first place is that they didn't have to pay anything for land or services. Houses in the upgraded areas are now going up for sale—not perhaps in alarming proportions, but sufficiently to prompt us to ask where their previous occupants are moving to. . . . When they move to an area where drainage is poor and we have rains like those falling on Lusaka this year, they have moved into greater misery and greater risk to life and health. . . . If the Government wants to improve the standard of housing in the nation without either subsidizing it or forcing some people to give up equally or even more important priorities like food or education, there is no other way than to raise people's incomes.[44]

A 1980 study by Richard Stren of the sites and services project in Dar-es-Salaam, Tanzania, financed by an IDA credit in 1974, revealed that six year later "consolidation," the term used by World Bank officials to denote completion of houses on assigned plots, "was very slow in the sites and services area, and most of the houses that were built appear to have cost considerably more than the original 'target population' for this scheme should have been able to afford." In Kijitonyama, an area which contained a relatively high proportion of finished houses, "the houses in the scheme appeared to be in the cost range of Shs. 100,000 to Shs. 150,000 although in principle the income of allocattees should not have permitted them to build houses for more than Shs. 50,000."[45] A Tanzanian scholar quoted by Stren discovered through interviews how the bureaucracy handled the income guidelines for plot applicants:

As Mgullu points out, the Project Agreement specified that plots in the sites and services schemes must be allocated preferentially to applicants whose *household* incomes were less than Shs. 750/month. This was to ensure that "low income groups" benefitted from the project. . . . In any case, because applications were not forthcoming, the upper limit was raised from Shs. 750 – Shs. 1,000/month in 1975. The next year the Ministry of Lands, Housing and Urban Development obtained an agreement that 25% of the project plots would be issued to individuals "regardless" of the income earned.[46]

Stren provides considerable evidence that the legal process of applying for sites and loans for building materials presented formidable obstacles to poor people, both in money terms (the application for a loan to purchase building materials required "the equivalent of close to one month's gross salary" just for the processing of the papers, quite apart from mortgage repayments and land rents for plots), and in terms of the time required to travel to and wait in the various government offices—time that poor people would have to take out of their working day. Stren concluded:

> Those who have connections, education and wealth in Tanzania have almost certainly been able to take disproportionate advantage of the system of land and building loan allocation in the sites and services scheme, as they have already done in the "normal" [i.e., pre-World Bank—C.P.] plot allocation system, and various other state-supported institutions in the urban areas.[47]

Shlomo Angel has made a survey of the effects of granting tenure to squatters in a number of Third World cities. His general conclusions tend to support the charge of Rod Burgess that tenure increases the cost to residents. Angel found that secure tenure is a necessary (but not sufficient) condition for generating significant domestic investments in house building. He also found that legal titles do have the effect of raising property values. On the other hand, the effects on poor people are serious, particularly the displacement of poorer residents by higher income groups. He warns that "tenure granting programs, unless properly conceived, may harm the poor rather than assist them, and may in the long run benefit the not-so-poor."[48]

Indeed, the World Bank admits as much: "As these communities are improved, it is inevitable that some of those who live in them will be unable to afford even a minimal level of improvements. To insist on cost recovery in these instances may force the poorest residents out of the communities."[49] Having admitted the problem, two courses are open to the planners: either they revise their procedures to prevent such injustice or they rationalize the process as inevitable and continue as before. The Bank paper makes a stab at the first alternative by mentioning some experiments that have been attempted, but admits immediately that "these measures have their limits, however, and it may not be possible to keep some residents—usually fewer than 5 percent—from being forced out."

The chief response to this shocking problem is rationalization. First, the numbers are minimized. It may be well that in some cases the number is less than 5 percent (5 percent of the population of Tondo is 9000 people) but as we have seen, Bank estimates of this type have not been found trustworthy by independent observers. Other references in the same publication mention the difficulty of reaching the "lowest decile" (10 percent) or even the lower two deciles. But, it is explained in extenuation:

> The lowest decile of the income distribution in any low-income urban settlement contains significant numbers of transients who often show no income at all. In view of the large flow of migrants in and out of cities, it is not surprising to find these job-seekers showing up temporarily at the bottom of the income scale. In addition, much of the lowest decile of the population in income may consist of the "young unemployed, the old unemployables, the aged, and the infirm." To these could be added the mentally and physically handicapped.

"The problems of groups such as these," it continues, "are too complex to be solved merely by provision of shelter, water supply, health facilities, and other public services."[50]

What should be noted about this statement? First, there is the inclusion of "young unemployed" in a category that otherwise includes people genuinely unable to work. The real problem, it is implied, is the lack of an income, but surely we already knew as much about the bottom 10 percent of the population of an underdeveloped country! This is, on another level, exactly the point: in terms of reaching the hard core of poverty, the slum upgrading financed by the Bank is frivolous and irrelevant. But worse, it does uproot people. And whatever problems the lowest 5, 10, or 20 percent of the population may endure, these will only be intensified if they lose their housing to an upgrading program. Though it may be admirable that the Bank admits the problem, the effect of this rationalization is to justify a sort of complacency: What can we do? Life is unfair, let's get on with the job.

Unfortunate, yes, that these poorest of the poor will have to suffer even more as the Bank juggernaut rolls on, improving property values in urban slums. But hypocritical, too, because surely these in the "lowest decile" are those of whom Robert McNamara spoke when he deplored (in the preface to this document) "absolute poverty: a condition of life so limited by malnutrition, disease, illiteracy, low life expectancy, and high infant mortality as to be beneath any rational definition of human decency" as he made another pitch for more funds for the World Bank.

12
Inside the Bank

This book has argued that the currently dominant style of development projects is strongly biased toward the accumulation of wealth and power by those who are already wealthy and powerful. Such a process necessarily implies the deepening impoverishment of the poor and the powerless. The interests of the World Bank, or rather of the powers behind it, lie in keeping its borrowing countries open to foreign investment, and, further, in ensuring that conditions within those countries are attractive to foreign investors.

The interests of local elites are roughly congruent to those of the World Bank, but by no means identical. In general, these interests lie in preserving their own position of power and in extracting resources from their subordinate populations.

For the benefit of public opinion a charade is performed by both parties. Third World leaders blame the poverty of their countries on the inequitable international system. In domestic rallies and international conferences they point to unequal trading relationships, insufficiency of foreign aid flows, and the need for debt relief. At the same time, the leaders of the rich nations (and the World Bank) urge domestic reforms in the poor countries: they point to great inequalities of income, the subjugation of women, the need for land reform, and more. In practice, each side has entered into an infernal pact with the other which permits both to extract labor and rob resources from the poor.

The results of this pact can be seen in the social effects of World Bank projects and the policies attached to them. Specifically, the influence of the pact is clear in the Bank's use of leverage on borrowers and its attachment of conditions to loans.

On issues which are of importance to the powers controlling the World Bank, such as an "open door" for multinational corporations, leverage is strong and persistent. But on poverty-related issues (also environmental, women's rights, etc.)—trumpeted so loudly in the Bank's propaganda—case after case shows that the Bank's attempts to exert leverage are weak or nonexistent. In practice, where the issue of access for multinationals is not in question, the borrowing country elites not only are permitted to do pretty much what they want to their subject populations, but are assisted financially in so doing.

For the most part this book has been limited to the question of what the policy of the Bank *is*, and the consequences of this policy for the people who are affected. I have treated the Bank as a "black box" which produces policy and practice. While fascinating stories of bureaucratic feints and parries doubtless lie behind the smooth facade of sector policy papers and gray cover appraisals, lack of information keeps me from telling them here. Only in a few cases, such as recent decisions on oil and gas lending, was there enough information about the companies that were consulted, and the alternatives that were suppressed, to allow even speculative conclusions.

The Bank and the Indians: Brazil's POLONOROESTE Project

The professed aim of the Bank, as stated in public relations brochures and press releases, is concern for improving the lives of the poor. Its real intentions, as enforced by the bureaucracy under the leadership of the controlling powers, are to keep the territories of its borrowing countries open to capitalist penetration and their policies attractive to multinational corporations, or to aid the designs of an important member government. The truth about the system is revealed when there is an open conflict between its professed aims and its real agenda.

I have discovered one case study of how the Bank responded to information that a large project in a very important borrowing country would probably destroy several indigenous communities. The country is Brazil, the largest borrower from the International Bank for Reconstruction and Development (IBRD), whose overhanging debt burden is currently giving the financial markets some of their worst headaches. The project is a huge and extremely costly plan to develop a large area in Brazil's northwest, an area already invaded by mining companies and ranchers. The project, called the POLONOROESTE, will cover the entire state of Rondonia and eight and a half counties in neighboring Mato Grosso, an area larger than the state of California. The five-year project, currently budgeted at $1.6 billion, includes construction of a paved 1,500-kilometer all-weather road between the cities of Cuiabá in Mato Grosso and Port Velho in Rondonia. A dirt road currently connects the two. The new trunk road, and a lateral road system feeding into it, will permit planned colonization in which workers from other areas of Brazil would be brought into the region to develop a modern, market-oriented agriculture.

However, the project represents a grave threat to more than thirty different indigenous groups who inhabit the area, totalling approximately 8,000 people. These peoples, already decimated by disease, have been deprived of most of the land they once possessed by the encroachment of commercial ranchers, miners, and colonization projects, which have cut down the tropical forest and herded the Indians out of their way. The plight of these peoples, and particularly of one group, the Nambiquara, attracted the attention of anthropologists and support groups interested in the protection of cultural minorities.

Brazil requested the World Bank in 1979 to supply about one-third of the project's required funding. Initially receptive, the Bank intended, as usual, to reformulate the project design to make it compatible with Bank specifications. And when the Bank became aware of the threat to the Indian communities, it told the Brazilian government that it would help finance the project only if the rights of these native peoples were adequately safeguarded. The Bank also made contact with several anthropologists with field experience in Brazil.

At first, Brazil balked at the Bank's request to make sure that Indian rights would be protected and that Indian people would benefit from development of the area. The Brazilian authorities withdrew temporarily from the loan negotiations, then returned with a counter-proposal that their own national Indian agency, FUNAI, do something for the Indians with Brazil's own money. Outside monitoring would not be permitted. The World Bank agreed to these provisos.

In June 1980 David Price was invited to give a talk at the Bank about the probable effect of this planned influx of population from other parts of Brazil on indigenous communities of the POLONOROESTE area. An anthropologist with extensive experience with Indian communities in the affected area, Dr. Price agreed to be interviewed by me by telephone in May 1981. He is the major source of information for material in this section. Price was cordially received at the Bank and told he would be kept informed of Bank efforts to safeguard Indian rights. When he later found that no progress was being made, he told me, "I knew I would have to do something, or ten years from now, when these people had been wiped out, I would not be able to forgive myself." He started a letter-writing campaign, urging the Bank to insist on adequate safeguards for Indian interests, and began to carry his message to meetings of anthropologists and Native Americans, who also sent letters of protest.

Apparently the Bank then persuaded Brazilian authorities to accept outside consultants, for Price was offered the chance to go to Brazil as the anthropological consultant on a project-preparation mission. "I guessed that they wanted to co-opt me, or shut me up, or at least keep me too busy to cause trouble, but if I had refused to participate they could say that they had asked me and that I was unwilling to help." His suspicions were reinforced, he said, when he recieved an "irate" phone call from a high official in the Latin American projects office asking why he continued to organize protests even though he had agreed to join the mission.*

The official said he was "shocked" to find out Price was agitating and accused him of taking an "adversary position"

---

*Price supplied the names of all individuals concerned to me; I have not used them because I consider this a matter of structural rather than personal responsibility.

toward the Bank. Price denied this, telling the official that if the Bank was really concerned with the Indians' welfare, they were both on the same team. The Bank invited Price to Washington. On August 26, after a long conference, Bank officials asked him to agree to a memorandum stating that he understood the Bank was sincerely concerned for the Indians and would not bring further pressure against the Bank. Price says:

> It was understood that I would not be invited to go to Brazil unless I agreed with this. I was willing to agree that the Bank was, at the moment, sincere. I refused, however, to agree that I would not seek to bring pressure against the Bank in the future. That, I maintained, would depend on the Bank's future acts and I intimated that making my consultancy conditional on my acceptance of the point could be construed as an attempt at blackmail.

The offending statement was dropped, and Price agreed verbally to the text as amended.

Price flew to Brasilia September 20, 1980, for a three-week mission with two full-time Bank employees. He was to evaluate the project submitted by FUNAI for the protection of the Indians and their integration into the POLONOROESTE project and to evaluate FUNAI's capability to execute the project. His mandate was specifically restricted to only one group of Nambiquara Indians, not the entire indigenous population of the area.

The first few days of the mission were spent in Brasilia, where Price tried to find out what the FUNAI project—the third version they had submitted to the Bank—meant. It was hardly a project proposal, but simply a "shopping list" of proposed purchases and salaries, with no explanation of or justification for the project. Price worked with the two people who had prepared the proposal, neither of whom had any direct knowledge of Indians or had tried to make contact with FUNAI field workers. One was very recently hired, which given the recent reorganization of FUNAI (discussed below) had grave implications. Nor had they any technical knowledge of agriculture or of the machinery on their shopping list, and Price was "astounded" at their apparent lack of concern over their own ignorance.

In the field he found further difficulties. The promised transportation proved very erratic, but despite some lost time he succeeded in visiting every major village in the Guaporé Valley, the area covered by his limited mandate. He also determined the approximate extent of the land traditionally used by each village, the key to protection of their territorial rights. Upon his return Price produced a fifty-page report. Since by the terms of his contract the report is the property of the Bank, he could not make it available to me, but he described its contents in general terms.

In the first place, while accepting the geographical limits of his assignment, he emphasized that he treated the Guaporé Valley as a "spot check" on FUNAI designs for all thirty communities in the affected area. "It would be very convenient," he told me, "for FUNAI to focus on this one small group of Nambiquara as a 'showcase' project. These Indians have received a lot of international publicity; people know they are there, and it will be difficult to conceal what is happening to them. But the Indians in the Guaporé Valley represent only 3 or 4 percent of the total that will be affected by POLONOROESTE."

His appraisal of FUNAI was scorching. The agency had been recently taken over by military men, several of whom were previously posted with Security and Information, a kind of secret police, and at least one of whom is alleged to have been involved with the torture of political prisoners. These "colonels" had no previous experience with Indian affairs and have purged the agency of most of its qualified and committed career Indianists. Price declared both FUNAI and its project totally unacceptable as guardians of Indian rights and interests. The proposal was "so much at variance with real needs as to be unbelievable." FUNAI must not believe that the World Bank was seriously concerned about Indians, Price concluded, or it would not have submitted such a farce.

His report did not receive wide distribution within the Bank; no more than three or four people close to the situation ever read it, Price said. Though he admits the Bank was perfectly within its rights to limit distribution of the report which they had paid for, he was outraged at the alteration of his findings in the mission report. His "blanket condemnation" of the FUNAI program was suppressed. Instead, the Bank's report suggested that the FUNAI program would be acceptable if a few specific difficulties were remedied.

After reading the draft mission report, Price complained in letters to Robert McNamara and to his mission chief that the document "systematically distorts material that I furnished so as to make it support conclusions radically opposed to my own." In the letter to the mission chief he detailed the specific points which he felt had been distorted. His letter to McNamara was answered by the director of country programs for the Latin American and Caribbean region, who coldly informed him that the final report was the responsibility of the mission leader, not one of its members, and that Price's findings had been given "due consideration" in preparing the report.

Price also was disturbed to learn that an internal Bank report on POLONOROESTE supported the colonels' drive to decentralize the FUNAI and give more decision-making capabilities to its regional offices. "What I recommended was getting more input from the Indian agents at the local level about what the Indians really need," he said. "This is something very different. Decentralization means, first, that anti-Indian business interests will be able to exert much more pressure at the local level; and second, if atrocities occur, FUNAI will be able to deny that this is national policy."

Given the record of Brazil's treatment of the Indians and the type of people who are now running FUNAI, Price says he has little doubt atrocities will happen. By allowing FUNAI to design and run its Indian project, he says, the World Bank is supporting a racist policy that will have genocidal consequences.

This is not to imply that the Bank consciously intends or supports genocide. But to face up to the implications of the actions of its local partners in Brazil would force the Bank to utilize its leverage in ways that might threaten a breach in that partnership. We may infer that the breach is more feared by the Bank than by Brazil, as it is the Bank which seems most eager to avoid a confrontation. In some cases the Bank has withdrawn funding in order to save its public image. In the case of the Chico River dam in the Philippines, for example, it technically withdrew its funding in the face of armed resistance and popular protest, while continuing to fund other projects of its implementing agency, the National Power Corporation (NPC), elsewhere in the country. As money is fungible, this puts no pressure on the NPC to alter its own designs for the region. In the case of POLONOROESTE, however, the Bank approved the project, announcing three loans totaling $320 million in December 1981. David Price was told by officials at the Bank that there would be no point in obstructing POLONOROESTE, for if the Bank did not fund this project it would fund projects elsewhere in Brazil that would enable Brazil to use its own funds to implement POLONOROESTE. He commented, "By this logic, it is a waste of time and money for the Bank to evaluate any project."

Because it is well aware that its funding can allow a government to direct its own spending elsewhere, on matters close to the interests of international capital, the Bank insists on the right to dictate policy on all activities, nationwide, in the affected sector. If the Bank were as devoted to the interests of poor and indigenous peoples as it is devoted to the open door for international capital, it could even insist that the government of Brazil institute adequate safeguards for Indian interests wherever these interests are threatened by development projects, regardless of whether the Bank was directly funding any particular project.[1]

The Question of Motive

My purpose is not to impugn the character and humanitarian motives of everyone who is employed by the Bank in a professional capacity. But it is specious to argue that because some of the officials employed by the Bank (typically friends of the arguer) are nice people, the institution must be achieving some good works.

The World Bank is a large bureaucracy. Even if a majority of its employees were sincerely concerned with improving the lives of the poor, this proves nothing: a bureaucracy is not a democracy. A bureaucracy is controlled from the top down; the personnel in key positions in the line of command must transmit decisions from above and ensure their implementation by subordinates. While the ideology of the Bank attempts to gain the concurrence of these underlings for policies they administer, the organization does not depend on their voluntary cooperation.

It probably would be incorrect to infer that even the highest and most reliable officials of the bureaucracy are conscious of their role in suppressing the poor. They work within a capitalist system which holds, internationally as well as within their own countries, that what is good for business must necessarily be good for the entire population. Ralph Miliband's remarks about the governments of the advanced capitalist states—the states which control the policies of the World Bank—is apposite here:

> [I]t is easy to understand why governments should wish to help business in every possible way, yet do not at all feel that this entails any degree of bias towards particular classes, interests, and groups. For if the national enterprise is in fact inextricably bound up with the fortunes of capitalist enterprise, apparent partiality toward it is not really partiality at all. On the contrary, in serving the interests of business and in helping capitalist enterprise to thrive, governments are really fulfilling their exalted role as guardians of the good of all. . . . And they do so because they accept the notion that the economic rationality of the capitalist system is synonymous with rationality itself, and that it provides the best possible set of human arrangements in a necessarily imperfect world.[2]

While to a certain extent the Bank is a collection of competing factions and interest groups, they do not all compete equally. For instance, I suspect that the recently added offices on environmental issues and on the position of women, which nominally have to approve all Bank lending, have no real power to change or veto practices which contravene their purpose.

Social scientists are another such group: the Bank makes a show of requesting and "taking into account" their recommendations, but in practice these professions are subordinated to the real purposes of the Bank. Anthropologists and social scientists are used chiefly as intermediaries to elicit cooperation and defuse opposition of affected communities to Bank designs which are in no way based on their own needs and desires. Price said one anthropologist employed by the Bank scolded another anthropologist for protesting the POLONOROESTE project, because it would be approved and carried out whether or not the Indians are taken care of. This Bank employee argued that it would be counterproductive for anthropologists to continue to oppose the Bank on the issue, for it would make the Bank annoyed with them as a group, with the result that they would not be consulted at all in the future!

In the intra-bureaucracy struggle of competing interest groups, some interests consistently win and others usually lose. Policy and practice may be subject to influence on some questions which do not touch the vital interests of the ruling group, but the debates and power struggles must stay within some clearly defined but usually invisible limits.

One might visualize these limits as a cage with glass walls. Within this barrier the bureaucrats and technocrats work, argue, debate, cooperate or fall out with one another, attempting to aggrandize their own position or to defeat opponents. They have the illusion of freedom because the barrier is invisible, and they become aware of it only when they collide with it. The smart or ambitious ones, having once experienced or observed such a collision, remember where the barrier is and avoid it thereafter; those who are slower, stubborn, or angry continue to beat their heads against it until they are bloody. The recruitment and promotion practices naturally favor the smart ones who don't have bloody heads.

From a study of the Bank's actual practice we now have a rough map of where these barriers stand. A more precise chart would have to be supplied by a perceptive insider. And while such a design would be useful, it is not really necessary for our conclusions. It is clear that the Bank is neither an instrument of progressive assistance nor an effective advocate for liberating reform in its borrowing countries.

The Impact of Reagan and Clausen

In fact, some observers claim that with the advent of Ronald Reagan as president of the United States in January 1981, and

A. W. Clausen, formerly of the Bank of America, as president of the World Bank in the following July, regressive policy changes are underway in the global financial institution. The Reagan administration is seen as hostile to foreign aid, and Clausen is characterized as a "monetarist" who will turn the World Bank into a clone of the International Monetary Fund (IMF) and abandon McNamara's poverty-oriented lending in favor of a more tender regard for the wishes of multinational corporations.[3]

A close reading of recent news reports and some familiarity with the substance of World Bank activity behind its public relations curtain show that such analyses exaggerate the changes of 1981. First, while some members of the Reagan administration are clearly hostile to the *image* of foreign aid as it has been presented for public consumption, other administration members are aware that foreign aid and the World Bank are essential to the security and profitability of U.S. capitalism. Treasury Secretary Donald Regan, late of the Wall Street brokerage firm Merrill Lynch, is probably the strongest foreign aid advocate in the administration. Testifying before a Senate subcommittee in April 1981, he stressed that multilateral development banks "are essential to America's strategic interests around the world and should continue to receive U.S. support." He added:

> We have to do something for those countries whose minds we have to capture and whose social structures we are trying to preserve. . . .
> If the United States ceases its support, the system of international cooperation, particularly among the Western powers, could begin to unravel, and the Soviet Union would become the major beneficiary.[4]

The Reagan administation does not speak with a single voice or have a widely agreed policy on foreign aid and the multilateral development banks, and it may be that the treasury secretary will not have the last word on policy. He was nevertheless echoed by Secretary of State Alexander Haig, Jr., in another congressional appearance. The most serious opposition to U.S. participation in the IMF and World Bank comes, as before, from the Congress, and the real danger to those institutions is that an ambivalent or divided executive may not be able to strong-arm Congress into voting fresh billions of dollars for IDA.

Administration hostility to foreign aid arises from two sources: ignorance of the real functions of the World Bank and related institutions as supports for capitalism; and the opposition of some Reagan advisers to "bailing out" large commercial banks. The latter understand that a major function of money channeled through the IMF and the World Bank is precisely the rescue of the bad loans of those large banks. This viewpoint has been expressed by Edward J. Feulner, Jr., president of the Heritage Foundation (a right-wing think tank), and by supply-side theorist Jude Wanniski.[5]

The World Bank bureaucracy is dominated by the president, and a new president certainly will bring changes in both style and substance. To hold that A. W. Clausen is more devoted to the interests of multinational capital than Robert McNamara, however, would be unjust to both men. Clausen has not, to my knowledge, uttered one word of criticism of McNamara's presidency or policies. His first annual address to the Board of Governors displayed both his willingness to oppose right-wingers in Congress and in the Reagan administration on two key questions, the Bank's proposed new energy affiliate and the importance of IDA, and his adoption of the McNamara rhetoric on poverty. In a later speech Clausen vowed that the Bank would refuse to finance projects that "seriously compromise health and safety" or cause serious environmental problems. He also pledged that the Bank would not finance a project that "displaces people without adequate provision for resettlement."[6] While such pledges must be taken with as much skepticism as similar pronouncements by McNamara, they are in the same liberal tradition.

McNamara, on the other hand, would be indignant at any implication that he saw conflict between the needs of multinationals and the needs of the poor. It would be hard indeed to make the World Bank any more responsive to the interests of international capital than it was under McNamara, who joined the board of Royal Dutch Shell upon stepping down from the World Bank presidency. In the last years of McNamara's presidency the Bank had already begun to shift its emphasis away from so-called poverty-oriented lending to programs—structural adjustment lending and energy in particular—that would more directly aid international capital by helping to meet the debt crises of its borrowers.

What we *are* seeing under Reagan is a decrease, largely for budgetary reasons, in the U.S. appropriations for IDA. What we are seeing in Clausen's World Bank is a marked change in the rhetoric of Bank public relations to meet the criticism of right-wing opponents. The ultimate irony is that all that needs to be done is to strip away the public facade of concern for the poor and begin boasting of what they have been doing all along. A good example of this is the study issued by the U.S. Treasury Department in February 1982, which confirms many of the points made in this book about the Bank's assistance to foreign investors and U.S. influence on World Bank policies.[7]

Perhaps the best example of the new type of public relations required by the new political situation is an op-ed piece written by a Bank employee that appeared in the *New York Times* on August 23, 1981. In an article entitled "Where the Supply-Side Path is Old Hat," Keith Marsden attempts to counter right-wing criticism of the Bank and other aid agencies by boasting that "many third-world economies are very dynamic and have benefitted from exactly the sorts of incentives advocated by the new breed of American economists. In a sense, supply-side economics is alreay there." He names South Korea, Singapore, Malaysia, Mauritius, the Ivory Coast, and Brazil as countries that "have pursued supply-side policies for several years," citing generous tax holidays, concessions to investors, low rates of personal taxation, and "flexible" wage policies. His claim that the World Bank has played an important role in this development only confirms the analysis contained in the body of this book—and gives the lie to the Bank's earlier professions of concern for the poor. Unfortunately for Marsden, he did not foresee David Stockman's subsequent confession that "supply-side economics" is just another name for "trickle-down" theories, and a ruse for reducing the taxes of the rich.[8]

Conclusion: Is There a Better Way?

This book has been more than a critique of one immensely powerful bureaucracy; it raises some fundamental questions about the nature of capitalist development. For some, it may seem to call into question the very concept of progress. Is not civilization itself predicated on the exploitation of agriculturalists? Is it possible to construct reservoirs without uprooting people? Many will demand that I deliver proof that it can be done, that it *has* been done, sometime, somewhere.

As Michael Parenti acidly observed, "People who insist on being presented with a blueprint for change before they move an inch are probably not very interested in change."[1] Some critics will infer that I am against progress because I would be willing to see institutions like the World Bank go out of business without a suggestion for some close substitute to be erected in its place. But if the charges in this book of the damage done to the lives of poor and working people by the class-biased development of the World Bank have validity, why should we need to put anything in its place? If I wrote an attack on the Mafia no one would demand to know what I would put in its place.

I do believe in the possibility of progress and the urgency of change. I wrote this book because the activities of the World Bank offend my notions of what progress should mean, and actively block the best possibilities for constructive change. Capitalist development of the Third World has been ideologically justified by the notion that it should bring a higher development of the productive forces, and immediately or eventually lead to a better life for all, including the poorest. The reality of capitalist development has been very different, and it should not be legitimized by fantasies that are merely disguised forms of the discredited "trickle-down" theory.

One of the most serious indictments of the World Bank, and the developed capitalist governments which support and control it, is that it consistently uses its considerable financial resources to block the forces of progressive change, whether incrementalist attempts to improve wages and working conditions or increase national control over an economy, or revolutionary change which challenges the survival of governments assisted by the Bank. I have no wish to glorify revolution; I deeply and fervently wish that progressive change could be effected by milder means. But the lessons of history, and most especially recent history, have shown that this is hardly possible, and that the violence of the exploiters always precedes and provokes the violence of the oppressed.

The question of humane economic development cannot be separated from the question of war and revolution. Too many well-meaning liberals who harangue aid agencies on the need to increase popular participation and local control in particular projects are repelled and frightened by popular participation in armed insurrections, which is too often the only hope oppressed people have for their very survival. As progressive people in the affected nations clearly realize, the important task for those in the wealthy countries who are concerned with international solidarity is to actively fight to end the flow of foreign aid to Third World oligarchies, not to decorate appropriations bills with pretty amendments on appropriate technology or on the role of women in development. In the most extreme cases, as in the later years of the Indochina War or currently in the case of El Salvador, broad sections of the population in the richer capitalist countries become aware of the extremely pernicious role of "aid" and actively lobby to oppose or limit it. But these cases are only the tip of the iceberg; even the "normal" operations of foreign aid programs are functioning to hold back progressive development, not to finance it.

The Role of Foreign Aid

The advocates of foreign aid insist that the presently under-developed nations cannot pull themselves out of poverty without a boost from U.S. capital and technology. It is true, at a very general level, that some capital and some technology are essential to improving the material conditions of peoples, but as Harry Magdoff has pointed out in a fine essay on the subject, "the trouble with these simple truths is that when they have to be applied, they end up as fetishes—fetishes that tend to obscure the real issues."² The real issue, he indicates, is *who controls* the capital and technology that is exported to the poorer countries. Under present forms of foreign aid this capital and technology is embodied in relations of production that deny its benefits to the peoples of those countries, and the entire structure of aid and imperialism prevent these societies from controlling and utilizing their own resources as capital and their own capacity for technological development.

The chart overleaf clarifies the major types of aid relationships. On the vertical axis are two types of aid agency. The first represents most existing capitalist governments and the international organizations they control. The primary purpose of these "donor" agencies is to preserve and defend their own economic and political interests in the recipient country. This typically requires a great deal of support for the local social classes that are allied with international capital. The second type of agency is genuinely concerned about development for people, rather than for international capital, and wishes to promote genuine self-reliance as a means to national independence. A few governmental and private organizations might fall into this category, though I am unwilling to endorse any in particular.

On the horizontal axis are two types of recipient state. On the left are states ruled by comprador elites. These states may not have interests that are identical with international capital but have achieved a symbiosis in which each side receives more or less what it desires from the system of government. Most, but not all, existing Third World states belong in this category. The second group of states I have called socialist. Though I am using

Recipient Social Structures

	Comprador elites (most of states currently ruling in the Third World)	Socialist states (e.g., Mozambique, Nicaragua, Vietnam)
Imperialist: dedicated to preservation and reproduction of capital; includes World Bank, IMF, most large bilateral programs	Class-biased development: no hope for abolition of poverty and oppression; includes projects described in the body of this book	Small amounts of aid, deployed for the purpose of strengthening "market forces," right-wing groups, the military; subverting socialist purposes
"Good" agencies, concerned about development for people and self-reliance	Generally ineffective in face of repressive local and international structures; at best ameliorative of individual problems of a few people	Inherent contradiction of "aid for self-reliance" Ideally: no aid for recurrent consumption expenditures or for projects which will require external servicing or spare parts; limited aid for specific bottlenecks on a case-by-case basis, or deliberately planned to be phased out

Aid Agencies

this term loosely, to mean states willing to challenge the prerogatives of capital in the interests of improving the lives of their poorer citizens, I would not include in this category many Third World governments which term themselves socialist. The examples of socialist states which I use as illustrations in the chart are Mozambique, Nicaragua, and Vietnam.

The type of development which has been described in this book belongs in the upper left-hand corner of the chart, in the category of class-biased development. This holds out no hope for the abolition of poverty and oppression, even though it may help some individuals. As the book has been devoted to the exposition of this type of aid, it needs no further discussion here.

The type of aid in the upper right-hand corner, from imperialist institutions to socialist states, includes a few World Bank projects not treated elsewhere in this book. The amount of aid in this category is extremely small; in many cases those who control and fund the aid agencies are so hostile that no funds at all will be extended. The World Bank did make one loan to Vietnam in 1978, but in December 1979 President McNamara, in order to retain U.S. congressional support for World Bank funding, was forced to promise Congress that there would be no more loans to that country. When aid is extended, it is typically deployed to strengthen "market forces" (meaning right-wing groups and classes), or to attempt to divert the government from its socialist objectives. Aid from the Carter administration of the United States to Nicaragua after the 1979 victory of the Sandinistas was clearly of this type, but under the Reagan administration those who prefer an absolute boycott of socialist governments to this type of "subversive" aid have gained the upper hand.

In some cases the socialist governments, despite their poverty and the difficulties of transition to a different type of society, will refuse aid from large capitalist-controlled aid institutions because they suspect the lender's motives and the conditions attached to the aid. An example is Mozambique, which so far has declined to join the IMF and the World Bank.

In summary, aid from capitalist institutions to socialist governments is minor in amount and inherently problematic. When such aid is offered, the intent of the donors will be to subvert the socialist principles of the government and to transform it (either gradually and peacefully, or by violent change) into one more hospitable to foreign capital. This conclusion should be pondered deeply by well-meaning citizens who lobby for official governmental aid to countries they consider to be "good."

In the lower left corner is aid that flows from governmental or private agencies which may be sincerely concerned about distributive justice to governments or privately administered projects in states ruled by comprador elites. Such aid projects, I would maintain, are doomed to be ineffective because they are swimming against a powerful current of political repression and regressive redistribution of wealth. At best they can only ameliorate some individual problems. But worse, they will often be co-opted and distorted by the local power structure to serve its own ends. John Briscoe's study of health projects sponsored by voluntary agencies in Bangladesh provides evidence for such a conclusion.[3]

Worse, the proponents of capitalist aid frequently use the existence of a few such projects to justify the entire enterprise of foreign aid, both governmental and private. The total amount of aid in such projects is extremely small compared with official aid from capitalist-controlled institutions. Those who argue the case for aid on the basis of these projects do so on the grounds of the benevolent intentions of the donors rather than a hard-nosed assessment of the real effects of such projects, which may not be so beneficial. It is not legitimate to justify all foreign aid by extrapolating from such minor and unrepresentative programs. As Briscoe remarks.

> It is my definite impression . . . that the role of external inputs into the successful programs is greatly overestimated. It is not the money available but rather the people involved which is exceptional. Even if these successes do owe something to the funds supplied by foreign voluntary organizations, *a judgement of this type has to be made in the light of the full effect of such foreign aid and not on the basis of one or two successes.*[4] (Emphasis added)

The final category, in the bottom right corner, is that of aid from "good" institutions to "good" countries. Here if anywhere a case can be made for the usefulness of foreign aid. But even here we must be aware of the inherent problems and dangers of aid. It would be amusing (if it were not so appalling) to see how "good" aid agencies rush to throw money at countries which subscribe to the objectives of "self-reliance." They do not seem to realize that there is an inherent paradox in funding self-reliance with outside resources; self-reliance must mean, if it means anything, a renunciation of outside assistance. Tanzania, the prime example of the aid-attractive powers of slogans of self-reliance, is far more deeply dependent today on outside financing than it was when the principle was first proclaimed.[5] The availability of aid from external sources always brings with it the threat of dependence and corruption, and the larger the amounts of aid the most serious the danger.

Even if unlimited aid were available to support the economic programs of a socialist government, I would argue that to have the best effect, it should be granted only in limited quantity for specific, well-thought-out needs, on a case-by-case basis. This approach is obviously poles away from the massive quantities of money calculated on the basis of gross formulae to cover "resource gaps," as called for by the Brandt Commission and the presidents of the World Bank.

As a general rule no aid should be granted for recurrent consumption expenditures. This principle might be bent to permit some assistance in basic consumption goods so long as these are deliberately phased out within a specified period. I am reluctant to make even this exception, as it is all too clear that exceptions are the camel's nose which regularly precedes the whole huge beast of aid and import dependency.

There may be a role for material aid for investment expenditures, but again this should be decided on a specific, case-by-case basis, and used only to remove bottlenecks to development in which a relatively small amount of foreign-built machinery can be used to catalyze the utilization of much greater quantities of domestic resources. No aid should be extended for projects which will require continued and repeated servicing, or spare parts which can be obtained only from abroad. If this seems a severe requirement, its intent is to prevent the perpetuation of dependence on foreign technology, and its implementation will create very specific demands for the development of truly appropriate technology.

Technological development can be promoted by hiring foreign experts, but they should be vetted carefully to ensure both the soundness of their technical competence and the extent to which they share the social aims of the government employing them. This is a particularly difficult problem as capitalist definitions of economic development are deeply embedded within the very parameters of technical knowledge developed by capitalism. The attempt must nevertheless be made, and foreign experts can be hired cheaply, relative to the high cost of technology embodied in capital imports and technical assistance tied to massive recurrent expenditures on imports. Such experts would not be cheap, of course, if they gave bad advice, but there is no reason to believe high-priced consultants have more to contribute to the cause of self-reliant development than those who are willing to accept a modest salary and live in a style not too far removed from the people they will be working among.

Rethinking the Alternatives

But it will be objected, development must inevitably claim some victims. Civilization requires roads and ports, industry requires electric power, and small farmers are always exploited under any political system. Is it not futile to blame the World Bank for its role in a process that would proceed inexorably toward the same ends in any case? Would not the alternative be stagnation and standstill, the romanticization of poverty and a nostalgia for the irrecoverable?

Such questions come, of course, from those who are demanding detailed blueprints, not from those who are striving to bring about progressive change with whatever poor tools they have available. My answer must necessarily be brief, but I see no reason at all why economic development, which is justified as the means of creating a better life for all, must necessarily always hurt the poor. If one's goal is the betterment of the lives of the wretched of the earth, then a type of development which imposes yet deeper sufferings on the very people it advertises as beneficiaries must be rejected. It is time to state loud and clear that if this is the only development which is offered, then indeed standstill and stagnation are to be preferred. But this is not what I, nor most socialists, are advocating.

It should be apparent from the body of the text that by exerting itself to influence the shape of the projects it finances and the sectoral policies which frame these projects, the World Bank is *opposing* alternative ways of achieving similar ends. By insisting, for example, on foreign partnerships in industrial enterprises, or on the calculation of rates of return based on world market prices, the Bank is throwing its weight on the side of export-oriented industrialization and against protection and import substitution. This is in itself evidence that there is more than one way of pursuing economic development.

It cannot be assumed, however, that all policies opposed by the World Bank are therefore progressive, for this is clearly not the case. When the choice is between an alternative pushed by a corrupt and autocratic government supported by large amounts of aid from the World Bank on the one hand, and the solution proposed by the World Bank on the other hand, we are faced with no choice that speaks to the real needs of the masses of the people. While, for example, a policy of industrial protectionism will benefit primarily local business elites with few real benefits for workers and consumers, the World Bank's prescription of outward-oriented industrialization has demonstrably *worsened* conditions in the countries where it has been adopted. Too often the struggle over conditions attached to World Bank loans is one between false alternatives, from the standpoint of the welfare of the poorest people. In order to envision a truly progressive development, it will be necessary to get outside the narrow framework of alternative forms of *capitalist* development in which these questions are usually posed. Let us briefly run through some examples of the type of rethinking of development projects which will be necessary if the interests of poor people are to be served.

Roads

As we saw in Chapter 4, road building under capitalism is designed to extract surplus from the countryside and mines in order to facilitate the accumulation of wealth in the major cities and thence to ship it overseas to metropolitan markets. Such a network connects rural areas and small towns to the world market but has the effect, if not the intent, of separating the smaller communities from one another. Carol LaGrasse has suggested that "the natural pattern of progressive, civilizing development is an intricate network of back roads or footpaths." Former Senator José Diokno of the Philippines has expressed a similar concern:

> Look at the expressways. Most of the cars that go through are private cars. Who owns the private cars in this country? The elite. And did you notice one more thing? All of these expressways converged in Manila when we should have been building roads connecting the different barrios to the población (town) and one barrio to another so that the flow of goods would not all go in one direction, which is towards an outgoing port, but would have been circulating internally.[6]

Dams

In order to discuss alternative ways of building dams we must consider a wide range of issues. First, what purposes do dams serve? And which classes are presently served by the functions performed by dams? There is a growing body of opinion that challenges the need for *large* dams for hydroelectric power and even questions the efficiency of centralized systems of electrical generation and distribution. Some analysts suggest that a society's energy needs may be better served by larger numbers of small dams, or by the utilization of other sources of energy.[7] If we nevertheless accept, for the sake of argument, the need for large dams and the reservoirs to feed them, a new range of questions appears: for one, why are these dams so often situated in areas where they will displace tens of thousands of people, often of cultures and races different from that of the government? Dorothy Friesen and Gene Stolzfus raise this question after observing the site of several projected dams in the Philippines; a group of native Americans displaced by the Missouri River development in North Dakota asked why they, and not white communities, were being forced to move:

> We see on the plans and maps of the proposed Missouri River development, that five great dams are to be built across the river. Four of these dams are carefully located above the white com-

munities of Yankton, Chamberlain and Pierre in South Dakota, and Bismark in North Dakota. . . . Our Indian community is larger than some of the cities which have been so carefully safeguarded by the original plan.[8]

The implication of such questions is that national planners tend to be much more wanton in dispersing groups of minority peoples than they would be in displacing settlements of wealthy and politically influential citizens. (Indeed, who has ever heard of a *city* which had to be displaced because it occupied the best site for a reservoir?) The cost of compensating and resettling existing populations on sites of proposed reservoirs is an important factor which influences planners' choice of sites, but the "costs" now considered are the narrow ones of minimal expenditure on the relocation of powerless peoples, whereas a true social cost-accounting would take into account the production foregone in perpetuity from the indundation of the lands as well as non-economic considerations such as the value of cultural diversity.

Taking the argument a step further, let us assume that it is deemed vital to build a large dam and reservoir and that it will not be possible to avoid uprooting a community of people living there. How should such people be compensated? They could perhaps be allowed to negotiate their own figure, which should be a large one to indemnify them for the loss of their homes and their livelihoods (the reader might ask what sum he or she would demand for such a loss). Or why should not the community which sits upon an energy resource of such vital importance to the larger society not be compensated as if they were the owners of petroleum deposits capable of producing an equivalent amount of energy? These suggestions are, I hasten to add, mischievous ones, as I do not believe that sums of money, however large, are the correct solution to this problem; but they do serve to point out how easily planners assume that poor people can be pushed around at will. A more serious suggestion is that a system of collectivized agriculture would at least permit the insertion of the dislocated people into units in which they would have a claim to a share of the produce of the soil, whereas under a system of private agriculture they will usually be doomed to remain landless laborers after they lose their own land.

Agriculture

The design of a socialist agricultural system is a complex problem, and will not be solved here with a few sentences. The choice of a suitable agriculture for each country will depend on many factors, including the historical legacy, the means of production and land tenure system inherited by the government which intends to make changes, and the production and distribution goals of that government. A reorientation of farm production to augment the domestic supply of basic foodstuffs is desperately needed in many Third World countries; yet a post-revolutionary society will face heavy pressure to maintain production and exports in their existing form, and a restructuring of agriculture will probably involve some short-term disruption of production and most likely a permanent drop in availability of resources for export.

I do not believe that an agricultural policy designed to aid small farmers is likely to lead to a just or egalitarian society. So long as the farmers remain geographically and politically isolated, they are likely to be manipulated and exploited by government or by merchants; if they organize in political associations they are likely to demand subsidies and special treatment which may not be reconcilable with the overall needs of society. Further, stratification of rural society arises spontaneously from even the most egalitarian pattern imposed by land reforms so long as private property remains the basis of the land tenure system, with the result that, as in World Bank programs, aid supposedly targeted for "small farmers" is actually going to relatively prosperous ones, and there is no help at all for the landless.

A large body of recent literature has emphasized that small farmers are the most efficient in the utilization of land resources. While not disputing these findings, I would point out that small farmers are efficient because they are forced to be by economic pressures. In any case it is also widely acknowledged that the world food problem is not one of efficient production, but of equitable distribution. And it is because of its potential for promoting more equitable distribution of income, more than for any real or imagined superiority in production, that I feel that some form of collectivized agriculture is the best answer to the problem of rural poverty in the Third World. However, no single policy prescription can do justice to the complexity of agricultural problems around the world. In the short term, in some countries, a redistributive land reform would at least give poor people some means with which to feed themselves, even though it is not an answer to the larger problem of building a new society.

Industry

As the World Bank well knows, one must look beyond the level of individual projects to broader sectoral and national issues. (I do not disagree at all on this point; my quarrel is with the content of the conditions they impose at these higher levels.) One cannot meaningfully discuss the need for a fertilizer plant or a tire factory without debating the issues of capitalism versus socialism; of export-oriented production versus concentration on local needs; of production of elite goods versus goods for mass consumption. Only when these larger issues have been decided can one get down to choosing what kind of factories are needed. Within these limits there is definitely a place for some kind of social cost-benefit analysis to ensure that the nation will not have to pay more heavily for a given project than is justified by the goods and services it will provide. This will, however, certainly be different from the short-term profit-oriented calculations of capitalist firms or the highly doctored post facto figures offered by the World Bank in justification of its choices.

Mining

The exploitation of mineral wealth poses special problems. Whereas agricultural resources are widely distributed, so that most nations have the potential capacity to feed their own populations, economic deposits of minerals are concentrated in relatively few countries and international trade is imperative for their utilization. This does not, of course, imply that the presently existing pattern of international trade is the best or fairest one might imagine; on the contrary, the overwhelming proportion of the world's mineral wealth is utilized by the wealthy countries, a shocking proportion of which goes for the production of weapons of war.

As long as the world is divided into states arbitrarily demarcated by colonial powers for the purpose of "divide and rule," and these states own or control the rights over their mineral deposits, those without any significant resources to use or to trade will be at a serious disadvantage. A transcendence of the existing state system would be needed to introduce any kind of equity in this respect. For the time being, however, we will eschew utopian speculations and concentrate on the optimum policy for states who do control significant mineral resources and want to exploit these for the best interests of their present and future populations.

The World Bank prescription for mineral development is a good model of what a responsible government should *not* do. The World Bank advises immediate exploitation of all commercial deposits (as defined by the corporations which will own the mines or purchase their output), on terms which are very advantageous to the corporations and will leave very little income, proportionally, to the host government. It must not be forgotten that at present what income there is will be consumed unproductively by corrupt and unrepresentative governments in a number of these states. In periods such as the present (the early 1980s) when market conditions are depressed and the countries' negotiating strength therefore weak, the option of nonaction, of letting the minerals rest in the ground for a while, must be seriously considered. A country with enough autonomy to make such a decision could then wait until market conditions became more favorable to minerals suppliers and they could obtain better terms for their exports. Norman Girvan has even suggested that Third World countries should gradually and progressively phase out their mineral exports to center countries, because "every ton of petroleum and minerals exported to the center represents that much less indigenous resources available for present or future use as an input into the local productive system for the satisfaction of the people's needs."[9]

Oil and gas exploration

Girvan also emphasizes the need for local geographical exploration, which raises the thorny problem of who pays for this expensive and risky operation. As shown in Chapter 7, the large oil companies will make such expenditures only if they are assured of control over subsequent finds and such development fits into their global supply strategy, while unsuccessful attempts financed by governments of poor countries will be an impossible financial burden. Given this situation, an early proposal from the World Bank staff for a revolving fund extending loans which would be repaid (by a percentage of the production) only if exploitable resources were found makes very good sense. It should be remembered that this staff proposal was killed by the opposition of the oil companies and the U.S. Treasury.

Forestry

The protection and renewal of forest resources can be guaranteed only by a government which makes allowance for the immediate needs of its poorest people for land to cultivate and for firewood, as well as providing for long-term needs for conserving land and water resources through forestry. In many cases, a reform of the land tenure system which gives poor people access to the richer lands of the nation will be a prerequisite for rational exploitation of the forests. Poor people whose basic needs are not otherwise provided for, and who see commercial timber corporations despoiling the forests with the connivance of their government, will not be amenable to tree-planting programs which displace the social costs of commercial deforestation onto the poorer residents of the area.

Housing

The provision of decent housing for the millions of inhabitants of Third World slums and shantytowns is a difficult assignment that will not be fulfilled overnight. In order to make a dent in this massive problem, it will be necessary to devise low-cost solutions; thus, I have no quarrel per se with the World Bank's emphasis on "affordability." But that is only one part of the solution. It is also necessary to *raise the incomes* of the slum dwellers if even the cheapest of housing options are not to remain out of their reach. It is, furthermore, unlikely that afford-able housing can be provided to the poorest people so long as a private land and private housing market determines rents. The experience of China and of Cuba suggests that an urban land reform and the nationalization of housing are prerequisites for the provision of affordable housing.[10]

These comments have necessarily been brief and superficial. I offer them in order to make the point that there are alternatives to the way the World Bank wants things done, and that there are people with technical expertise who are working on these prob-lems and suggesting alternative solutions. But most of these alternatives require a challenge to the international corporations and to local elite structures of which the World Bank is not capable. A socialist government without technical competence will probably grapple unsuccessfully with these enormous prob-lems, but it is equally true that only under a government which is genuinely committed to and supported by its poor and labor-ing people will the best technical solutions have any chance to work.

Toward a Socialist Philosophy of Development

And so we have arrived at the usual conclusion of a work like this, that a social revolution will be the precondition for a differ-ent and more humane development policy. But this is not enough. Voices are multiplying which insist that the presently existing socialist states have done no better than the capitalist ones in this respect; that there, too, people are displaced for development projects; that there, too, forests are uprooted and the land eroded; in short, that there, too, the poor and powerless are the victims of development.

This is not the place for detailed examination of the validity of those charges. My impression is that they contain a partial truth.

On the one hand, they ignore many innovative experiments in new types of economic development which have been pioneered by socialist states; on the other hand, cases exist where socialist development projects have had detrimental impacts on poor people and the environment which rival those of capitalist development. Quite often, I suspect, this has been true because the socialist states, instead of inventing a new, humanistic type of development, have preferred instead to copy capitalist models. If socialist states can do no better in this regard than capitalist ones, then socialism must be considered to be bankrupt. When the interests of poor people are forgotten in an infatuation with large dams and world-class factories there is little reason for anyone except the bureaucrat-rulers of these states to prefer socialist economic development over capitalistic development.

I do not write this because I believe that socialism holds out no more hope than capitalism; on the contrary, I believe it is the only hope. But there are many different forms of socialism, as the existing socialist states demonstrate; the range of potential forms which have not yet been embodied in state form is surely even greater. I wish primarily to underline the fact that socialism is not "the answer"; it is the beginning of the search for answers.

Frequently radical scholars, when presented with demands for blueprints for change, retort that the question itself presumes an elitist and racist assumption that "we" should decide the future for others. The peoples of the Third World, they say, will design their own future society out of their own particular conditions and felt needs, after they have made their socialist revolution.

This response is correct, but again it is not enough. If peoples in revolution are determined to effect change, with or without a blueprint, this does not imply that they would not be grateful for some blueprints; not, to be sure, detailed and authoritarian ones, but partial and suggestive ones derived from the sharing of experiences of other countries. Those who have had to fight a war to achieve state power are typically ill-prepared to manage an economy, which requires quite different skills, and the recent experience of countries such as Zimbabwe, Mozambique, Vietnam, and Nicaragua would seem to suggest that winning the war was the easier half of the task.

To be sure, given the heavy ideological content of Western economic theory, ignorance of the currently received opinions may be a positive advantage to a party or movement trying to create a new kind of society. But if bourgeois economics cannot be trusted to provide guidelines for organizing a socialist society, some alternative is desperately needed. Armchair radicals such as myself, who have not been able to change the nature of our own imperialist states and the organizations which these states control, can perhaps make a modest contribution to international solidarity by performing scholarly tasks for which the revolutionaries on the spot have no time and few resources. It is in this spirit that this book is offered. But more is needed; and what is needed is no less than a socialist philosophy of development, a guideline for what has to be done after the conquest of political power is achieved.

A number of revolutionary movements calling themselves socialist have come to power in different nations in this century. There is a need for careful study and comparison of the post-revolutionary political and administrative experiences of all these societies for the purpose of assessing and evaluating the successes and the failures of various policies in different countries, with the aim of eliciting some general principles for the guidance of other societies in revolution. Such an enterprise will inevitably attract contention from those with ideological vested interests on both the Left and the Right, but that is a mark of its significance, not a reason to avoid the enterprise.

In such an endeavor, it will be necessary to avoid the error of taking all *previous* experience as definitive, by holding that nothing should be attempted unless it has already been tried, successfully, somewhere else. The enemies of progress are guilty of this for the good reason that their real interest is in preventing change by proving that it is impossible. But the Left is also prone to a subtle form of this fatalism, as is demonstrated by the confusion and disarray shown by many when the "Chinese model," which had been so often cited as the proof that progressive change is possible, seemed to disintegrate before their eyes when repudiated by a new leadership. The response of some has been to retreat to the "Albanian model." I think there is a need to reject the use of models altogether. No country, with its unique constellation of resources and history, can serve as a model for any other. But worse, the use of models inhibits rather than stimulates original thinking about the solution to social problems. It is necessary to remind ourselves that when the Bolsheviks took power in Russia, they had no predecessor socialist government whatsoever on which to model themselves. The new government had to *invent* the meaning of socialism. When we remember this, the wonder is not that there were so many mistakes, failures, and even crimes committed by the leadership of the Soviet Union, but that so much that is truly impressive was achieved. It is essential to analyze both the successes and the failures, in order to discern where (if at all) there is some necessary connection between the two, or whether it might not after all be possible to throw out the bath water to save the baby. Similarly, when the Chinese Communist Party came to power, it had the "Soviet model" from which to borrow experience (and material aid), but it had no "Chinese model." That had to be invented by the Chinese. If we have now lost the living breathing prototype of the "Chinese model," we have no right to feel disheartened in our own quest for the outlines of progressive change. Much less do we have any right to feel "betrayed" by the turn of events. Clearly humankind would be doomed to stagnation if all work in science and technology were absolutely limited by what had been done before, yet many people do not hesitate to deny that any progress can be made in the organization of society on the grounds that no revolution has yet created the particular utopia that would appeal to them.

If we must at all costs avoid the extreme of defeatism, however, we must also avoid the opposite error of believing that faith alone can move mountains or abolish exploitation. We must not disdain the lessons of previous experience, any more than we must consider ourselves limited to it. Both theoretical and practical experiments must be directed to finding solutions to the challenge of socialist development. The project of "sharing experiences" is one of considerable urgency. At stake is no less than the reclamation of the natural resources of earth and the full promise of human technology for the benefit of the vast majority of humankind.

Notes

Preface and Acknowledgments

1. John S. Furnivall, *Colonial Policy and Practice* (New York: New York University Press, 1956), p. 545.
2. Aart van de Laar, *The World Bank and the Poor* (The Hague: Martinus Niijhoff, 1980), p. 7
3. My chapters do not follow the Bank's sector categories exactly. For example, the Bank does not treat water resources as a sector, and it subsumes mining under "industry," and forestry under agriculture.

1: The Institution and Its Power

1. World Bank, *Co-Financing*, August 1980, Annex 1, p. 17. From the time of its establishment the Bank has tried to augment its own resources by selling "participation" in the loans that it makes to private investors. At its high point in 1961–1962 outside participation in Bank loans yielded $319 million, in a year when total Bank loan commitments were only $882 million. Accelerated inflation in the 1960s and 1970s made the Bank's fixed-interest portfolio unattractive to private investors, however, so in 1974 the Bank inaugurated a new policy to attract cofinancing from private institutions. Under the new regime the private banks are to make a separate loan at the same time a World Bank loan for a particular project is negotiated. The borrower and the private bank agree on the terms of their loan, which follow precedents established in the Eurodollar markets, i.e., floating interest rates pegged to the London Interbank Offer Rate, management and commitment fees, syndication of loans, and so on. The loans are linked by (a) cross-default and other cross-reference clauses in the two agreements, which effectively provide a World Bank guarantee to the private lender; and (b) a written memorandum of agreement between the two lenders providing for exchange of information and consultation on matters affecting the implementation of the project or the borrowers' ability to meet its repayment obligations. This provision assures greater than usual access by private

lenders to the plethora of country and project information that the World Bank collects and analyzes in the normal course of its activities. Each party, however, retains the right to withhold confidential information.

2. Edward S. Mason and Robert E. Asher, *The World Bank Since Bretton Woods* (Washington: D.C.: Brookings Institution, 1973), pp. 56–58.

3. World Bank, *Annual Report 1980* (Washington, D.C.: World Bank, 1981), p. 77.

4. See Rosemary Galli, "The UNDP, 'Development,' and Multinational Corporations," *Latin American Perspectives* 4, no. 4 (Fall 1977).

5. Just Faaland, ed., *Aid and Influence: The Case of Bangladesh* (London: Macmillan, 1981), p. 111; and Aart van de Laar, *The World Bank and the Poor* (The Hague: Martinus Nijhoff, 1980), pp. 44–45.

6. Figures compiled from World Bank news releases.

7. Personal communication.

8. For example, Teresa Hayter, *Aid as Imperialism* (Baltimore: Penguin, 1971); and Cheryl Payer, *The Debt Trap: The IMF and the Third World* (New York: Monthly Review Press, 1975).

9. Ansel F. Luxford, quoted in Mason and Asher, *The World Bank Since*, p. 19.

10. Robert W. Oliver, *Early Plans for a World Bank*, (Princeton, N.J.: Princeton Studies in International Finance, no. 29, 1971), p. 3.

11. IBRD Articles of Agreement, Article 5, Section 9, quoted in Mason and Asher, *The World Bank Since*, p. 31.

12. Mason and Asher, *The World Bank Since*, p. 40.

13. Quoted in A. A. Fatouros, "The World Bank," in J. B. Howard, ed., *The Impact of International Organizations on Legal and Institutional Change in the Developing Countries* (New York: International Legal Center, 1977), p. 23.

14. Quoted in Mason and Asher, *The World Bank Since*, pp. 60–61.

15. Mason and Asher, *The World Bank Since*, p. 43; van de Laar, *The Bank and the Poor*, p. 99.

16. Mason and Asher, *The World Bank Since*, p. 271.

17. George D. Woods, address before The Pilgrims (London: World Bank, November 29, 1965), p. 2. For small farmer projects, see Gavin Williams, "The World Bank and the Peasant Problem," in J. Heyer, P. Roberts, and G. Williams, eds., *Rural Development in Tropical Africa* (London: Macmillan, 1981), p. 21.

18. David E. Lilienthal, *The Harvest Years 1959–1963*, vol. V of *The Journals of David E. Lilienthal* (New York: Harper & Row, 1971), entry for June 20, 1963, p. 480.

19. Fatouros, "The World Bank," p. 13.

20. For a cutting assessment of McNamara's personality and previous achievements, see David Halberstam, *The Best and the Brightest* (New York: Fawcett, 1972), *passim*.

21. van de Laar, *The Bank and the Poor*, pp. 225–27.

22. Ibid., p. 232.

23. Ibid.
24. Escott Reid, "McNamara's World Bank," *Foreign Affairs* (July 1973).
25. van de Laar, *The Bank and the Poor*, p. 235.
26. Ronald T. Libby, "International Development Association: A Legal Fiction Designed to Secure an LDC Constituency," *International Organization* 29, no. 4 (autumn 1975): 1065–72.
27. My discussion of IBRD finances is based on the following sources: Mason and Asher, *The World Bank Since*, ch. 5; van de Laar, *The Bank and the Poor*, pp. 18–27; Eugene H. Rotberg, *The World Bank: A Financial Appraisal* (Washington, D.C.: World Bank, 1976 and 1978); and World Bank, *Annual Report 1981*.
28. Rotberg, *World Bank: Financial*, p. 18.
29. Ibid., p. 19
30. World Bank Information and Public Affairs, "Facts of the World Bank," handout (1981).
31. Rotberg, *World Bank: Financial*, 1978, p. 19 and annex. V. H. Oppenheim, "Whose World Bank?" *Foreign Policy* 19 (summer 1975), accused the Bank of subservience to OPEC politics, including a tolerant line on oil price increases and acquiescence in a boycott of Israeli officials in missions sent to Mideast nations.
32. Rotberg, *World Bank: Financial*, 1978, p. 20.
33. See *New York Times* August 25 and 31, September 23 and 26, 1981.
34. *International Herald Tribune*, October 8–9, 1980.
35. Mason and Asher, *The World Bank Since*, p. 380.
36. Ibid., pp. 387–88.
37. Ibid., p. 386.
38. van de Laar, *The Bank and the Poor*, p. 66.
39. Ibid., p. 59.
40. Ibid., pp. 81–82.
41. Rotberg, *World Bank: Financial*, 1978, p. 26.
42. Ann Crittendon, "Foreign Aid Has Friends Back Home: Businessmen," *New York Times*, July 30, 1978.
43. Jane Chudy, "Why Canadian Business Is Not Getting More World Bank Contracts," *Development Directions* (August/September 1978): 23.
44. Richard Newfarmer, *Transnational Conglomerates and the Economics of Dependent Development: A Case Study of the International Electrical Oligopoly and Brazil's Electrical Industry* (Greenwich, Conn.: JAI Press, 1980), *passim*.
45. Ibid., p. 294.
46. Ibid., p. 295.
47. In Seymour J. Rubin, ed., *Foreign Development Lending—Legal Aspects* (Leiden and Dobbs Ferry, N.Y.: Oceana, 1971), p. 219.
48. Ibid., p. 222.
49. Newfarmer, *Transnational Conglomerates*, p. 296.
50. World Bank news release, June 23, 1978.

51. Crittenden, "Foreign Aid."
52. Escott Reid, *Strengthening the World Bank* (Chicago: The Adlai Stevenson Institute, 1973), p. 194.
53. Clyde H. Farnsworth, "Bank of America's Chief Chosen by Carter to Head World Bank," *New York Times,* October 31, 1980.
54. National Advisory Council on International Monetary and Financial Policies, *Annual Report 1979.*
55. A recent exploration of this network of influence on executive power is found in Holly Sklar, ed., *Trilateralism: The Trilateral Commission and Elite Planning for World Management* (Boston: South End Press, 1980).
56. The best discussion of this is James R. Morrell, "Foreign Aid: Evading the Control of Congress," *International Policy Report* 3, no. 1 (January 1977).
57. van de Laar, *The Bank and the Poor,* p. 78.
58. Graham Hovey, "White House Is Fighting to Prevent Congress Crippling of World Bank," *New York Times,* March 28, 1978.
59. Clyde Farnsworth, "World Bank Loans Not Just Money," *New York Times,* August 7, 1977.
60. Shirley Hobbs Scheibla, "McNamara's Band Sour," *Barron's,* December 3, 1979.
61. Even this was not really new as the McCarthy "witch hunts" in the 1950s had affected U.S. members of the Bank staff.
62. Payer, *Debt Trap,* ch. 5.
63. The story of the U.S. effort to get a World Bank loan for Saigon is told by Gabriel Kolko, "The United States Effort to Mobilize World Bank Aid to Saigon," *Journal of Contemporary Asia* 5, no. 1 (1975): 42–52.
64. Mason and Asher, *The World Bank Since,* pp. 170–1.
65. John Waterbury, *Hydropolitics of the Nile Valley* (Ithaca, N.Y.: Syracuse University Press, 1980), pp. 101–7.
66. Howard, ed., *The Impact of International Organizations,* ch. 3.
67. Jim Morrell, "Back-door Aid Abroad," *New York Times,* April 1, 1981; "Total Aid Package for El Salvador May Reach $523 million," April 1981; and Department of the Treasury, *United States Participation in the Multilateral Development Banks in the 1980s* (Washington, D.C.: Dept. of Treasury, 1982), p. 61
68. David E. Lilienthal, *The Harvest Years,* entry for December 19, 1963, p. 538.
69. van de Laar, *The Bank and the Poor,* p. 78.
70. Rotberg, *World Bank: Financial,* 1978, p. 13.
71. van de Laar, *The Bank and the Poor,* p. 24.
72. Robert S. McNamara, address to the Board of Governors, September 30, 1980, p. 37.
73. Ibid., p. 38.
74. van de Laar, *The Bank and the Poor,* p. 26.
75. Rotberg, *World Bank: Financial,* 1978, p. 11.
76. Ibid., p. 12.
77. van de Laar, *The Bank and the Poor,* p. 38.

78. Rotberg, *World Bank: Financial*, 1978, pp. 11–12.
79. Payer, *Debt Trap*, p. 202.
80. The executive director's report to the congressional subcommittee was published in *Inter-American Economic Affairs* 30, no. 2 (1976): 81–91.
81. Mason and Asher, *The World Bank Since*, pp. 224–25.
82. Ibid., p. 226.
83. Rotberg, *World Bank: Financial*, 1976, p. 18.
84. "Clausen Will Help Those Who Help Themselves," interview, *Euromoney*, December 1980, p. 35.
85. Notably Mason and Asher, *The World Bank Since*, pp. 217–21; van de Laar, *The Bank and the Poor*, pp. 15–16.
86. Rotberg, *World Bank: Financial*, 1976, p. 21.
87. *World Business Weekly*, May 11, 1981, p. 47.
88. *New York Times*, January 6, 1982.

2: Malignant Growth: A Preliminary Explanation

1. Ronald L. Meek, ed., *Marx and Engels on the Population Bomb*, 2nd ed. (Palo Alto, Cal.: Ramparts Press, 1971), pp. 5–6.
2. Michael Perelman, "Marx, Malthus, and the Concept of Natural Resource Scarcity," *Antipodes* 2, no. 2 (1979): 81.
3. Robert S. McNamara, address to the Board of Governors, 1979.
4. "A Report from Africa and a Conversation with Robert McNamara," *Bill Moyer's Journal*, WNET/13, February 6, 1975.
5. Mahbub ul Haq, "Changing Emphasis of the Bank's Lending Policies," *Finance and Development* 15, no. 2 (June 1978): 13.
6. Ernest Feder has written amusingly of the military terminology favored by Bank ideologists; see "The New World Bank Programme for the Self-Liquidation of the Third World Peasantry," *Journal of Peasant Studies* 3, no. 3 (April 1976): note 20.
7. See, e.g., "Editorial Commentary: Blood and Treasure," *Barron's*, June 16, 1980, p. 7; and Ho Kwon Ping, "End of the McNamara Era," *Far Eastern Economic Review*, September 19, 1980, p. 108.
8. ul Haq, *Changing Emphasis*, p. 13.
9. World Bank, *Papua New Guinea: Economic Situation and Development Prospects*, July 14, 1976 (Washington, D.C.: World Bank), annex 1, p. 4.
10. See Chapter 11.
11. Karl Marx, "The so-called primitive accumulation," *Capital* (New York: International Publishers, 1975), vol. I, part VIII.
12. Ibid., p. 706.
13. Ibid., p. 636.
14. Engels' letter to Davidson, January 9, 1895, excerpted in Meek, ed., *Marx and Engels*, p. 122.
15. The destruction of the Indian cotton industry is an example here. Karl Marx,

"The British Rule in India," *Selected Works I* (New York: Progress, 1969), p. 490.

16. Robert McNamara, interview with Leonard Silk, *New York Times*, April 1, 1978.

17. The Bank does argue for *Redistribution with Growth* (the name of a book edited by Hollis Chenery and published by the Bank), a hypothetical position that the poor can be helped by allocating to them a small additional percentage of future increments to growth. The argument has been appropriately roasted by Ernest Feder in "McNamara's Little Green Revolution: The World Bank Scheme for the Liquidation of the Third World Peasantry," *Comercio Exterior* 22, no. 8 (August 1976); and in "Monopoly Capital and Agricultural Employment in the Third World," unpublished, July 1980.

18. Harry Braverman, *Labor and Monopoly Capital* (New York: Monthly Review Press, 1974).

19. Frances Stewart, *Technology and Underdevelopment* (London: Macmillan, 1977), p. 47.

20. For an account of this process, see John Kurien, "Entry of Big Business into Fishing: Its Impact on Fish Economy," *Economic and Political Weekly*, September 9, 1978, pp. 1557–68.

21. Garrett Hardin, "The Tragedy of the Commons," *Science* 162 (December 13, 1968): 1244.

22. David Waite, "Copper," in Cheryl Payer, ed., *Commodity Trade of the Third World* (New York: Halsted Press, 1975), p. 51.

23. Michael Perelman, *Farming for Profit in a Hungry World* (Montclair, N.Y.: Allanheld, Osmun, 1977), pp. 53–59.

24. Jack Shepherd, *The Forest Killers: The Destruction of the American Wilderness* (New York: McKay, 1975), pp. 378–38.

25. Robert S. McNamara, address to the Board of Governors, 1979. The Bank is also frank in admitting its failure to solve the employment problem in *Shelter*, Poverty and Basic Needs Series (Washington, D.C.: World Bank, September 1980), pp. 21–23.

26. David L. Gordon, "The Bank and the Development of Small Enterprises," *Finance and Development*, March 1979, p. 19.

27. See for example Louis T. Wells, Jr., "Economic Man and Engineering Man," in C. Peter Timmer et al., *The Choice of Technology in Developing Countries* (Cambridge, Mass.: Center for International Affairs, 1975), p. 78.

28. Gordon, "The Bank and the Development," p. 20.

29. Ibid., p. 19.

30. Ibid., p. 21.

31. Ibid.

32. For those who are concerned with the issue of alternative technology, Frances Stewart, *Technology and Underdevelopment*, should be required reading. Her case study of cornmeal in Kenya illustrates the absurdity of any simple ratios of capital to labor by revealing that technologically inefficient

methods (in terms of input-output ratios) can still be the most profitable due to questions of price, consumer preference, and organizational form.

33. David Dickson, *The Politics of Alternative Technology* (New York: Universe Books, 1974), p. 152.

3: Project Lending: Some General Considerations

1. The short descriptions of the six stages quoted here are taken from Warren C. Baum, "The World Bank Project Cycle," *Finance and Development* (December 1978): 3.
2. Judith Tendler, *Inside Foreign Aid* (Baltimore: Johns Hopkins University Press, 1975), p. 104.
3. Fawzi Mansour, "The World Bank: Present Role and Prospects," United Nations African Institute for Economic Development and Planning, Dakar, December 1979, p. 30.
4. Aart van de Laar, *The World Bank and the Poor* (The Hague: Martinus Nijhoff, 1980), pp. 227–28.
5. Baum, *World Bank Project*, p. 5.
6. Edward S. Mason and Robert E. Asher, *The World Bank Since Bretton Woods* (Washington, D.C.: The Brookings Institution, 1973), p. 234.
7. Ibid., p. 313.
8. K. W. Taylor, quoted in van de Laar, *The Bank and the Poor*, p. 86.
9. Jacques Berthelot, "Développement du Tiers Monde et Methodes de Selection des Projects," *Mondes en Developpement* 31 (1980).
10. The chief textbooks used as guides for World Bank project evaluations are I. M. D. Little and J. A. Mirrlees, *Manual of Industrial Project Analysis in Developing Countries*, vol. II, Social Cost Benefit Analysis (Paris: OECD, 1969); and L. Squire and H. van der Tak, *Economic Analysis of Projects* (Baltimore: Johns Hopkins University Press, 1975).
11. R. G. Layard, quoted in Frances Stewart, "A Note on Social Cost-Benefit Analysis and Class Conflict in LDC's," *World Development* 3, no. 1 (1975); reprinted in Charles K. Wilber, ed., *The Political Economy of Development and Underdevelopment*, 2nd ed. (New York: Random House, 1979), pp. 297–98.
12. Stewart, "Note on Social," pp. 299, 302.
13. Ibid., p. 303.
14. Ibid., p. 306.
15. Stewart thinks it is a "puzzle" that governments should use shadow prices in SCB rather than simply changing the prices in reality. The introduction of the aid agency as advocate of shadow wages is a more satisfactory solution than her own, Stewart, "Note on Social," p. 306.
16. Berthelot, "Développement du Tiers Monde," section 4.2.1.
17. Frances Stewart, "Social Cost-Benefit Analysis in Practice," *World Development* 6, no.2 (1978): 153–65.

18. Berthelot, "Développement du Tiers Monde," section 3.3.
19. Personal communication from Robert Williams, November 1981.
20. Stewart, "Social Cost-Benefit," p. 158.
21. Berthelot, "Développement du Tiers Monde," section 2.2.3.
22. Ibid., section 1.1.1.
23. van de Laar, *The Bank and the Poor*, p. 221.
24. Personal communication from Stephen Zorn. The project appraisal for the copper-nickel mine in Botswana ends with such a somber warning about risks that one suspects that the technical staff was registering a protest against a political decision to proceed with the loan despite the risks because the corporate sponsors and the Botswana government wished it.
25. Aart van de Laar, "The World Bank and the World's Poor," *World Development* 4, nos. 10–11 (1976): 845.
26. David Hart, *The Volta River Project* (Edinburgh: University Press, 1980).
27. Andres Federman, "Poverty's Strange Bedfellows," *South* (June 1981): 10.
28. A. A. Fatouros, "The World Bank," in J. B. Howard, ed., *The Impact of International Organizations on Legal and Institutional Change in the Developing Countries* (New York: International Legal Center, 1977), pp. 39–40.
29. Ibid., p. 18.
30. Ibid., pp. 46–50.
31. World Bank Report no. 2539, *Mexico: Impact Evaluation Report: Third Irrigation Project*, June 18, 1979, pp. 18–20.
32. Ibid., para. 2.39, p. 20.
33. van de Laar, *The Bank and the Poor*, p. 205 and note 33, p. 208.
34. World Bank press releases of February 23, 1978, and November 28, 1978.

4: *Infrastructure: The Traditional Sectors*

1. Edward S. Mason and Robert E. Asher, *The World Bank Since Bretton Woods* (Washington, D.C.: The Brookings Institution, 1973), p. 151.
2. World Bank, *Transportation:* sector working paper, 1972, p. 3. Also published in *World Bank Operations* (Baltimore: Johns Hopkins University Press, 1972). I have underlined the key words to emphasize the consonance of this statement with the overall development theory and strategy of the Bank. It may also be compared with the quotations from the sector policy papers on agriculture and rural development in Chapter 8.
3. Ibid., p. 4.
4. Ibid., pp. 34–36.
5. M. K. McCall, "Political Economy and Rural Transport: A Reappraisal of Transportation Impacts," *Antipode: A Radical Journal of Geography* 9, no. 1 (February 1977): 61.
6. M. K. McCall, "Political Economy and Rural Transport: An Appraisal of Western Misconceptions," *Antipode: A Radical Journal of Geography* 9, no. 3 (December 1977): 98.

7. J. S. Furnivall, *Colonial Policy and Practice*, (New York: New York University Press, 1956), p. 322.
8. Thanks to Carole LaGrasse and Peter Hayes for these points.
9. World Bank, *Transportation*, p. 5.
10. McCall, "Western Misconceptions," p. 99.
11. McCall, "Transportation Impacts," p. 59.
12. Ibid., p. 63.
13. Personal communication from Carole LaGrasse, March 31, 1981.
14. The Amazon tragedy has been documented in many accounts, including *The Geological Imperative* (1976) and other publications of the Anthropology Resource Center, Cambridge, Mass. The northwest Brazil road is critically examined in Jason W. Clay, "The POLONOROESTE Project," in Cultural Survival, *The Path of POLONOROESTE: Endangered Peoples of Western Brazil* (Washington, D.C.: Government Printing Office, 1981). Clay closely examines the Bank's project appraisal and finds serious omissions and deceptions.
15. McCall, "Transportation Impacts," pp. 64–65.
16. John A. King, Jr., *Economic Development Projects and Their Appraisal* (Baltimore: Johns Hopkins University Press, 1967), pp. 386–88.
17. Michael Stahl, *Ethiopia: Political Contradictions in Agricultural Development* (Uppsala: Political Science Association, 1974), pp. 85–86.
18. Ibid., p. 129.
19. Quoted in McCall, "Transportation Impacts," p. 65.
20. Keith Griffin, *Land Concentration and Rural Poverty* (New York: Macmillan, 1976), pp. 244–45.
21. Colin Clark and Margaret Haswell, *The Economics of Subsistence Agriculture* (New York: St. Martin's Press, 1964), p. 213.
22. World Bank News Release 81/34, "Chile gets $42 Million World Bank Loan for Highway Reconstruction," December 11, 1980.
23. King, *Economic Development*, p. 333.
24. Ibid., pp. 334, 335.
25. Ibid.
26. Ibid. Similar pressures for international competitive bidding were exerted in Spain, see p. 431.
27. World Bank, *Transportation*, p. 14 and Table 2, p. 12.
28. Mason and Asher, *The World Bank Since*, p. 664.
29. King, *Economic Development*, p. 404.
30. World Bank, *The World Bank Group in Africa 1963*, pp. 51, 60.
31. *Development Finance* 1, no. 3 (September–October 1978): 12.
32. Martin S. Brown and John Butler, *The Production, Marketing, and Consumption of Copper and Aluminum* (New York: Praeger, 1968), p. 12.
33. *Financial Times*, special supplement on aluminium, October 6, 1977, p. 37.
34. Victor L. Urquidi, *The Challenge of Development in Latin America* (New York: Praeger, 1964), pp. 56–57.
35. Judith Tendler, *Electric Power in Brazil* (Cambridge, Mass.: Harvard University Press, 1968), p. 227.

36. Ibid., pp. 196–97.
37. Miguel S. Wionczek, "Electric Power," in Raymond Vernon, ed., *Public Policy and Private Enterprise in Mexico* (Cambridge, Mass.: Harvard University Press, 1964), p. 89.
38. Ibid., p. 106.
39. Ibid., p. 104.
40. Ibid., p. 105.
41. Mason and Asher, *The World Bank Since*, p. 239.
42. E.g., Albert O. Hirschman, *Development Projects Observed* (Washington, D.C.: The Brookings Institution, 1967), pp. 153–59; and Judith Tendler, *Inside Foreign Aid* (Baltimore: Johns Hopkins University Press, 1975), p. 104.
43. A. Fatouros, "The World Bank," in J. B. Howard et al., *The Impact of International Organizations on Legal and Institutional Change in the Developing Countries* (New York: International Legal Center, 1977), p. 57.
44. Fernando Cepeda Ulloa, "Colombia and the World Bank," in Howard et al., *Impact of International*, p. 127.
45. Fatouros, "The World Bank," pp. 59–60.
46. As quoted in ibid., p. 61.
47. Mason and Asher, *The World Bank Since*, p. 239.
48. Ibid., p. 437.
49. Cepeda Ulloa, "Colombia," p. 126.
50. Wionczek, "Electric Power," p. 95.
51. Cepeda Ulloa, "Colombia," p. 128.
52. Fatouros, "The World Bank," p. 60.
53. Walden Bello, Peter Hayes, and Lyuba Zarsky, "500 Mile Island: The Philippine Nuclear Reactor Deal," *Pacific Research* 10, no. 1 (1979): 19.
54. H. S. Plunkett, "Social Effects of Rural Electrification: An Examination of Data from Pakistan," 1979, reprinted in *Rural Electrification in Bangladesh*, a documentation packet prepared by the Reading Service of Bangladesh.
55. "Dazzling Darkness," editorial, *Economic and Political Weekly* (Bombay), December 15, 1979; reprinted in *Rural Electification in Bangladesh*.
56. Douglas V. Smith, "Rural Electrification or Village Energization?" *Interciencia* 5, no. 2 (March–April 1980): p. 87.
57. Bello et al., "500 Mile Island," p. 16.
58. *Rural Electrification in Bangladesh*, p. 6, and letter of Sahela Begum, reprinted in ibid. from *Bangladesh Observer*, January 9, 1980.
59. Bello et al., "500 Mile Island," p. 19.

5: Industry

1. See Cheryl Payer, *The Debt Trap: The IMF and the Third World* (New York: Monthly Review Press, 1975), especially ch. 7; Cheryl Payer, "Pushed into the Debt Trap: South Korea's Export 'Miracle,'" *Journal of Contemporary Asia* 5, no. 2 (1975); Peter Evans, *Dependent Development: The Alliance of*

Multinational, State and Local Capital in Brazil (Princeton, N.J.: Princeton University Press, 1979), pp. 314–20.

2. Edward S. Mason and Robert E. Asher, *The World Bank Since Bretton Woods* (Washington, D.C.: The Brookings Institution, 1973), p. 375.

3. World Bank, *Development Finance Companies*, sector policy paper, 1976, pp. 12–13.

4. "Interview: William S. Gaud of the International Finance Corporation," *Finance and Development* 7, no. 1 (March 1970): 14.

5. John A. King, Jr., *Economic Development Projects and Their Appraisal: Cases and Principles from the Experience of the World Bank*, Economic Development Institute of the IBRD (Baltimore: Johns Hopkins University Press, 1967).

6. Shareholder Agreement, Loan 1660 BR, Valesul Aluminum, March 7, 1979, pp. 4–5.

7. World Bank, *The IFC in Africa*, August 1971, p. 13 (Nigeria) and p. 17 (Tunisia).

8. "Interview: William S. Gaud," p. 14.

9. Cyril H. Davis, "The Bank Group Meeting," *Finance and Development* 6, no. 4 (December 1969): 7.

10. V. V. Bhatt, *Aspects of Development Banking Policy*, seminar paper no. 12, Economic Development Institute of the World Bank, 1975, p. 14.

11. Ibid., pp. 21–23.

12. World Bank, *Industry*, sector working paper, April 1972; published in *World Bank Operations* (Baltimore: Johns Hopkins University Press), 1972.

13. World Bank, *Development Finance Companies*, p. 21.

14. Ibid., p. 22.

15. World Bank, *Annual Report, 1979*, appendix 1, pp. 182–83.

16. International Finance Corporation (IFC), *Annual Report, 1969*, p. 6.

17. Mason and Asher, *The World Bank Since*, p. 356.

18. Ibid., p. 347.

19. International Finance Corporation, *Annual Report, 1980*, p. 30.

20. Taken from IFC *Annual Reports*, 1957 through 1970. For agribusiness investments of IFC see Chapter 8.

21. International Finance Corporation, *Annual Report, 1979*, pp. 13, 22–23.

22. IFC, *IFC: What It Is, What It Does, How It Does It*, August 1971.

23. IFC, *Annual Report, 1979*.

24. Dorothea Mezger and Hildegarde Harlander, *Development Banking in Africa: Seven Case Studies* (Munich: Weltforum Verlag, June 1972).

25. World Bank, *Development Finance Companies*, pp. 10–13.

26. Examples are given in S. K. Basu, *Theory and Practice of Development Banking: A Study in the Asian Context* (London: Asia Publishing House, 1965), p. 133; James C. Baker, *The International Finance Corporation* (New York: Praeger 1968), pp. 48–49, 146; IFC, *The IFC in Africa*, August 1971, p. 16.

27. World Bank, *Development Finance Companies*, p. 13.

28. Ibid., p. 14.
29. Ibid.
30. Ibid.
31. Joseph A. Kane, *Development Banking: An Economic Appraisal* (Lexington, Mass.: Lexington Books, 1975), pp. 110–11.
32. Ibid., p. 110.
33. World Bank, *Development Finance Companies*, p. 12.
34. Asian Development Bank, *Industrial Development Banks in Asia*, 1974.
35. World Bank, *Development Finance Companies*, annex 3.
36. Kane, *Development Banking*, p. 28; Dorothea Mezger, "The Banque Ivorienne de Développement Industriel (BIDI), Ivory Coast," in Mezger and Harlander, *Banking in Africa*, p. 275.
37. Mezger, "The Banque Ivorienne," p. 278.
38. Agon Eze, "Nigeria: An Appraisal of Development Banking," *Intereconomics* (Hamburg), April 1971, p. 122.
39. Shirley Boskey, *Problems and Practices of Development Banks* (Baltimore: Johns Hopkins University Press, 1959), p. 20.
40. William Diamond, ed., *Development Finance Companies: Aspects of Policy and Operation* (Baltimore: Johns Hopkins University Press, 1968).
41. Manfred Nitsch, "Entwicklungsfinanzierung in Lateinamerika—dargestellt am Beispiel Columbiens," Institut für Ibero-amerika Kunde, Schriftenreihe, Band 16 (Stuttgart: Ernst Klett Verlag, 1970), p. 40.
42. Example taken from Douglas Gustafson, "Financial Policy Problems of Development Finance Companies," in Diamond, ed., *Development Finance*, p. 62.
43. Ibid., p. 66.
44. Ibid.
45. Ibid.
46. Mezger and Harlander, *Banking in Africa*, p. 281.
47. Kane, *Development Banking*, p. 114.
48. Mezger, "The Banque Ivorienne," p. 283–84.
49. P. M. Mathews, "Relations Between Governments and Development Finance Companies," in Diamond, ed., *Development Finance*, pp. 96–97.
50. Ibid.
51. Kane, *Development Banking*, p. 109.
52. Business International, *Doing Business in the Middle East* (Geneva: Business International, 1975).
53. World Bank, Report 259a—IRN, appraisal of IMDBI, January 15, 1974, para. 2.17.
54. Ibid., annex 1; *International Herald Tribune*, December 31, 1979.
55. Mezger, "The Banque Ivorienne," pp. 289, 295.
56. Eze, "Nigeria," p. 123.
57. L. C. Gupta, *The Changing Structure of Industrial Finance in India: The Impact of Institutional Finance* (Oxford: Clarendon Press, 1969), p. 112.
58. Mathews, "Relations," pp. 98–99.

59. Mezger, "The Banque Ivorienne," p. 304.
60. World Bank, *Development Finance Companies*, p. 44.
61. Mathews, "Relations," p. 107.
62. Kane, *Development Banking*, p. 48.
63. Mathews, "Relations," p. 94.
64. *Oil, Paint and Drug Reporter*, November 14, 1966.
65. Ibid., June 19, 1967.
66. Usha Menon, "World Bank and Transfer of Technology: Case of Indian Fertilizer Industry," *Economic and Political Weekly* (Bombay) (August 23, 1980): 1440–41; and Francine F. Frankel, "India's New Strategy of Agricultural Development," *Journal of Asian Studies* 28, no. 4 (August 1969): 704.
67. *Oil, Paint and Drug Reporter*, December 26, 1966.
68. Menon, *World Bank*, p. 1441.
69. Ibid., p. 1442.
70. World Bank, *Staff Appraisal Report: Brazil, COPESUL Petrochemical Project*, April 12, 1978, para. 3.03.
71. Ibid., para. 2.21.
72. Evans, *Dependent Development*, pp. 237–38.
73. World Bank, *Staff Appraisal Report*, para. 3.03.
74. Most of this data is from *Business Latin America*, June 28, 1978, p. 205.
75. World Bank, *Staff Appraisal Report*, para. 2.23.
76. Francisco Colman Sercovich, *State-owned Enterprises and Dynamic Comparative Advantage in the World Petrochemical Industry: The Case of Commodity Olefins in Brazil*, development discussion paper no. 96 (Cambridge, Mass.: Harvard Institute for International Development, May 1980), p. 23.
77. Ibid., p. 30.
78. Ibid., p. 5.
79. Ibid., p. 84.
80. Ibid., p. 7.
81. Ibid., p. 43.
82. Ibid., p. 53.
83. World Bank, *Staff Appraisal Report*, para. 7.08.
84. Kurt Lanz, *Around the World with Chemistry* (New York: McGraw-Hill, 1980), p. 366.
85. *Chemical Week*, December 1, 1979.
86. *Business Latin America*, June 28, 1978.
87. World Bank, *Staff Appraisal Report*, para. 7.04.
88. Ibid., para. 4.03.
89. Ibid., paras. 4.22 and 4.23.
90. Ibid., para. 10.02 (iv).
91. World Bank, *Annual Report, 1980*, p. 68.
92. Quoted in Ann Crittenden, "World Bank in Shift, Lending for Trade Debts," *New York Times*, May 26, 1980.

93. Eduardo Lachica, "World Bank Gives Philippines Special Loans and Calls for Tough Administrative Reform," *The Asian Wall Street Journal*, October 8, 1980.

94. World Bank, *Philippines: Industrial Development Strategy and Policies*, May 1980, p. 2, para. 7.

95. Bela Balassa, "Korea during the Fifth Five-Year Plan Period (1982–86): An advisory report prepared for the Government of the Republic of Korea," preliminary, July 31, 1980.

96. Walden Bello and John Kelly, "The World Bank Writes Off Marcos and Co.," *Nation*, January 31, 1981, p. 106.

97. World Bank, *Philippines*, para. 116, p. 32.

98. Ibid.

99. All these points are made in Folkar Fröbel, Jürgen Heinrichs, and Otto Kreye, *The New International Division of Labor* (Cambridge, England: Cambridge University Press, 1980), part III. A good short introduction to export processing zones is Tsuchiya Takeo, "Free Trade Zones in Southeast Asia," *Monthly Review* 29, no. 9 (February 1978): 29–39. For the World Bank's more positive view, see Barend A. de Vries and Carl D. Goderez, "Exports of manufactures provided a boost by EPZ," *Report: News of the World Bank Group*, September-October 1978, pp. 1ff.

100. World Bank, *Philippines*, para. 4 on p. 2, and para. 26, p. 9.

101. Quoted in Bello and Kelly, "The Bank Writes Off," p. 105.

102. Payer, *Debt Trap*. For a discussion of the structural adjustment loan in the Philippines, see Robin Broad, "New Directions at World Bank: Philippines as Guinea Pig," *Economic and Political Weekly* (Bombay), November 21, 1981, pp. 1919–22. She examines structural adjustment lending in her Ph.D. dissertation, Princeton University, forthcoming.

6: Mining

1. World Bank, *Annual Report, 1978*, pp. 20–21.

2. This description is taken from several sources, notably Dorothea Mezger, *Copper in the World Economy* (New York: Monthly Review Press, 1980); and Marian Radetzki and Stephen Zorn, *Financing Mining Projects in Developing Countries: A United Nations Study* (London: Mining Journal Books, 1979). Theodore Moran portrays the contrasting strategies of "old-style" Anaconda and "new-style" Kennecott in Chile in *Multinational Corporations and the Politics of Dependence* (Princeton, N.J.: Princeton University Press, 1974).

3. Pierre Bonté, "Multinational Corporations and National Development: MIFERMA and Mauritania," *Review of African Political Economy* 2 (1975): 95.

4. "Sangaredi—an African Plateau of Bauxite," *Engineering and Mining Journal* (August 1977): 83, 85.

5. Radetzki and Zorn, *Financing Mining Projects*, p. 110. Infrastructure costs were inflated by Botswana's insistence on building its own power plant rather than importing power from South Africa as the Bank recommended. The power plant was not financed by the Bank, but by another aid donor.

6. The very complicated successive corporate restructurings are detailed in Greg Lanning with Marti Mueller, *Africa Undermined* (London: Penguin, 1979), pp. 336–45.

7. James H. Cobbe, *Governments and Mining Companies in Developing Countries* (Boulder, Colo.: Westview Press, 1979), pp. 195, 200–1.

8. *Engineering and Mining Journal* (February 1980): 55.

9. Richard M. Westebbe, *The Economy of Mauritania* (New York: Praeger, 1971), p. 51.

10. Bonté, "Multinational Corporations," p. 94.

11. It is not clear how this statement by Westebbe *(Economy of Mauritania)* can be reconciled with the assertion in a World Bank publication (John A. King, Jr., *Economic Development Projects and their Appraisal* [Baltimore: Johns Hopkins University Press, 1967], p. 299) that "MIFERMA experienced favorable marketing conditions and brought its annual capacity to about 6 million tons in 1966 instead of 1968 as originally planned," except that Westebbe, writing unofficially, may be franker.

12. Westebbe, *Economy of Mauritania*, p. 51.

13. Bonté, "Multinational Corporations," table 8, p. 101.

14. Samir Amin, *Neo-Colonialism in West Africa* (New York: Monthly Review Press, 1973), p. 80.

15. Bank news release No. 80/1, July 16, 1979.

16. For Mauritania, Bonté, "Multinational Corporations," p. 105; for Botswana, Cobbe, *Governments and Mining Companies*, p. 201.

17. Raymond Mikesell, *New Patterns of World Mineral Development* (London: British-North America Committee, 1979), p. 71.

18. Christian Kirchner et al., *Mining Ventures in Developing Countries* (Deventer, Holland: Kluwer, 1979), pp. 114–16.

19. John Deverell and the Latin American Working Group (LAWG), *Falconbridge: Portrait of a Canadian Mining Multinational* (Toronto: James Lorimer & Co., 1975), p. 56.

20. Ibid., p. 129.

21. Ibid.

22. Ibid., p. 63.

23. Ibid.

24. Ibid., p. 130.

25. Fred Goff, "Falconbridge—Made in USA," *NACLA's Latin America and Empire Report* 8, no. 4 (April 1974): 13.

26. Ibid. and Deverell and LAWG, *Falconbridge: Portrait*, p. 141.

27. Deverell and LAWG, *Falconbridge: Portrait*, p. 135.

28. The story of Hanna Mining and the coup is given in an account (sympathetic to Hanna) by Raymond F. Mikesell, "Iron Ore in Brazil: the Experience of

Hanna Mining Company," in Raymond Mikesell, ed., *Foreign Investment in the Petroleum and Mineral Industries* (Baltimore: Johns Hopkins University Press, 1971), pp. 345–64; and in another (critical of Hanna) by Edie Black and Fred Goff, "The Hanna Industrial Complex," *NACLA Newsletter* 2, no. 3 (1968). A short account is given in Shelton H. Davis and Robert O. Matthews, *The Geological Imperative* (Cambridge, Mass.: Anthropology Resource Center, 1976), pp. 28–31.

29. *Fortune,* April 1965, quoted in Davis and Mathews, *Geological Imperative,* p. 29.

30. *New York Times,* November 4, 1964, quoted in Black and Goff, "Hanna Industrial Complex."

31. "African Plateau of Bauxite," p. 85. My account is based mainly on this article.

32. Ibid.

33. Michel Beaud, Pierre Danjon, and Jean David, *Une Multinationale Fran-çaise: Pechiné Ugine Kuhlmann* (Paris: Seuil, 1975), p. 151.

34. The best account in English is Fred Goff, "Exmibal: Take Another Nickel Out," in Susanne Jonas and David Tobis, eds., *Guatemala* (Berkeley: NACLA 1974), from which my account is condensed.

35. Ibid., p. 160.

36. Rex Bosson and Benison Varon, *The Mining Industry and the Developing Countries* (New York: Oxford University Press for the World Bank, 1977).

37. Ibid., pp. 161–63.

38. Ibid., pp. 163–65.

39. Ibid., pp. 165–66.

40. Ibid., pp. 166–73.

41. Ibid., p. 173.

42. Craig Emerson, "Taxing Natural Resource Projects," *Natural Resources Forum* 4, no. 2 (April 1980): 125. This article also includes two tables which illustrate the advantage to host governments and the disadvantage to corporations of alternative tax regimes, including royalties and production sharing: Table 10, p. 140, and Table 11, p. 141. Emerson and other advocates of the so-called resource rent tax argue that if a country is to efficiently tax the "resource rent" (excess profits) of mining projects, instant depreciation must be offered to the foreign investors as a trade-off for the forfeiture of bonanza profit in later years. See Ross Garnaut and Anthony Clunies-Ross, "Uncertainty, Risk Aversion and the Taxing of Natural Resource Projects," *Economic Journal* (June 1975): 272–87.

43. IDA Development Credit Agreement, #455-BO, section 3.04.

44. World Bank Report No. 2309-BO, staff appraisal report, "Bolivia: National Mineral Exploration Fund Project," June 5, 1979.

45. Malcolm Gillis et al., *Taxation and Mining: Nonfuel Minerals in Bolivia and Other Countries* (Cambridge, Mass.: Ballinger, 1978).

46. Meyer Bucovetsky, Malcolm Gillis, and Louis T. Wells, "Comparative Mining Taxes," in ibid., p. 123.

47. World Bank, "Bolivia: National Mineral Exploration." Sam Pintz told me that the comparison with Asian tin producers is misleading as tin is not highly taxed by minerals standards.
48. IBRD Report 2195-BO, "Economic Memorandum on Bolivia," November 3, 1978, para. 47.
49. Goff, "Exmibal," p. 163.
50. IBRD Report, "Economic Memorandum on Bolivia." Emphasis mine.
51. World Bank, "Bolivia: National Mineral Exploration," para. 2.09.
52. Ibid., para. 3.04.
53. Ibid.
54. IBRD Report, "Economic Memorandum on Bolivia," para. 46.
55. Ibid., para. 44.
56. *World Business Weekly,* March 23, 1981, p. 43, and May 18, 1981, p. 42.
57. Mezger, *Copper in the World,* pp. 150–51 and 224–26.
58. Ibid., pp. 146–47.
59. Radetzki and Zorn, *Financing Mining Projects,* p. 114.
60. *International Herald Tribune,* June 26, 1980; *World Business Weekly,* August 24, 1981, p. 42.
61. On ICSID and its effect on national judiciaries, see Stanley D. Mezger, "Private Foreign Investment and International Organizations," in Richard N. Gardner and Max Millikan, eds., *The Global Partnership: International Agencies and Economic Development* (New York: Praeger, 1968), p. 301.

7: Oil and Gas

1. World Bank, *Annual Report, 1978,* p. 21.
2. "Towards Third World Oil Independence: An Interview with Michael Tanzer," *Multinational Monitor* (May 1980): 13.
3. Michael Tanzer, *The Energy Crisis* (New York: Monthly Review Press, 1974), pp. 108–9.
4. World Bank, "Transportation," sector working paper, *World Bank Operations* (1972), p. 154.
5. World Bank, *Energy in the Developing Countries,* August 1980, para. 3.25.
6. Ibid., para. 3.40.
7. Something of the sort has been charged by Stanton R. Smith (for electric power generation) in his article "Outline Program of Hydro-electric Development in West Africa to 1980," in Neville Rubin and William M. Warren, eds., *Dams In Africa: An Inter-Disciplinary Study of Man-made Lakes in Africa* (London: Frank Cass, 1968), pp. 174–75. As Smith is employed by Kaiser Engineering, a firm deeply involved in hydroelectric development, his testimony is biased but is not necessarily for that reason wrong. I remain an agnostic on this issue.
7. Peter R. Odell, "Oil," in Cheryl Payer, ed., *Commodity Trade of the Third World* (New York: Halsted Press, 1975), pp. 16–17.

9. Christian H. Walser, "The Role of the World Bank in Supporting Mineral Development," paper prepared for the workshop on Mining Legislation and Mineral Resources Agreements, Gabarone, Botswana, October 9–14, 1978.

10. Ibid., para. 7, p. 3.

11. Ibid., para. 31, p. 12.

12. Text of communiqué reprinted in *Keesing's Contemporary Archives,* July 29, 1977.

13. World Bank, *Annual Report, 1978,* p. 22.

14. Ibid.

15. Walser, "World Bank in Mineral Development," para. 33, p. 12.

16. Ibid., para. 35, p. 13.

17. "The World Bank's Flier in Oil," *Business Week,* July 10, 1978, p. 64.

18. *International Herald Tribune,* December 5, 1979. Dr. Hansen's views on the World Bank's role are set forth in his article, "OPEC's Role in a Global Energy and Development Conference," *Journal of Energy and Development* 5, no. 2 (Spring 1980): 182–93.

19. Walser, "World Bank in Mineral Development," para. 10, p. 4.

20. Efrain Friedmann and Raymond Goodman, "Prospects for Oil and Gas Production in the Developing World," *Finance and Development* (June 1979): 8–9.

21. "Third World Oil Independence," p. 13.

22. *Business Week,* July 10, 1978.

23. Described in Walser, "World Bank in Mineral Development," para. 40, p. 14.

24. *New York Times,* August 22, 1979.

25. United States Government Accounting Office, "Issues related to Foreign Oil Supply Diversification," ID-79-36, B-178205, May 1979, p. 7.

26. Ibid., pp. 7–8. Text of the communiqué can be found in *Keesing's Contemporary Archives,* November 10, 1978.

27. U.S. GAO, "Foreign Oil Supply," p. 11.

28. World Bank press release, January 17, 1979, pp. 3–4.

29. *Oil and Gas Journal,* October 2, 1978, p. 64.

30. U.S. GAO, "Foreign Oil Supply," p. 11.

31. Quoted in ibid., pp. 11–12.

32. Ibid., pp. 13–14.

33. Ibid., p. 12.

34. The exchange of letters was published in *Nation,* July 28–August 4, 1979, p. 69.

35. U.S. GAO, "Foreign Oil Supply," p. 13.

36. *International Herald Tribune,* December 6, 1979.

37. *New York Times,* August 22, 1979. They would be even less happy to see the state oil companies acquire experience.

38. *International Herald Tribune,* December 6, 1979; also *Oil and Gas Journal* March 16, 1981, p. 49.

39. Walser, "World Bank in Mineral Development," para. 39, p. 14.

40. Friedmann and Goodman, "Oil and Gas Production," p. 9.

41. Ibid., pp. 9–10.
42. IDA News Release No. 80/97, June 12, 1980, Somalia.
43. World Bank News Release No. 80/77, April 17, 1980, Morocco.
44. World Bank News Release No. 80/111, June 2, 1980, Honduras.
45. World Bank News Release No. 80/128, June 26, 1980, Argentina.
46. IDA News Release No. 80/107, June 26, 1980, People's Democratic Republic of Yemen.
47. World Bank News Release No. 81/24, November 20, 1980, Turkey.
48. World Bank News Release No. 80/26, December 13, 1979, Thailand.
49. *New York Times*, August 22, 1979.
50. *New York Times*, October 2, 1980; U.S. Department of State, Bureau of Intelligence and Research, "Disputes Involving U.S. Private Direct Investment: March 1, 1977–February 29, 1980, Report No. 1441, August 18, 1980, p. 34.
51. World Bank News Release No. 81/24; *New York Times*, April 6, 1981.
52. "Third World Oil Independence," p. 14; Mohan Ram, "India No Longer Goes It Alone," *Far Eastern Economic Review* (December 26, 1980): 38–39; *Petroleum Economist* (November 1980): 495–96; *World Business Weekly* March 2, 1981, p. 37.
53. World Bank, Report 3101–IN, Second Bombay High Offshore Development Project, staff appraisal report, Nov. 5, 1980, p. 15.
54. Quoted in Tanzer, "Third World Oil Independence, p. 14.
55. "U.S. Derails Energy Plan for Third World," *Science* 212 (April 3, 1981): 21–23.
56. Department of the Treasury, Office of the Assistant Secretary for International Affairs, *An Examination of the World Bank Energy Lending Program* (Washington, D.C.: Department of the Treasury, 1981).
57. Ibid., p. 25.
58. Ibid., p. 27.
59. Ibid., pp. 33–34.
60. Ibid., p. 39.
61. Ibid., p. 22.
62. Ibid., p. 41.
63. Matthew Rothschild, "U.S. Treasury Blasts World Bank Plan to Finance Third World Energy Development," *Multinational Monitor*, September 1981, pp. 9ff.
64. *World Business Weekly*, September 7, 1981, p. 18.

8: Agriculture and Rural Development

1. Craig L. Dozier, "Mexico's Transformed Northwest: The Yaqui, Mayo, and Fuerte Examples," *The Geographical Review* 53 (October 1963): 548–71.
2. David E. Lilienthal, *The Harvest Years 1959–1963*, vol. V, *The Journals of David E. Lilienthal* (New York: Harper & Row, 1971), p. 538.

3. Frances Moore Lappé and Joseph Collins, *Food First: Beyond the Myth of Scarcity* (Boston: Houghton Miflin, 1977), pp. 259–60; Maureen McIntosh, "Fruits and Vegetables as an International Commodity: The Relocation of Horticultural Production and its Implications for the Producers," *Food Policy* 2, no. 4 (November 1977): 286–87; 290–91.

4. John W. Lowe, "The IFC and the Agribusiness Sector," *Finance and Development* (March 1977): 28.

5. Ernest Feder, "Agricultural Resources in Underdeveloped Countries: Competition Between Man and Animal," *Economic and Political Weekly* 14, nos. 30, 31 (August 1979): 1347.

6. Beverly Keene, "Incursiones del Banco Mundial en Centroamérica," in Hugo Assman, ed., *El Banco Mundial: un caso del "progresismo conservador"* (San José, Costa Rica: Departamento Ecumenico de Investigaciones, 1980), p. 201.

7. Feder, "Agricultural Resources," p. 1345.

8. Keene, "Banco Mundial en Centroamérica," p. 202.

9. World Bank, *Agricultural Credit*, sector policy paper, 1975, p. 25.

10. Donald J. Pryor, "Livestock: The Recognition of a Stepchild," *Finance and Development* (September 1970): 23.

11. Feder, "Agricultural Resources," p. 1363 and table 5.

12. Keene, "Banco Mundial en Centroamérica," p. 210–11.

13. Edward S. Mason and Robert E. Asher, *The World Bank Since Bretton Woods* (Washington: The Brookings Institution, 1973), p. 682.

14. Lappé and Collins, *Food First*, chap. 17.

15. Mason and Asher, *The World Bank Since*, p. 672.

16. Ibid., p. 653.

17. Ibid., p. 712.

18. World Bank, *Agricultural Credit*, p. 22. Also see Ronald J. Herring and Charles R. Kennedy, Jr., "The Political Economy of Farm Mechanization Policy: Tractors in Pakistan," in Raymond F. Hopkins, Donald J. Puchala, and Ross B. Talbot, eds., *Food, Politics and Agricultural Development* (Boulder, Colo.: Westview Press, 1979), pp. 193–226.

19. "World Bank-supported Project Opposed by Natives in the Area," *Canada Asia Currents* (Winter 1979): 14. Also see Bernard Wideman, "Philippine Mt. People Declare War on Chico Dam Project," *AMPO* 10, no. 3 (1978): 24–29.

20. World Bank country report, *Papua New Guinea: Economic Situation and Development Prospects*, July 14, 1976, p. 18.

21. Cynthia Hewitt de Alcantara, *Modernizing Mexican Agriculture: Socioeconomic Implications of Technological Change 1940–70* (Geneva: United Nations Research Institute for Social Development, 1976), pp. 265–56, quoting E. H. Spicer's work.

22. Ibid., p. 268.

23. Ibid., pp. 271–72.

24. Ibid., pp. 319–20.

25. World Bank, *Rural Development*, sector policy paper, 1975, p. 3.

26. Ibid., p. 16.

27. World Bank, *Agricultural Credit*, p. 5.

28. Ibid., p. 20.

29. Montague Yudelman, "Agriculture in Integrated Rural Development: the Experience of the World Bank," *Food Policy* (November 1976): 369.

30. Cf. Gavin Williams, "The World Bank and the Peasant Problem," in J. Heyer, P. Roberts, and G. Williams, eds., *Rural Development in Tropical Africa* (London: Macmillan, 1981), p. 29.

31. Irrigation is an exception to this generalization, if its benefits are accessible at reasonable cost to the small farmer. In practice this is seldom the case.

32. Yudelman, "Agriculture in Rural Development," p. 374.

33. On the day this paragraph was first drafted, a *New York Times* article reported a "rice glut" in Asia, with governments forced to sell surplus rice at prices much lower than they paid farmers to encourage production. James P. Sterba, "A Bounty of Rice in Asia: Forecast Disproved by Crop Surplus," *New York Times*, April 4, 1979.

34. John Higgs, "Land Settlement in Africa and the Near East: Some Recent Experiences," *Land Reform, Land Settlement and Cooperatives*, no. 2 (1978): 13.

35. For example see the Loan Agreement (Rural Development Project) between Jamaica and the IBRD (Loan 1484 JM), June 29, 1977. World Bank loan agreements and IDA credit agreements and supplementary agreements are published and available in most UN depository libraries.

36. The "religious" secessionist war of the Moro Liberation Front in the southern Philippines is actually a land war, a legacy of the settler schemes of President Magsaysay, who gave away Muslim-occupied land in Mindanao to land-hungry peasants who had supported the Hukbalahap movement in Central Luzon.

37. For example, the paramilitary Young Pioneers group in Malawi has benefited from settlement projects in that country, but many areas have been abandoned because they did not stick with the farming. *Area Handbook for Malawi* (Washington, D.C.: Government Printing Office, 1975), p. 98.

38. IBRD (Loan 1484), June 29, 1977.

39. Lappé and Collins, *Food First*, ch. 34.

40. "With all highly labour-intensive crops, at the present stage of economic growth in the developing countries, smallholdings have the advantage of lower labor costs." H. Blume, *Organisational Aspects of Agro-Industrial Development Agencies* (Munich: Weltforum Verlag, 1971), p. 30.

41. Ernest Feder calls these "agricultural cottage industries" in "Monopoly Capital and Agricultural Employment in the Third World," unpublished ms., July 1980, p. 38.

42. World Bank, *Land Reform*, sector policy paper, 1975, p. 44.

43. World Bank, *Agricultural Credit*, p. 37.

44. Nicola Swainson, *The Development of Corporate Capitalism in Kenya, 1918–1977* (Berkeley: University of California Press, 1980), pp. 250–64.

45. World Bank, project appraisal, Oil Palm Development Project, Zaire, 1978.
46. Stephen Baier, "Economic History and Development: Drought and the Sahelian Economics of Niger," *African Economic History* 1 (Spring 1976): 3–5.
47. Ibid., pp. 6–7.
48. Ibid., pp. 8–9; see also Richard W. Franke and Barbara H. Chasin, *Seeds of Famine* (Montclair, N.J.: Allanheld Osman, 1980), ch. 4.
49. Claude Meillassoux, "Development or Exploitation: Is the Sahel Famine Good Business?" *Review of African Political Economy*, no. 1 (August–November 1974): 32.
50. See for example Higgs, "Land Settlement in Africa," p. 9.
51. Meillassoux, "Development or Exploitation"; Richard Stryker, "The World Bank and Agricultural Development," *World Development* 7, no. 3 (1979).
52. Personal communication, August 28, 1981.
53. This process is illustrated in a case study from Kenya in Paul Spencer, *Nomads in Alliance* (New York: Oxford University Press, 1973), pp. 182–83, 190.
54. Uma Lele, *The Design of Rural Development* (Baltimore: Johns Hopkins University Press, 1975), p. 59.
55. "Rapport de synthèse sur la situation alimentaire et nutritionelle dans le Sahel," C.I.L.S.S./COM 1/73/Inf. 7; August 1974. Quoted in Comité Information Sahel, *Qui se nourrit de la famine en Afrique?* (Paris: Maspéro, 1974), p. 162.
56. World Bank, *Agriculture Sector Survey, Nigeria*, vol. I, January 26, 1973, para. 3.60, p. 24.
57. "Many of the past initiatives of the government have been received with considerable suspicion by the Masai." Lele, *Design of Rural Development*; Spencer, *Nomads in Alliance*, pp. 186–87; Ian Livingstone, "Economic Irrationality Among Pastoral Peoples: Myth or Reality," *Development and Change* 8 (1977): 209–30.
58. In addition to the livestock lending in Latin America mentioned earlier in the chapter, the bank has also promoted commercial ranching in Ethiopia, Kenya, and other African countries. Most of these funds go to large privately owned ranches, not to rural development projects for nomadic herders.
59. See Livingstone, "Economic Irrationality."
60. Ernest Feder makes the point that large farmers and ranchers receive World Bank loans with a much lighter burden of conditions and supervision, i.e., they are trusted, as small farmers are not, to develop commercial agriculture. "El crédito agricola nacional e internacional y el campsino mexicano," *Uno más uno*, May 11, 1978.
61. Hannes Lorenzen, unpublished thesis on the Papaloapan Basin project (Mexico), University of Bielefeld, 1979.
62. In Malawi's Lilongwe Development Project, for example, the ratio of farmers to extension agents inside the project area was 250:1 while outside the ratio was 2000:1. Jaap Mieuwenhuize, *Investeringen van de Wereldbank in de landbouw, en haar "strijd" tegen de armoede in Malawi* (Wageningen: De Uitbuyt, 1975), p. 41.

63. On Tanzania, see James Mittelman, *Underdevelopment and the Transition to Socialism: Mozambique and Tanzania* (New York: Academic Press, 1981), pp. 194–98.

64. Yudelman, "Agriculture in Rural Development," p. 377.

65. World Bank, *Rural Development*, p. 40.

66. Ibid., p. 21.

67. Ibid., p. 40.

68. Betsy Hartmann and James Boyce, "Bangladesh: Aid to the Needy?" *International Policy Report* (Center for International Policy) 4, no. 1 (May 1978): 6.

69. Ibid.

70. Michael Stahl, *Ethiopia: Political Contradictions in Agricultural Development* (Uppsala: Political Science Association, 1974), p. 123.

71. *The Aid Debate: Assessing the Impact of U.S. Foreign Assistance and the World Bank* (San Francisco: Institute for Food and Development Policy, 1979), p. 23.

72. This has happened to agriculture in the richer countries as well. For the United States in the 1940s and 1950s, see Grant McConnell, *The Decline of Agrarian Democracy* (New York: Atheneum, 1969).

73. Ernest Feder has predicted and described this process in several articles, including "McNamara's Little Green Revolution: The World Bank Scheme for the Liquidation of the Third World Peasantry," *Comercio Exterior* 22, no. 8 (August 1976): 296–306; and "Capitalism's Last-ditch Effort to Save Underdeveloped Agricultures: International Agribusiness, the World Bank, and the Rural Poor," *Journal of Contemporary Asia* 7, no. 1 (1977): 56–78.

74. Elizabeth Colson, "The Impact of the Colonial Period on the Definition of Land Rights," in Victor Turner, ed., *Colonialism in Africa*, vol. 3 (Cambridge: Cambridge University Press, 1970), p. 199. Also see Melville J. Herskovits, "Economic Change and Cultural Dynamics," in Ralph Braibanti and Joseph J. Spengler, eds., *Traditional Values and Socio-Economic Development* (Durham, N.C.: Duke University Press, 1961), p. 132.

75. The country was described in 1975 as "having a greater proportion of those in regular paid employment working outside the nation than within." J. C. Mills, *Price Responses of Malawian Smallholder Farmers* (Zomba: University of Malawi, Department of Economics, 1975), p. 2.

76. World Bank, *Land Reform*, p. 42.

77. IBRD Loans 256 (Kenya), May 1960, and 253 (Rhodesia), March 1960.

78. *Area Handbook for Malawi*, p. 243.

79. Barbara Rogers, "Women and Land Rights," *ISIS International Bulletin* 11 (Spring 1979): 5–8.

80. For examples, I. Gerschenberg, "Customary Land Tenure as a Constraint on Development: A Re-evaluation," *East African Journal of Rural Development* 4, no. 1 (1971): 51–62; and Beverly Brock, "Customary Land Tenure, 'Individualization,' and Agricultural Development in Uganda," *East Africa Journal of Rural Development* 2, no. 2 (1969): 1–27.

81. Lord Hailey, *African Survey*, rev. ed. (New York: Oxford University Press, 1957), p. 807.

82. R. N. Kettlewell, "Agricultural Change in Nyasaland: 1945–1960," *Food Research Institute Studies* 5, no. 3 (1965): 250.

83. Rowton Simpson, "The New Land Law in Malawi," *Journal of Administration Overseas* 6, no. 4 (1967): 227. For a good case study of the World Bank's rural development program in Malawi see Mieuwenhuize, *Investeringen van de Wereldbank*. Also see Brian Phipps, "Evaluating Development Schemes: Problems and Implications, A Malawi Case Study," *Development and Change* 7 (1976): 469–84.

84. Montague Yudelman, *Africans on the Land* (Cambridge, Mass.: Harvard University Center for International Affairs, 1964), pp. 112–13.

85. Ibid., pp. 113–14. In May 1979 I asked Mr. Yudelman whether he still held these views. He responded that it was somewhat unfair to bring up a book published so long ago, and that his opinions had changed a great deal: he now believed that the emphasis should be on providing incentives for farmers to produce. He did not directly repudiate the message of the book, however.

86. Yash Tandon, "Food Production in East Africa: The Tanzanian Case," *Outlook* 8 (April–May 1978): 17.

87. Adrian Adams, "The Senegal River Valley: What Kind of Change?" *Review of African Political Economy* 10 (September–December 1977): 41.

88. Tina Wallace, "Agricultural Projects and Land in Northern Nigeria," *Review of African Political Economy* 17 (January–April 1980): 69.

89. "The Plight of Federal Land Development Authority Settlers in Malaysia," *Berita Socialis* 2, no. 4, reprinted in *Journal of Contemporary Asia* 3, no. 3 (1973): 367–68.

90. Gavin Williams, "World Bank and Peasant Problem," p. 17.

91. Rodolphe de Koninck, "The Integration of the Peasantry: Examples from Malaysia and Indonesia," *Pacific Affairs* 52, no. 2 (1979): 289.

92. *The Aid Debate*, p. 28.

9: Water Resources

1. Douglas V. Smith, "Management of Water Resources," mimeo, April 1980, p. 1. I am indebted to this article for many of the ideas developed in this chapter.

2. Herbert Addison, *Land, Water and Food*, 2nd. ed. (London: Chapman and Hill, 1961), p. 105.

3. Ibid., p. 234.

4. Richard B. Reidlinger, "Institutional Rationing of Canal Water in Northern India: Conflict Between Traditional Patterns and Modern Needs," *Economic Development and Cultural Change* 23, no. 1 (October 1974): 87.

5. John Waterbury, *Hydropolitics of the Nile Valley* (Syracuse: University of Syracuse Press, 1979), p. 148.

6. Reidlinger, "Rationing of Canal Water," p. 88.

7. Herbert Bernstein, "An Exploration of the World Bank's Treatment of Water Resources Projects," mimeo, 1977, p. 7.

8. Ibid., table 1, p. 6.

9. Robert Wade, "How Not to Redistribute with Growth: The Case of India's Command Area Development Program," *Pacific Viewpoint* 17 (1976): 95.

10. Thayer Scudder, "Resettlement," in N. F. Stanley and M. P. Alpers, eds., *Man-made Lakes and Human Health*, (New York: Academic Press, 1975).

11. Most of the information about Kariba in the following paragraphs comes from an unpublished seminar paper by Patrick J. McNally, "The River God Is Angry: The Impact of the Kariba Dam Project," May 1980.

12. Antony Martin, quoted in ibid., p. 2.

13. *Wall Street Journal,* November 13, 1956, quoted in ibid., p. 4.

14. Montague Yudelman, *Africans on the Land* (Cambridge, Mass.: Harvard University Center for International Affairs, 1964), p. 46; IBRD Loan Agreement 145 RN, Rhodesia.

15. McNally, "The River God Is Angry," p. 5.

16. See for example M. H. Webster, "Medical Aspects of the Kariba Hydroelectric Scheme," in Stanley and Alpers, *Man-made Lakes and Human Health*.

17. Scudder, "Resettlement,"p. 455.

18. Scudder, quoted in McNally, "The River God Is Angry," p. 8.

19. Scudder, "Resettlement," p. 456.

20. Ibid., p. 462.

21. Webster, "Medical Aspects of Kariba," p. 74.

22. Elizabeth Colson, "Land Rights and Land Use Among the Valley Tonga of the Rhodesian Federation," in Daniel Biebuyck, ed., *African Agrarian Systems* (London: Oxford University Press, 1963), p. 149.

23. Ibid., p. 151.

24. David Hart, *The Volta River Project: A Case Study in Politics and Technology* (Edinburgh: University Press, 1980).

25. Ibid., p. 63.

26. Ibid., pp. 49–50.

27. "Imperialism and the Volta Dam," *West Africa,* March 24, 1980, p. 523.

28. John A. King, Jr., *Economic Development Projects and Their Appraisal* (Baltimore: Johns Hopkins University Press, 1967), p. 135.

29. Nicholas Burnett, "Kaiser Shortcircuits Ghanaian Development," *Multinational Monitor* 1, no. 1 (February 1980): 9.

30. Hart, *Volta River Project,* p. 64.

31. Ibid., p. 66; Burnett, "Kaiser Shortcircuits," p. 8.

32. Quoted in Burnett, "Kaiser Shortcircuits," p. 8.

33. "Imperialism and the Volta Dam—II," *West Africa,* March 31, 1980, p. 572.

34. Burnett, "Kaiser Shortcircuits," p. 8.

35. King, *Economic Development Projects,* p. 136.

36. Edward S. Mason and Robert E. Asher, *The World Bank Since Bretton Woods* (Washington, D.C.: The Brookings Institution, 1973), pp. 132, 668.

37. Hart, *Volta River Project,* p. 30.
38. Quoted in Hart, *Volta River Project,* p. 78.
39. Hart, *Volta River Project,* p. 79.
40. Ibid., pp. 80–82.
41. Ibid., pp. 83, 86.
42. Ibid., pp. 84–85.
43. Ibid., p. 85.
44. Ibid., p. 88.
45. Ibid., p. 97.
46. See Chapter 8.
47. [Lindy Washburn], "The Right and the Power? Militarization and the National Power Corporation in Lanao del Sur," *MSPC Communications,* no. 32, Mindanao Sulu Pastoral Conference, October 1979, p. 32.
48. Lindy Washburn, "Our Lake for Others? The Maranao and the Agus River Hydroelectric Project," *Research Bulletin,* Dansalan Research Center, Marawi City (Philippines), November–December 1977, p. 1.
49. Ibid., p. 3.
50. IBRD Loan Agreements 325-0 and 491-0, Philippines.
51. Washburn, "Maranao and Agus River Project," p. 11.
52. Lindy Washburn, "On the Rise and Fall of Lake Lanao," *Research Bulletin,* Dansalan Research Center, Marawi City (Philippines) July–August 1978.
53. Washburn, "Maranao and Agus River Project," pp. 7–8.
54. King, *Economic Development Projects,* p. 219.
55. Quoted in Helmut Richards, "Land Reform and Agribusiness in Iran," *MERIP Report* no. 43 (December 1975): 12.
56. David E. Lilienthal, *The Road to Change 1955–59,* vol. IV, *The Journals of David E. Lilienthal* (New York: Harper & Row, 1969), p. 214.
57. Ibid., p. 293.
58. King, *Economic Development Projects,* p. 219.
59. Lilienthal, *Road to Change,* p. 277.
60. Oddvar Arevik, *The Agricultural Development of Iran* (New York: Praeger, 1976).
61. Richards, "Land Reform and Agribusiness," p. 14.
62. Food and Agriculture Organization, *Iran: Country Development Brief,* April 1974, p. 45.
63. International Finance Corporation Press Release 73/2, February 9, 1973.
64. Lilienthal, *Road to Change,* p. 214.
65. Quoted in Richards, "Land Reform and Agribusiness, p. 14.
66. Ibid.
67. Richards, "Land Reform and Agribusiness," p. 17.
68. Ibid.
69. Frances Moore Lappé and Joseph Collins, *Food First,* rev. ed. (New York: Random House, 1978), p. 387.
70. Christophe Batsch, "Les Mésaventures d'une entreprise de maraîchage au Senegal," and Claud Reboul, "Modernisme et réalités locales," both in *Le Monde Diplomatique,* September 1980, p. 10.

71. Reboul, "Modernisme et réalités locales."
72. Quoted in Batsch, "Entreprise de maraîchage au Senegal."
73. Ibid.
74. Claude Meillassoux, "700,000 Paysans de la Vallée du Senegal," *Le Monde Diplomatique*, May 1980.
75. A poignant account of how a locally initiated irrigation project in the Senegal Valley was appropriated by the national government and by AID is found in Adrian Adams, "An Open Letter to a Young Researcher," *African Affairs* 78 (October 1979): 451–79.
76. Quoted in *International Herald Tribune*, August 21, 1979.
77. Reboul, "Modernisme et réalités locales." Bernstein's review of World Bank water control projects also accused the Bank's appraisal work of slighting "the ecological and social impact of upstream storage moderating the annual floods, particularly in the interval before irrigation can replace traditional agriculture." "World Bank's Water Resources Projects," p. 56.
78. Personal communication from Ben Crow, July 18, 1980. As Mason and Asher comment, "A number of big dams have not resulted in the increase in irrigated farmland and agricultural output that had been forecast . . . it is one thing to collect water behind a dam and another thing to move it from behind the dam or from the main distributary channels to individual farm plots." *World Bank Since*, p. 711.
79. Cynthia Hewitt de Alcantara, *Modernizing Mexican Agriculture* (Geneva: United Nations Research Institute for Social Development, 1976): p. 164.
80. World Bank Project Appraisal, *Rahad Irrigation Project, Sudan*, February 16, 1973, p. 5, para. 3.01, and Annex 2.
81. Ibid., para. 4.01, p. 7.
82. Ibid., p. 19.
83. Martin E. Adams, review article in *Economic Development and Cultural Change* 28 (April 1980): 636.
84. World Bank, *Rahad Irrigation Project*, para. 6.10, p. 23.
85. Paul Duane, "A Policy Framework for Irrigation Water Charges," World Bank staff working paper no. 218, July 1975.
86. IBRD Loan Agreement 434-0, Muda River Irrigation Project, Malaysia, 1965.
87. Personal communication from Ben Crow, July 18, 1980.
88. Daniel W. Bromley, Donald C. Taylor, and Donald E. Parker, "Water Reform and Economic Development: Institutional Aspects of Water Management in the Developing Countries," *Economic Development and Cultural Change* 28, no. 2 (January 1980): 368.
89. Ibid., p. 372.
90. Anne Booth, "Irrigation in Indonesia: Part I," *Bulletin of Indonesian Economic Studies* 13, no. 1 (March 1977): 52–53.
91. Anne Booth, "Irrigation in Indonesia: Part II," *Bulletin of Indonesian Economic Studies* 13, no. 2 (July 1977): 49.
92. Ibid., p. 52.
93. Ibid., pp. 58, 67.

94. Ibid., p. 73.
95. Ibid., p. 71, 72.

10: Forestry and Tree Farming

1. World Bank, *Forestry*, sector policy paper, 1978, p. 5.
2. Norman Myers, *The Sinking Ark* (London: Pergamon, 1979), pp. 120–21.
3. Personal communication from Jack Westoby, September 7, 1981.
4. World Bank, *Forestry*, p. 18.
5. Ibid., p. 14.
6. Ibid., p. 33.
7. Eric Eckholm, *Losing Ground: Environmental Stress and World Food Problems* (New York: Norton, 1976), p. 39.
8. Ibid., p. 177.
9. World Bank, *Forestry*, p. 33.
10. "Our Disappearing Forests," *Report: News and Views of the World Bank* (May–June 1978): 4.
11. Jack Shepherd, *The Forest Killers: The Destruction of the American Wilderness* (New York: McKay, 1975), p. 382.
12. Myers, *The Sinking Ark*, p. 173.
13. Kevin Young, Willem C. F. Bussink, and Parvez Hasan, *Malaysia: Growth and Equity in a Multiracial Society* (Baltimore: Johns Hopkins University Press, 1980), table 9.11, p. 276.
14. Food and Agriculture Organization, *Forest Resources in the Asia and Far East Region* (Rome: FAO, 1976), p. 91.
15. World Bank Report no. 1696a-PH, November 4, 1977, para. 2.04.
16. Afrim Resource Center, "Mindanao Report," mimeo, Davao City, Philippines, 1980, pp. 67–68.
17. Ibid., p. 69.
18. World Bank, *Philippines: Water Management and Erosion Control Project* (June 10, 1980), para. 1.07.
19. Afrim Resource Center, "Mindanao Report."
20. Young et al., *Malaysia*, p. 277.
21. *International Herald Tribune*, October 4–5, 1980.
22. First National City Bank, *Indonesia: The Timber Industry* (1969).
23. Shepherd, *The Forest Killers*, p. 319; Myers, *The Sinking Ark*, pp. 194–202.
24. Ingrid Palmer, *The Indonesian Economy Since 1965: A Case Study of Political Economy* (London: Frank Cass, 1978), p. 120.
25. Quoted in ibid., pp. 122–23, 126.
26. World Bank, *Forestry*, p. 27.
27. Ibid., p. 6.
28. Ibid., p. 28.
29. Young et al., *Malaysia*, p. 277.
30. World Bank, *Forestry*, p. 7.

31. Ibid., p. 49.
32. Ibid., p. 50.
33. World Bank, *Ivory Coast Forestry Project*, staff appraisal report no. 2403, June 7, 1979, para 1.06.
34. World Bank, *Jamaica Forestry Project*, staff appraisal report, April 7, 1979, p. 42.
35. World Bank, *Forestry*, p. 47.
36. Ibid., pp. 34–35.
37. Hans M. Gregerson and Arnoldo H. Contreras, *Economic Analaysis of Forestry Projects*, case study no. 1 (Rome: FAO, 1980), p. 1.
38. Ibid., p. 3, para 9.
39. Afrim Resource Center, "Mindanao," pp. 64, 67, 68.
40. Gregerson and Contreras, *Economic Analysis of Forestry*, p. 3.
41. John S. Spears, Bank Forestry Adviser, in "Our Disappearing Forests," p. 6.
42. Letter postmarked March 10, 1981.
43. World Bank, *Philippines: Water Management*.
44. Ibid., para. 2.07.
45. Ibid., para. 2.06.
46. Dorothy Friesen and Gene Stolzfus, *Filipino Newsletter* 2, no. 4 (April 1978).
47. World Bank, *Philippines: Water Management*, para. 1.07.
48. Ibid., paras. 4.05, 4.06.
49. Ibid., para. 4.06.
50. Myers, *The Sinking Ark*, p. 137.
51. World Bank, *Ivory Coast Forestry Project*, para. 5.01 and 5.08.
52. Ibid., para. 1.04.
53. Ibid., para. 1.08 and 5.01.
54. Ibid., para. 1.16.
55. Ibid., paras. 1.10, 2.07, and 5.08.
56. Eric Eckholm, *Planting for the Future: Forestry for Human Needs*, Worldwatch Paper 26 (Washington, D.C.: Worldwatch Institute, 1979), p. 46, quoting a German study.
57. Vincent S. R. Brandt, "The New Community Movement," *Journal of Asian and African Studies* 13, nos. 3–4 (July–October 1978): 206. An even harsher critique of the movement is Phyllis Kim, "SAEMAUL Agriculture: South Korean Farmers Prop Up Export-Oriented Economy," *AMPO* 12, no. 1 (1980): 2–11, and no. 5 (1980): 56–65.
58. Eckholm, *Planting for the Future*, p. 55.
59. Vandana Shiva, H. C. Sharatchandra, and J. Bandyopadhyay, *Social and Ecological Impact of Social Forestry in Kolar* (Bangalore: Indian Institute of Management, 1981).
60. Myers, *The Sinking Ark*, pp. 212–13.
61. Ibid., p. 154.

11: Urban "Shelter" Projects

1. Friedrich Engels, Introduction to Karl Marx, "The Class Struggles in France 1848 to 1850," in Karl Marx and Friedrich Engels, *Selected Works* vol. I (Moscow: Progress Publishers, 1969), p. 199. Engels was writing not only of Paris but of "big cities" in Europe generally, including the new working-class districts of Berlin.
2. Two examples are Alan Riding, "Mexico, Crushing a Maverick, Razes a Neighborhood," *New York Times*, March 19, 1981; and Loren Jenkins, "Bulldozers Push Turkish Workers' Town to Self-rule," *International Herald Tribune*, September 4, 1980.
3. World Bank, *Shelter* (Washington, D.C.: Poverty and Basic Needs Series, September 1980), p. 2.
4. *Report: News and Views of the World Bank*, March-April 1976, p. R-4.
5. World Bank, *Housing*, sector policy paper, May 1975, p. 15.
6. Robert Nicholas Grose, "Squatting and the Geography of Class Conflict: Limits to Housing Autonomy in Jamaica," mimeo, Cornell University, International Studies in Planning, June 1979, p. 2.
7. World Bank, *Housing*, p. 25.
8. Ibid., p. 28.
9. Ibid., p. 30.
10. Ibid., p. 19.
11. Ibid., pp. 19–24, annexes 7–9.
12. Ibid., p. 24.
13. Ibid., p. 36.
14. Ibid., p. 37. The Bank's policy in this respect follows closely that of some national governments, notably Mexico and Peru, and the writings of John Turner, e.g., *Housing by People: Towards Autonomy in Building Environments* (New York: Pantheon, 1977).
15. World Bank, *Housing*, p. 29.
16. Ibid.
17. Rod Burgess, "Petty-Commodity Housing or Dweller Control? A Critique of John Turner's Views on Housing Policy," *World Development* 6, nos. 9/10, (1978): 1129.
18. World Bank, *Housing*, pp. 29–30.
19. Ibid., p. 30.
20. Ibid., p. 19, note 2.
21. Shlomo Angel, *Land Tenure for the Urban Poor* (Bangkok: Human Settlements Division, Asian Institute of Technology, 1980), p. 40.
22. World Bank, *Housing*, p. 41.
23. For details see the chapter on the Philippines in Cheryl Payer, *The Debt Trap: The IMF and the Third World* (New York: Montly Review Press, 1975); and Cheryl Payer, "Seeds of a New Vietnam," *The Progressive*, September 1974.
24. Data from Walden Bello, "The New Dollar Diplomacy," *Nation*, November

20, 1976; and Center for International Policy, "World Bank Sets $2.9 billion in Loans to Human Rights Violators for Fiscal Year 1979," research study, n.d.

25. The citation and all information about the events of Vancouver Habitat are taken from a pamphlet, "A Report on Tondo Happenings at Vancouver Habitat," June 30, 1976, which reproduces new stories and other related documents.

26. Interestingly, some of the demolished structures had legal titles—a pertinent reminder that titles are not synonymous with security of tenure. A government can use its power of eminent domain against property with legal tenure as well as squatters.

27. Information on the happenings at the IMF-World Bank Annual Meeting in Manila (1976) is taken from articles by David Andelman in the *New York Times* October 7, 1976, and Bernard Wideman in the *Washington Post* October 6, 1976.

28. "Revolutionary ideas of 1972 becoming today's convention," *Report: News and Views from the World Bank*, September–October 1979, p. 1ff.

29. World Bank, *Philippines: Third Urban Development Project*, staff appraisal report, no. 2703a, February 26, 1980, para. 1.25, p. 13. Another visitor to Tondo found the area seemed "depopulated" by comparison with previous years. Dorothy Friesen, personal communication.

30. Oberndorfer report, typescript, p. 2.

31. Information on the Obendorfer report and the Bank's response can be found in an article written by Walden Bello and released by the AMLC-FFP Congress Task Force (September 6, 1980), which also provided me with a copy of the report itself.

32. World Bank, *Philippines: Manila Urban Development Project*, staff project report, May 1976, para. 5.13, p. 61.

33. Ibid., para. 5.17, p. 64.

34. World Bank, *Philippines: Third Urban Development*, para. 3.05, p. 27.

35. Ibid., para. 5.06, p. 44.

36. Ibid., Table on p. 45.

37. Ibid., para. 2.10, p. 18.

38. Ibid., para. 4.10, p. 31.

39. Ibid., para. 5.10, p. 46.

40. Ibid., para. 6.02, p. 47.

41. Ibid., para. 6.04, p. 47. The Bank's concern for the market value of real estate is also noted in Laurence A. G. Moss, "Implementing Sites and Services," Ph.D. diss., University of California, Berkeley, 1979.

42. *South*, December 1981, pp. 66–67.

43. Robert J. Ledogar, "Food, Incomes, and Housing Options: Observations from a Nutrition Survey in Chawama Complex," mimeo, Lusaka, April 1977, p. 5.

44. Ibid., pp. 7–8.

45. Richard E. Stren, "Squatting and the State Bureaucracy: A Case Study of Tanzania," unpublished paper, University of Toronto, 1980, pp. 25–26.

46. Dissertation by Francis Mgullu, cited in Stren, "Squatting and the State," p. 27.
47. Stren, "Squatting and the State," p. 30.
48. Angel, *Land Tenure*, pp. 4, 46, and 48.
49. World Bank, *Shelter,* p. 17.
50. Ibid., p. 9.

12: Inside the Bank

1. For more on this subject see Cultural Survival, *In the Path of POLONORESTE: Endangered Peoples of Western Brazil* (Cambridge, Mass.: Cultural Survival, 1981).
2. Ralph Miliband, *The State in Capitalist Society* (New York: Basic Books, 1969), p. 75.
3. Matthew Rothschild, "The U.S. pushes World Bank and IMF to be supports for global corporations," *Multinational Monitor*, November 1981, pp. 16ff.
4. Reported by InterPress Service, April 29, 1981.
5. *New York Times*, March 1, 1981.
6. Reported in *International Herald Tribune*, November 14–15, 1981.
7. Department of the Treasury, United States Participation in the Multilateral Development Banks in the 1980s (Washington, D.C.: Government Printing Office, 1982).
8. William Greider, "The Education of David Stockman," *The Atlantic Monthly*, December 1981, p. 47

Conclusion: Is There a Better Way?

1. Michael Parenti, *Democracy for the Few* (New York: St. Martins Press, 1974), p. 298.
2. Harry Magdoff, "Capital, Technology, and Development," in *Imperialism: From the Colonial Age to the Present* (New York: Monthly Review Press, 1978), p. 223.
3. John Briscoe, "Are Voluntary Agencies Helping to Improve Health in Bangladesh?" *International Journal of Health Services* 10, no. 1 (1980): 47–68.
4. Ibid., p. 67.
5. James H. Mittelman, *Underdevelopment and the Transition to Socialism: Mozambique and Tanzania* (New York: Academic Press, 1981), p. 227.
6. Quoted in *Ibon* 60 (February 15, 1981), p. 5.
7. See for example Peter Hayes, "Atoms for the Poor?" unpublished ms.
8. Quoted in Arthur Morgan, *Dams and Other Disasters* (Boston: Porter Sargent, 1971), p. 44.
9. Norman Girvan, *Corporate Imperialism: Conflict and Expropriation* (New York: Monthly Review Press, 1978), ch. 5.
10. For Cuba see Maruja Acosta and Jorge E. Hardy, *Urban Reform in Revolutionary Cuba* (New Haven: Yale University Antilles Research Program, 1973).

Index

409